A SEAT AT THE TABLE

A SEAT AT THE TABLE

Black Women Public Intellectuals
in US History and Culture

Edited by Hettie V. Williams
and Melissa Ziobro

University Press of Mississippi / Jackson

Publication of this work was made possible in part due to the generous support of the Grant in Aid of Creativity awarded by the Wayne D. McMurray School of Humanities and Social Sciences at Monmouth University.

The University Press of Mississippi is the scholarly publishing agency of the Mississippi Institutions of Higher Learning: Alcorn State University, Delta State University, Jackson State University, Mississippi State University, Mississippi University for Women, Mississippi Valley State University, University of Mississippi, and University of Southern Mississippi.

www.upress.state.ms.us

The University Press of Mississippi is a member of the Association of University Presses.

Any discriminatory or derogatory language or hate speech regarding race, ethnicity, religion, sex, gender, class, national origin, age, or disability that has been retained or appears in elided form is in no way an endorsement of the use of such language outside a scholarly context.

Copyright © 2023 by University Press of Mississippi
All rights reserved

First printing 2023
∞

Library of Congress Cataloging-in-Publication Data

Names: Williams, Hettie V., editor. | Ziobro, Melissa, editor.
Title: A seat at the table : Black women public intellectuals in US history and culture / edited by Hettie V. Williams and Melissa Ziobro.
Other titles: Black women public intellectuals in US history and culture
Description: Jackson : University Press of Mississippi, [2023] | Includes bibliographical references and index.
Identifiers: LCCN 2023020199 (print) | LCCN 2023020200 (ebook) | ISBN 9781496847515 (hardcover) | ISBN 9781496847522 (trade paperback) | ISBN 9781496847539 (epub) | ISBN 9781496847546 (epub) | ISBN 9781496847553 (pdf) | ISBN 9781496847560 (pdf)
Subjects: LCSH: African American intellectuals—History. | African American women—Intellectual life. | African Americans—Intellectual life. | African American women—Political activity—History. | African Americans—Politics and government. | African American intellectuals—Biography. | African American women—Biography.
Classification: LCC E185.89.I56 S43 2023 (print) | LCC E185.89.I56 (ebook) | DDC 305.48/896073—dc23/eng/20230522
LC record available at https://lccn.loc.gov/2023020199
LC ebook record available at https://lccn.loc.gov/2023020200

British Library Cataloging-in-Publication Data available

If they don't give you a seat at the table, bring a folding chair.
—Shirley Chisholm

DEDICATION

This book is dedicated to Hettie's beloved aunt Ann Quinnett Cunningham, a frontline medical worker who passed away during the height of the coronavirus pandemic. She was much loved by her family, especially her children.

Ann was a gentle and loving soul. She was the sixth of fourteen children. Ann moved to Michigan from Sylvester, Georgia, in the late 1960s. While in Detroit, Michigan, she married, started a family, and divorced. Ann had four children, three grandchildren, and one great-grandchild. She cherished her children and grandchildren; they were her entire life and she lived for them. Ann loved life! Her unexpected transition on April 9, 2020, left a tremendous hole in the hearts of those that loved and adored her.

Ann favored taking care of sick people. She especially enjoyed taking care of the elderly and terminally ill communities. As a result, she spent over thirty-one years of her life working in the nursing profession providing support to these individuals.

Ann was incredibly independent, and she loved plants, sewing, singing, and dancing. She was an avid reader, and her library collection would rival those in the literary community. To some, Ann was a literary genius, interpreting the works of many scholars, a gift given to her by God. In fact, her lifelong dream was to become a literature professor; although she never realized that goal, she supported her children and others in achieving their academic dreams in higher education. Ann was an incredible spirit and a great lady.

CONTENTS

Acknowledgments XIII

Introduction 3
Hettie V. Williams

Part I. Foundations of Black Women's Public Intellectualism

Summary 17

Chapter 1. "Fired with a Holy Ambition": Maria W. Stewart
and the Foundations of Black Women's Jeremiadic Tradition 19
Lacey P. Hunter

Chapter 2. "Did Not Mary *First* Preach the Risen Savior?"
Black Preaching Women as Public Intellectuals 45
Hettie V. Williams

Part II. Politics and Black Women's Public Intellectualism

Summary 65

Chapter 3. "Our Group of Women": Mary McLeod Bethune,
Nannie Helen Burroughs, Charlotte Hawkins Brown, and
Black Women in the Christian Intellectual Tradition 68
Tejai Beulah

Chapter 4. We Led the Way: Black Women and the
Civil Rights Movement at Morgan State College 89
Simone R. Barrett

Chapter 5.   Elreta Melton Alexander: A Theoretical Approach. 107
Virginia L. Summey

Chapter 6.   More Than an Icon:
Taking Shirley Chisholm at Her Word. 123
Marissa Jackson Sow

Chapter 7.   Lenora B. Fulani:
Distinguished Postmodern Revolutionary 148
Omar H. Ali and Tiera C. Moore

Part III. Black Women's Public Intellectualism in Art, Media, and the Culture Wars

Summary 173

Chapter 8.   "Whoever Heard of a Woman Running a Newspaper?"
The Public Life and Intellectual Odyssey of Charlotta Bass 176
John Portlock

Chapter 9.   "She Did It for the Culture": Black Women
Visual Artists as Public Intellectuals in the New Negro Era 194
Lauren T. Rorie

Chapter 10.   Mildred Fay Jefferson and the Pro-Life Movement:
A Conservative Black Woman Public Intellectual 215
Hettie V. Williams

Chapter 11.   Naked Truths: Dr. Joycelyn Elders,
Public Health, and Sex Education in the 1990s 236
Tedi A. Pascarella

Chapter 12.   What She Knows for Sure:
Oprah Winfrey and the Tradition of Black Spiritual
but Not Religious Writing. 256
Tejai Beulah

Part IV. Black Women's Patriotism: The National Good, Military Service, and Everyday Intellectualism

Summary 275

Chapter 13. "Know Where You Are Going and . . . Remember Where You Came From": Black Women in the Army during World War II 278
Sandra Bolzenius

Chapter 14. Seizing Opportunity: African American Women in the Postwar Military 305
Tanya L. Roth

Chapter 15. "Regardless of What Life Presents You": Black Women Public Intellectuals in the Post-Vietnam US Military. 327
Carol Fowler and Melissa Ziobro

About the Editors and Contributors .353

Index 359

ACKNOWLEDGMENTS

No book is written or compiled in a vacuum. We as the editors of this volume owe many a debt of gratitude including to our contributors, colleagues, family, and friends. First, we would like to thank all of the authors for their powerful contributions to this book. This volume would have been impossible without their thoughtful assessments of Black women intellectuals in US history. Second, we would like to thank the anonymous peer reviewers who thoughtfully assessed all of the chapters and made helpful suggestions that strengthened the final product. Thanks, too, to acquisitions editor Emily Bandy for her faith in our topic and thoughtful guidance throughout. We appreciate the support of our colleagues at Monmouth University, especially Dr. Christopher DeRosa, chair of the Department of History and Anthropology, and Dr. Richard Veit, interim dean of the Wayne D. McMurray School of Humanities and Social Sciences. We are also forever grateful to Lisa Munro and her team of editors for the copyediting work that they completed on this volume. And last, but not least, we thank all the women memorialized in the following pages. As noted in our introduction, the title of this book is inspired by a quote from Shirley Chisholm, the first African American woman elected to the US Congress and the first Black woman to run for the office of US president on a major party ticket. She also once said, "I'd like them to say Shirley Chisholm had guts. That's how I'd like to be remembered." Well, every one of the women discussed in this book had "guts," and their grit has made things a bit easier for those of us who come after them. Let's honor their legacy by remembering their stories and continuing to use our intellectual abilities to work toward equality for all.

A SEAT AT THE TABLE

INTRODUCTION

HETTIE V. WILLIAMS

A Seat at the Table is about Black women public intellectuals in United States history with a focus on recent American history.[1] The chapters collected in this book present an overview of African American women as public intellectuals in politics, culture, and public service from the early twentieth century to the present. The book's title is derived from the words of Shirley Chisholm, the first African American woman elected to the US Congress and the first Black woman to run for the office of US president on a major party ticket. She once stated, "If they don't give you a seat at the table, bring a folding chair." Chisholm was an educator, a civil rights activist, a politician, and a public intellectual who participated in the major debates of her day regarding human equality, first as a public-school teacher and then as a member of the US House of Representatives and presidential candidate. Currently only a few book-length projects are devoted to Black women's intellectual history—*A Seat at the Table* seeks to fill this void in the scholarly literature concerning African American women within the larger context of American intellectual history. Major volumes on American intellectual history tend to exclude the words and ideas of Black women. That said, Black women's intellectual history continues to grow as an important subfield in historical studies.

This volume includes chapters on women in politics, art, government, journalism, media, education, and the military, with chapters on women such as Shirley Chisholm, Oprah Winfrey, Charlotta Bass, and Mildred Fay Jefferson. A summary begins each of the book's four parts. The first part is a necessary discussion of foundational women in the history of Black women's public intellectualism in the nineteenth century, and the remaining parts cover Black women in twentieth-century US history.

This volume is in many respects a follow-up, or second volume, to my previous book *Bury My Heart in a Free Land: Black Women Intellectuals in Modern U.S. History* (Praeger, 2017). *Bury My Heart* as a text is more broadly conceived in that, using a topical chronological approach, chapters included trace the history of Black women's intellectualism from the era of enslavement to the present, with chapters on Black women abolitionists, writers, civil rights activists, artists, and poets. In contrast, *A Seat at the Table* is guided by the central theme of Black women's public intellectualism, with a focus on the twentieth century to the present. While *Bury My Heart* is a work that focuses on traditional Black women intellectuals such as Zora Neale Hurston, Toni Morrison, and Pauli Murray, *A Seat at the Table* incorporates analyses of lesser-known women such as Mildred Fay Jefferson, a medical doctor and antiabortion advocate, and civil rights pioneer Judge Elreta Melton Alexander and their work as public intellectuals. Some of the chapters in this text concentrate on individual women, such as with Oprah Winfrey, while other chapters explore groups of women who used public space to claim authority and influence society for the public good.

Another distinct aspect of this collection is a focus on Black women and the culture wars of the 1990s. This focus is represented in the chapters on Oprah Winfrey, Joycelyn Elders, and Mildred Fay Jefferson—three African American women public intellectuals who were central to conversations about religion, sex education, and abortion during the height of the culture wars. Winfrey, without a classical education, and author of nearly a dozen books, has a profound influence on American culture as a self-made billionaire who often refers to herself as "preacher" or "teacher." Her influence encompasses media, literature, education, religion, and politics (her endorsement of Barack H. Obama for US president likely secured millions of votes for the then-unknown politician), and she accomplished this outside of the confines of more traditional intellectual spaces, in the public square. Elders was a polarizing figure caught up in the midst of public debates about sex education while a member of the administration of President Bill Clinton. Though she was dismissed from her post as surgeon general for her controversial views on sex, she made some important contributions to discourses about human sexuality before, during, and after her role in the Clinton administration. Jefferson, a Harvard-educated medical doctor, was among a contingent of conservative intellectuals who turned away from traditional academic institutions in the 1990s to embrace life as a public intellectual, with the goal of shaping public policies such as abortion legislation. *A Seat at the Table* places these Black women, among others discussed in this volume, into the larger narrative of US intellectual history.

Myriad thinkers and their ideas constitute the canonical intellectual tradition in US history. This history often begins with the Puritan vision, through the American Enlightenment and First Great Awakening, to ideas about unionism in the Civil War era in terms of the colonial and Early Republic periods. Most collections on US intellectual history that concern the colonial period and the Early Republic include names such as John Winthrop, Anne Hutchinson, Roger Williams, Benjamin Franklin, Thomas Paine, Thomas Jefferson, Charles Grandison Finney, and Sarah Moore Grimké. Despite their erasure from key anthologies of early American intellectualism, African American women such as Phillis Wheatley, Maria Stewart, and Jarena Lee have always been part of this subfield, and it is a racist proposition to suggest otherwise.

Wheatley was active in the major conversations on religion, politics, race, and slavery in the eighteenth century. She inserted herself into these discourses by mastering the classics and acquiring an education while enslaved. In 1773, Wheatley became the first woman of African descent in the North American colonies to publish. She was a key producer of knowledge as a writer of eulogies, elegies, poems, and letters on a variety of subjects in the Revolutionary era. Wheatley is an ideal example of an intellectual. She fits the definition of intellectual "as one who engages in an activity of the mind, produces writings, and participates in public debates."[2] Arlette Frund contends that "with the writing and publication of her letters and poems," Wheatley in fact "entered the literary, intellectual, and public spheres of Boston."[3] Frund further argues that Wheatley participated in the larger intellectual discussion of the Enlightenment with her elegies, poems, and letters, which overcame the boundaries of race and gender by "exercising discursive practices of a literary genre such as poetry."[4]

Jarena Lee wrote her spiritual biography before the first slave narrative by a Black woman was published, and Maria Stewart was the first woman in US history to address an interracial crowd of men and women.[5] Lee's public intellectualism led her to challenge the authority of men in the African Methodist Episcopal (AME) Church. Marilyn Richardson, in her book *America's First Black Woman Political Writer*, has identified Stewart as the first Black woman political writer in US history. Stewart engaged in the major political debates of the day in the public sphere, and she wrote things down. Wheatley was, perhaps, an "intellectual" in the classical sense, while Stewart and Lee were public intellectuals who nonetheless wrote down their ideas and participated in important public debates on issues such as women's power in the church and abolitionism.

Secularism, progressivism, the extension of democracy through the civil rights era, identity politics, and the new conservatism in contemporary America are dominant themes in American intellectual history from 1865 to the present. African American women clearly played central roles in the emergence of the Black church and the long civil rights movement. However, scholars of intellectual history continue to ignore the contributions of Black women to this tradition, from the colonial era to contemporary times. By focusing on Black women in the public square, this volume brings Black women from the margin to the center of the American intellectual tradition.

According to Mia Bay, Farah J. Griffin, Martha S. Jones, and Barbara D. Savage in their text *Toward an Intellectual History of Black Women* (University of North Carolina Press, 2015), there is a "distinctive tradition" of Black women's intellectualism.[6] Historically, as the editors note, Black women have rarely worked out of "the academy or research institutes."[7] That said, "black women's intellectual history can never be explained by way of a mere genealogy of ideas."[8] Given that these women have been routinely closed out of prominent academies and institutions on the account of race and gender, their ideas have always been "produced in dialogue with lived experience"[9] as shaped by their social condition. More restrictive definitions of the term "intellectual" limit the meaning to one who makes her living through an activity of the mind and produces written work that is often attached to academies or research institutes, which is sometimes inadequate when defining Black women intellectuals, who often have been self-taught and preoccupied with concerns of race and gender outside of academia. Terms such as "organic intellectual," "activist intellectual," and sometimes "public intellectual" tend to be more applicable when considering Black women intellectuals in the context of US history.[10] Social ethicist Jean Bethke Elshtain has argued that intellectuals in American history have always been "members of a wider public" who "favored practical results over systems" and have "come in a number of modes" while using "a variety of approaches."[11] This term "intellectual" is abundantly applicable to many Black women thinkers in US history and their traditions given Elshtain's comprehensive definition of American intellectuals.

American intellectual history is directly connected to the lives, thought, and activism of Black preaching women, writers, politicians, artists, and journalists. This volume brings together chapters that analyze the place of Black women within the broader framework of American intellectual history as public intellectuals. Black women preachers, writers, and political figures collectively had a pervasive influence on the formation of not only the Black church but the American intellectual tradition as a whole. This concept of the public intellectual is intimately bound up with American religious history, as historian of American religion Tejai Beulah notes in her chapter on Black women in the Black Christian intellectual tradition. Elshtain has further contended that for many American public intellectuals, moral concerns were intricately connected to political questions throughout much of US history from the First Great Awakening to the civil rights era.[12] This preoccupation with moral and religious concerns is a constant in Black women's thought, from Maria Stewart to Oprah Winfrey.

Patricia Hill Collins has identified the core themes in Black women's feminist consciousness in her text *Black Feminist Thought: Knowledge, Consciousness, and the Politics of Empowerment* (Routledge, 1990). Collins identified the core themes from Black women's perspective as the legacy of struggle, interdependence of experience and consciousness, consciousness and the struggle for a self-defined standpoint, and lastly, the interdependence of thought and action.[13] The legacy of the struggle against racism and sexism is a constant theme in Black women's writings through the nineteenth century and beyond, while at the same time, the *consciousness* that many Black women *experienced* sexual violence during enslavement and after is a core subject of Black women's writings in both spiritual autobiographies and slave narratives. Black women have used writing as a means to self-articulation, understanding that cultivating a self-defined standpoint is integral to Black women's liberation.

An interdependence of thought and action is revealed in both the writings and activism of Black women preachers, abolitionists, and creative writers. This reform-minded Black feminist consciousness, which first emerged in the National era and evolved in the nineteenth century, arose from a tradition of activist intellectualism in the public square that continued through the twentieth century. African American women preachers and writers wrote spiritual biographies and participated in the major reform movements through the nineteenth century and beyond, laying the foundations of Black women's public intellectualism. This volume moves beyond Black preaching women in the public square to include Black women entertainers, journalists, activists, public servants, and educators with a focus primarily on the twentieth century.

Several historians have made notable contributions to the development of African American women's history by assiduously documenting the lives and thoughts of Black women in the historical record, as demonstrated with an array of texts. These historians include Paula Giddings, Hazel Carby, Darlene Clark Hine, Evelyn Brooks Higginbotham, Nell I. Painter, Deborah Gray White, Mia Bay, Bettye Collier-Thomas, Martha Jones, and a contingent of others. The chapters that follow include histories of Black women in the era of enslavement, Black women's religious activism in the Black church, histories of the Black women's club movement, and intellectual biographies of women such as Ida B. Wells and Sojourner Truth. In analyses covering a broad range of subjects, scholars have demonstrated the trajectory of Black women's ideas about empowerment with writings that have cogently revealed the importance of intersectionality in the history of Black's women's thought while identifying a clear tradition of Black women's intellectualism.

Several key works written in the 1980s helped to define the field of African American women's history. Giddings's book *When and Where I Enter: The Impact of Race and Sex in America* (William Morrow, 1984), which focuses on women such as Ida B. Wells and Julia Cooper, provided the first historical survey on how Black women, through their reform activism, confronted the dilemma of race and sex, while White's *Ar'n't I a Woman?: Female Slaves in the Plantation South* (W. W. Norton, 1985) is the first historical survey on Black women in slavery. Carby's *Reconstructing Womanhood: The Emergence of the Afro-American Woman Novelist* (Oxford University Press, 1987), with its emphasis on nineteenth-century Black women such as Harriet Jacobs, Frances E. W. Harper, and Anna Julia Cooper, helped to shape the emerging field of Black women's intellectual history.

Hine's voluminous works, including her edited volume *We Specialize in the Wholly Impossible: A Reader in Black Women's History* (Carlson Publishing, 1995), have become essential readings in Black women's history, alongside works by several other aforementioned historians. Higginbotham's *Righteous Discontent: The Women's Movement in the Black Baptist Church, 1860–1920* (Harvard University Press, 1993) details the origins of Black women's social activism within in the Black church. Higginbotham argues in *Righteous Discontent* that Black Baptist women forged a feminist theology defined by an "aggressive womanhood that felt personal responsibility to labor no less for men, for the salvation of the world."[14] Painter's groundbreaking biography of Sojourner Truth, *Sojourner Truth: A Life, A Symbol* (W. W. Norton, 1999), influenced the rise of intellectual biographies on Black women such as Bay's *To Tell the Truth Freely: The Life of Ida B. Wells* (Hill and Wang, 2009),[15] one of the more comprehensive intellectual biographies on the life and thought of Wells.

Collier-Thomas's *Jesus, Jobs, and Justice: African American Women and Religion* (Alfred A. Knopf, 2011) and, more recently, Betty Livingston Adams's *Black Women's Christian Activism: Seeking Social Justice in a Northern Suburb* (New York University Press, 2016) have drawn important conclusions regarding Black women's thought and Christian activism.[16] Collier-Thomas builds on the work of scholars such as Higginbotham, concerning the self-defined feminist standpoint of Black women, to contend that Black women's broadly defined feminism "did not exclude racial issues" and that Black women "recognized that in black America women's status was often defined by sex, necessitating an internal struggle for their rights as women."[17] In *Black Women's Christian Activism*, Adams contends that Black churchwomen such as Florence Spearing Randolph and Violent Johnson "advocated a politics of *civic righteousness*" to transform American secular institutions by "placing morality and justice in the realm of public policy, laws, and institutions."[18]

More recently, African American women's intellectual history has come to maturity with edited volumes specifically dedicated to Black women's thought. Two of the first such texts edited by historians include the aforementioned *Toward an Intellectual History of Black Women* edited by Mia Bay, Farah J. Griffin, Martha S. Jones, and Barbara D. Savage, with chapters that cover the early colonial era and the Black Atlantic to twenty-first-century politics, and *Bury My Heart in a Free Land: Black Women Intellectuals in Modern U.S. History*, which includes chapters on Black women intellectuals from Black preaching women to writers such as Toni Morrison. *A Seat at the Table* is a volume that helps to further substantiate the field of Black women's intellectual history by focusing on Black women's public intellectualism in various aspects of US society and culture. With innovative ideas about human liberation, African American women have repeatedly turned to the public square to combat racism and sexism, many times out of necessity, as much of the scholarship on Black women's thought and activism has demonstrated.

This phrase, "public intellectual," has been variously defined. In a broad sense, as Richard Posner notes, it is a term that is linked to the practice of engagement with the public. Stefan Collini, professor of literature and history at the University of Cambridge, argues that the public intellectual is one who has reached a point of achievement in a given field, has access to media to express her ideas, and advances ideas that engage a larger public. Patricia Hill Collins, however, notes that because of racism and sexism, "the gender politics of the public/private split" often denies Black women positions as public intellectuals.[19] The "machinery of racism,"[20] coupled with sexism, has kept Black women out of prominent academies and the intellectual circles of elites for centuries. These women nonetheless have turned to the public square for redress and to be heard. Political scientist Corey Robin has stated that public intellectuals use writing as "a transformative mode of action"[21] in an essay that appeared in the *Chronicle of Higher Education* (based on a speech he gave at the annual conference of the Society for US Intellectual History in 2016). It is pertinent to state here that Black women's intellectualism was built on a foundation of public intellectualism. These women sought to transform the racial state defined by enslavement in writing their spiritual autobiographies and slave narratives that were subsequently used to promote the abolitionist movement. Ta-Nehisi Coates, one of the foremost public intellectuals in the US today, has defined the public intellectual as an interlocutor who "communicates to a larger public" in an "original way."[22] Maria Stewart, Jarena Lee, and Harriet Jacobs advanced an intersectional approach to Black empowerment that was an original way of thinking that they deployed in public addresses, and in their writings, in an effort to transform society, thereby producing what Robin suggests are "thought deeds in the world."[23] Considering the definitions offered by both Robin and Coates: public intellectuals are those who engage a larger public, either through the written or spoken word, and participate in conversations or public debates while seeking to advance ideas that change society in fundamental ways, ideally for the betterment of humanity as a whole. *A Seat at the Table* is a volume that considers the thoughts and deeds of women who do this work.

African American intellectuals have been preoccupied with human liberation from the era of enslavement to the rise of Jim Crow segregation and to the structural crises of the present. Historically, these intellectuals have united thought with action. Frederick Douglass, with his *Narrative of the Life* and eloquent orations against slavery, comes to mind when we think of the African American intellectual in the era of enslavement, while W. E. B. Du Bois, America's most prominent Black intellectual in the twentieth century, and his *Souls of Black Folk* are envisioned when we think of the fight against Jim Crow segregation. Though Ida B. Wells was organizing, writing, and entering public spaces for the cause of Black equality alongside Du Bois, she is often relegated, as many scholars of Black women's thought have noted, to the category of activist—when she was in fact a public intellectual. Wells, like Douglass and Du Bois, combined thought with praxis as a cofounder of the National Association for the Advancement of Colored People (NAACP). In the civil rights era, Martin Luther King Jr., also a theologian and philosopher, is often recognized as the leading public intellectual of his generation, while Septima Clark, educator and civil rights advocate; Rosa Parks; and Jo Ann Robinson, an architect of the Montgomery bus boycott, are reduced to roles as mere activists when they were in fact public intellectuals who engaged in activism while advancing original ideas about Black equality in public spaces. *A Seat at the Table* details the history of Black women public intellectuals who have often been viewed through a reductionist lens despite the fact that these women meet the criteria of intellectuals in various contexts over time—and in every sense of the term "intellectual."

The four parts of this book are defined by pivotal topics in history as complemented with a chronological framework. Part I consists of two essays authored by Lacey P. Hunter and Hettie V. Williams, respectively. Hunter's chapter on Maria Stewart is an important intervention in terms of the place of Stewart in history, as an architect of the Black women's jeremiad, while Williams traces the public intellectualism of Jarena Lee, who authored the first spiritual autobiography written by a Black woman in North America, and includes some discussion of other Black preaching women of the nineteenth century such as Zilpha Elaw. These foundational chapters provide a framework for understanding the elements, structure, and concerns central to Black women public intellectuals.

Part II focuses on Black women in the Black Christian intellectual tradition, the civil rights era, and modern politics, with chapters written by Tejai Beulah, Simone R. Barrett, Virginia L. Summey, Marissa Jackson Sow, and Omar H. Ali and Tiera C. Moore. These writers explore the politics of Black women's public intellectualism by placing Black women at the center of Black church politics, the civil rights era, and twentieth-century American politics.

Part III contains chapters authored by John Portlock, Lauren T. Rorie, Hettie V. Williams, Tedi A. Pascarella, and Tejai Beulah that discuss journalist Charlotta Bass; Black women artists in the New Negro era; antiabortion activist Mildred Fay Jefferson; Joycelyn Elders, a public servant and former surgeon general; and America's foremost Black woman influencer, Oprah Winfrey. This section is particularly focused on Black women in society and culture in the twentieth century, with an emphasis on the positioning of Black women in the culture wars of the late twentieth century.

Lastly, part IV concerns Black women and their ideas about public service—particularly military service. In this section, Sandra Bolzenius writes about Black women in the army during World War II, Tanya L. Roth discusses Black women in the post-WWII military, and Carol Fowler and Melissa Ziobro contribute a chapter on Black women and military service more generally. These authors make extensive use of interviews and oral histories to craft a picture of the everyday intellectualism of Black women and their thoughts about military service.

A Seat at the Table is an important volume that helps to establish the validity and existence of Black women's intellectual traditions in the public square.

NOTES

1. Some portions of this introduction are included from the introduction to my previous edited volume, *Bury My Heart in a Free Land*.
2. Arlette Frund, "Phillis Wheatley, A Public Intellectual," in *Toward an Intellectual History of Black Women*, ed. Mia Bay, Farah J. Griffin, Martha S. Jones and Barbara Savage, 37.
3. Frund, "Phillis Wheatley."
4. Frund, "Phillis Wheatley," 38.
5. Marilyn Richardson, preface to *Maria W. Stewart*, xiii.
6. Bay, Griffin, Jones, and Savage, introduction to *Toward an Intellectual History of Black Women*, 1.
7. Bay, Griffin, Jones, and Savage, introduction to *Toward an Intellectual History of Black Women*, 5.
8. Bay, Griffin, Jones, and Savage, introduction to *Toward an Intellectual History of Black Women*, 4.
9. Bay, Griffin, Jones, and Savage, introduction to *Toward an Intellectual History of Black Women*, 4.
10. The phrase "organic intellectual" is borrowed here from the writings of Italian neo-Marxist Antonio Gramsci, who states in "The Intellectuals," which appears in *An Anthology*

of Western Marxism from Lukacs and Gramsci to Socialist Feminism, pp. 113–19, edited by Roger S. Gottlieb (New York: Oxford University Press, 1989), an essay from volume 3 of his *Prison Notebooks*, that "all men are intellectuals" (115). Gramsci further contends in this same section of his *Prison Notebooks* that the category of intellectual is multiple and that everyone has the capacity to think; therefore, there are only categories of intellectuals, and "nonintellectuals do not exist" (115). In the tradition of African American history, the phrase "activist intellectual" has been utilized by scholars of the Black experience to connote the dialogic relationship between lived experience, the formation of ideas, and the production of knowledge as stated in *Toward an Intellectual History of Black Women*: "The result is intellectual history 'black woman-style,' an approach that understands ideas as necessarily produced in dialogue with lived experience and always inflected by the social facts of race, class, and gender" (4). Jürgen Habermas, in *The Structural Transformation of the Public Sphere: An Inquiry into a Category of Bourgeois Society* (Cambridge, MA: MIT Press, 1988), has defined the public intellectual as one who makes "public use of reason," as quoted in Frund, "Phillis Wheatley," 35. Frund, in this same essay, goes on to define the term "intellectual" as an "individual who engages in an activity of the mind, produces written work, and participates in public debates," 35. These terms are used in this article as derived from the writings of Gramsci, Habermas, Frund, and the editors of *Toward an Intellectual History of Black Women*.

11. Elshtain, "Why Public Intellectuals?," 43–44.
12. Elshtain, "Why Public Intellectuals?," 44.
13. Collins, *Black Feminist Thought*, 22–33.
14. Higginbotham, *Righteous Discontent*, 139.
15. For more notable studies on Wells, see Paula Giddings, *Ida: A Sword Among Lions, Ida B. Wells and the Campaign against Lynching* (New York: Amistad, 2008); James West Davidson, *"They Say": Ida B. Wells and the Reconstruction of Race* (New York: Oxford University Press, 2008); and Linda O. McMurry, *To Keep the Waters Troubled: The Life of Ida B. Wells* (New York: Oxford University Press, 1998).
16. There is an ever-expanding compendium of scholarly analyses on women as prophets and preachers. Some notable works that analyze this subject matter include Daniella J. Kostroun and Lisa Vollendorf, eds., *Women, Religion, and the Atlantic World, 1600–1800* (Toronto: University of Toronto Press, 2009), which examines women in an international context with some coverage of Black women and religion before the nineteenth century; Marilyn J. Westerkamp, *Women and Religion in Early America, 1600–1850: The Puritan and Evangelical Traditions* (New York: Routledge, 1999) contains some discussion of Black women and Methodism and prophesying women; Beverly Mayne Kienzie and Pamela J. Walker, eds., *Women Preachers and Prophets through Two Millennia of Christianity* (Berkeley: University of California Press, 1998) provides a collection of essays on women preachers and prophets in the history of Christianity through the twentieth century; "Producing the Voice, Consuming the Body: Women Prophets of the Seventeenth Century," in *Women, Writing, History, 1640–1740*, edited by Isobel Grundy and Susan Wiseman, 139–58 (Athens: University of Georgia Press, 1992 explores the relationship between women's agency and prophecy in the early modern era.
17. Collier-Thomas, *Jesus, Jobs, and Justice*, 121.
18. Adams, *Black Women's Christian Activism*, 3.

19. Collins, "Black Public Intellectuals," 26.
20. Coates, "What It Means to Be a Public Intellectual."
21. Robin, "How Intellectuals Create a Public."
22. Coates, "What It Means to Be a Public Intellectual."
23. Robin, "How Intellectuals Create a Public."

REFERENCES

Adams, Betty Livingston. *Black Women's Christian Activism: Seeking Social Justice in a Northern Suburb*. New York: New York University Press, 2016.

Andrews, William L., ed. *Sisters of the Spirit: Three Black Women's Autobiographies of the Nineteenth Century*. Bloomington: Indiana University Press, 1986.

Baer, Hans. "The Limited Empowerment of Women in Black Spiritual Churches: An Alternative Vehicle to Religious Leadership." *Sociology of Religion* 54, no. 1 (Spring 1993): 65–82.

Barstow, Anne Llewellyn. "Mystical Experience as a Feminist Weapon: Joan of Arc." *Women's Studies Quarterly* 13, no. 2 (Summer 1985): 26–29.

Bay, Mia, Farah J. Griffin, Martha S. Jones, and Barbara D. Savage. *Toward an Intellectual History of Black Women*. Chapel Hill: University of North Carolina Press, 2015.

Carby, Hazel V. *Reconstructing Womanhood: The Emergence of the Afro-American Women Novelist*. New York: Oxford University Press, 1987.

Coates, Ta-Nehisi. "What It Means to Be a Public Intellectual." *The Atlantic*, January 8, 2014. https://www.theatlantic.com/politics/archive/2014/01/what-it-means-to-be-a-public-intellectual/282907/.

Collier-Thomas, Bettye. *Daughters of Thunder: Black Women and Their Sermons, 1850–1979*. San Francisco: Jossey-Bass, 1998.

Collier-Thomas, Bettye. *Jesus, Jobs, and Justice: African American Women and Religion*. New York: Alfred A. Knopf, 2011.

Collins, Patricia Hill. *Black Feminist Thought: Knowledge, Consciousness, and the Politics of Empowerment*. New York: Routledge, 1991.

Collins, Patricia Hill. "Black Public Intellectuals from Du Bois to the Present." *Contexts* 4, no. 4. 2005, 22–27.

Collins, Patricia Hill. "What's in a Name? Womanism, Black Feminism, and Beyond." *Black Scholar* 26, no. 1 (2001): 9–17.

Dodson, Jualynne. *Engendering Church: Women, Power, and the A.M.E. Church*. Lanham, MD: Rowman and Littlefield, 2002.

Elshtain, Jean Bethke. "Why Public Intellectuals?" *Wilson Quarterly* 25, no. 4 (Autumn 2001).

Gates, Henry Louis, Jr., and Nellie Y. McKay, eds. *The Norton Anthology of African American Literature*. New York: W. W. Norton, 2004.

Giddings, Paula. *When and Where I Enter: The Impact of Black Women on Race and Sex in America*. New York: William Morrow, 1984.

Guy-Sheftall, Beverly, ed. *Words of Fire: An Anthology of African American Feminist Thought*. New York: The New Press, 1995.

Higginbotham, Evelyn Brooks. *Righteous Discontent: The Women's Movement in the Black Baptist Church, 1880–1920*. Cambridge, MA: Harvard University Press, 1993.

Logan, Shirley Wilson. *We Are Coming: The Persuasive Discourse of Nineteenth Century Black Women*. Carbondale: Southern Illinois Press, 1999.

Maffly-Kipp, and Kathryn Lofton, eds. *Women's Work: An Anthology of African American Women's Historical Writings from Antebellum America to the Harlem Renaissance*. New York: Oxford University Press, 2010.

Ouimet, Lorraine. "The Ins and Outs of Public Intellectualism." *Thought and Action* 17, no. 1, (Summer 2001): 51–60.

Richardson, Marilyn, ed. *Maria W. Stewart, America's First Black Woman Political Writer: Essays and Speeches*. Bloomington: Indiana University Press, 1987.

Robin, Corey. "How Intellectuals Create a Public." *Chronicle of Higher Education*. January 22, 2016. https://www.chronicle.com/article/How-Intellectuals-Create-a/234984.

Sterling, Dorothy, ed. *We Are Your Sisters: Black Women in the Nineteenth Century*. New York: W. W. Norton, 1984.

Waters, Kristin, and Carol B. Conaway, eds. *Black Women's Intellectual Traditions: Speaking Their Minds*. Burlington: University of Vermont Press, 2007.

White, Deborah Gray. *Too Heavy a Load: Black Women in Defense of Themselves, 1894–1994*. New York: W. W. Norton, 1999.

Williams, Hettie V., ed. *Bury My Heart in a Free Land: Black Women Intellectuals in Modern U.S. History*. Santa Barbara, CA: Praeger, 2017.

Part I

Foundations of Black Women's Public Intellectualism

SUMMARY

Part I of *A Seat at the Table*, "Foundations of Black Women's Public Intellectualism," includes two chapters, "'Fired with a Holy Ambition': Maria W. Stewart and the Foundations of Black Women's Jeremiadic Tradition" by Lacey P. Hunter and "'Did Not Mary *First* Preach the Risen Savior?' Black Preaching Women as Public Intellectuals" by Hettie V. Williams. These two chapters focus on the origins and foundations of Black women's public intellectualism in US history. Though this volume focuses primarily on the twentieth century as a whole, these chapters are necessary in that they illustrate the genesis of a Black woman's intellectual tradition by detailing the major concerns and theoretical approaches of early Black women public intellectuals.

This section helps to establish the tradition of public intellectualism developed by Black women in the face of racism and sexism. These women challenged racial slavery and demanded a space for women in the public square. Black women's intellectual traditions begin with Black women abolitionists and preachers, a tradition that then extended down to Black women writers, artists, journalists, and entertainers. The book focuses on Black women public intellectuals across various arenas in American life, including in religion, where it all began, as well as education, media, and the arts. African American women stood on the shoulders of women such as Maria Stewart and Jarena Lee. This section shows that these women fit the definition of intellectual, broadly construed. Stewart inaugurated a tradition of Black women's public intellectualism that continues to the present, and this is a historical fact.

Stewart, the first American woman to speak publicly to an interracial crowd of men and women, might be considered the first woman public intellectual in US history. Scholars have long considered her to be the first Black woman politician. Black woman preachers such as Jarena Lee, explored by Williams in the second chapter of this section, are second only to Stewart as the first Black women intellectuals in that they were the first Black women to author extended autobiographies. They, too, were public intellectuals given that, as itinerant ministers, they traveled extensively, preaching and extending Black women's intellectual traditions through the written word while embracing an intersectional approach to Black empowerment.

Born free in Hartford, Connecticut, in 1803, Maria Miller was orphaned at a young age. She went on to serve as a domestic worker in the home of a white clergyman. Later, she moved to Boston, where she married a veteran of the War of 1812 and solidly middle-class merchant named James, adopting both his surname, Stewart, and his middle initial, W. Sadly, Stewart was quickly widowed. Deprived of any inheritance from his estate, she again turned to domestic work to support herself.

From these inauspicious beginnings, with no formal education save Sunday school and against all odds, Stewart built herself a career as a journalist, orator, and outspoken champion of women's rights and abolition. One cannot overestimate how difficult this must have been at a time when "respectable" women of both races were relegated to the private sphere. But Stewart remained undeterred by these difficulties. In her own words: "Shall I, for fear of feeble man who shall die, hold my peace? Shall I for fear of scoffs and frowns, refrain my tongue? Ah, no!" As Lacey P. Hunter writes, Stewart is "a foremother of Black women's jeremiadic discourse and a prime example of the creative ways in which African American women worked in the public sphere to defend and protect their race."

The second chapter in this section concentrates on the life and work of Black women preachers such as Jarena Lee and Zilpha Elaw. Williams situates these Black women preachers within the larger context of the Black Atlantic, alongside several other early Black women preachers. These women produced spiritual autobiographies integral to the advancement of Black women's intellectual traditions, were abolitionists, and were concerned with women's empowerment within and beyond the Black church. They traveled extensively throughout North America and abroad to places such as England. Their preaching activities were international in scope. Their public intellectualism laid the foundation for the development of a Black women's intellectual tradition in the public sphere.

Chapter 1

"FIRED WITH A HOLY AMBITION"

Maria W. Stewart and the Foundations of Black Women's Jeremiadic Tradition

LACEY P. HUNTER

> Where is the soul amongst us that is not fired with a holy ambition? Has not everyone a wish to excel in order to encourage those benevolent hearts who are making every exertion in our behalf.... The day star from on high is beginning to dawn upon us, and Ethiopia will soon stretch forth her hands unto God.[1]

When she began her public speaking career in the 1830s, Maria W. Stewart stepped onto a stage prime for her emergence. The mingling of nationalist sentiment, revolutionary idealism, religious fervor, and economic anxieties provided a rich backdrop for her to articulate the specific concerns of Black communities as the United States edged toward greater industrialization. Stewart's moment of emergence was also underscored by the vigorous writing, oratory, and activism occurring in African American communities around the nation. Though her public speaking career was ephemeral, Stewart's life work as a public intellectual and activist reveals the significance of Black women in the development of larger African American intellectual communities. More than this, however, Stewart's work highlights her importance to Black women's distinct intellectual traditions. Specifically, her use and adaptation of the American jeremiad indicate a wider trend among her peers in free Black communities.

A discourse that emphasizes the United States' city-on-a-hill identity by linking its democracy to divine purpose, the language of the jeremiad permeated American political discourse from the eighteenth century through the nineteenth. As American intellectuals strained to ascertain the direction of a changing nation, many of them relied on the jeremiad to emphasize the importance of its early revolutionary ideals. They also issued warning about the secular and spiritual consequences of veering away from these ideals.[2] In her writing and oratory, Stewart gleaned heavily from the revolutionary language and ideals of the American War for Independence, positioning herself as a divinely chosen representative of American civic religion. Infusing this language with nineteenth-century abolitionist, feminist, and temperance philosophy, Stewart fashioned a new style of jeremiadic discourse that laid the foundations for its evolution in Black women's intellectual communities. A pillar in the emergence of Black women's jeremiadic discourse, Maria Stewart is not merely a Black female Jeremiah who falls within the existing canon of thinkers considered in the tradition, such as Frederick Douglass and W. E. B. Du Bois. Rather, she is a forerunner in the creation of a discourse marked by its use of American revolutionary ideals to centralize the experiences of free and enslaved women in the larger national debates about democracy and citizenship. Black women's jeremiad also valorized Black womanhood in public forums by relying on claims of spiritual authority and purity to substantiate their demands for greater sociopolitical inclusion in American society. In their adaptation of the jeremiad, Maria W. Stewart and others rejected the idea that African American people were naturally inferior to white Americans, while also challenging the stereotypes about Black hypersexuality and immorality. Hence, as she openly rejected slavery, racism, sexism, sexual violence, and religious hypocrisy, Stewart forged a jeremiadic discourse that critiqued democracy and Judeo-Christian belief in the United States. Emphasizing the oppression of free and enslaved African American communities throughout the United States and the country's unwillingness to realize the revolutionary ideals of its inception and the spiritual pillars of its professed faith traditions would inevitably garner long-term consequences. The road to redemption, Stewart suggested, would not be paved by those in power. Only the virtuous example and activism of "the least of these" in the nation could clear this path.[3]

From the Early Republic through the antebellum period, use of the jeremiad focused acutely on the budding market revolution. Many Americans believed that the cultural shifts looming as a result of the new market threatened to entice the nation away from its republican virtues. Though they feared changes that seemingly undermined the moral and ethical foundations of the United States, critics of the market economy also believed that the country could redeem itself by maintaining the sacred values of their forebears. From benevolent societies to moral and religious intellectuals, challengers of the market economy maintained that its transitions would eventually undermine the basic moral and ethical foundations of the nation. Many argued that a commercial economy would destroy the value and importance of small farmers and skilled craftsmen.[4] Others asserted that a market economy would gradually lead to deteriorating wage labor conditions—some even contended that a growing market would reduce wage laborers to a status worse than slaves.[5] Slave labor was a particularly challenging dimension in the nation's debates about the market economy, and economists, politicians, religious leaders, and business owners struggled to sift morality from the notion of a "free market." Antislavery and abolitionist proponents, however, hinged their challenges of the new economy on the idea that forced labor was inherently immoral and unethical. Hence, many argued that the changing economy appeared to signal the beginning of the nation's moral declension to many.[6]

By the 1830s, evidence of the nation's waning moral values was seemingly clear in the rise of mob violence in many of its states and developing territories. Several of these instances of violence were race riots that exacerbated economic disparities among Black and ethnic white Americans. Added to this were the realities of poverty and high mortality and crime rates that worsened conditions for urban residents and workers throughout the nation.[7] For African Americans, these realities were aggravated by higher rates of poverty, chronic illness, infant and adult mortality, poor housing, criminalization, public derision, sexual violence, and unemployment. The new market also represented increased exploitation of Black labor and further restrictions on the civic freedoms and education of free Black communities.[8] Still, for African American leaders, slavery remained the most pressing concern about the development of economic commercialization. In effect, the new market signaled the continuation and extension of the system of slavery. To African American women, the shifting economy, and its foreseeable sociopolitical consequences, also denoted the extension of sexual violence experienced by free and unfree women alike.[9] Family separation and kidnap were another set of serious concerns for African American women as the slave market expanded and cotton production increased in the South. Consequently, Maria Stewart positioned these concerns at the center of her discourse as she established her early career.

Throughout her career, Stewart argued that the circumstances of African American people—and Black women in particular—were a testimony against the founding principles of the United States and its profession of Christian ethics. In her first book, *Religion and the Pure Principles of Morality*, Stewart asserted that the nation failed to realize its democratic ideologies and that its insistence on maintaining a racial hierarchy that demeaned African American people was antithetical to God. She asserted that African Americans had a right to claim their freedom and political inclusion because God made them equal to all other racial groups in the nation. "This is the land of freedom," she wrote. "Many think, because your skins are tinged with a sable hue, that you are an inferior race of people." Despite this, Stewart noted, "God does not consider you as such . . . he hath bestowed upon you reason and strong powers of intellect . . .

and according to the Constitution of the United States, he hath made all men free and equal."[10] Denial of African American rights, she observed, was a function of white racial prejudice and discrimination—a characteristic that undermined American democracy and morality. While Americans made a concerted effort to flourish "in arts and sciences, and in polite literature . . . [and] . . . to excel in political, moral and religious improvement," she argued, "very few are there among them that bestow one thought upon the benighted sons and daughters of Africa, who have enriched the soils of America with their tears and blood."[11] Indeed, she asserted, if "every gentlemen in America" were suddenly destined "to become bondmen, and their wives, their sons, and their daughters, servants forever to Great Britain . . . their countenance would be filled with horror, every nerve and muscle would be forced into action."[12] If Americans could never foresee themselves in permanent servitude to any other nation, she questioned, "Why have not Afric's sons the right to feel the same?"[13] Consequently, Stewart argued that the nation's unwillingness to secure the full freedom of Black men and women would result in divine punishment.

The underlying contradiction and prejudice that fueled America's racial and gender inequalities represented an undoing of all that made the nation virtuous in the eyes of its people. Stewart's suggestion that this virtue was shallow, because of its failures to include African Americans, underlined her insistence that the country's failure to manifest the ideals it upheld as pillars in the founding of the nation would inevitably create long-term social and political repercussions throughout. In this vein, she argued that racial injustice would not stand for many more generations. "Oh America," she lamented, "foul and indelible is thy stain! Dark and dismal is the cloud that hangs over thee, for thy cruel wrongs and injuries to the fallen sons of Africa." In its continued practice of slavery, she argued, the United States had "become drunken with the blood of . . . [Africa's] slain . . . and . . . hast caused the daughters of Africa to commit whoredoms and fornications." Still, she warned, "Upon thee be their curse." The nation's powerful and wealthy, she cautioned, "will call for rocks and mountains to fall upon you, and to hide you from the wrath of the Lamb."[14] Racism and slavery represented national sins against America and gave urgency to African American calls for a new republic in which they would be included on equal terms through divine intervention. "Charity begins at home," Stewart noted, "and those that provide not for their own are worse than infidels." If the nation's political leaders failed to address its injustices, she maintained, "our cry shall come up before the throne of God."[15] Stewart prophesied that divine intervention would lead to dire consequences for the United States, comparable to "the ten plagues of Egypt." She also declared that African Americans would fully assert their rights and "tell you that our souls are fired with the same love of liberty and independence with which your souls are fired." "It is the blood of our fathers," she continued, "and the tears of our brethren that have enriched your soils and we claim our rights."[16]

Stewart's assertions here parallel the prophetic tradition of the Old Testament. *Religion and the Pure Principles of Morality* was replete with references to one of the Major Prophets—Jeremiah. Chosen from his youth to speak to the house of Israel, Jeremiah criticized the Babylonian empire for its corruption and called on his people to refrain from adopting their customs and spiritual practices. Neglecting their traditions and core beliefs, he warned, would give them over to ruin and distance them from God.[17] Similarly, Maria Stewart viewed herself as a divinely chosen orator, and she positioned herself as a living prophet calling the nation to change. "In 1831," she explained, "I made a public profession of my faith in Christ," and this inspired her lifelong work for equality in African American communities. As she would explain in her farewell address merely two years later, Stewart believed she had been called by God "to drink of that cup that I have drank of," and she "felt that [she] had a great work to perform." Her conviction led her to begin public oration, and as she argued, "I have every reason to believe that it is the divine influence of the Holy Spirit operating upon my heart."[18] Hence, in many of her speeches, letters, and poems, Stewart compared herself to Jeremiah and drew parallels between her own sense of rejection and that of Jesus and his disciples.[19] The negative responses Stewart faced from the well-to-do free Black community in Boston—particularly from its male leadership—fueled her convictions. Specifically, the disproval she confronted during her public speaking career convinced her that African Americans were also guilty of prejudice and corruption against poor people and women—which threatened their ability to achieve full justice and equality.

In her writing, teaching, and oration, Stewart maintained that realizing the nation's revolutionary principles of freedom and equality did not fall squarely on the shoulders of its white population. Rather, she stressed that Black people were just as American as their white counterparts and, therefore, were equally obligated to live up to their country's high moral ideals. Stewart insisted that freedom from oppression depended on the spiritual purity of the people calling on God for its fruition. "Never will the chains of slavery and ignorance burst," she argued, "till we become united as one and cultivate among ourselves the pure principles of piety, morality, and virtue." Adding to this, she claimed that if African Americans dedicated themselves to moral uplift, they would subsequently "become fired with a holy zeal for freedom's cause."[20] In her 1832 lecture to the Anti-Slavery Society of New England, Stewart declared, "The prayers and tears of Christians will avail the finally penitent nothing; neither will the prayers and the tears of the friends of humanity avail us anything unless we possess a spirit of virtuous emulation within our breasts."[21] Still, she asserted, "the hand of God has touched us," and it was therefore the responsibility of African Americans to raise the nation's standards of morality higher.

Stewart's arguments underscored an early Black theology that positioned African Americans as a divinely chosen people. Similar to the prophets of the Old Testament tradition, she called on her people to avoid the pitfalls of turning away from their race and their God.[22] In this tradition, she urged free Black communities to work toward a higher moral standard. Stewart contended that when free African Americans allowed the liberties and leisure of their class to undermine the larger objectives of freedom and equality, the entire race suffered. Class divisions and prejudice, therefore, stymied full Black civic equality and the abolition of slavery. She reflected on this in frustration, noting:

> When I consider how little improvement has been made the last eight years; the apparent indifferent state of the children of God . . . when I see the greater part of our community following the vain bubbles of life with so much eagerness . . . I really think we are in as wretched and miserable a state as was the house of Israel in the days of Jeremiah.[23]

Complacency among the well-to-do in free Black communities, Stewart argued, upheld their oppression as a racial group and was, essentially, sinful. As she perceived it, the privileged class of free Black people were lax in their dedication to African American freedom and equality. They were also guilty of adopting prejudicial attitudes against poor Black people and women that mirrored discriminatory sentiments in larger American society. "I see this people lying in wickedness," she argued, adding, "Were it not for a few righteous that are to be found among us, we should become as Sodom, and like unto Gamorrah."[24] Taking aim at African American religious leadership, she asserted,

> Had the ministers of the gospel shunned the very appearance of evil; had they faithfully discharged their duty, whether we should have heard them or not, we should have been a very different people from what we now are, but they have kept the truth, as it were, hid from our eyes, and have cried "Peace!" "Peace!" when there was no peace; they have plastered us with an untempored mortar, and have been as it were blind leaders of the blind.[25]

Here, Stewart echoes the themes of the book of Jeremiah, specifically its emphasis on the insidious nature of corruption among Israel's class of priests and prophets. Her accusations were a serious charge against African American male leadership, since few denominations permitted women to lead congregations.[26] In another sense, Stewart's criticism of Black religious leaders reified her own position as a Christian disciple and prophet. Indeed, as she declared, "God has fired my soul with a holy zeal for his cause," and "I expect to be hated of all men, and persecuted even unto death, for righteousness and truth's sake."[27] Standing on this authority, she charged African American men beyond the church to take greater incentive to secure the liberation and equality of the race.

In her 1833 lecture at the African Masonic Hall in Boston, Stewart argued that the lack of accomplishment among African American people was a function of the "want of energy" among its Black male leadership. To this she added that they seemed to "have long been willing to bear the yoke of oppression."[28] "We have made ourselves appear altogether unqualified to speak in our own defence," she asserted, "and now, if we complain, it is considered as the height of impertinence."[29] Class leisure and self-interest, she maintained, detracted from the needs of the race. "It is astonishing to me," she explained, "that our fine young men are so blind to their own interest and the future welfare of their children as to spend their hard earnings on frivolous amusement, for it has been carried on to such an unbecoming extent that it has become disgusting." Black wealth, she contended, was "being thrown away" and would be best spent on "schools and seminaries of learning for our children and youth." In a biting rebuke, she asserted, "Had those men among us who had an opportunity, turned their attention as assiduously to mental and moral improvement as they have to gambling and dancing, I might have remained quietly at home and they stood contending in my place."[30] While Stewart's words here were clearly a charge that Black men were negligent in their responsibilities to their families and communities, it was also an underlying challenge to the gender constraints of the day. Nineteenth-century social mores did not offer women opportunities to act as leaders in or outside of their communities—particularly when their ambitions meant that they could assert their authority over men. Stewart's critique of Black male leadership suggests that their failures necessitated Black women's interjection and influence. It also directly challenged the sexism born out of nineteenth-century gender norms. Additionally, Stewart's challenging remarks highlighted the ways in which Black male sexism frustrated the progress of the race, by reinforcing the subjugation of Black women.

As she argued throughout her career, African Americans could not challenge their exclusion from larger national society while supporting the marginalization and exclusion of women in their communities. She defended this point in her farewell speech in 1833 when she told her audience that "holy women ministered unto Christ and the apostles; and women of refinement in all ages, more or less, have had a voice in moral, religious and political subjects."[31] "Wherefore, my friends," she stated, "let us no longer talk of prejudice, till prejudice becomes extinct at home." She continued, "Let us no longer talk of opposition, till we cease to oppose our own."[32] Stewart's melancholy sentiments in this instance echoed her arguments in a lecture she delivered to the Afric-American Female Intelligence Society in 1832: "It appears to me that there are no people under the heavens so unkind and so unfeeling towards their own, as are the descendants of fallen Africa."[33] Consequently, intra-racial prejudice was as detrimental as white racial discrimination, and Stewart believed that it hindered racial progress and undermined Black spirituality. Gender prejudice and sexism within Black communities were also impediments, and Stewart believed that the prevalence of gender inequalities among African American people jeopardized the spiritual growth and intellectual development of Black women. Women's equal sociopolitical inclusion in African American communities, she contended, was a critical factor in the process of Black liberation. Accordingly, Stewart suggested that the challenges Black women faced as they sought to uplift their communities doubled the burden on the entire race.

Unique to Black women's jeremiadic discourse was the insistence that their active contribution to and participation in religious and political development was a vital part of realizing the nation's early democratic goals and securing African American freedoms. For Maria Stewart and her contemporaries, ignorant and inactive women represented another hindrance in the long struggle for freedom and equality. Obtaining Black civil rights, therefore, was contingent on the uplift and equality of African American women. As Stewart suggested, the materialization of democratic freedoms for African Americans also entailed redefining Black womanhood, the preservation of Black motherhood, and full sociopolitical inclusion of African American women through education. Collectively, these three areas represent the core themes of Black women's jeremiad, and they emerge frequently in the writing and oration of several Black women leaders of the nineteenth century.[34]

It is important to note, however, that although the political discourse of early African American women leaders was couched deep in the Judeo-Christian rhetoric of the nineteenth century, it was not merely a parroting of a popular or acceptable public discourse. Rather, it was a strategic means of pushing the boundaries of democracy, citizenship, and gender norms. Gleaning from anti-slavery, temperance, feminist, and Christian philosophies, African American women intellectuals joined the broader dialogues occurring around the nation and aligned their causes with that of several powerful political factions across the country. Grounding their calls for freedom and equality in Judeo-Christian ideals also allowed African American women to build on the tradition of syncretized spiritual belief. In many ways, their reliance on Christian principles bolstered an Afrocentric world view that emphasized the infinite relationship between the secular and the spiritual, and the active role of an omnipotent creator in the lives of the vulnerable.[35] In this respect, African American women were prime conduits for divine manifestation since they represented one of the nation's most unprotected populations.

For Stewart, demonstrations of the potential of African American people were best illustrated through the accomplishments of their women. Accordingly, she encouraged free Black women to use every means available to show themselves capable and honorable. In her early plea for racial uplift, Stewart called the "daughters of Africa" to "arise ... distinguish yourselves ... show forth to the world that ye are endowed with noble and exalted faculties." The time had come for Black women to "immortalize your names beyond the grave" and to set examples "before the rising generation."[36] The posterity and fate of the race, she posited, depended on the value of its women. This value was intimately tied to virtue and integrity, or "the principles formed within the soul."[37] Black women's moral integrity, therefore, served as a scaffold for the redemption of the race in the eyes of the nation and God.

For Stewart, the low social values ascribed to African American women, and their acceptance of low moral standards in Black communities, promoted a lack of interest in virtue among African American people and extended public scorn against them. Pointing to this, she asked, "Where is the maiden who will blush at vulgarity? And where is the youth who has written upon his manly brow a thirst for knowledge; whose ambitious mind soars above trifles, and longs for the time to come, when he shall redress the wrongs of his father and plead the cause of his brethren?"[38]

Though she did not directly blame Black women for the distractions and laxity she believed plagued their communities, Stewart did link disinterest in achieving Black liberation among African American youth to a shortage of strong female examples. "Did the daughters of our land possess a delicacy of manners, combined with gentleness and dignity; did their pure minds hold vice in abhorrence ... would not their influence become powerful?" The ambition of Black women, she asserted, would inevitably inspire the efforts of their male counterparts to "distinguish themselves ... [and] ... display their talents." Consequently, Stewart charged that it was the responsibility of all able African American women to "strive to excel in merit and virtue ... [and to] ... store thy mind with useful knowledge." It was only through this effort, she posited, that "able advocates would arise in our defence. Knowledge would begin to flow, and the chains of slavery and ignorance would melt like wax before the flames."[39]

Black women's moral leniency, Stewart noted, was not merely a danger to the race, it also undercut the position of Black women who stood as examples of virtue and as legitimate leaders. In one way, Stewart's contentions suggested that any laxity on the part of few Black women was a poor reflection on all. In another, however, her arguments also spoke to the underlying gender prejudice against Black women within their own communities. And, as she observed, "I am sensible of former prejudices; but it is high time for prejudices and animosities to cease from among us. I am sensible of exposing myself to calumny and reproach; but shall I, for fear of feeble man who shall die, hold my peace? . . . Ah, no! I speak as one that must give an account at the awful bar of God."[40]

Stewart's direct approach to addressing the gender prejudice of her time is noteworthy for several reasons. Foremost among these is that she was complicating the ideology of "True Womanhood."[41] While she certainly gleaned from and adapted the language of domesticity to emphasize the dignity and virtue of Black women, Stewart also rejected the idea that nature relegated them exclusively to the realm of domestic affairs. Given the labor conditions of free and enslaved African American women, Stewart's commentary signaled the need for their balanced representation in the public and private spheres. Extending this, her commentary on the "former prejudices" within the race suggested a rejection of Black male leadership as the natural path to achieving racial equality.

Stewart's rejection of gender prejudice also challenged the power dynamics in her community in its assertion that her selection by, and instructions from, God superseded African American male authority. Yet her arguments also served as a direct criticism of African American men, whose acquiescence to patriarchy and sexism was detracted from the larger goal of racial liberation. Without a full demonstration of equality, how could African American people expect freedom or justice in the United States? In effect, African American failure to extend equality to all those within Black communities was a mere reproduction of larger American democratic flaws. Consequently, Stewart implied that this hypocritical practice within Black communities was in direct conflict with their national aspirations and with the order of God. Gender prejudice, in turn, was a sinful practice that demoralized the race and hampered the virtue of Black women.

In addition to their roles as moral examples to and for African American people, Stewart maintained that Black women's integrity and virtue also served as a bridge between Black and white communities. Specifically, Stewart maintained that a demonstration of ambition and virtue among women would foster greater abolitionist support among sympathetic white activists. In her celebratory comments on the Second Annual Convention of the People of Color held in Philadelphia, Stewart wrote, "These Anti-Slavery societies, in my opinion, will soon cause many grateful tears to flow, and many desponding hearts to bound and leap for joy." It was not, she explained, "the applause of men" that encouraged white allies. Rather, it was the virtuous character of those whose efforts "will raise and elevate us above our present condition, and cause our aspirations to ascend up in unison with theirs [antislavery advocates]."[42] These efforts, she continued, exemplified the founding principles of the United States and furthered the cause of freedom.

Yet the virtue of African American people was not enough to secure Black-white alliances, and to this point, Stewart argued that white supporters should do more to eliminate racial prejudice within their communities. Namely, she called for greater access to employment opportunities for Black laborers. Economic independence and stability, she noted, was an important means of rejecting white racism by chipping away at dependent economic relationships between the communities. Limited employment opportunities—outside of those that mirrored slave labor—prevented many African Americans from aspiring beyond a lifetime of servitude. Black women's employment opportunities were limited to domestic labor, where their conditions were often identical to those of domestic slave laborers.[43] Hence, in her 1832 lecture to the New England Anti-Slavery Society she explained that "the free people of color throughout these United States are neither bought nor sold . . . but few, if any, have an opportunity of becoming rich and independent."[44]

"Tell us no more of southern slavery," she argued, "for with few exceptions . . . yet I consider our condition but little better than that."[45] To emphasize this point, Stewart made comparisons between Black and white women, noting that their most prominent differences were linked to the opportunities and resources afforded to both groups. Although white women may have agreed that Black women deserved more opportunities, she explained, they refused to act on these beliefs for fear of retaliation or alienation within their communities. "I have asked several individuals of my sex," she explained, "who transact business for themselves, if providing our girls were to give them the most satisfactory references, they would not be willing to grant them an equal opportunity with others?" Stewart further explained that while the general consensus was agreeable to Black female laborers, they would not hire Black women since "it was not the custom, were they to take them into their employ, they would be in danger of losing the public patronage."[46] As a result of "the powerful force of prejudice," she argued, "it is impossible for scarce and individual of them to rise above the condition of servants."[47]

These barriers to economic mobility, Stewart contended, created social ills and immorality in Black communities. Lifetimes of harsh physical labor and limited access to education crippled African Americans' humanity and even minimized their love of life. "Few white persons of either sex," she argued, "are willing to spend their lives and bury their talents in performing mean, servile labor." The imposition of this reality, she continued, was enough to persuade anyone to "gladly hail death as a welcome messenger." It was, she admitted, a "horrible idea, indeed! to possess noble souls aspiring after high and honorable acquirements, yet confined by the chains of ignorance and poverty to lives of continual drudgery and toil."[48] Stewart continued, "We are neither lazy nor idle; and considering how little we have to excite or stimulate us, I am almost astonished that there are so many industrious and ambitious ones to be found." Poor labor conditions and lack of opportunity, she insisted, "irritates our tempers and sours our dispositions . . . and we care but little whether we live or die."[49] Encouraging white women to increase their efforts to support Black freedom, she reminded them that "had we had the opportunity that you have had, to improve our moral and mental faculties, what would have hindered our intellects from being as bright, and our manners from being as dignified as yours?"[50]

Stewart's emphasis on Black women's virtue and piety was also rooted in the idea that it would garner divine justice and hasten the legal end of slavery. The manifestation of abolition and divine retribution, however, was linked to their concerted efforts to turn away from acts that cemented their public derision. Here too, she noted, prejudice within African American communities bolstered the "hissing" and "reproach" against them.[51] As she explained to the Afric-American Female Intelligence Society of America, "God has said that Ethiopia shall stretch forth her hands unto him," but this called for "the rising generation [to] manifest a different temper and disposition towards each other from what we have manifested." Change would only come "in convincing the world by our own efforts, however feeble, that nothing is wanting on our part but opportunity."[52] In this respect, Black women who countered public stereotypes about African American people, she asserted, nudged the country closer to abolition. It was through their examples, she maintained, that African American people could dismantle justifications for the continuation of slavery on the basis that Black people were naturally incapable of handling the responsibilities of legal freedom or citizenship. "O woman," she pleaded, "upon you I call; for upon your exertions almost entirely depends whether the rising generation shall be anything more than we have been or not."[53]

In her insistence that the future of African American people rested on the morality of their women, Stewart redefined them as soft, refined, noble, and beautiful. She challenged the idea that Black women were naturally licentious by reminding her audiences that the conditions of slavery and the abuses of domestic labor subjected Black women to "whoredom" and "fornication."[54] Stewart also pointed out that untruths about African American women prevailed because they had no means of defending themselves. With few public forums outside of churches, revivals, prayer meetings, and the homes of other women, African American women faced many obstacles to establishing a place in the public sphere. Stewart's call for Black women to step forward by using their moral influence helped to create a platform on which other Black women leaders could launch similar campaigns. Her appeal also mirrored the discourse of white feminists who relied on a language of moral influence to uplift the nation.[55] Yet Stewart's use of moral persuasion was multifaceted in its application to and use among African American women.

Primarily, Stewart's discourse linked the struggles of Black women to those of their white counterparts and helped to integrate issues of race into the larger nineteenth-century feminist movement that had grown out of the failure to grant women equal political rights during the period of the Early Republic.[56] It also limited the ability of detractors to challenge Black women's right to civic equality by demonstrating their ability to engage in nuanced political discourse, while her use of moral persuasion further cemented African American women's rightful inclusion in the definition of woman. Additionally, Stewart's moral suasion language offered her the opportunity to argue for the importance of Black motherhood in racial politics. Her emphasis on dignified Black womanhood, then, supported her contention that motherhood was at the center of African Americans' national destiny.

Motherhood, as Stewart argued, was a sacred obligation, and it was through the wisdom and virtue of Black mothers that the public image and future success of the race could be secured. Mothers had the potential, she maintained, to influence generations of African Americans and to persuade Black youth that high moral standards could redeem their race before God and the nation. Theirs, she asserted, was a tremendous responsibility. "You have souls committed to your charge," she argued, "and God will require a strict account of you." Motherhood required women to develop "a thirst for knowledge, the love of virtue, the abhorrence of vice, and . . . a pure heart" in Black youth. Virtuous motherhood, she claimed, was a protective measure for African American children who were inexperienced, but it was also a means of securing the redemption of the race through a deep-seated value system that prized integrity and education over material gain or short-term pleasures. This value system, in turn, promised to cultivate a genuine spirit of self-help and racial uplift in Black communities. In particular, Stewart suggested that the freedom of Black women could maximize the basic skills and knowledge they had to foster greater industry and independence in their families and their communities. "How long," she asked,

> shall the fair daughters of Africa be compelled to bury their minds and talents beneath a load of iron pots and kettles? How long shall a mean set of men flatter us with their smiles and enrich themselves with our hard earnings; their wives fingers sparkling with rings, and they themselves laughing at our folly?[57]

Use of their skills for community development and diligence in the effort to build Black institutions, she argued, were the most important means of showing younger generations the power of collective support and self-sustenance. Stewart suggested that Black women could and should fundraise so that they could "lay the cornerstone for the building of a high school that the higher branches of knowledge might be enjoyed by us."[58] She also emphasized the importance of community investment, arguing that Black women should "begin to promote and patronize each other."[59] Seemingly marginal efforts, she maintained, could make a significant difference and could also lay the foundations for growing a Black economy. To Stewart, this was an integral part of fostering a sense of community investment in African American youth. It was also a potent means of detracting from public scorn.

Personal industry and economic prudence fell in sync with the nation's own Protestant work ethic and its mantra of republican virtue.[60] No doubt, the prevailing post-Revolutionary public discourse about the virtue—or lack thereof—of America's body politic infused Stewart's own sense of what it meant for Black women to utilize their skill sets for financial stability in their communities. These efforts had already begun among a small fraction of the free Black population through the private ownership of businesses, churches, leisure spaces, and residences. As they demonstrated their ability to secure and sustain economic growth without the help of white Americans, Stewart suggested African American people also dismantled the idea that they were state dependents incapable of such ventures outside of white instruction or supervision. Underlining this point, she asserted that the minimal financial capital within Black communities could serve as formidable pillars of economic stability. "We have spent more than enough for nonsense," she quipped, "to do what building we should want." She argued that the lack of patronage within Black communities had, therefore, undercut African Americans' "opportunity of displaying our talents; therefore the world thinks we know nothing." Hence, she urged her audience to "possess the spirit of independence" found among white Americans and "the spirit of men, bold and enterprising, fearless and undaunted."[61] For their part, then, African American women could act as agents in the cultivation of an industrious spirit in their communities. This, in turn, bolstered Stewart's call for Black people to act as a nation within a nation and to prove their value before American society and God.

In her calls for Black motherhood that spurred community virtue and industry, Stewart was also modifying the notion of Republican motherhood. Black women's responsibilities lay in and outside of their homes, she explained, and their influence came primarily through virtuous womanhood. Yet for Stewart, the economic influence of Black women was just as important as their reproductive abilities or their responsibilities in marriage. There was space to maximize Black racial potential through the domestic sphere, and she encouraged Black women "to excel in good housewifery, knowing that prudence and economy are the road to wealth."[62] In her directive to "practice what we do know," Stewart was emphasizing the integral relationship between

Black women's domestic labor in and outside of their communities as a source of untapped power. Still, she was careful not to overemphasize this point or to encourage behavior or habits that might stretch the definition of "true womanhood" too far beyond its traditional use. Just as the redefinition and protection of Black womanhood was vital for the longevity of the race, the preservation Black motherhood was essential for the development of African Americans as a nation of people. The political potential of the race lay in the labor and virtue of Black mothers, even as it also rested on their concerted efforts to build up African American communities and to spur greater political agitation. In their efforts to challenge anti-Black racism, Stewart argued that African Americans must show themselves politically fit for inclusion in the American republic. They, too, she argued, were heirs of the Revolution and had been inspired by the same desires for freedom that compelled white Americans to action against the British Empire. Likewise, African Americans were equally ambitious and talented, and Stewart maintained that their calls for abolition and political equality were justified by these evidences. Specifically, she asserted that Black contributions to the American Revolution and the War of 1812 had proven their abilities. Nonetheless, she maintained that African Americans' fears, internal class divisions, and complacency in class privilege deterred the continuation of their fight for liberation.

Stewart rested the charge for these shortcomings partly on the men in African American communities. Their failure, she argued, to make a demonstrated effort toward political inclusion left the race without the protection it needed. Motherhood, therefore, was an important means of circumventing the deleterious effects of this vulnerability. Here, Stewart's use of the theme of motherhood buttressed another underlying dimension of republican virtue—concern for the well-being of the people of the republic. Active efforts by Black mothers could, in effect, spur political resistance to oppression. While Stewart undoubtedly maintained suspicions about a larger society she viewed as "those who now point at us with the finger of scorn," and whose outright refusal to acknowledge Black rights were rooted in a belief that they were "a ragged set, crying for liberty," she was also convinced that collective effort to challenge their oppression would favorably sway public opinion. Black mothers, therefore, could lead this charge by fostering racial pride, economic self-help, and piety within their communities. Most of all, Stewart's use of Black motherhood as a thematic lens for envisioning a more equal democratic system was a means of claiming the humanity of her race. Employing this theme cemented the humanity, dignity, and value of Black women and emphasized their ability to help the nation realize its revolutionary ideals. The important roles of African American women, however, hinged on their ability to educate themselves and their race. For Stewart, education was the only means of securing the position of the race in the future progress of the United States. Stewart maintained that formal education was critical for the inclusion of African American people into the body politic. Here, too, she insisted that women were vital to this integration. Through Black women's access to education, she argued, they would act as teachers within their communities. Their education would also serve as a continued affront to the system of slavery and to racial and gender oppression.

For many free African Americans living through the first half of the nineteenth century, education was prohibited, underfunded, or inaccessible. Stewart herself acquired education informally from her adolescence through her teenage years as she worked in domestic servitude for the family of a clergyman.[63] Her experiences were similar to many free Black youths living in the nation's urban centers, where public education was under intense scrutiny and heated debate. Only some states were willing to fund the education of poor and working-class youth, and these were primarily ethnic white children. Schools created for African Americans were often privately funded by benevolent societies, religious groups, or wealthy sympathetic philanthropists. In the first few decades of the nineteenth century, these schools proved to be dangerous ventures when mobs of white vigilantes burned them down or when frustrated residents complained to local officials about the schools. Funding Black schools was an equally challenging feat, and many African Americans and their white allies struggled to keep their institutions open once they were established.[64]

It was with these realities in mind that Maria Stewart argued physical labor and denial of basic education dulled the intellectual faculties of poor African Americans. "I have learnt by bitter experience," she wrote, "that continual hard labor deadens the energies of the soul, and benumbs the faculties of the mind." Creativity became severely restricted, she argued, and "the ideas become confined, the mind barren, and, like the scorching sands of Arabia, produces nothing; or like the uncultivated soil brings forth thorns and thistles." Careful not to disparage the work many African Americans depended on for sustenance, Stewart noted, "I do not consider it derogatory, my friends, for persons to live out to service." Still, she insisted, "Where constitutional strength is wanting, labor of this kind in its mildest form is painful."[65] Nonetheless, Stewart maintained that without education, African American people were also denied the means to uplift themselves and to live in the fullness of their humanity. "What literary acquirement can be made," she asked, or useful knowledge derived, from either maps, books, or charts, by those who continually drudge from Monday morning until Sunday noon?"[66] Although Stewart's arguments clearly highlight the ways in which educational restrictions intersected with economic conditions, her words also reminded the nation that the denial of Black education was, in itself, a means of continuing enslavement. Without the means to expand their potential, she suggested, Black communities would be confined to the low ceiling of their own socioeconomic realities and to the will of sympathetic white Americans.

Similar to the legal practice of slavery, which denied education to enslaved people, laws and policies that undermined Black education replicated the "sin of slavery" and further tarnished the nation's philosophical ideals of freedom and equality.[67] Additionally, Stewart's assertion that a lack of education "deadens the energies of the soul" spoke to the insidious nature of racism that permeated Northern states. While most began to end the legal practice of slavery through gradual manumission laws, freed African American people were not included in the fabric of life in most northern states, cities, and towns. Complicating this even further was the rise of punitive legislative measures taken throughout the North to prevent the socioeconomic, political, and physical mobility of African American people throughout the region. Between the 1820s and the 1840s, Pennsylvania, New York, and Massachusetts had all passed—or attempted to pass—racially restrictive legislature that denied Black property ownership, raised taxes, or prohibited Black migration into their states. Several Northern states also extended the reach of slavery by enforcing fugitive slave laws within their boundaries.[68] Consequently, Stewart's tone and urgency carried with them the weight of political criticism and accusation.

Underneath her criticisms, however, was an implicit charge against the religious factions in the North. In the mid-Atlantic and New England, strong Protestant communities flourished with and around slave labor. And in this way, Stewart was challenging the validity of their values. Hence, she warned that the nation would face divine retribution for its hypocrisy and told of a time when "Ethiopia shall stretch forth her hands."[69] As she perceived it, the signs of Black racial progress had already begun in communities where notable achievements were visible among the few. Still, Stewart asserted, African Americans could be more effective if they insisted on improving themselves with or without the nation's support. "I am rejoiced to reflect that there are many able and talented ones among us," she noted, "but 'I can't' is a great barrier in the way. I hope it will soon be removed, and 'I will,' resume its place."[70] By working to break barriers on their own, she argued, African Americans could extend their own reach into the future. Black parents, she argued, should pool their resources to have their children "taught in the first rudiments of useful knowledge and then you can have private teachers who will instruct them in the higher branches." Rather than hoping for public funding that would provide qualified or willing teachers, she suggested, the community should select its own educators. "Their intelligence will become greater than ours," she wrote, "and their children will attain to higher advantages, and their children still higher, and then, though we are dead, our works shall live."[71]

Stewart also believed that formal education had the ability to bolster African Americans' love of liberty and knowledge—a legacy she argued they carried as heirs of the Revolution. Though driven by the same ambitions, Stewart asserted that African American people were stunted by racial oppression and fear. Nonetheless, Stewart reminded her audiences that their experiences of exclusion and oppression should not prevent their diligent efforts to dismantle the racial hierarchy that inhibited their progress. "I am sensible," she reflected, "that many of you have been deprived of advantages, kept in utter ignorance, and that your minds are now darkened, and if any one of you have attempted to aspire after high and noble enterprises, you have met with so much opposition that your souls have become discouraged."[72] Yet she encouraged her readers not to give up since, "for this very cause, a few of us have ventured to expose our lives in your behalf to plead your cause against the great." If they focused their energies on "knowledge and improvement," she asserted, God would supplement their inefficiencies and "fill you with wisdom and understanding."[73] Here, too, Stewart drew from her own experiences as a testament to the elevating power of faith and dedication to self-education. It was, after all, her faith that compelled her to champion virtue and piety among the race, and the very same bolstered her efforts to publicly grapple with issues of political inequality. If granted the right to educate themselves, she maintained, African American ambitions would buttress their sociopolitical achievements and help to integrate the race fully into the American body politic. For African American women, she argued, this was critical. Their educational access would also open new economic doors that Stewart asserted were invaluable for the uplifting of the race.

Domestic labor and servitude relegated Black women to the lowest sociopolitical and economic conditions, stifling their ability to prove themselves intelligent and virtuous members of the democratic republic. Yet it also cemented their positions as "the servants of servants" in their own communities—by supporting existing attitudes of sexism within them. Without the virtuous and knowledgeable leadership of Black women, she argued, African American youth would continue to struggle to uphold the moral standard she believed God was calling the race to uphold. Without education, African American women would be unable to fulfill the sacred calling of their womanhood in and around their communities. This was particularly important since many African American women among the well-to-do in their communities acted as teachers or private tutors in traditional and religious subjects.[74] Black education, then, was a primary means of unlocking Black potential as well as an essential venue for spiritual instruction. It was through the training and examples of African American women that Black youth would learn and extend the intellectual and faith traditions of their forebears. Black women's education and teaching, therefore, were a cornerstone of racial virtue.

Stewart's emphasis on virtue and morals in African American education was another means of reinforcing their values as potential citizens of the United States. The discourse of Black virtue, and certainly of Black women who represented the core of that morality, underscored their humanity and affirmed Stewart's argument that African Americans should not be excluded from the virtuous republic. If, as Stewart argued, the nation's Black population was as dedicated to the welfare and progress of their society as their white counterparts, they were indeed an important part of its national virtue. Black political inclusion, therefore, was the sole means of rectifying America's discordant posture toward the God many believed had favored the nation and its body politic. Beyond this, however, Stewart's call for Black women's teaching and learning provided another means to underscore their purity and further cement their status as model citizens and spiritual authorities.

For many African American women, teaching was a spiritual calling that allowed them to fulfill their roles as virtuous change agents and moral guardians in their communities. It was primarily through education that most African American women believed they could train the next generation to strive for progress and inclusion. No doubt these messages carried over into the latter nineteenth century precisely because of women like Maria Stewart, Sojourner Truth, Jarena Lee, and many others who served as teachers in free communities across the nation well into their later lives. Their work, therefore, laid the foundation for the development of national organizations such as the National Association of Colored Women. They also forged a dynamic set of practices through their intellectual communities and traditions that enabled future generations of Black women to defend themselves against undue public scrutiny and racial and gender inequalities.

Though short-lived, Maria Stewart's public speaking was a remarkable feat. Her unwillingness to succumb to social pressure and her insistence on higher standards for African Americans mark her as a striking example of a Black woman Jeremiah. Nonetheless, Stewart's limitations and the gender discrimination she faced forced her to adapt the jeremiad to her own lived realities. Similar to women such as Jarena Lee and Sojourner Truth, Stewart drew on powerful tropes of spiritual purity and femininity to ground and support her calls for racial equality. In her writing and discourse, Stewart melded the concerns of free and enslaved Black women with the larger issues facing the nation and placed her own voice at the center. To ignore her was to ignore God. As she claimed divine authority, Stewart defied the popular notion that Black bodies—and especially Black women's bodies—were impure and invaluable outside of physical labor. Yet she also imbued herself with authority that could not be granted or taken away by whites or by Black men. In this way, Maria Stewart is indeed a foremother of Black women's jeremiadic discourse and a prime example of the creative ways in which African American women worked in the public sphere to defend and protect their race.

NOTES

1. Maria W. Stewart, "Cause for Encouragement," in *Maria W. Stewart*, 43.

2. See Perry Miller's *The New England Mind* and *Errand into the Wilderness*, and Sacvan Bercovitch's *The American Jeremiad*.

3. In New Testament biblical tradition, Jesus urged his followers to offer as much consideration to the vulnerable in their societies as they did the powerful. In her advocacy for African American women and communities, Stewart invoked this idea to persuade her audiences that racism and sexism were antithetical to God and Christianity. Reference to Matthew 25:40–45.

4. See for further discussion Charles Grier Sellers, *The Market Revolution: Jacksonian America, 1815–1846* (New York: Oxford University Press, 1991).

5. For a full discussion on moral debates during the nineteenth century market revolution, see James L. Huston, "Abolitionists, Political Economists, and Capitalism," *Journal of the Early Republic* 20, no. 3 (Fall 2000): 487–521; Paul Goodman, "The Manual Labor Movement and Origins of Abolitionism," *Journal of the Early Republic* 13 (Fall 1993), 355–88.

6. Schantz, "Religious Tracts, Evangelical Reform"; Huston, "Abolitionists, Political Economists, and Capitalism."

7. For more details see Richard Maxwell Brown's *Strain of Violence Historical Studies of American Violence and Vigilantism* (New York: Oxford University Press, 1975).

8. Freedman, "African-American Schooling"; Rury, "The New York African Free School"; Christopher M. Span, "Learning in Spite of Opposition: African Americans and Their History of Educational Exclusion in Antebellum America," *Counterpoints* 131 (2005): 26–53; Hilary J. Moss, *Schooling Citizens: The Struggle for African American Education in Antebellum America* (Chicago: University of Chicago Press, 2009).

9. Brenda E. Stevenson, "What's Love Got to Do with It? Concubinage and Enslaved Women and Girls in the Antebellum South," *Journal of African American History* 98 (Winter 2013): 99–125; Deborah Gray White, *Ar'n't I a Woman? Female Slaves in the Plantation South*, rev. ed. (New York: W. W. Norton, 1999); Darlene Clark Hine, "Rape and the Inner Lives of Black Women: Preliminary Thoughts on the Culture of Dissemblance," *Signs* 14 (Summer 1989): 912–20; Wilma King, "'Prematurely Knowing of Evil Things': The Sexual Abuse of African American Girls and Young Women in Slavery and Freedom," *Journal of African American History* 99, no. 3 (Summer 2014): 173–96.

10. Maria W. Stewart, "Religion and the Pure Principles of Morality," in *Maria W. Stewart*, 39.

11. Stewart, "Religion and the Pure Principles of Morality," in *Maria W. Stewart*, 34–35.

12. Stewart, "Religion and the Pure Principles of Morality," in *Maria W. Stewart*, 34–35.

13. Stewart, "Religion and the Pure Principles of Morality," in *Maria W. Stewart*, 38–39.

14. Stewart, "Religion and the Pure Principles of Morality," in *Maria W. Stewart*, 38–39.

15. Stewart, "Religion and the Pure Principles of Morality," in *Maria W. Stewart*, 38–39.

16. Stewart, "Religion and the Pure Principles of Morality," in *Maria W. Stewart*, 40.

17. For warning see reference in Jeremiah 7:1–15 KJV. For a full discussion on the significance of these passages in Jewish and Christian history and tradition see Christopher J. H. Wright, *The Message of Jeremiah: Against Wind and Tide* (Downers Grove, IL: IVP Academic, 2014); J. A. Wilcoxen, "The Political Background of Jeremiah's Temple Sermon," in *Scripture in History and Theology: Essays in Honor of J. Coert Rylaarsdam*, ed. Arthur L. Merrill and Thomas W. Overholt (Pittsburgh Theological Monograph Series, no. 17, Pittsburgh: Pickwick Press, 1977); Pearle Felicia Stone, "The Temple Sermons of Jeremiah," *American Journal of Semitic Languages and Literatures* 50, no. 2 (January 1934): 73–92; Carolyn J. Sharp, "The Call of Jeremiah and Diaspora Politics," *Journal of Biblical Literature* 119, no. 3 (2000): 421–38.

18. Maria Stewart, "Mrs. Stewart's Farewell Address to Her Friends in the City of Boston," in *Maria W. Stewart*, 66–67.

19. Maria W. Stewart made many explicit and implicit references to herself as a divinely chosen orator, disciple, and prophet. Stewart's references appear in each of the works referenced here, but they also appear in her poetry submissions to *The Liberator*. See for example "Untitled Poem," *The Liberator*, May 19, 1832. Stewart's poem drew a parallel between her own rejection as a spiritual authority in her Boston community and the foretold rejection of Jesus's disciples. See reference Matthew: 10:14–16 KJV. In this passage, Jesus instructed his disciples on how to respond to those who rejected their message. In her poem, Stewart relied on the same language, noting that she would shake the dust from her feet rather than fighting to prove herself to her peers.

20. Stewart, "Religion and the Pure Principles of Morality," in *Maria W. Stewart*, 30–31.

21. Stewart, "Religion and the Pure Principles of Morality," in *Maria W. Stewart*, 49.

22. For Black theology see Cone, *A Black Theology of Liberation*; for African Americans as divinely chosen people see Eddie S. Glaude, *Exodus!*

23. Stewart, "Religion and the Pure Principles of Morality," in *Maria W. Stewart*, 32.

24. Stewart, "An Address Delivered Before the Afric-American Female Intelligence Society of America," in *Maria W. Stewart*, 51.

25. Stewart, "An Address Delivered Before the Afric-American Female Intelligence Society of America," in *Maria W. Stewart*, 53.

26. The power of Black women in their religious institutions was frequently limited by male dominance, and often women operated in their ministries outside of church jurisdiction. Women who received recognition from their organizations were typically permitted to act as "exhorters" (traveling proselytizers) or community caretakers. See for full discussion TeResa Green, "A Gendered Spirit: Race, Class, and Sex in the African American Church," *Race, Gender and Class* 10, no. 1 (2003): 115–28; Bettye Collier-Thomas, *Jesus, Jobs, and Justice: African American Women and Religion* (New York: Alfred A. Knopf, 2010); Hans A. Baer, "The Limited Empowerment of Women in Black Spiritual Churches: An Alternative Vehicle to Religious Leadership," *Sociology of Religion* 54, no. 1 (1993).

27. Stewart, "An Address Delivered Before the Afric-American Female Intelligence Society of America," in *Maria W. Stewart*, 52.

28. Stewart, "An Address Delivered at the African Masonic Hall," in *Maria W. Stewart*, 56.

29. Stewart, "An Address Delivered at the African Masonic Hall," in *Maria W. Stewart*, 57.

30. Stewart, "An Address Delivered at the African Masonic Hall," in *Maria W. Stewart*, 60.

31. Stewart, "Mrs. Stewart's Farewell Address to Her Friends in the City of Boston," in *Maria W. Stewart*, 68.

32. Stewart, "Mrs. Stewart's Farewell Address to Her Friends in the City of Boston," in *Maria W. Stewart*, 71.

33. Stewart, "An Address Delivered Before the Afric-American Female Intelligence Society of America," in *Maria W. Stewart*, 53.

34. References to each of these themes reoccur in the writings of several antebellum African American women intellectuals and activists. See for examples Andrews, *Sisters of the Spirit*; Delores S. Williams, "Visions, Inner Voices, Apparitions, and Defiance in Nineteenth-Century Black Women's Narratives," *Women's Studies Quarterly* 21, no. 1/2 (Spring 1993): 81–89. For Black motherhood see Crystal Lynn Webster, "In Pursuit of Autonomous Womanhood: Nineteenth-Century Black Motherhood in the U.S. North," *Slavery and Abolition* 38, no. 2 (April 3, 2017): 425–40. For Black womanhood see Dunbar, *A Fragile Freedom*; Bert James Loewenberg and Ruth Bogin, *Black Women in Nineteenth-Century American Life: Their Words, Their Thoughts, Their Feelings* (University Park: Pennsylvania State University Press, 1976).

35. See Cone, *God of the Oppressed*. John S. Mbiti, *African Religions and Philosophy* (London: Heinemann, 1969); John S. Mbiti, *Concepts of God in Africa* (London: Society for Promoting Christian Knowledge, 1970); Albert J. Raboteau, *A Fire in the Bones: Reflections on African American Religious History* (Boston: Beacon Press, 1995); Bert Hamminga, "Epistemology from the African Point of View," in *Knowledge Cultures: Comparative Western and African Epistemology*, ed. Bert Hamminga (New York: Radopi, 2005), 57–85.

36. Stewart, "Religion and the Pure Principles of Morality," in *Maria W. Stewart*, 30.

37. Stewart, "Religion and the Pure Principles of Morality," in *Maria W. Stewart*, 29.

38. Stewart, "Religion and the Pure Principles of Morality," in *Maria W. Stewart*, 31.

39. Stewart, "Religion and the Pure Principles of Morality," in *Maria W. Stewart*, 31.

40. Stewart, "Religion and the Pure Principles of Morality," in *Maria W. Stewart*, 30.

41. Barbara Welter, "The Cult of True Womanhood," *American Quarterly* 18, no. 2 (Summer 1966): 155–74. For excellent discussions on the ways in which Black women adapted and modified this concept see Carby, *Reconstructing Womanhood*; Sharon Harley, "For the Good of Family and Race: Gender, Work, and Domestic Roles in the Black Community, 1880–1930," *Signs: Journal of Women in Culture and Society* 15, no. 2 (Winter 1990): 336–49; Linda M. Perkins, "The Impact of the 'Cult of True Womanhood' on the Education of Black Women," *Journal of Social Issues* 39, no. 3 (Fall 1983): 17–28.

42. Stewart, "Cause for Encouragement," in *Maria W. Stewart*, 43.

43. Horton and Horton, *In Hope of Liberty*; Jennifer Hull Dorsey, *Hirelings: African American Workers and Free Labor in Early Maryland* (Ithaca, NY: Cornell University Press, 2011); James Oliver Horton, "Freedom's Yoke: Gender Conventions among Antebellum Free Blacks," *Feminist Studies* 12, no. 1 (1986): 51–76. For Black women's labor conditions see Jones, *Labor of Love, Labor of Sorrow*; Elizabeth Fox-Genovese, *Within the Plantation Household: Black and White Women of the Old South* (Chapel Hill: University of North Carolina Press, 1988).

44. Stewart, "Lecture Delivered at the Franklin Hall," in *Maria W. Stewart*, 47.

45. Stewart, "Lecture Delivered at the Franklin Hall," in *Maria W. Stewart*, 45.

46. Stewart, "Lecture Delivered at the Franklin Hall," in *Maria W. Stewart*, 45.

47. Stewart, "Lecture Delivered at the Franklin Hall," in *Maria W. Stewart*, 46.

48. Stewart, "Lecture Delivered at the Franklin Hall," in *Maria W. Stewart*, 46.

49. Stewart, "Lecture Delivered at the Franklin Hall," in *Maria W. Stewart*, 47.
50. Stewart, "Lecture Delivered at the Franklin Hall," in *Maria W. Stewart*, 48.
51. Stewart, "An Address Delivered before the Afric-American Female Intelligence Society of America," in *Maria W. Stewart*, 53.
52. Stewart, "An Address Delivered before the Afric-American Female Intelligence Society of America," in *Maria W. Stewart*, 53.
53. Stewart, "An Address Delivered before the Afric-American Female Intelligence Society of America," in *Maria W. Stewart*, 55.
54. See notes 10 and 13.
55. For a discussion about Black use of moral suasion see Bracey, Meier, and Rudwick, *Blacks in the Abolitionist Movement*; George A. Levesque, "Black Abolitionists in the Age of Jackson: Catalysts in the Radicalization of American Abolitionism," *Journal of Black Studies* 1, no. 2 (1970): 187–201; Tunde Adeleke, "Philosophizing Non-Violence: Free Blacks in Antebellum America," *American Studies* 21 (December 2004): 69–86; Tunde Adeleke, "Afro-Americans and Moral Suasion: The Debate in the 1830's," *Journal of Negro History* 83, no. 2 (March 1998): 127–42.
56. See Sylvia D. Hoffert, *When Hens Crow: The Women's Rights Movements in Antebellum America* (Bloomington: Indiana University Press, 1995); Shirley Samuels, *The Culture of Sentiment: Race, Gender, and Sentimentality in Nineteenth-Century America* (New York: Oxford University Press, 1992); Epstein, *The Politics of Domesticity*; Carol Mattingly, *Appropriate[ing] Dress: Women's Rhetorical Style in Nineteenth-Century America* (Carbondale: Southern Illinois University Press, 2002).
57. Stewart, "Religion and the Pure Principles of Morality," in *Maria W. Stewart*, 38.
58. Stewart, "Religion and the Pure Principles of Morality," in *Maria W. Stewart*, 37.
59. Stewart, "Religion and the Pure Principles of Morality," in *Maria W. Stewart*, 38.
60. See Dagger, *Civic Virtues*.
61. Stewart, "Religion and the Pure Principles of Morality," 38.
62. Stewart, "Religion and the Pure Principles of Morality," 37.
63. See Marilyn Richardson ed. *Maria W. Stewart: America's First Black Woman Political Writer*, (Bloomington: Indiana University Press, 1987), 3–4.
64. See note 8. For specific examples of African American struggles to secure educational institutions for themselves see Harry C. Silcox, "Delay and Neglect: Negro Public Education in Antebellum Philadelphia, 1800–1860," *The Pennsylvania Magazine of History and Biography* 97, no. 4 (1973): 444–64. Hilary J. Moss, "The Tarring and Feathering of Thomas Paul Smith: Common Schools, Revolutionary Memory, and the Crisis of Black Citizenship in Antebellum Boston," *New England Quarterly* 80, no. 2 (June 2007): 218–41; David Freedman, "African-American Schooling in the South Prior to 1861," *Journal of Negro History* 84, no. 1 (January 1999): 1–47.
65. Stewart, "Lecture Delivered at the Franklin Hall," in *Maria W. Stewart*, 47.
66. Stewart, "Lecture Delivered at the Franklin Hall," in *Maria W. Stewart*, 48.
67. Anti-slavery activists often used this term to highlight the immorality of slavery. For a full discussion see Molly Oshatz, *Slavery and Sin: The Fight against Slavery and the Rise of Liberal Protestantism* (New York: Oxford University Press, 2012).
68. Horton and Horton, *In Hope of Liberty*; Rael, *Black Identity and Black Protest*; Winch, *Between Slavery and Freedom*.

69. Stewart, "An Address Delivered Before the Afric-American Female Intelligence Society of America," in *Maria W. Stewart*, 53.

70. Stewart, "Religion and the Pure Principles of Morality," in *Maria W. Stewart*, 35.

71. Stewart, "Religion and the Pure Principles of Morality," in *Maria W. Stewart*, 36.

72. Stewart, "Religion and the Pure Principles of Morality," in *Maria W. Stewart*, 36.

73. Stewart, "Religion and the Pure Principles of Morality," in *Maria W. Stewart*, 41.

74. Johnson, Pitre, and Johnson, *African American Women Educators*.

REFERENCES

Alexander, Estrelda Y. *Black Fire: One Hundred Years of African American Pentecostalism*. Downers Grove, IL: IVP Academic, 2011.

Andrews, William L., ed. *Sisters of the Spirit: Three Black Women's Autobiographies of the Nineteenth Century*. Bloomington: Indiana University Press, 1986.

Ball, Erica L. *To Live an Antislavery Life: Personal Politics and the Antebellum Black Middle Class*. Athens: University of Georgia Press, 2012.

Bassard, Katherine Clay. *Spiritual Interrogations: Culture, Gender, and Community in Early African American Women's Writing*. Princeton, NJ: Princeton University Press, 1999.

Bassard, Katherine Clay. *Transforming Scriptures*. Athens: University of Georgia Press, 2010.

Bercovitch, Sacvan. *The American Jeremiad*. Madison: University of Wisconsin Press, 1978.

Bracey, John H., August Meier, and Elliott M. Rudwick. *Blacks in the Abolitionist Movement*. Belmont, CA: Wadsworth, 1971.

Butler, Jon. *Awash in a Sea of Faith: Christianizing the American People*. Cambridge, MA: Harvard University Press, 1990.

Carby, Hazel V. *Reconstructing Womanhood: The Emergence of the Afro-American Woman*. New York: Oxford University Press, 1987.

Cawardine, Richard J. *Evangelicals and Politics in Antebellum America*. New Haven, CT: Yale University Press, 1993.

Collier-Thomas, Bettye. *Daughters of Thunder: Black Women Preachers and Their Sermons, 1850–1979*. San Francisco: Jossey-Bass Publishers, 1998.

Cone, James H. *A Black Theology of Liberation*. 20th anniversary ed. Maryknoll, NY: Orbis Books, 1990.

Cone, James H. *God of the Oppressed*. Rev. ed. Maryknoll, NY: Orbis Books, 1997.

Cooper, Valerie C. *Word Like Fire: Maria Stewart, the Bible, and the Rights of African Americans*. Charlottesville: University of Virginia Press, 2011.

Dagger, Richard. *Civic Virtues: Rights, Citizenship, and Republican Liberalism*. New York: Oxford University Press, 1997.

Dunbar, Erica Armstrong. *A Fragile Freedom: African American Women and Emancipation in the Antebellum City*. New Haven, CT: Yale University Press, 2008.

Epstein, Barbara Leslie. *The Politics of Domesticity: Women, Evangelism, and Temperance in Nineteenth-Century America*. Middletown, CT: Wesleyan University Press, 1981.

Freedman, David. "African-American Schooling in the South Prior to 1861." *Journal of Negro History* 84, no. 1 (January 1, 1999): 1–47.

Glaude, Eddie S. *Exodus! Religion, Race, and Nation in Early Nineteenth-Century Black America*. Chicago: University of Chicago Press, 2007.

Hardesty, Nancy A. *Women Called to Witness: Evangelical Feminism in the Nineteenth Century*. Knoxville: University of Tennessee Press, 1978.

Harrell, Willie, Jr. "A Call to Political and Social Activism: The Jeremiadic Discourse of Maria Miller Stewart, 1831–1833." *Journal of International Women's Studies* 9, no. 3 (2008): 300–319.

Harrell, Willie, Jr. *Origins of the African American Jeremiad: The Rhetorical Strategies of Social Protest and Activism, 1760–1861*. Jefferson, NC: MacFarland, 2011.

Harris, Leslie. *In the Shadow of Slavery: African Americans in New York City, 1626–1863*. Chicago: University of Chicago Press, 2003.

Horton, James Oliver, and Lois E. Horton. *In Hope Of Liberty: Culture, Community, and Protest among Northern Free Blacks, 1700–1860*. New York: Oxford University Press, 1997.

Howard-Pitney, David. *The African American Jeremiad: Appeals for Justice in America*. Philadelphia: Temple University Press 2005.

Hume, Janice. *Popular Media and the American Revolution: Shaping Collective Memory*. New York: Routledge, 2014.

Johnson, Karen A., Abul Pitre, and Kenneth L. Johnson, eds. *African American Women Educators: A Critical Examination of Their Pedagogies, Educational Ideas, and Activism from the Nineteenth to the Mid-Twentieth Century*. Lanham, MD: Rowman and Littlefield Education, 2013.

Jones, Jacqueline. *Labor of Love, Labor of Sorrow: Black Women, Work and the Family, from Slavery to the Present*. New York: Basic Books, 2010.

King, Wilma. *The Essence of Liberty: Free Black Women during the Slave Era*. Columbia: University of Missouri Press, 2006.

Lasser, Carol, and Stacey Robertson. *Antebellum Women: Private, Public, Partisan*. Lanham, MD: Rowman and Littlefield, 2010.

McHenry, Elizabeth. "'Dreaded Eloquence': The Origins and Rise of African American Literary Societies and Libraries." *Harvard Library Bulletin* 6, no. 2 (June 1995): 32–56.

Miller, Perry. *Errand into the Wilderness*. Cambridge, MA: Harvard University Press, 1956.

Miller, Perry. *The New England Mind: The Seventeenth Century*. Cambridge, MA: Harvard University Press, 1939.

Moses, Wilson Jeremiah. *Black Messiahs and Uncle Toms: Social and Literary Manipulations of a Religious Myth*. University Park: Pennsylvania State University Press, 1982.

Peterson, Carla L. *Doers of the Word: African-American Women Speakers and Writers in the North (1830–1880)*. New York: Oxford University Press, 1995.

Rael, Patrick. *Black Identity and Black Protest in the Antebellum North*. Chapel Hill: University of North Carolina Press, 2002.

Richardson, Marilyn. *Maria Stewart: America's First Black Woman Political Writer*. Bloomington: Indiana University Press, 1987.

Roberts, Rita. *Evangelicalism and the Politics of Reform in Northern Black Thought, 1776–1863*. Baton Rouge: Louisiana State University Press, 2010.

Rockman, S. "Liberty Is Land and Slaves: The Great Contradiction." *OAH Magazine of History* 19, no. 3 (May 1, 2005): 8–11.

Rothman, Joshua D. "The Hazards of the Flush Times: Gambling, Mob Violence, and the Anxieties of America's Market Revolution." *Journal of American History* 95, no. 3 (December 2008): 651–77.

Rury, John L. "The New York African Free School, 1827–1836: Conflict over Community Control of Black Education." *Phylon* 44, no. 3 (September 1983): 187–97.

Rury, John L. "Philanthropy, Self Help, and Social Control: The New York Manumission Society and Free Blacks, 1785–1810." *Phylon* 46, no. 3 (September 1985): 231–41.

Schantz, Mark S. "Religious Tracts, Evangelical Reform, and the Market Revolution in Antebellum America." *Journal of the Early Republic* 17, no. 3 (Fall 1997): 425–66.

Scully, R. "Slavery and Sin: The Fight against Slavery and the Rise of Liberal Protestantism." *Journal of American History* 99, no. 2 (September 1, 2012): 590–91.

Sinha, Manisha. "To 'Cast Just Obliquy' on Oppressors: Black Radicalism in the Age of Revolution." *William and Mary Quarterly* 64, no. 1 (January 2007): 149–60.

Stanley, Amy. "Dominion and Dependence in the Law of Freedom and Slavery." *Law and Social Inquiry* 28, no. 4 (September 1, 2003): 1127–34.

Stewart, Maria W. *Maria W. Stewart: America's First Black Woman Political Writer*. Edited by Marilyn Richardson. Indianapolis: Indiana University Press, 1987.

Sundue, Sharon Braslaw. "Confining the Poor to Ignorance? Eighteenth-Century American Experiments with Charity Education." *History of Education Quarterly* 47, no. 2 (Summer 2007): 123–48.

Tate, Gale T. *Unknown Tongues: Black Women's Political Activism in the Antebellum Era, 1830–1860*. East Lansing: Michigan State University Press, 2003.

Winch, Julie. *Between Slavery and Freedom: Free People of Color in America from Settlement to the Civil War*. Lanham, MD: Rowman and Littlefield, 2014.

"DID NOT MARY *FIRST* PREACH THE RISEN SAVIOR?"

Black Preaching Women as Public Intellectuals

HETTIE V. WILLIAMS

Jarena Lee, Zilpha Elaw, and Mary Prince helped to inaugurate the activist tradition that is so fundamental to the historical development of Black intellectualism within the larger framework of the American intellectual tradition. These women occupy a distinct place in this history. Lee and Elaw, among others, helped to inaugurate the Holiness tradition in American Christianity, embraced an intersectional approach to Black women's empowerment as abolitionists, advocated temperance, and supported women's rights. These preaching women advanced an activist approach to knowing, provided the groundwork for American feminist thought, wrote spiritual biographies that predate Black women's slave narratives, and facilitated the development of evangelical Christianity into the first four decades of the nineteenth century. This chapter situates the thought and activism of Black preaching women in the National era of early US history within the larger context of American public intellectualism.

"If then, to preach the gospel, by the gift of heaven, comes by inspiration solely, is God straitened; must he take the man exclusively? May he not, did he not, and can he not inspire a female to preach the simple story of the birth," implores Jarena Lee in her autobiography entitled *The Life and Religious Experience of Jarena Lee, A Coloured Lady, Giving an Account of Her Call to Preach the Gospel*, first published in 1836.[1] Black women such as Lee who were concerned with religious questions and ideas about women's rights were the first Black women intellectuals. As writers of poems, letters, autobiographies, memoirs, and speeches and as evangelists, these women are among the earliest intellectuals in the history of the African diaspora. Scholarly literature on the National era in the history of the United States tends to overlook the thought of Black women, and this essay seeks to fill this void. Focusing primarily on the spiritual autobiographies of Black women such as Jarena Lee and Zilpha Elaw, this analysis, as largely a work of historical synthesis, situates Black women within the context of American intellectual history. A synthesis such as this is necessary given the continued erasure of Black women intellectuals from some of the canonical texts on American intellectual history.

Black women preachers and their ideas are integral to the discussion of the American intellectual tradition. Women preachers such as Lee and Elaw helped to inaugurate the activist approach that is so fundamental to the evolution of Black thought past and present. This tradition was further cultivated by Black women preachers such as Florence Spearing Randolph in the late nineteenth century and Pauli Murray in the twentieth century. African American women preachers have often been overlooked in the development of American intellectual history. Black women preachers of the Early Republic, in particular, occupy a distinct place in the American intellectual tradition for multiple reasons. These preaching women helped to facilitate the advance of evangelical Christianity in nineteenth-century America while advocating for the end of human bondage. Furthermore, a discussion of the major debates of the nineteenth century is incomprehensible without a sustained discussion of Black preaching women who were active during this time.

According to Mia Bay, Farah J. Griffin, Martha S. Jones, and Barbara D. Savage, the editors of the first significant edited volume on Black women intellectuals, *Toward an Intellectual History of Black Women*, there is a "distinctive tradition" of Black women's intellectualism.[2] Historically, as the editors note, Black women have rarely worked out of "the academy or research institutes."[3] That said, "black women's intellectual history can never be explained by way of a mere genealogy of ideas."[4] Given that these women have been routinely closed out of prominent academies and institutions on the account of race and gender, their ideas have always been "produced in dialogue with lived experience"[5] as shaped by their social condition.

American intellectual history is directly connected to the lives, thought, and activism of Black preaching women. Black women preachers collectively had a pervasive influence on the formation of not only the Black church but the American intellectual tradition as a whole. This concept of the public intellectual is intimately bound up with American religious history and, specifically, the thoughts of Black church women who provided a foundation for Black women's public intellectualism.

There have been important works published on Black preaching women and religion. Chanta M. Haywood's *Prophesying Daughters: Black Women Preachers and the Word, 1823–1913* (2003), Evelyn Higginbotham's *Righteous Discontent* on

Black Baptist women, Jualynne E. Dodson's *Engendering Church: Women, Power, and the AME Church* (2002), Bettye Collier-Thomas's *Jesus, Jobs, and Justice: African American Women and Religion* (2011), and more recently Betty Livingston Adams's *Black Women's Christian Activism: Seeking Social Justice in a Northern Suburb* (2016) have made important conclusions regarding Black women's thought and Christian activism.[6] In her analysis of the writings of women such as Lee and Elaw, Haywood demonstrates that Black women used prophesying as a means to gain some authority in and beyond the male-dominated Black church as preachers and "prophesying women."[7] In *Righteous Discontent*, Higginbotham argues that Black Baptist women forged a feminist theology defined by an "aggressive womanhood that felt personal responsibility to labor no less for men, for the salvation of the world."[8] Dodson's history of Black women in the AME Church also reveals the importance of "black churchwoman's feminist activity," as do works by Higginbotham and Collier-Thomas.[9]

Jesus, Jobs, and Justice by Collier-Thomas and *Black Women's Christian Activism* by Adams are critically significant works on Black women and religion. Collier-Thomas's text includes material on both the nineteenth and twentieth centuries. Collier-Thomas builds on the work of other scholars concerning the self-defined feminist standpoint of Black women, specifically Higginbotham, to contend that Black women's broadly defined feminism "did not exclude racial issues" and that Black women "recognized that in black America women's status was often defined by sex, necessitating an internal struggle for their rights as women."[10] In *Black Women's Christian Activism*, Adams contends that Black churchwomen such as Florence Spearing Randolph and Violet Johnson "advocated a politics of *civic righteousness*" to transform American secular institutions by "placing morality and justice in the realm of public policy, laws, and institutions."[11]

This chapter continues in this tradition by arguing that Black women indeed embraced an intersectional approach to empowerment by forging alliances across race, class, and gender lines through the National era and into the nineteenth century as they moved from the margins to the center of the major debates in US society as public and organic intellectuals. These women engaged in acts of self-naming, as evidenced in their autobiographies, claiming power, and prophesying, defining an activist way of knowing that formed the basis of Black women's intellectualism in US history. Most of the historical analyses on Black women and religion tend to focus on the nineteenth century or on a specific geographic location. In this study, Black women in early American history and in an Atlantic World context are at the center.[12]

Paul Gilroy, in his pivotal text *The Black Atlantic: Modernity and Double Consciousness*, defines the Black Atlantic as an "intercultural and transnational formation" that connects people of the African diaspora through travel and resettlement in and between Africa, the Americas, and Europe.[13] In this Black Atlantic space, Black writers, artists, and intellectuals such as Phillis Wheatley made contributions to the development of modernity. These contributions are particularly evident in their conversations about religion, race, slavery, and freedom as exemplified in narratives and autobiographies. Some of the more recognizable Black Atlantic authors include Olaudah Equiano, James Gronniosaw, and Ottobah Cugoano. Equiano, traveler, writer, and abolitionist, authored *The Interesting Narrative of the Life of Olaudah Equiano* in 1789, detailing the harrowing story of his enslavement in the Americas and Britain, considered by most to be one of the first published slave narratives. Stories of harsh punishment, renaming, and separation are a constant "changing-same" in Black Atlantic narratives of enslavement. That said, much of what has been written about the Black Atlantic focuses on the lives of Black men who wrote narratives, such as Equiano, despite the fact that Black women were writers, poets, and travelers in this Black Atlantic world as well.

Rebecca Protten, Phillis Wheatley, Anne Hart Gilbert, Elizabeth Hart Thwaites, and Mary Prince, among others, were producers of knowledge in a Black Atlantic context. In the early Black Atlantic world, several women participated in conversations about religion and human freedom. Some wrote things down. Protten is visible largely in letters or testimonials on religious subjects, while Wheatley was a prolific writer of poems, letters, and elegies. She likely authored as many as 145 poems. All of these women had some access to education, were literate, and in the case of Wheatley, Prince, and later Mary Seacole, produced a body of written knowledge about their experiences. In all these Black Atlantic discourses produced by women, we primarily see a concern about faith, but Wheatley in particular wrote on subjects related to religion, literature, death, and human bondage. Both Protten and the Hart sisters were mixed-race women married to white men, and most scholars agree that they occupied a liminal space in the Black Atlantic context. Seacole refers to herself as a "Creole" on the first page of her narrative while at the same time declaring that she has "good Scotch blood coursing" through her veins.[14] There is no explicit interrogation of racial slavery in most of the writing by these women (although the lack of a direct challenge to slavery is clearly evident in the work of Prince, who lived in the home of a prominent British abolitionist when she related her story), but there is a negotiation with the idea of race in their lives that is at times alluded to in these writings. For the majority of these women, the main literary concern was religion.

Protten, born a slave of mixed-race ancestry on the West Indian island of Saint Thomas in 1718, is considered by her biographer to be the first woman of African descent to be ordained in a Western Christian denomination.[15] At the time of her manumission at about the age of fifteen, it remained a custom for some slavers to allow enslaved persons to acquire their freedom after conversion, though this practice had declined steeply by the late eighteenth century. Protten played a role in the Moravian movement to convert African slaves to Christianity in the Americas in the eighteenth century. She learned to read and write at a young age and became an active evangelist in the Moravian Church, eventually traveling to Germany and subsequently to Africa. Protten was instrumental in establishing the first Black church in the Americas and traveled extensively to "two islands, on two continents, and in two hemispheres."[16]

Moravian missioners and Blacks both free and enslaved helped to lay the foundation of the Black church in the Americas. According to Sylvia R. Frey and Betty Wood in their text *Come Shouting to Zion*, "Moravians presented a different view of the world, one that carried an implicit promise of a new social order. While Moravians accepted slavery as part of God's structured universe, they also welcomed slaves into the interracial communities they created in the Caribbean."[17] Frey and Wood go on to state that the Moravians were one of "the most open and inclusive Protestant churches" in that they incorporated into their worship practices "such as the kiss of peace, laying on of hands, and the ritual washing of feet."[18] Protten's Christian marriage in 1738 to a white Moravian missionary was sanctioned by the Moravian church, though it is not known if this was a type of negotiated freedom by a mixed-race woman who gained her liberty through conversion. Though scholars must continue to make visible the life of Protten in the historical record, there are some conclusions we can make about her life. She occupied a middle ground between slavery and freedom, but at the same time, she understood the liberatory value of religion. It is not yet clear if her actions were more reflective of a complex process of identity formation.

Anne and Elizabeth Hart, born free and of mixed-race heritage in Antigua in the mid-eighteenth century, were also concerned with religious questions. Some of the same issues raised concerning the life of Rebecca Protten are relevant to the lives of the Hart sisters. As mixed-race women of property who could read and write, the two sisters married white men but were also engaged in religious and education reform efforts on the island of Antigua.[19] They operated schools for the disadvantaged in the early 1800s and were involved in the moral, educational, and social uplift of communities both Black and white, free and enslaved, through their association with the Methodist Church. These sisters actively worked to improve the lives of the enslaved in Antigua but largely within the confines of religious moralism. Natasha Lightfoot has argued that the Hart sisters, like other free people of color in Antigua who were associated with the Methodist Church, "used all avenues" to "gain status and undermine white dominance in Antigua."[20] That said, the sisters also understood the limitations of their place as women and people of color.

While this matter remains largely ambiguous in the case of Protten and the Hart sisters, Phillis Wheatley and Mary Prince make clear assertions regarding slavery and human freedom in their writings. Wheatley was "snatch'd from Afric's fancy's happy seat" at age seven, as she relates to us in a poem, and came to live in the home of prominent Bostonians Susanna and John Wheatley circa 1760, where she was taught to read and write.[21] In her studies, she became familiar with the Bible, astronomy, geography, and literature. Her instruction included readings of Greek and Latin writers such as Homer and Ovid, as well as authors such as John Milton and Alexander Pope. By age eighteen, Wheatley had written more than twenty-five poems. She wrote primarily on religious matters and elegies for notable people but demonstrated a concern for human bondage, such as in her "On the Death of General Wooster," stating, "they disgrace / And hold in bondage Afric's blameless race."[22] These poems are primarily religious lamentations, but they are not without abolitionist sentiments. While it is not possible to label Protten or the Hart sisters as abolitionists, this is not the case with Wheatley, who also wrote on other subjects, including matters discussed in Enlightenment circles such as deism.

Born into slavery in Bermuda in 1788, Mary Prince, after having been sold several times and separated from her immediate family, came to England in 1828, where she made connections with members of the Anti-Slavery Society such as Thomas Pringle. While working in the home of Pringle, Prince dictated the narrative of her life to Susanna Strickland. Her narrative entitled *The History of Mary Prince, a West Indian Slave* was published in 1831 as the first complete narrative of a Black woman in Britain. Though we might consider that Prince had associations with members of the British abolitionist community, where slavery had been outlawed, her account of her enslavement is no less poignant than the words of Equiano: "I have been a slave—I have felt what a slave feels, and I know what a slave knows; and I would have all the good people in England to know it too, that they may break our chains, and set us free."[23]

While enslaved, Prince lived in Bermuda, Antigua, and England. She sometimes suffered harsh treatment, which she relates in her narrative. She also reveals a concern for enslaved women in particular by relating the brutal abuse of an enslaved woman named Hetty who was brutally beaten while pregnant, leading to her death. This narrative by Prince parallels the earlier narratives written by Equiano and others in terms of the separation of families and the brutality of slavery.

Black women's public intellectualism in the National era, particularly the work of Maria Stewart and the Black preaching women, laid the foundation of an intellectual tradition. Stewart was the first Black woman to publicly express and record the core themes of Black women's thoughts on liberation. Stewart was born free as Maria Miller in Hartford, Connecticut, in 1803 and later orphaned at the age of five. She was as an indentured servant until age fifteen. She later supported herself as a domestic servant and eventually moved to Boston. In 1826, she married James Stewart, an independent Black shipping agent and a veteran of the War of 1812. In Boston, among the region's Black elite, the Stewarts made the acquaintance of Thomas Paul, founder of the African Baptist Church, and the ardent Black abolitionist David Walker. James died in 1829, and Maria was forced to reenter domestic service upon the confiscation of her inheritance by white businessmen who claimed to be the executors of her husband's estate. In 1831, following a profound experience of religious conversion, Stewart wrote the essay "Religion and the Pure Principles of Morality, the Sure Foundation on Which We Must Build," which was published in William Lloyd Garrison's *Liberator*.

In her various writings and speeches, Stewart recognizes the interlocking nature of race, gender, and class oppression while advancing a belief in Black women's activism as mothers, teachers, and leaders of the community.[24] The writings and speeches of Stewart also reveal an awareness of sexual politics.[25] Stewart's writings and speeches served as a call to action, as revealed in her essay on religion and the principles of morality:

> O, ye daughters of Africa, awake! Arise! No longer sleep nor slumber, but distinguish yourselves. Show forth to the world that ye are endowed with noble and exalted faculties. O, ye daughters of Africa! What have ye done to immortalize your names beyond the grave? What examples have ye set before the rising generation? What foundation have ye laid for generations yet unborn?[26]

In the same essay, she urged "the daughters of Africa" to preach, teach, and actively build up the infrastructure of the Black community:

> Let every female heart become united, and let us raise a fund ourselves, and at the end of one year and a half, we might be able to lay the cornerstone for the building of a High School, that the higher branches of knowledge might be enjoyed by us; and God would raise us up, and enough to aid us in our laudable designs.[27]

Stewart developed the foundation of Black feminist thought, and several Black church women engaged in preaching, writing, and public addresses were Stewart's contemporaries. The core themes of Black feminist thought first advanced by Stewart are present in the writings and public addresses of Black church women.

The Black church served as a major conduit through which African American women claimed identity and voice in the nineteenth century by challenging the monopolization of authority by Black men in the organizational structure of the Black church. Black women's public voice, in many respects, begins with the activism of Black church women. The development of the Black church in America involved the public activism of Black women on multiple levels through church auxiliary groups and mutual aid societies such as the Daughters of Conference created by African American Episcopal Church (AME) women in 1816. Jualynne E. Dodson has noted that through mutual aid societies such as the Daughters of Conference, the Independent Daughters of Hope, and the Sisters of the Good Shepherd, the Black church movement expanded dramatically.[28] These societies not only attracted new members but raised substantial funds to support Black churches.[29] Many Black women began to openly challenge the autonomy of Black men in the church by demanding to speak publicly as a result of the organizational work of Black women's church-based mutual aid societies.[30]

Some Black women turned to spiritualism as an alternative means to religious leadership and to claim the power of voice. Hans A. Baer has argued that "women have often compensated for their relative powerlessness cross culturally by participating in spiritual movements within and beyond the organizational structures of religious institutions."[31] In fact, women in various religious traditions, including the Black church, have relied on spiritualism as a type of feminist weapon to secure power within religious institutions. Anne Llewellyn Barstow contends that mysticism (those claiming a direct connection to God) was both an integrative and activating force, used particularly by medieval women, who were able to parlay a claim of private channel to the spirit world out of the reach of male control, employing it as a feminist weapon.[32]

African American church women, similar to the women of the medieval past, declared that they were "called by God" to speak. By claiming a direct connection to God, many Black women gained both personal and structural recognition in the Black church movement during the nineteenth century. Specifically, within the Black Baptist church and Black Methodism, African American women were able to acquire leadership roles in the Black church and used their positions to advocate for a broad-based program of social reform. Jarena Lee, Zilpha Elaw, and Julia Foote all claimed that God had chosen them to preach and teach the Gospel of Jesus Christ. Lee, Elaw, and Foote are likely the most prominent Black church women of the nineteenth century. These three women were among some of the first American women to publish book-length works and establish a public voice for African Americans through the nineteenth century as public speakers, writers, and active reformers.

Lee and Elaw were active in the free Black community in the North. Lee, born in 1783 in New Jersey, began experiencing spiritual "visions" as a child that led her, as an adult, to tell Richard Allen, founder of the AME Church in Philadelphia, that God "spoke to her" to preach the Gospel. Lee would go on to deliver hundreds of sermons across thousands of miles, as far north as Canada and as far south as Maryland. Lee was also one of the first American women to have her work, titled *Life and Religious Experience of Jerena Lee* (1836), reach a mass audience through print. Elaw, born near Philadelphia, Pennsylvania, to free Black parents, was an itinerant minister and one of the earliest published African American female ministers along with Lee. In her autobiographical narrative *Memoirs of the Life, Religious Experience, Ministerial Travels and Labours of Mrs. Zilpha Elaw, an American Female of Colour*, she proclaims that a spiritual awakening influenced her to become a preacher. Elaw founded a school in Burlington, New Jersey, for Black women in 1823 and included in her sermons discussions about her status as a woman and how Christianity made it possible for her to attack the injustice of racism and women's inequality. She would eventually go on to preach in homes, revival camps, and welcoming pulpits in America and England.

Julia Foote, daughter of former slaves, born in Schenectady, New York, was the first woman to be ordained a deacon in the AME Zion Church and the second ordained female elder in the AME Zion Church. Foote was initially criticized by her church, parents, and husband when she insisted that she had been called by God to preach and was sanctioned by her minister for conducting services in her home. She eventually went on to preach in New York, various New England states, and Canada. Julia Foote published her autobiography *A Brand Plucked from the Fire* in 1879. African American women were able to use the Black church as an apparatus to forge pathways into public leadership as well as auxiliary agencies such as the Female Union and Daughters of Zion throughout the nineteenth century.

Spiritual autobiographies advanced by Black men and women espoused a gospel of divine knowledge that was connected to a deep sense of self-awareness.[33] The spiritual autobiographers and the slave narratives written later allowed Black writers to "accrue authority and power via the word."[34] God's word as appropriated for individual purposes signified an audacious form of self-authorship on the part of Black men and women who wrote spiritual autobiographies in the nineteenth century. William L. Andrews has argued that the intellectual foundation of Black reformist thought was first developed by men and women who authored spiritual autobiographies by stating:

> The black spiritual autobiographer had to lay the necessary intellectual groundwork by proving that black people were as much chosen by God for eternal salvation as whites. Without the black spiritual autobiography's reclamation of the Afro-Americans spiritual birthright, the fugitive slave narrative could not have made such a cogent case for black civil rights in the crisis years between 1830 and 1865.[35]

Black women spiritual autobiographers such as Lee and Elaw laid the "groundwork" for the reform-minded feminist consciousness that led to the rise of the Black women's club movement at the end of the nineteenth century. Harriet Jacobs's *Incidents in the Life of a Slave Girl* (1861) has long been considered the first slave narrative written by a Black woman; however, this narrative was not the first autobiography written that made Black female self-determinism a fundamental theme.

In the first decades of the nineteenth century, the Second Great Awakening produced a flood of evangelical Christian activism, particularly among denominations such as the Methodists and Baptists, two groups that placed a great emphasis on salvation by free will. Spiritual autobiographies reveal that Black women, through their claim of sanctification by the spirit, combined a feminist consciousness with the pronounced individualism of evangelical Christianity. This combination would not only lead to reform within the Black church but also, by the turn of the century, to the emergence of a new Black church movement known as Pentecostalism. Pentecostalism as a movement is defined by the "gifts of the spirit." It is rooted in the history of nineteenth-century perfectionism and the Second Great Awakening. Black women's spiritual writings are an integral part of defining this history.

Lee's 1836 autobiography *The Life and Experience of Jarena Lee* challenged male autonomy in the Black church by examining traditional female roles among whites as well as Blacks. Lee's text is likely the first sustained discussion of Black women's roles in the church as coupled with a discussion concerning resistance to these traditional roles. Lee described her call to preach with utter surprise: "But to my utter surprise there seemed to sound a voice which I thought I distinctly heard, and most certainly understood, which said to me, "Go preach the Gospel!"[36] Lee was subsequently told by Richard Allen that the denomination "did not call for women preachers."[37] In response to Allen, Lee provided a rationale as to why woman should be allowed to preach, stating that "nothing is impossible with God" and further, "And why should it be thought impossible, heterodox, or improper for a woman to preach? Seeing the Saviour died for the woman as well as the man."[38] Lee then provides a more eloquent defense of woman preachers:

> If a man may preach, because the Savior died for him, why not the woman? Seeing he died for her also. Is he not a whole Savior, instead of a half one? As those who hold it wrong for a woman to preach, would seem to make it appear. Did not Mary *first* preach the risen Savior, and not the doctrine of the resurrection the very climax of Christianity ... then did not Mary, a woman, preach the gospel? For she preached the resurrection of the crucified Son of God.[39]

Lee goes on to conclude that she was called to preach by "the gift of heaven" and divine inspiration, stating, "As for me, I am fully persuaded that the Lord called me to labor according to what I have received, in his vineyard."[40] The notion of the "sanctification of the spirit" was later deployed by church women such as Elaw and Foote.

Zilpha Elaw's *Memoirs* and Julia Foote's *A Brand Plucked from the Fire* follow the pattern of Lee's autobiography while at the same time exhibiting some of the core themes of Black feminist consciousness. Elaw speaks of her conversion at a camp meeting, saying, "It was at one of these great meetings of the saints in the wilderness."[41] Elaw describes her conversion in evocative terms, saying, "I saw no personal appearance while in this stupendous elevation, but I discerned bodies of resplendent light; nor did I appear to be in this world at all, but immensely far above those spreading trees."[42] Foote's autobiography begins with a retelling of her mother's enslavement:

> She had one very cruel master and mistress. This man, whom she was obliged to call master, tied her up and whipped her because she refused to submit herself to him, and reported his conduct to her mistress. After the whipping, he himself washed her quivering back with strong salt water. At the expiration of a week she was sent to change her clothing, which stuck fast to her back. Her mistress, seeing that she could not remove it, took hold of the rough tow-linen under garment and pulled it off over her head with a jerk, which took the skin with it, leaving her back all raw and sore.[43]

The recounting of gender-specific sexualized violence is one of the core themes of Black feminist consciousness. Foote's conversion and call to preach is as evocative as Lee's and Elaw's in that Foote said that an angel came to her declaring that she must follow the commands of God.[44]

Lee, Elaw, and later Foote, in their autobiographical writings, inaugurate and advance a tradition of Black women's intellectualism that became a basis for later slave narratives, written by women, through what some scholars have called self-life writing. They were the first Black women intellectuals, writing primarily in the Early National era, and it is these women who initiated the tradition identified by the editors of *Toward an Intellectual History of Black Women*. African American women have forged a distinct tradition of intellectualism through public address and self-life writing. Stewart's speeches, combined with these spiritual autobiographies, are forms of political discourse that merge the personal with the political as amplified by an intersectional approach to empowerment. This is apparent in works such as autobiography and memoir, which exist at times as a type of "scriptotherapy,"[45] a form particularly evident in the genre of Black women's slave narratives. They should be understood as an oppositional way of knowing within the larger historical continuum of American intellectualism.

Joanne M. Braxton, in her *Black Women Writing Autobiography: A Tradition within a Tradition*, argues that Black women have been "knowers" who have "not been known."[46] These women turned to self-life writing as a response to enslavement, sexual violence, and Jim Crowism, and to become known through literary acts of self-articulation.[47] The process of enslavement led to the loss of indigenous African languages in the New World context as well as ownership of the body for the enslaved population. This attempt to become known through literary processes inaugurates a tradition of Black women's self-life writing that is defined by a reclamation of words, language, the body, and image.[48] For these women, the ownership of words is an act of self-liberation. Braxton posits that these Black women writers, "through the juxtaposition of oral and literary forms,"[49] functioned as a type of "outraged" mother voice that spoke for and to the Black masses.[50] This outraged mother is defined by Braxton as "a variation of the articulate hero archetype"[51] evident in the autobiographical writings of Black men.

These outraged mothers wrote about the violence of racial oppression and sexual assault as a form of catharsis or scriptotherapy, evident in memoirs as a form of re-memory/reenactment that seeks public validation for suffering through testimony; and henceforth, these are political discourses.[52] However, Trauma does not overtake agency or action in Black women's self-life writing, given that a core theme in Black autobiographical writing is action and not contemplation.[53] Thus, a unique tradition of Black women's self-life writing was born, defined by the trope of a Black mother who seeks redress and action through the written word, a tradition that is intrinsic to understanding Black women's intellectualism. This is illustrated in both literary and oral traditions from the era of enslavement through the twentieth century. Ma Rainey's lesbian song of self-affirmation "Prove It on Me" is as autobiographical in nature as Anne Moody's participant history *Coming of Age in Mississippi*. These women, as those who speak in mother tongues that fuse the personal and the political, fashioned a tradition of Black women's self-life writing that "challenges ways of knowing"[54] often defined by the voices of (white) men.

By the mid-nineteenth century, African American women were preaching, writing, speaking, and organizing efforts to call for the end to slavery. In the 1830s, the Female Literary Society of Philadelphia was formed, and in Boston the Afric-American Female Intelligence Society was created. William Lloyd Garrison's New England Anti-Slavery Society invited Black women to join and write for *The Liberator*. Black women in the Black church movement provided the foundation of Black leadership in the abolitionist movement. Williams Lloyd Garrison's New England Anti-Slavery Society was formed in 1832, the same year that the first women's antislavery society—the Female Anti-Slavery Society, later the Salem Female Anti-Slavery Society—was founded by Black women in Salem, Massachusetts. Founded in 1833, the development and activities of the American Anti-Slavery Society involved the participation of several prominent African Americans such as James Forten, Frederick Douglass, and Sarah Remond. Jarena Lee joined the American Anti-Slavery Society movement after publishing her autobiography, believing that the abolition of slavery would lead to a more Christian nation. Maria Stewart, also divinely inspired, wrote for Garrison's *Liberator* on subjects related to abolitionism and women's rights, while Sojourner Truth is likely the most formidable preacher-abolitionist Black woman of the nineteenth century.

African American women such as Margaretta Forten helped to organize both the Philadelphia Anti-Slavery Society in 1833 and the Salem Female Anti-Slavery Society in 1834. Sarah Paul was instrumental in the formation of the Massachusetts Female Anti-Slavery Society. African American women abolitionists such as Truth and Harriet Tubman are well known, but several other Black women made abolitionism a subject of their speeches, writings, and activism. Sara Duncan, as a member of the AME Church, and Florence Spearing Randolph, through AME Zion, among others, secured positions as stewardesses, evangelists, and deaconesses by the late nineteenth century. These women founded women's missionary societies and clubs such as the Women's Home and Foreign Missionary Society and the New Jersey Federation of Colored Women's Clubs to maintain leadership positions and advance social causes.

Black church women reformed the Black church in fundamental ways that ultimately led to a new and independent Black church movement at the turn of the century, as illustrated in movements such as Pentecostalism that is predicated on spiritual gifts and sanctification. We must look to Black women's intellectualism in the form of speeches, public addresses, and spiritual autobiographies, in the National era, to understand more succinctly the evolution of nineteenth-century perfectionism and the development of evangelical Christianity. More importantly, the Black women authors of spiritual autobiographies laid the foundation of Black women's public intellectualism. Black women's Christian activism continued into the twentieth century.

African American women in contemporary America have built on the protofeminist/nationalist way of knowing, and conceptions of the divine, that first emanated from the womanist theology that developed in the National era. Feminist notions of the Black woman as divine have now become transfigured in Black popular culture. Kelly Brown Douglas, in her text *The Black Christ*, on the history of the idea of the Black Christ as image and metaphor, contends that from the era of enslavement to the present, a womanist approach to Christ "confronts black women's struggles with the wider society as well as with the black community" that ultimately allows for a prophetic ministry beyond race.[55] In other words, the "sustaining and liberating Christ of black faith"[56] defined by color and the relationship to Black people's struggles must now extend beyond race to include sex/gender to remain a sustaining force in Black life or a "system of doing theology that is accountable to the survival and liberation of black women."[57] Douglas argues that there are many possibilities of imagining Christ in the world. Christ might be imagined as Black, female, same-sex oriented, and economically disadvantaged to remain as a sustaining and liberating force within Black culture more generally.

African American women have persistently presented themselves as prophets, while many have also called themselves divine, in an attempt to sustain the image of a liberating god. This is evident from the National era through the nineteenth century to the present. These women have played key roles in the development of the American intellectual tradition by calling for the abolition of slavery, supporting the campaign for women's liberation, and helping to lead the temperance movement. Black women turned to the public square because, historically, they were often turned away from the leading intellectual institutions/academies on account of race and gender. Nonetheless, they were producers of knowledge illustrated in their writings, spiritual biographies, sermons, and public addresses. African American women are a part of the American intellectual tradition, and this is evidenced in their words, deeds, and actions.

NOTES

1. Jarena Lee, *The Life and Religious Experience of Jarena Lee, A Coloured Lady, Giving an Account of Her Call to Preach the Gospel* (Philadelphia, 1836) in *Three Black Women's Autobiographies of the Nineteenth Century*, ed. William L. Andrews, 37.

2. Mia Bay, Farah J. Griffin, Martha S. Jones, and Barbara D. Savage, eds., introduction, to *Toward an Intellectual History of Black Women* (Chapel Hill: University of North Carolina Press, 2015), 1.

3. Bay et al., introduction, 5.

4. Bay et al., introduction, 4.

5. Bay et al., introduction, 4.

6. There is an ever-expanding compendium of scholarly analyses on women as prophets and preachers. Some notable works that include analysis of this subject matter include Daniella J. Kostroun and Lisa Vollendorf, eds., *Women, Religion, and the Atlantic World,*

1600–1800 (Toronto: University of Toronto Press, 2009), which examines women in an international context with some coverage of Black women and religion before the nineteenth century; Marilyn J. Westerkamp, *Women and Religion in Early America, 1600–1850: The Puritan and Evangelical Traditions* (New York: Routledge, 1999) contains some discussion of Black women and Methodism and prophesying women; Beverly Mayne Kienzie and Pamela J. Walker, eds., *Women Preachers and Prophets through Two Millennia of Christianity* (Berkeley: University of California Press, 1998) is a collection of essays on women preachers and prophets in the history of Christianity through the twentieth century; "Producing the Voice, Consuming the Body: Women Prophets of the Seventeenth Century," in *Women, Writing, History, 1640–1740*, ed. Isobel Grundy and Susan Wiseman (Athens: University of Georgia Press, 1992), 139–58, explores the relationship between women's agency and prophecy in the early modern era.

7. Chanta M. Haywood, *Prophesying Daughters: Black Women Preachers and the Word, 1823–1913* (Columbia: University of Missouri Press, 2003), ix–xi.

8. Higginbotham, *Righteous Discontent*, 139.

9. Dodson, *Engendering Church*, 6.

10. Collier-Thomas, *Jesus, Jobs, and Justice*, 121.

11. Betty Livingstone-Adams, *Black Women's Christian Activism: Seeking Social Justice in a Northern Suburb* (New York: New York University Press, 2016), 3.

12. Paul Gilroy in *The Black Atlantic: Modernity and Double Consciousness* (Cambridge, MA: Harvard University Press, 1993) first defines the concept of a Black Atlantic culture that is composed of the shared experiences of Blacks in North America, the Caribbean, and Britain; for some important early works on the idea of the Black Atlantic see Sylvia R. Frey and Betty Wood, *Come Shouting to Zion: African American Protestantism in the American South and British Caribbean to 1830* (Chapel Hill: University of North Carolina Press, 1998); Michelle M. Wright, *Becoming Black: Creating Identity in the African Diaspora* (Durham, NC: Duke University Press, 2004) concerning how Black writers responded to discourses on racism and sexism with an emphasis on the ideas of Black women such as Carolyn Rodgers, Joan Riley, and Audre Lorde in particular. For an early Black intellectual history of the Black Atlantic see James Sidbury, *Becoming African in America: Race and Nation in the Early Black Atlantic* (New York: Oxford University Press, 2007), containing a discussion on how Black writers such as Phillis Wheatley negotiated questions of identity and freedom in their writings, and associations in the Early National Period.

13. Gilroy, *The Black Atlantic*, ix.

14. Mary Seacole, *The Wonderful Adventures of Mrs. Seacole in Many Lands* (New York: Penguin Classics, 2005), 11.

15. Jon F. Sensbach, *Rebecca's Revival: Creating Black Christianity in the Atlantic World* (Cambridge, MA: Harvard University Press, 2005), 7.

16. Sensbach, *Rebecca's Revival*, 4.

17. Frey and Wood, *Come Shouting to Zion*, 83–84.

18. Frey and Wood, *Come Shouting to Zion*, 84.

19. Natasha Lightfoot, "The Hart Sisters of Antigua: Evangelical Activism and 'Respectable' Public Politics in the Era of Black Atlantic Slavery," in Bay et al., *Toward an Intellectual History of Black Women*, 53.

20. Lightfoot, "The Hart Sisters of Antigua," 56.

21. Phillis Wheatley, "To the Right Honorable William, Earl of Dartmouth," in *The Collected Works of Phillis Wheatley*, ed. John Shields (New York: Oxford University Press, 1988), 74.

22. Phillis Wheatley, "On the Death of General Wooster," in Shields, *Collected Works*, 149.

23. Mary Prince, *The History of Mary Prince, a West Indian Slave* (New York: Penguin Classics, 2004), 21.

24. Prince, *The History of Mary Prince*, 21.

25. Collins, *Black Feminist Thought*, 23.

26. Maria Miller Stewart, "Religion and the Pure Principles of Morality, the Sure Foundation on Which We Must Build," in Guy-Sheftall, *Words of Fire*, 27.

27. Stewart, "Religion and the Pure Principles," 28.

28. Dodson, *Engendering Church*, 46.

29. Dodson, *Engendering Church*, 46.

30. Dodson, *Engendering Church*, 47.

31. Baer, "The Limited Empowerment of Women."

32. Barstow, "Mystical Experience as a Feminist Weapon."

33. Andrews, introduction to *Sisters of the Spirit*, 1.

34. Andrews, introduction to *Sisters of the Spirit*, 1.

35. Andrews, introduction to *Sisters of the Spirit*, 1–2.

36. Lee, *The Life and Religious Experience of Jarena Lee*, 35.

37. Lee, *The Life and Religious Experience of Jarena Lee*, 36.

38. Lee, *The Life and Religious Experience of Jarena Lee*, 36.

39. Lee, *The Life and Religious Experience of Jarena Lee*, 36.

40. Lee, *The Life and Religious Experience of Jarena Lee*, 37.

41. Zilpha Elaw, *Memoirs of the Life, Religious Experience, Ministerial Travels of Mrs. Zilpha Elaw*, in Andrews, *Sisters of the Spirit*, 66.

42. Elaw, *Memoirs of the Life*, 66–67.

43. Julia Foote, *A Brand Plucked from the Fire: An Autobiographical Sketch by Mrs. Julia Foote*, in Andrews, *Sisters of the Spirit*, 166.

44. Foote, *A Brand Plucked from the Fire*, 201.

45. Suzette A. Henke, *Shattered Subjects: Trauma and Testimony in Women's Life-Writing* (New York: St. Martin's Press, 2000), xii.

46. Joanne M. Braxton, *Black Women Writing Autobiography: A Tradition within a Tradition* (Philadelphia: Temple University Press, 1989), 1.

47. Braxton, *Black Women Writing Autobiography*, 2.

48. Braxton, *Black Women Writing Autobiography*, 2.

49. Braxton, *Black Women Writing Autobiography*, 5.

50. Braxton, *Black Women Writing Autobiography*, 3.

51. Braxton, *Black Women Writing Autobiography*, 10.

52. Henke, *Shattered Subjects*, xi–xii.

53. Braxton, *Black Women Writing Autobiography*, 5.

54. Alice A. Deck, "Autobiography as Activism: Three Black Women of the Sixties," *African American Review* 36, no. 3 (Fall 2002): 3.

55. Kelly Brown Douglas, *The Black Christ* (New York: Orbis Books, 1993), 97.

56. Douglas, *The Black Christ*, 2–3.

57. Collier-Thomas, *Jesus, Jobs, and Justice*, 474.

REFERENCES

Andrews, William L., ed. *Sisters of the Spirit: Three Black Women's Autobiographies of the Nineteenth Century*. Bloomington: Indiana University Press, 1986.
Baer, Hans. "The Limited Empowerment of Women in Black Spiritual Churches: An Alternative Vehicle to Religious Leadership." *Sociology of Religion* 54, no. 1 (Spring 1993): 65–82.
Barstow, Anne Llewellyn. "Mystical Experience as a Feminist Weapon: Joan of Arc." *Women's Studies Quarterly* 13, no. 2 (Summer 1985): 26–29.
Carby, Hazel V. *Reconstructing Womanhood: The Emergence of the Afro-American Woman Novelist*. New York: Oxford University Press, 1987.
Collier-Thomas, Bettye. *Daughters of Thunder: Black Women and Their Sermons, 1850–1979*. San Francisco: Jossey-Bass, 1998.
Collier-Thomas, Bettye. *Jesus, Jobs, and Justice: African American Women and Religion*. New York: Alfred A. Knopf, 2011.
Collins, Patricia Hill. *Black Feminist Thought: Knowledge, Consciousness, and the Politics of Empowerment*. New York: Routledge, 1991.
Collins, Patricia Hill. "What's in a Name?" Womanism, Black Feminism, and Beyond." *Black Scholar* 26, no. 1 (2001): 9–17.
Dodson, Jualynne. *Engendering Church: Women, Power, and the A.M.E. Church*. Lanham, MD: Rowman and Littlefield, 2002.
Gates, Henry Louis, Jr., and Nellie Y. McKay, eds. *The Norton Anthology of African American Literature*. New York: W. W. Norton, 2004.
Giddings, Paula. *When and Where I Enter: The Impact of Black Women on Race and Sex in America*. New York: William Morrow, 1984.
Guy-Sheftall, Beverly, ed. *Words of Fire: An Anthology of African American Feminist Thought*. New York: New Press, 1995.
Higginbotham, Evelyn Brooks. *Righteous Discontent: The Women's Movement in the Black Baptist Church, 1880–1920*. Cambridge, MA: Harvard University Press, 1993.
Logan, Shirley Wilson. *We Are Coming: The Persuasive Discourse of Nineteenth Century Black Women*. Carbondale: Southern Illinois Press, 1999.
Maffly-Kipp, Laurie F., and Kathryn Lofton, eds. *Women's Work: An Anthology of African American Women's Historical Writings from Antebellum America to the Harlem Renaissance*. New York: Oxford University Press, 2010.
Scully, Pamela, and Diana Paton, eds. *Gender and Slave Emancipation in the Atlantic World*. Durham, NC: Duke University Press, 2005.
Sterling, Dorothy, ed. *We Are Your Sisters: Black Women in the Nineteenth Century*. New York: W. W. Norton, 1984.
Tate, Claudia, ed. *The Works of Katherine Davis Chapman Tillman*. New York: Oxford University Press, 1991.
Waters, Kristin, and Carol B. Conaway, eds. *Black Women's Intellectual Traditions: Speaking Their Minds*. Burlington: University of Vermont Press, 2007.
White, Deborah Gray. *Too Heavy a Load: Black Women in Defense of Themselves, 1894–1994*. New York: W. W. Norton, 1999.

Part II

Politics and Black Women's Public Intellectualism

SUMMARY

Several chapters in part II speak to the history of Black women's public intellectualism. These include chapters by Tejai Beulah and Simone R. Barrett. Beulah points out that the state of Christian public intellectualism in the twenty-first century has increasingly become a topic of interest for both scholars and journalists. These discussions often explore the history of Christian public intellectualism but often exclude the contributions of African American women. While some women have surely been lost to history, others, such as Mary McLeod Bethune, Nannie Helen Burroughs, and Charlotte Hawkins Brown have not.

Though articles, book chapters, and biographies on these women are available, they are usually lumped in the broad category of "Black women in history" and are not specifically identified as Christian public intellectuals. Tejai Beulah seeks to remedy this in "'Our Group of Women': Mary McLeod Bethune, Nannie Helen Burroughs, Charlotte Hawkins Brown, and Black Women in the Christian Intellectual Tradition." In this chapter Beulah writes, "First, this chapter offers a more complex explanation of why Black women Christian intellectuals of the early twentieth century have been overlooked as subjects in histories, particularly intellectual histories." She applies definitions of Black Christian public intellectuals "to make the case that Bethune, Burroughs, and Brown were significant public contributors to Black intellectual life in the early twentieth century as school founders and as social commentators." She closes the essay with "an urgent plea for scholarship that updates and continues the important work . . . that emphasizes the Black Christian public intellectual work of not only early twentieth-century women thinkers but also contemporary leaders."

Just as Black women are often written out of the history of Christian public intellectualism, so too are they often written out of (or deprioritized in) the story of the civil rights movement. Simone R. Barrett seeks to fix this in her chapter, "We Led the Way." She writes, "While we should continue to recognize men, who were instrumental in the movement, it is equally important to recognize that courageous, dedicated women, like Rosa Parks, Fannie Lou Hamer,

Ella Baker, and Daisy Lee Bates, were at the forefront of several well-known and influential civil rights initiatives. Women of the civil rights movement suffered from triple oppression of race, class, and gender." This chapter has a regional focus, examining:

> ... the role of Black women intellectuals within the context of Black female student involvement in the civil rights movement while highlighting Morgan State College, Baltimore, and the state of Maryland. Black women intellectuals such as Lucy Diggs Slowe, Lillie Carroll Jackson, Juanita Jackson Mitchell, Thelma Bando, and Gloria Richardson influenced and provided a strong and indelible foundation for Morgan State's female students and their supporters as they fought against racial oppression and inequality. These Black women were "intellectuals" who throughout their careers sought to elevate Black women's experiences by training and mentoring the next generation of Black women "intellectuals" who changed the racial and political complexity of the nation.

In the next chapter, "Elreta Melton Alexander: A Theoretical Approach," Virginia L. Summey examines the life and career of a trailblazing African American attorney and judge. Born in 1919 in North Carolina, Alexander's parents were middle class: her father was a Baptist minister, and her mother was a schoolteacher. Alexander attended college, and become a teacher like her mother. She married a doctor in 1938. The couple had one child in 1950, but they divorced in 1968. In 1979, Alexander married again, to John D. Ralston. In what we might now identify as an early example of "leaning in," Alexander pursued her more traditional personal life and her pioneering professional life in tandem. After becoming the first Black woman to graduate from Columbia Law School in 1945, she would go on to be the first African American woman to practice law in North Carolina. In 1968, Alexander became the first African American woman to become an elected district court judge. As Summey writes,

> In spite of her many accomplishments, her story has gone largely overlooked in southern, intellectual, and civil rights history. While the work of other Black, female attorneys, such as Sadie Tanner Mossell Alexander, Constance Baker Motley, and Florynce Kennedy, has been noted in books examining African American women's history, Elreta Alexander has been excluded. This chapter attempts to rectify that exclusion and examines Judge Alexander's intellectual contributions as well as her place within existing theoretical frameworks.

This part of the book moves from Alexander, impartial arbiter of justice, to an unapologetic politician in Marissa Jackson Sow's exploration of the place and legacy of the first Black woman elected to the United States Congress in "More Than an Icon: Taking Shirley Chisholm at Her Word." The chapter on Chisolm, both the first woman to run for the Democratic Party's presidential nomination and the first woman to appear in a United States presidential debate, segues naturally to the next on "Lenora B. Fulani: Distinguished Postmodern Revolutionary." Fulani is often overlooked by historians of women and politics, yet she was the first American woman to have her name placed on the ballot as a presidential candidate in all fifty states during a presidential election.

Chapter 3

"OUR GROUP OF WOMEN"

Mary McLeod Bethune, Nannie Helen Burroughs, Charlotte Hawkins Brown, and Black Women in the Christian Intellectual Tradition

TEJAI BEULAH

In September 2016, Professor Alan Jacobs published "The Watchmen: What Became of the Christian Intellectuals?" in *Harper's Magazine*.[1] The article documents and laments the declining influence of Christian public intellectuals on American popular culture over the course of the late twentieth century. Jacobs pointed to the career of Reinhold Niebuhr to demonstrate how Christian intellectuals emerged at the outset of World War II to serve as the necessary interpreters of the religious issues that surfaced in the war and in public discourse. In Jacobs's estimation, however, Christian public intellectualism declined when the "liberal establishment" went beyond advocating an antiracist and antiwar agenda to also embracing the platform for women's rights. The Christian intellectuals that Jacobs uses as examples reduced their understanding of "women's rights" to the issue of a woman's right to have an abortion. Jacobs's intellectuals thought that abortion went against their ideas about Christian ethics.[2] According to Jacobs, these thinkers, mostly Protestant white males, felt that they were becoming irrelevant, minority speakers in national conversations that now included the prominent voices of Black leaders and women, and they retreated from public discourse.

Jacobs's essay sparked lively responses from a variety of scholars and other critics online, including an extended commentary from Vincent Lloyd and Joshua L. Lazard on the digital magazine formerly known as Religion Dispatches.[3] Lloyd, a scholar of religion and race, agreed with Jacobs. Lloyd also saw the need for a more defined and active public Christian intellectual tradition. However, he pointedly calls for a "public black theology for the 21st century" in his essay response to "The Watchmen."[4] In short, Lloyd argues for

Black Christian public intellectuals to serve as "translator[s] of both Christian and Black concerns to a white, secular public that is attuned to racial injustice."[5]

Lloyd's essay identifies a group of contemporary Black scholars, including Melissa Harris-Perry and Eddie Glaude, who write about the religion of Christianity and spirituality but "do not frame their public engagements as motivated by their Christian commitments, and they do not employ a thickly theological idiom."[6] Further, Lloyd asserts that these individuals speak primarily to white audiences on primetime networks and in popular magazines, thereby limiting their ability to directly connect with Black communities to organize for social and political change. While these individuals maintain a high degree of visibility, Lloyd does not view them as suitable spokespersons for the thoughts and concerns of Black Christians. Rather, he points to the historical subjects featured in his influential book, *Black Natural Law*, as exemplars for reviving the Black Christian public intellectual tradition. These individuals include Frederick Douglass, Anna Julia Cooper, W. E. B. Du Bois, and Martin Luther King Jr.

For Lloyd, his subjects represent the religious thinkers who grappled with "God's law" in a manner that spurred organizing in Black communities as a powerful tool to challenge white supremacist ideologies. Further, Lloyd suggests that these individuals are the principal forerunners to two groups of contemporary Black leaders that emerged over the last thirty years. The first group, "black religious experts," such as Rev. Jesse Jackson and Rev. Al Sharpton, maintained high public profiles as Christian spokesmen on social issues during the eighties and nineties. The second group, Black scholars of religion, includes Cornel West, J. Kameron Carter, and Willie Jennings. In Lloyd's opinion, these thinkers and writers have "reinvigorated . . . the radical project of constructing a theology that begins with the Blackness of God" in the theological academy.[7]

Joshua L. Lazard, a writer and administrator in religious education, wrote a scathing response to Lloyd's essay. Among Lazard's issues with Lloyd's piece is the absence of early Black Christian intellectuals such as Mordecai Johnson and Benjamin Elijah Mays. Johnson and Mays seem to stand out for Lazard because both men were "renowned preachers" and college presidents who wrote and spoke extensively about how their Christian faith informed their social and political thought and practice in the segregated South.[8] This is a valid critique considering that Lloyd's book, *Black Natural Law*, does not consider early twentieth-century Black intellectuals who had clearly defined roles within Christian churches and denominations, with the exception of Martin Luther King Jr. However, by his own admission, Lazard's list of early Black Christian public intellectuals excludes women. Curiously, rather than proceeding with naming and briefly examining Black women Christian intellectuals who were contemporaries of Johnson and Mays, Lazard explains how women were left out of history books because of "social and gender norms that did not give them voice."[9]

Lazard's explanation for excluding women from his essay is problematic for three reasons. First, Vincent Lloyd's inclusion of Dr. Anna Julia Cooper in his work on Black Christian public intellectuals is evidence that Black women were indeed included in historical narratives on Black intellectuals.[10] Cooper's presence in Lloyd's work is significant because studies typically present her as a "womanist foremother" and not solely as a Black Christian public intellectual.[11] Second, Lazard does not name any particular history books or branches of history that Black women were left out of. However, if we consider the historiography of Black intellectuals in the early twentieth century, it is rare to find much discussion on Mordecai Johnson and Benjamin Mays. Certainly, these men are the subjects of countless articles and chapters on the history of Black education in the United States.[12] Yet from Kevin K. Gaines's influential 1996 book on Black leaders and thinkers of the twentieth century to Vincent Lloyd's book mentioned above and the recently published *New Perspectives on the Black Intellectual Tradition*, Black church leaders—men and women—are typically left out of those particular history books.[13] While Lazard correctly identifies Johnson and Mays as two important contributors to the Black Christian intellectual tradition, his critique of Lloyd is shortsighted because Lazard himself does not fully consider the nuances of why Black men like Johnson and Mays have been excluded from conversations on Black intellectualism that do not take religion, specifically Christianity, into account.

Finally, by 2016, dozens of articles and book chapters and, in some cases, full-length biographies had been published on Mary McLeod Bethune, Nannie Helen Burroughs, and Charlotte Hawkins Brown. These three influential women were of Johnson's and Mays's generation, and in some cases, they had organizational affiliations with these particular men. Further, they fit into Lazard's examples of a Black Christian intellectual. He could have easily made mention of any one of them to fully flesh out his ideas about the contributions of Black religious thinkers to public life in the early twentieth century.

For Lazard, a Black Christian intellectual is someone who writes and speaks about how their "social and political ideology is shaped and critiqued by . . . Christian ethics."[14] Further, Lazard considers a Black Christian intellectual to be someone who "occupies the public square . . . in a large and visible way—a way that is accessible by many public entry points."[15] Lazard's definition aptly describes the careers of Mordecai Johnson and Benjamin Mays, *and* of Mary McLeod Bethune, Nannie Helen Burroughs, and Charlotte Hawkins Brown. These women are typically examined in studies that are broadly defined as "African American Women's History" and/or "African American religious history."

However, few scholars have mined these women's thought for an intellectual study. Their lives and work are the subject of this chapter.

There are three critical tasks central to this narrative. First, this chapter offers a more complex explanation of why Black women Christian intellectuals of the early twentieth century have been overlooked as subjects in histories, particularly intellectual histories such as the one that Joshua L. Lazard offered in his response essay to Vincent Lloyd. Second, both Vincent Lloyd and Joshua Lazard's definitions of Black Christian public intellectuals are used to make the case that Bethune, Burroughs, and Brown were significant public contributors to Black intellectual life in the early twentieth century as school founders and as social commentators. Finally, the chapter closes with an urgent plea for scholarship that updates and continues the important work of Mark Chapman, Clarence Taylor, and Barbara Dianne Savage that emphasizes the Black Christian public intellectual work of not only early twentieth-century women thinkers but also contemporary leaders such as Rev. Traci Blackmon and Bishop Yvette Flunder.[16]

Lazard is correct in naming social and gender norms as reasons for the exclusion of Black women Christian thinkers in histories on Black leaders and intellectuals. However, their exclusion is much more complicated than "male-centered voices" that overpowered the voices of women and others. Bethune, Burroughs, and Brown may have been considered unattractive subjects for Black intellectual histories because they were not prolific authors as much as they were productive and successful institution builders. In other words, unlike Dr. Anna Julia Cooper or even the renowned anti-lynching crusader and writer Ida B. Wells, they did not produce autobiographies and/or essay collections that fully explicated their social and political critique of American society and institutions.[17] Bethune, Burroughs, and Brown built schools. Much of their written work includes speeches, essays, and articles that supported the mission and funding of their schools. In the unique case of Nannie Helen Burroughs, she left behind a host of "how-to" guides that provided Black Baptist women with instructions on how to start and sustain various church offices and programs.[18] Among the papers of Charlotte Hawkins Brown are stories that promote good manners and decorum.

The examples from the papers of Nannie Helen Burroughs and Charlotte Hawkins Brown provide another critical insight into why they, along with Bethune, have not been considered as rigorous intellectuals by many scholars of Black intellectual history. These women began their public careers as teachers of children, specifically young girls, who they largely trained to become laborers and schoolteachers. As the examples of Mordecai Johnson and Benjamin Mays show, most commentators on Black Christian intellectual history look to those male historical figures who were university professors and administrators in addition to being well-known preachers as worthy historical subjects. Additionally, Mordecai Johnson and Benjamin Mays counted prominent public leaders such as Supreme Court Justice Thurgood Marshall and the Rev. Dr. Martin Luther King Jr. as graduates of their respective universities.[19]

Thinking about the kinds of students who attended the schools founded by Bethune, Burroughs, and Brown is important because it forces a reconsideration of who counts as a Black public intellectual, regardless of religious affinity or affiliation. In short, Bethune, Burroughs, and Brown each embraced Booker T. Washington's "accommodationist" strategy for educating Black people.[20] Their students were not among the "exceptional" individuals W. E. B. Du Bois championed as saviors of the Black race in his essay "The Talented Tenth."[21] Yet the evidence shows that Bethune, Burroughs, and Brown did not simply graduate pupils who only learned skills and trades, they also advocated the study of history, literature, and other liberal arts subjects in their curricula. In clarifying her school's mission, Burroughs once remarked, "We believe that an industrial and classical education can be simultaneously attained, and it is our duty to get both."[22]

Additionally, Mary McLeod Bethune, Nannie Helen Burroughs, and Charlotte Hawkins Brown instilled in their students a belief that they were valuable to God, and they modeled a set of ethical Christian values that encouraged their students to become pious and productive and self-sufficient community members. Lewis Baldwin and Rufus Burrow, two prominent scholars on the life and thought of Martin Luther King Jr., have shown that King's early ethical and intellectual beliefs were informed by the exact same teachings that Bethune, Burroughs, and Brown offered their students. While their pupils may not have become as renowned as Martin Luther King Jr., these three women educators and intellectuals inspired their students to become mechanics, teachers, doctors, farmers, and other valuable contributors to their communities.

A final reason why these women have been ignored as subjects for Black intellectual histories is that they have each been limited to examination of one or two aspects of their careers in scholarly writings on their lives. Therefore, scholars of intellectual histories may have simply been unaware of the complexity of these particular Black women's thoughts and ideas. Mary McLeod Bethune, for example, is generally presented as the founder of Bethune-Cookman University and as an influential Black clubwoman who had deep ties to the Franklin D. Roosevelt administration.[23] Little attention is paid to her Christian faith and how her religious beliefs informed her political ideas. Too much emphasis is placed on Nannie Helen Burroughs's role as founder of the Women's Convention of the National Baptist Convention and her groundbreaking school for Black girls and women in Washington, DC. However, as Barbara Dianne Savage and Jessica Gordon Nembhard show, Burroughs was an astute political and economic theorist. Finally, Charlotte Hawkins Brown did not have the same national political presence and influence that Bethune and Burroughs did. However, Brown's commitment to improving the lives of Black children and families in rural North Carolina made her an influential figure in the southern United States. Brown, like Bethune and Burroughs, was a highly visible leader who translated Christianity and Black concerns to public audiences with the intent of advocating for racial justice. This definition of a Black Christian public intellectual combines the definitions offered by Lloyd and Lazard. Throughout this chapter, examples of this definition in the careers of Bethune, Burroughs, and Brown are explored.

Bethune, Burroughs, and Brown have been grouped together for historical examination and analysis before. In 1948, *Negro History Bulletin* published a lesson plan on Bethune, Burroughs, and Brown for elementary school teachers. The lesson, titled "The Three B's (Builders)," had the general aim of encouraging the teachers "to teach such an interest in the 3 women that the children may wish to emulate them in some way."[24] In a 1961 letter, Gordon Hancock, a Baptist minister and professor, and close associate of Burroughs, wrote to her and expressed his grief over the recent death of Charlotte Hawkins Brown. Hancock wrote, "I believe it was the Romans who boasted of a great Triumvirate . . . and when I thought of you and Charlotte and Mrs. Bethune I always wanted to invent a Latin word, 'Trifeminate.' This may be bad Latin but it is mighty fine sentiment."[25] Barbara Dianne Savage named these women, along with Benjamin Mays, as a critical group of "earlier Southern black religious intellectuals," who laid the foundation on which Martin Luther King and his generation of intellectuals, preachers, and activists built their platforms of public ministry and service.[26] Savage's excellent 2008 book, *Your Spirits Walk Beside Us: The Politics of Black Religion*, should be credited as the first work to offer in-depth analysis of Mary McLeod Bethune and Nannie Helen Burroughs as contributors to the Black Christian public intellectual thought.[27] Finally, Audrey Thomas McCluskey offered a groundbreaking examination of the trio, along with Bethune's mentor, Lucy Laney, in her 2014 book, *A Forgotten Sisterhood: Pioneering Black Women Educators and Activists in the Jim Crow South*.[28]

However, Mary McLeod Bethune provided one of the earliest documentations of her connection to Brown and Burroughs. In a 1927 letter to Charlotte Hawkins Brown, Bethune wrote:

> I think of you and Nannie Helen Burroughs and Lucy Laney and myself as being in the most sacrificing class in our group of women. I think that the work we have produced will warrant love or consideration or appreciation or confidence that the general public may bestow upon us.

I have, unselfishly, given my best, and I thank God that I have lived long enough to the see the fruits from it.[29]

What did Bethune mean by the phrase, "our group of women"? What did they "sacrifice"? What was their "work"? What "fruits" did Bethune, Burroughs, and Brown see in their lifetimes from their work? Is there more "fruit" to be picked from the work that they left behind? These four questions will guide the remainder of the chapter as I make sense of who these women were as leaders and intellectuals.

The easy answer to the first question is that each of the women that Bethune named in her letter were founders of schools.[30] However, these women had much more in common with one another than their line of work. They were friends, colleagues, and contemporaries. They were each born between 1874 and 1883, and they each died between 1954 and 1962. Bethune, Burroughs, and Brown were the daughters and granddaughters of formerly enslaved women and men who ensured that they went to grade school.

Unlike Bethune and Brown, Burroughs did not have any additional educational training after high school. None of these women, however, graduated from college. Yet Burroughs, like Bethune and Brown, shared a deep commitment to the Christian faith that empowered them to become educators as acts of service to both God and their race, particularly southern Blacks. Understanding their shared identity as southern Black women is important to fully comprehending who they were as leaders and intellectuals. As mentioned, these women embraced the accommodationist educational philosophy of Booker T. Washington. However, they also embraced Washington's call for southern Blacks to "cast down your bucket" in southern communities.[31]

In his famous "Atlanta Compromise Speech," Booker T. Washington advised:

> To those of my race who depend on bettering their condition in a foreign land or who underestimate the importance of cultivating friendly relations with the Southern white man, who is their next-door neighbor, I would say, "Cast down your bucket where you are"—cast it down in making friends in every manly way of the people of all races by whom we are surrounded.[32]

In other words, Washington encouraged southern Blacks to remain in the South to prosper their own communities and to improve social conditions between Blacks and whites. It is beyond the scope of this chapter to provide a full historical overview and analysis of Washington's most well-known and discussed address. However, in consideration of the lives of Bethune, Burroughs, and Brown, these women proved to be beacons of hope and inspiration for southern Black communities in the post-Reconstruction era. The neighborhoods in which they founded and operated their schools challenged young Blacks—even those who could not afford to attend their schools—to envision possibilities for themselves that would move them beyond the humiliation of segregation and the threats of racialized terror and violence. For example, Bethune and her Daytona Literary and Industrial Training School for Negro Girls had a profound impact on the preeminent Black theologian, preacher, and educator Howard Thurman. In his autobiography, *With Head and Heart*, Thurman devotes several paragraphs to detailing the influence that Mary McLeod Bethune had on him personally and on their community in Daytona Beach.

Howard Thurman was five when Bethune's school opened in 1904, several blocks from the home he lived in with his mother, grandmother, and younger sister. Though his mother could not afford to send his sister to Bethune's school, Thurman credits Mary McLeod Bethune for teaching him about leadership and social influence. For example, he recalls Bethune attending his church to promote the work of her school and to advocate for temperance.[33] He further recalls encountering "Mrs. Bethune" on the streets of Daytona Beach, and she was always kind enough to greet him by name and ask about his family. Thurman was most impressed, however, with Bethune's ability to challenge the practice of segregated seating at public events. He noted that whenever Bethune delivered public addresses at his church, whites attended, but there were no segregated seating arrangements. Thurman was so deeply inspired by Bethune's "inner strength and authority" that he spent much of his own teaching career dedicated to "Mrs. Bethune's visionary crusade to uplift black women and young people."[34] Thurman and his wife, Sue Bailey Thurman, financially supported and worked directly with Bethune's National Council of Negro Women. Further, Thurman counted his role as eulogist for Mrs. Bethune when she died in 1955 as among his greatest privileges in life.

Nannie Helen Burroughs and Charlotte Hawkins Brown also had significant influences on the Southern communities in which they lived and worked. Burroughs completed high school in Washington, DC, and applied for teaching jobs in the public school system. However, she was constantly denied employment because of her dark complexion. She worked as a janitor and as an editor of several church-related magazines before stepping into the national spotlight as founder of the Women's Convention of the National Baptist Convention in 1900. Burroughs used her influence with the convention to fund her idea of opening a school that would give "all sorts of girls a fair chance, without political pull, to help them overcome whatever handicaps they might have."[35] Her National Training School for Women and Girls opened in Washington, DC, in 1909.

The school provided education for students in the seventh through twelfth grades, training classes for missionaries and Sunday school teachers, and trade classes for women and girls from the United States, Puerto Rico, and African countries. Her prominence as a race leader among working-class Blacks and an organizer for the Republican Party led to Burroughs's appointment by President Herbert Hoover as a chairperson of a special committee on Black housing in Washington in 1928.[36] Under Burroughs's leadership, the Committee on Negro Housing spent four years conducting research on housing in DC, and they reported their findings in *Negro Housing: Report of the Committee on Negro Housing*. The group recommended that the Hoover administration consider the construction of low-income housing, the removal of restrictive housing covenants, and an end to discriminatory practices with respect to lending and financing for potential Black homeowners. While Hoover's administration did not implement any of the committee's recommendations, Burroughs used the information she helped to gather through the committee to work with the Northeast Self-Help Cooperative, which she cofounded. The cooperative helped to address the economic needs of individuals who would have benefited from government supported low-income housing in Washington during the time of Hoover's presidential term.[37]

Charlotte Hawkins Brown's Palmer Memorial Institute had a transformative impact on the rural community of Sedalia, North Carolina. Brown was born in Henderson, North Carolina, but she spent her formative years in Cambridge, Massachusetts. After one year of college, in 1901 Brown returned to North Carolina to teach at the Bethany Institute, a school operated by the American Missionary Association (AMA). The following year, the AMA closed the institute, leaving Black children without a school to attend. Brown purchased a small cabin, and she opened the doors of her school in 1902. She named the school in honor of Alice Freeman Palmer, the president of Wellesley College. Palmer had provided financial support to Brown during her years as a high school and college student.[38]

Over the next several decades, Charlotte Hawkins Brown brought national prominence to the rural community of Sedalia. While the institute was initially founded as an industrial training school, Brown transformed it into a renowned college preparatory boarding school that attracted Black teenagers from throughout the United States and abroad. Many of the graduates of the institute went on to become educators, like the school's founder. Where Bethune's Daytona Beach school helped to challenge segregation, and Burroughs's school provided her with political influence in DC, Brown's role as a school leader allowed her to challenge the social climate of the South in another unique way. Brown used her influence as the leader of the all-Black Palmer Institute to mediate conversations between her students in North Carolina and white college students throughout the South.

For example, in December 1935, Brown organized her students' thoughts into a speech titled "What the Negro Youth Expects of the White Youth in Their Tomorrow." She delivered this address at a Friday morning chapel service at Berea College in Berea, Kentucky, before an all-white audience.[39]

Brown's speech provides an ample unpacking of the term "white privilege," which seems to dominate contemporary discourse on race in the United States. She explains to her all-white audience that the government, the industries, and the institutions of American society have already been "bequeathed" to them. Therefore, she stated that her Black students expected educated whites to "develop that sense of fairness and justice, that expression of neighborliness that will include them in your plan and program for the development of a finer and better America in which to live."[40]

A commentator on Brown's speech noted that "the students' eyes were fastened on the speaker and for a full forty minutes she held both teachers and students to an almost uncanny silence in her appeal for justice for her people."[41] It is unclear what impact Brown had on the white students who heard her speech. Did those particular white students go on to create opportunities for Black people through their careers after hearing Brown's address?[42] There is no evidence found among her papers to provide an adequate answer to that question. However, as stated, Brown—like Bethune and Burroughs—used her position as an educator and leader in a southern community to promote positive change in the social climate in a region that was still grappling with the aftermath of chattel slavery, as Washington advised Black leaders to do in his "Atlanta Compromise."

As southern Black women educators, Mary McLeod Bethune, Nannie Helen Burroughs, and Charlotte Hawkins Brown were indeed a unique group of women. Many Black southern women had to quit their teaching jobs upon marriage.[43] However, Bethune's, Burroughs's, and Brown's unique positions as school founders gave them an unprecedented amount of social freedom, influence, and power. Their unique positions appear to have cost them opportunities for happy romantic relationships.[44] While Burroughs never married or had children of her own, Bethune's husband abandoned her and their son three years after she opened her school. Charlotte Hawkins Brown was divorced twice. She often remarked, "I was not made for marriage."[45]

In addition to sacrificing the roles of "wife" and "mother," two hallmarks of the "cult of domesticity" that defined American womanhood in the eras in which Bethune, Burroughs, and Brown came of age and matured in order to accomplish their goals, these women sacrificed in other areas of their lives.

During the initial phases of their careers, Mary McLeod Bethune, Nannie Helen Burroughs, and Charlotte Hawkins Brown often lacked financing and other resources that were necessary to run their schools. However, as they rose in prominence as nationally known leaders, these three women became the first of their race and gender to enter into many of the public spaces that they inhabited. As such, they experienced loneliness because they were often the only Black people in the room. They felt humiliated because they knew that white people viewed them as tokens. Further, they endured the umbrage and critique of Black men who resented the high degree of visibility afforded to them. For example, Barbara Dianne Savage notes that E. Franklin Frazier, a distinguished sociologist and scholar at Morehouse College, criticized Mary McLeod Bethune for becoming increasingly arrogant and domineering as her influence in Washington, DC, expanded.[46] However, Savage, aptly points out that Bethune did not allow such critiques to prevent her from taking advantage of the privileges that came with her connection to President Franklin Roosevelt and First Lady Eleanor Roosevelt.

Savage argues that Bethune used her relationship with the White House to serve as a reminder to whites and Blacks that Black people—especially Black women—needed to be present and seen in powerful, public spaces. She includes a quote from Bethune's diary to emphasize her point. After attending an event with Eleanor Roosevelt at the White House, Bethune reflected:

> While I felt very much at home, I looked about me longingly for other dark faces. In all that great group I felt a sense of being quite alone . . . Then I thought how vitally important it was that I be here, to help these others get used to seeing us in high places. And so, while I sip tea in the brilliance of the White House, my heart reaches out to the delta land and the bottom land. I know so well why I must be here, must go to tea at the White House. To remind them always that we belong here, we are a part of this America.[47]

Bethune's diary entry is useful here for outlining the key ideas that framed not only her intellectual work but also the intellectual work of Nannie Helen Burroughs and Charlotte Hawkins Brown. These women understood that not only did they need to be seen, their ideas needed to be heard. Therefore, in addition to building schools and taking advantage of opportunities to network with political officials, Bethune, Burroughs, and Brown wrote essays and delivered addresses that communicated their thoughts about the condition of Black people in the United States. Next, I turn to the written work and speeches of Bethune, Burroughs, and Brown to explain their ideas on Christianity, equality, education, and justice and to demonstrate why these women must be considered for future work on Black Christian intellectual history.

Prior to Lloyd's and Lazard's 2016 essays on Black Christian intellectualism in the twentieth century, very few scholars had directly addressed the subject since the late 1970s.[48] Mark Chapman's 1996 *Christianity on Trial: African American Religious Thought before and after Black Power* examined five religious leaders, including Benjamin Mays, who represented various movements that interrogated the relevancy of Christianity to the African American struggle for freedom. While most of the religious leaders examined in Chapman's text were Christians, Chapman included Elijah Muhammad, leader of the Nation of Islam, to add diversity to his study. Delores Williams, a pioneer of womanist scholarship in the field of religious studies, is the only woman featured in that particular text.[49]

Clarence Taylor's *Black Religious Intellectuals: The Fight for Equality from Jim Crow to the 21st Century* stands out in this brief historiography for its emphasis on highlighting the careers of lesser-known Black male preachers, including Bishop Smallwood Williams. In short, Taylor's inclusion of Williams is significant because most Pentecostal preachers—Black and white—did not engage in civil rights activism. Taylor's book also stands out for his examination of Ella Baker and Pauli Murray. While Baker was not a preacher and probably would have identified as "spiritual, but not religious," she was a good choice for Taylor's study because of her thoughts on how to mobilize Black churches for activism. Murray, who became an Episcopal priest at the age of sixty-seven, had been involved in the Black freedom movement for her entire adult life. Taylor included her to show how she fought gender discrimination in the Episcopal Church.[50]

As noted earlier, Barbara Dianne Savage's *Your Spirits Walk Beside Us* is a significant text because it wrestles with Mary McLeod Bethune, Nannie Helen Burroughs, and Charlotte Hawkins Brown's thoughts on politics, Christian faith, and the role of Black churches in civil rights activity. Savage was not the first to examine any of these women; however, her presentation of them as "Southern black religious intellectuals" was an original reading of these three particular women's lives.[51] Savage provides broad biographical narratives on how these women contributed to denominational and public conversations on church politics, and the social and economic circumstances of the Black people living in their communities. What is unique about Savage's narratives of Bethune, Burroughs, and Brown is that these three women are examined primarily in conversation with other Black thinkers and intellectuals. What conversations did these women have with wider audiences that afforded them opportunities to become public translators of Black Christian thought with the intent of confronting racial injustices?

Bethune's essay "Certain Unalienable Rights" was the only piece written by a woman featured in Rayford Logan's edited volume, *What the Negro Wants*.[52] By 1945, the year in which the volume was published, Bethune was seventy years old, and she had already had an illustrious career as a teacher, educational administrator, clubwoman, and political leader.[53] She delivered countless addresses and wrote articles for publication in newspapers and club journals. However, her contribution to Logan's volume stands out for several reasons. First, it shows that many Black intellectuals of her era took her thought and work seriously. In other words, where most historians of Black intellectual history have overlooked Bethune, her contemporaries, namely Rayford Logan and Eugene Holmes, directly solicited and engaged her ideas.[54] Second, Logan selected Bethune to contribute to his project because he had hoped that her conservative views would add variety to the book. Logan was intentional in inviting several political militants, moderates, and conservatives to write essays. However, he and several reviewers were surprised that each contributor ultimately demanded an end to segregation as the main concern for all Black Americans. Finally, Bethune's contribution to *What the Negro Wants* stands out because her essay demonstrates how she employed her Christian theology in her ideas about what type of government and society the United States needed to be so that Black people would no longer live as second-class citizens.

Bethune begins "Certain Unalienable Rights" with a brief overview of the American Revolution with special interest in the Boston Tea Party. She explains how a small group of colonists decided to "take the law into their own hands" and "struck out against restrictions and tyranny and oppression." As a result, Bethune explains that those colonists "gave initial expression to the ideal of a nation 'that all men are created equal, that they are endowed by their Creator with certain unalienable rights.'"[55] Bethune then moves on to the 1943 race riot in Harlem and observes that when young, Black Americans have struck out against restrictions, tyranny, and oppression in their neighborhoods, they were either beaten, imprisoned, or, worse, killed by police officers. She then turns her attention to the plight of African American soldiers who were actively fighting in World War II as she was writing. Bethune writes:

> Along with other good Americans the Negro has been prepared to take his part in the fight against an enemy that threatens all these basic American principles. He is fighting now on land and sea to beat back forces of oppression and tyranny and discrimination. Why, then, should we be surprised when at home as well as abroad he fights back against these same forces?[56]

Bethune's commentary on Black soldiers is significant to her argument because she views them as the chief defenders of American democracy. Ultimately, she argues that Black people in the United States want to experience the freedoms established in the Declaration of Independence and the Constitution. She offers nine ways in which she believes that Blacks could experience those freedoms. In short, she called for the federal government to end segregation, to model democracy at home and abroad, to end all discrimination in the armed forces, to end lynching and ensure the civil rights of all Black people, the elimination of poll taxes, and equal access to employment, housing, and labor unions. Finally, Bethune states that Blacks desire interracial cooperation. Before closing her essay, Bethune makes five suggestions to Black people on how they might go about securing all that she has demanded of the federal government.

Bethune's theology shows up subtly in "Certain Unalienable Rights." For example, she argues that "Christianity works for equality." This is a rather interesting utterance from Bethune, considering that in 1944, when she would have been writing her essay, she was still a public member of the Methodist Church. This is significant because in 1939, the Methodist Church reunited its northern and southern factions as a segregated church in which Black congregations were a separate but equal conference. That Bethune believed Christianity was a religion that emphasized equality shows her sophistication in biblical hermeneutics, and the extent to which she rejected American Christianity. In short, Bethune held to those Christian scriptures that taught that believers in Christ were equals spiritually and, therefore, were equals as citizens of the United States. Further, she believed in Christian equality, even though the church she was affiliated with did not. There is evidence to suggest that Bethune may have remained connected to the Methodist Church as a means of securing funding for her school.[57] Exploring that evidence is beyond the scope of this paper, but it is mentioned here because it is clear from her essay that Bethune's belief in Christ was stronger than her belief in a Christian denomination.

The end of "Certain Unalienable Rights" concludes with Bethune asking, "In order for us to have peace and justice and democracy for all, may I urge that we follow the example of the great humanitarian—Jesus Christ—in exemplifying in our lives both by word and action the fatherhood of God and the brotherhood of man?"[58] Bethune's question demonstrates a high Christology or, in other words, a strong belief in both the personhood and divinity of Jesus. Further, she sees Christ as a model for promoting the human welfare of all human beings or, in her context, of Blacks and of whites in the United States.

"Certain Unalienable Rights" is the best representative of Bethune's work as a Black Christian public intellectual because, given the high-profile natures of the book's editor and contributors, she had to have known that the piece would be read broadly by Black and white critics. While her theology is subtle, it is clear that Mary McLeod Bethune saw the opportunity to contribute to Logan's book as an opportunity to present Christianity as a valuable tool in bringing about social and political change.

As a prominent leader in the National Baptist Convention, Nannie Helen Burroughs's entire career was focused on using her faith to bring about social and political change in the United States. Burroughs is distinguished in this trio of Black women intellectuals because she was much more militant and direct than Bethune and Brown when addressing Black *and* white audiences. Audrey Thomas McCluskey, a Burroughs biographer, has provided the most succinct and accurate description of Burroughs's writing and speaking projects. McCluskey explains, "Criticizing errant blacks and holding white Christian leaders' feet to the fire by calling them out on their racism was Burroughs's specialty."[59] Burroughs was a prolific writer of newspaper articles and pamphlets, and a highly sought-after speaker. She used every opportunity to demonstrate this specialty when conveying her ideas about how whites could develop better Christian character and community, and how Blacks could improve their plight in the US.

In an undated pamphlet titled "Making Your Community Christian," Burroughs addressed "intelligent white Southerners." She advised them to stop using racial epithets, to address Black folk with titles of respect, to learn Black history, and to encourage their preachers to preach about Christian unity. The pamphlet urges whites to support Black veterans and to donate to social agencies that assist Black laborers. Finally, Burroughs suggested that her audiences subscribe to Black periodicals. She proposed this idea to her audience because she believed that white southerners only knew Blacks who had worked for them "in some menial position."[60]

Burroughs's speech "What Must the Negro Do to Be Saved" stands out among her papers because it details the depth of her intellectual project.[61] While the work functions here to show her ideas about how Blacks could improve themselves socially and politically, other scholars have used it to represent Burroughs as a feminist foremother.[62] Delivered in 1933 at Bethel AME Church to a group of young adults, Burroughs relayed three messages to her audience. First, she advised the young people to live spiritually grounded lives. Second, she encouraged them to fight for their rights, even if it meant death. Further, she implored them not to wait for a savior. She exclaimed, "I like the quotation, 'Moses my servant is dead. Therefore, arise and go over Jordan.' There are no deliverers. They're all dead. We must arise and go over Jordan. We can take the Promised Land."[63] Finally, Burroughs advised them to create a new vision of Black women. Burroughs declared:

We must have a glorified womanhood that can look any man in the face—white, red, yellow, brown, or black, and tell of the nobility of character within black womanhood. Stop making slaves and servants of our women. We've got to stop singing—"Nobody works but father." The Negro mother is doing it all. The women are carrying the burden.[64]

Evelyn Brooks Higginbotham, perhaps the most prolific Burroughs scholar, has defined this particular speech as "the legacy of Nannie Helen Burroughs." For Higginbotham, it demonstrates the extent of Burroughs influence over young leaders by "asserting the crucial relationship between religion, politics, and gender."[65] For the purposes of this chapter, Burroughs's speech and the above pamphlet are included as examples of how she used the popular mediums of her day, pamphlets, newspaper articles, and speaking engagements, to assert a strong Black Christian intellectual tradition in the early twentieth century.

There is still much to mine through in the papers of Charlotte Hawkins Brown. However, what is clear is that much of her writing and speaking centered on her ideas about how to educate Black youth. Brown appears to have had a strong relationship with the administration of Berea College in Berea, Kentucky. As noted earlier, Brown spoke at a chapel service there in 1935. She delivered another undated address there titled "What to Teach to Negro Americans."[66] That Brown had an extensive relationship with Berea College is not surprising. When Berea opened its doors in the late 1860s, it became the first interracial institution of higher education in the South. However, in 1904, a segregation law in Kentucky prohibited Berea from admitting Black students. That law was struck down in 1950 and Berea resumed admitting Black students. The language in Brown's speech suggests that she may have delivered it soon after the school resumed admitting Black students. For example, she praises Berea as "one of the few opportunities of its kind given to white and Negro people residing so near to the states of southern tradition."

While Brown encouraged Berea's instructors to teach all of their students how to exhibit "enlightenment and industry," she focused on two major areas that Black students needed to excel. First, Brown emphasized several times throughout her speech the need for Berea to teach Black history and culture. She exclaimed, "Teach Negro youth to know themselves. By that I mean to give them an appreciable knowledge of the history of the race and its background." Second, she encouraged the teaching of Christian religion as a means to spur interracial "compassion and cooperation."

Brown's frequent appearances at Berea College suggest that her ideas about interracial cooperation and the educational needs of Black people were valuable to communities in the South beyond Sedalia, North Carolina. The extent to which Brown shaped the political climate of the South as a political leader has yet to be explored, but as more and more scholars look to the Black church tradition, it is clear that Brown's ideas are critical to study as a means of understanding the complexity and diversity of early Black thought in the twentieth century.

By 1962, Mary McLeod Bethune, Nannie Helen Burroughs, and Charlotte Hawkins Brown were dead. As Bethune suggested in her letter to Brown, each of these women had enjoyed the fruits of their labor. Over the span of their lengthy careers, they helped to transform southern communities by building schools for the children of former slaves and sharecroppers. Bethune's and Burroughs's schools continue to operate today.[67] These three women were pioneers in improving race relations in the South and throughout the nation. They were influential thinkers who produced essays, articles, and speeches that allowed them to translate Christianity as a viable ideal to address inequality and demand justice. As the field of Black Christian intellectualism builds on the work of Mark Chapman, Clarence Taylor, and Barbara Dianne Savage, the trio of women examined here deserve even more attention than what this chapter has shown them. Further, scholars who are interested in the Black Christian intellectual tradition would do well to follow the public careers of contemporary women preachers Traci Blackmon and Yvette Flunder, who are promoting Christianity as a viable ideal to think about the #BlackLivesMatter movement and LGBTQIA issues.

NOTES

1. Alan Jacobs, "The Watchmen: What Became of the Christian Intellectuals," *Harper's Magazine*, September 2016, https://harpers.org/archive/2016/09/the-watchmen/.

2. In other words, I am suggesting that the Christian intellectuals that Jacobs references did not consider other aspects of the women's rights movement—for example, the right to affordable birth control.

3. According to the website, Religion Dispatches is now known as Rewire.News.

4. Vincent Lloyd's essay "Why We Need a Public Black Theology for the 21st Century," was published on Religion Dispatches on September 16, 2016, http://religiondispatches.org/why-we-need-a-public-black-theology-for-the-21st-century/. Joshua L. Lazard's response, "To Be Christian, Intellectual, and Black: A Response to Vincent Lloyd," was published two weeks later on September 30, 2016, http://religiondispatches.org/to-be-christian-intellectual-and-black-a-response-to-vincent-lloyd/.

5. Lloyd, "Why We Need a Public Black Theology for the 21st Century."

6. Lloyd, "Why We Need a Public Black Theology for the 21st Century."

7. Lloyd, "Why We Need a Public Black Theology for the 21st Century."

8. There is a decent amount of scholarship available on both Benjamin Mays and Mordecai Johnson. For more information on Mays, see John Robert Roper Jr., *The*

Magnificent Mays: A Biography of Benjamin Elijah Mays (Columbia: University of South Carolina Press, 2012). For more information on Johnson, see Richard I. McKinney, "Mordecai Johnson: An Early Pillar of African American Higher Education," *Journal of Blacks in Higher Education* (Spring 2000): 99–104.

9. Lazard, "To Be Christian, Intellectual, and Black."

10. Anna Julia Cooper (1858–1964) was the fourth African American woman to earn a doctoral degree. Her essay collection, *A Voice from the South* (1892), remains influential for its commentary on race, gender, religion, and politics.

11. See for example Karen Baker Fletcher's 1994 book, *A Singing Something: Womanist Reflections on Anna Julia Cooper*. Alice Walker coined the term "womanist" in 1983 to define a wave of Black feminism that resonated with many Black women religious scholars of theology and biblical interpretation.

12. See for example McKinney, "Mordecai Johnson," 99–104.

13. See Kevin K. Gaines, *Uplifting the Race: Black Leadership, Politics, and Culture in the Twentieth Century* (Chapel Hill: University of North Carolina Press, 1996). Keisha Blain, Christopher Cameron, and Ashley D. Farmer are the editors the volume mentioned.

14. Lazard, "To Be Christian, Intellectual, and Black."

15. Lazard, "To Be Christian, Intellectual, and Black."

16. Blackmon, a minister within the United Church of Christ, has been at the forefront of the #BlackLivesMatter movement in Ferguson. Flunder is the presiding bishop of the Fellowship of Affirming Ministries, a coalition of churches that welcome and affirm LGBTQIA individuals.

17. Wells's autobiography, *Crusade for Justice*, and other writings have made her a rather accessible historical figure to examine.

18. Burroughs's pamphlet, "Twelve Things the Negro Must Do for Himself" is readily available online and is often cited in studies on her life and work.

19. Marshall graduated from Howard School of Law in 1933. King completed his undergraduate studies at Morehouse in 1948.

20. Booker T. Washington's easily accessible "The Atlanta Compromise Speech of 1895" spells out his strategy for Blacks to make peace with white supremacy by accommodating segregation and embracing vocational education.

21. See W. E. B. Du Bois, "The Talented Tenth," September 1903, http://teachingamericanhistory.org/library/document/the-talented-tenth/.

22. Earl H. Harrison, "An Abbreviated Story of the Life of Nannie Helen Burroughs and the National Trade and Professional School," Burroughs Papers, Manuscripts and Archives, Library of Congress.

23. Bethune served as an organizer of Roosevelt's Black Cabinet, an informal association of Black leaders and scholars who informed the president on race relations.

24. "Lesson Plan Grade III–VI," *Negro History Bulletin*, December 1948, 61.

25. Gordon Hancock to Nannie Burroughs, March 17, 1961, Burroughs Papers, Manuscripts and Archives, Library of Congress.

26. Savage, *Your Spirits Walk Beside Us*, 119–20.

27. Evelyn Brooks Higginbotham's extensive work on Burroughs also presents Burroughs as an intellectual. However, Savage's chapter on Burroughs focuses more on her public life outside of the National Baptist Convention.

28. Lucy Laney (1854–1933) operated one of the first schools for Black children in Georgia. Mary McLeod Bethune was heavily influenced by Laney.

29. Mary McLeod Bethune, "Letter to Charlotte Hawkins Brown" in McCluskey and Smith, *Mary McLeod Bethune*, 94.

30. For more information on Lucy Laney, see McCluskey, *A Forgotten Sisterhood*.

31. Booker T. Washington, "Atlanta Compromise Speech of 1895," http://historymatters.gmu.edu/d/39/.

32. Washington, "Atlanta Compromise Speech of 1895."

33. See Thurman, *With Head and Heart*.

34. Thurman, *With Head and Heart*, 23.

35. Easter, *Nannie Helen Burroughs*, 57.

36. This significant fact of Burroughs's life has not been fully unpacked. The most significant evidence of Burroughs's participation in Hoover's administration is the publication *Negro Housing: Report of the Committee on Negro Housing*, which lists her as the chair of the committee.

37. See Jessica Gordon Nembhard, *Collective Courage: A History of African American Cooperative Economic Thought and Practice* (University Park: Pennsylvania State University Press, 2014).

38. McCluskey, *A Forgotten Sisterhood*, 8.

39. Charlotte Hawkins Brown, "What the Negro Youth Expects of the White Youth in Their Tomorrow," Charlotte Hawkins Brown Papers, HOLLIS for Archival Discovery, Harvard University, https://hollisarchives.lib.harvard.edu/repositories/8/resources/4965/digital_only.

40. Brown, "What the Negro Youth Expects."

41. Brown, "What the Negro Youth Expects."

42. While I do not know the answer to the question I posed, I do know that Berea College was initially an interracial institution until state laws prohibited interracial education. Once those laws were struck down in 1950, the administration began to immediately accept Black students for enrollment.

43. See Lewis Baldwin, *There Is a Balm in Gilead: The Cultural Roots of Martin Luther King, Jr.* (Minneapolis: Augsburg Press, 1991). Baldwin explains how King's mother, Alberta, was a schoolteacher until she married. She quit as it was customary in the South for women to be unmarried as teachers.

44. There is no evidence to suggest that these women were involved in same-sex relationships. However, I try to keep an open mind regarding historical figures. They could have been happily involved in relationships, with men and/or women, and they managed to keep those relationships private.

45. McCluskey, *A Forgotten Sisterhood*, 79.

46. Savage, *Your Spirits Walk Beside Us*, 134.

47. Savage, *Your Spirits Walk Beside Us*, 135.

48. Henry J. Young, *Major Black Religious Leaders, 1755–1940* (Nashville: Abingdon Press, 1977); and Randall Burkett and Richard Newman *Black Apostles: Afro American Clergy Confront the Twentieth Century* (Boston: G. K. Hall, 1978) provided the earliest studies on Black religious intellectuals.

49. See note 11 for a brief overview of womanist scholarship.

50. Pauli Murray not only pushed the Episcopal Church on gender discrimination, she also pushed the church on its stances on human sexuality.

51. In addition to Audrey Thomas McCluskey's joint biography of Bethune, Burroughs, and Brown, their careers have been examined by Evelyn Brooks Higginbotham, Bettye Collier-Thomas, Clarence Newsome, and countless others. Still, there is a dearth of scholarship available on Brown.

52. For more information, see Logan, *What the Negro Wants*.

53. For more information, see Logan, *What the Negro Wants*.

54. Rayford Logan and Eugene Holmes were both professors at the time that *What the Negro Wants* published. While Logan served as editor of the volume, Holmes, a philosopher, wrote a book review and praised Bethune's pragmatic approach.

55. Mary McLeod Bethune, "Certain Unalienable Rights," in Logan, *What the Negro Wants*, 248.

56. Bethune, "Certain Unalienable Rights," 250.

57. See Clarence Newsome's essay "Mary McLeod Bethune and the Methodist Episcopal Church North: In but Out" in Weisenfeld and Newman, *This Far by Faith*, 124–39. Newsome documents Bethune's rocky relationship with the Methodist Church, an institution that provided funding for her school. Bethune battled with the Church over school governance, and it seems that she may have remained a member of the denomination since she was the school's founder and first president. In the later years of her life, she was more publicly involved with the Moral Re-Armament Movement than she was with Methodist circles.

58. Bethune, "Certain Unalienable Rights," 258.

59. McCluskey, *A Forgotten Sisterhood*, 107.

60. Nannie Helen Burroughs, "Making Your Community Christian," Burroughs Papers, Manuscripts and Archives, Library of Congress.

61. Nannie Helen Burroughs, "What Must the Negro Do to Be Saved," Burroughs Papers, Manuscripts and Archives, Library of Congress.

62. For example, see Evelyn Brooks Higginbotham, "Religion, Gender, and Politics: The Leadership of Nannie Helen Burroughs" in Weisenfeld and Newman, *This Far by Faith*, 140–57.

63. Burroughs, "What Must the Negro Do to Be Saved."

64. Burroughs, "What Must the Negro Do to Be Saved."

65. Higginbotham, "Religion, Gender, and Politics," 154.

66. Charlotte Hawkins Brown, "What to Teach to Negro Americans," Charlotte Hawkins Brown Papers, HOLLIS for Archival Discovery, Harvard University, https://hollisarchives.lib.harvard.edu/repositories/8/resources/4965/digital_only.

67. Bethune's school is now known as Bethune-Cookman University. Burroughs's school is now the home offices of the Progressive National Baptist Convention, and Brown's school has been transformed into a museum named in her honor.

REFERENCES

Chapman, Mark. *Christianity on Trial: African American Religious Thought Before and After Black Power*. Maryknoll: Orbis Press, 1996.

Collier-Thomas, Bettye. *Jesus, Jobs, and Justice: African American Women and Religion*. New York: Alfred Knopf, 2011.

Easter, Opal V. *Nannie Helen Burroughs*. New York: Garland Press, 1995.

Higginbotham, Evelyn Brooks. *Righteous Discontent: The Women's Movement in the Black Baptist Church, 1880–1920*. Cambridge, MA: Harvard University Press, 1993.

Logan, Rayford, ed. *What the Negro Wants*. Notre Dame, IN: University of Notre Dame Press, 2001.

McCluskey, Audrey Thomas. *A Forgotten Sisterhood: Pioneering Black Women Educators in the Jim Crow South*. Lanham, MD: Rowan and Littlefield, 2014.

McCluskey, Audrey Thomas, and Elaine M. Smith, eds. *Mary McLeod Bethune: Building a Better World: Essays and Selected Documents*. Bloomington: Indiana University Press, 1999.

Savage, Barbara Dianne. *Your Spirits Walk Beside Us*. Cambridge, MA: Belknap Press, 2008.

Taylor, Clarence. *Black Religious Intellectuals*. New York: Routledge, 2002.

Thurman, Howard. *With Head and Heart: Autobiography*. New York: Harcourt, Brace, Jovanovich, 1981.

Weisenfeld, Judith, and Richard Newman. *This Far by Faith: Readings in African American Women's Religious History*. New York: Routledge, 1996.

Archives

The Papers of Charlotte Hawkins Brown, Radcliffe College, Cambridge, MA.
The Papers of Nannie Helen Burroughs, Library of Congress, Washington, DC.

WE LED THE WAY

Black Women and the Civil Rights Movement at Morgan State College

SIMONE R. BARRETT

According to the editors of *Toward an Intellectual History of Black Women*, "Historical scholarship on black women has especially yet to map the broad contours of their political and social thought in any detail or to examine their distinctive intellectual tradition as often self-educated thinkers with a sustained history of wrestling with sexism and racism."[1] Since the Civil War, African American women have endured both the pain of racial segregation and discrimination from their male counterparts. African American women felt the urge to liberate themselves from economic, political, and social oppression just as deeply as did African American men and, perhaps at times, more deeply. However, during the civil rights movement, women were noticeably excluded from major publicity, while "the success of the civil rights movement hinged on the selfless dedication and hard work of a host of women whose names were less familiar."[2]

While we should continue to recognize men who were instrumental in the movement, it is equally important to recognize that courageous, dedicated women, like Rosa Parks, Fannie Lou Hamer, Ella Baker, and Daisy Lee Bates, were at the forefront of several well-known and influential civil rights initatives.[3] Women of the civil rights movement suffered from the triple oppressions of race, class, and gender. "Women routinely performed mundane office chores and rarely asked to chair meetings or engage in policymaking decisions. These grievances seem insignificant to some; however, they resulted in much wasted talent and experience because women of the movement did not perform jobs commensurable with their abilities. The assumptions of male superiority were as widespread, deeply rooted and as crippling to the women as the assumptions of white supremacy are to the African American."[4] These women, many unnamed and unknown, were the backbone of the long civil rights movement, while also facing the challenges of existing in a world that does not recognize or acknowledge them.

This essay will examine the role of Black women intellectuals within the context of Black female student involvement in the civil rights movement while highlighting Morgan State College, Baltimore, and the state of Maryland. Black women intellectuals such as Lucy Diggs Slowe, Lillie Carroll Jackson, Juanita Jackson Mitchell, Thelma Bando, and Gloria Richardson influenced and provided a strong and indelible foundation for Morgan State's women students and their supporters as they fought against racial oppression and inequality. These Black women were intellectuals who throughout their careers sought to elevate Black women's experiences by training and mentoring the next generation of Black women intellectuals who changed the racial and political landscape of the nation.

As a rule, most civil rights protests across the country included a woman or women as prominent figure(s) in their development and execution. Lillie Carroll Jackson and Juanita Jackson Mitchell were the women at the forefront of Baltimore's civil rights activities. Their roles as the president and legal counsel, respectively, of the Baltimore City NAACP allowed these women to work closely with Morgan's students beginning in the 1930s. This relationship was one of the defining factors in the success of many of the students' endeavors.[5]

This collaborative effort waged as part of the "Buy Where You Can Work" campaign also included supporting various national antilynching bills, marching on the statehouse in Annapolis, and picketing the segregated seating practices of Ford's Theatre in Baltimore. Under the guidance of Jackson, the Baltimore City NAACP provided transportation to protests in Annapolis, downtown Baltimore, and Gwynn Oak Amusement Park, as well as monies for bail and attorneys for students who needed these services.[6]

A large mass arrest occurred in February 1963, with 415 students, including women, detained and charged with disorderly conduct and/or criminal trespassing for picketing the Northwood Movie Theater. Of the students arrested, more than 200 women were jailed in hazardous conditions due to severe overcrowding. Seeing women treated in this manner outraged the public. Though men faced similar conditions, some whites allowed themselves to feel more protective of women, and the pictures of them in those conditions had a negative effect on the theater's racist policy.

Thelma Bando, Morgan's dean of women, along with other members of the faculty, empowered female students and supported them in their stand against discrimination while Jackson, Mitchell, and others negotiated with Baltimore City officials, including Mayor Philip Goodman, to secure their release and to integrate the theater. They succeeded when, on February 22, 1963, a headline of a *Baltimore Sun* article read, "Movie House Agrees to Admit Negroes If Protests Halt."[7] The integration of the movie theater, the culmination of a decade-long protest, completed the integration of the shopping center. Mass arrests made this victory possible.

This victory at Northwood Theater was one of many during the institution's years of active protest, which began in 1935 with the establishment of the college's NAACP chapter. When established, the chapter's membership included Elva Davis, Hazel Thompson, and Clara Graves. Additionally, the recording and correspondence secretaries for the chapter during the 1939–1940 academic year were also women, Betty Patterson and Gladys Anderson.[8]

By the early 1940s, African Americans were fighting and dying abroad for their country. At home, however, they were treated as second-class citizens. It was during this period that large numbers of Morgan students began to take an active role in improving the conditions for Blacks in Maryland and on Morgan's campus.[9]

In 1947, Elaine Blackwell and fellow Morgan students made their second protest march to the statehouse in a five-year period. According to Blackwell, "We marched to express to William Preston Lane Jr., governor of Maryland, our displeasure with the allotment of funds for Morgan State College."[10] The demands of the students included housing for veterans, more faculty, and updated facilities for the college. At the time, although there were nine hundred physical education majors, Morgan had no gymnasium. Several buses carrying over six hundred students traveled to Annapolis to participate. The climax of the demonstration was an hour-long meeting between Lane and a committee of four students, who informed the governor that there were inadequate facilities and limited equipment. He listened to them and said, "My hands are tied, there is nothing I can do . . . and the financial appropriations made to Morgan were adequate."[11] Although Lane's message was discouraging, nevertheless, there were changes made to the campus facilities, and new buildings were erected, including Truth Hall, Harper-Tubman dormitory, Hurt Gymnasium, and the refectory.

In 1948, students again aligned themselves with Lillie Carroll Jackson and the NAACP. Their protest efforts focused on Ford's Theatre, which had a seating policy that relegated African Americans to the balcony. Though female Morgan students were involved with this protest, research yielded few specific names. However, Adah Jenkins, a member of the Congress of Racial Equality (CORE), former Morgan music faculty, and then-theater critic for the *Baltimore Afro-American* newspaper, did participate. According to her obituary in the *Afro-American*, "She spent many long cold, hot or rainy nights demonstrating for what she believed were the rights of all people to patronize any restaurant or theater they so desired."[12] During the protests at Ford's, she received letters of support from both Black and white entertainers, including Ruby Dee, Ossie Davis, Charles Boyer, and Oscar Hammerstein.[13] Additionally, Jenkins picketed outside of the police station during the court hearings for those arrested during the July 1963 Gwynn Oak Park protest.[14] The role of Morgan women students expanded as the movement progressed. In the winter of 1955, Helena Hicks (nee Sorrell), a graduating senior at the college, was en route to school when she and her classmates walked into the Read's Drug Store at the corner of Howard and Lexington Streets in downtown Baltimore. Hicks and friends went in because they wanted to get out of the cold. She recounted the incident:

> So, the waitress said, "Well I can't serve you." So, we just sat there, and we didn't say anything; and finally, she went back and got the manager. And he came out and said, "You niggers get out of here!" And we just sat there; and finally, when his voice got to the point where we knew he was going to do something like call the police at Pine Street, which was three blocks away—only police station in the city, we decided to leave. And we got up and just came out of the place. We got the bus; we came on to school.[15]

Though this was an impromptu act by Hicks, it was not her first demonstration. Actually, she was a member of the NAACP's City-Wide Young People's Forum and accompanied her parents to a demonstration at Ford's Theatre long before attending Morgan. Hicks set the bar for the young women students who would follow. Her bravery and unwavering desire to be recognized as a human being by whites continued throughout her as career as a sociologist. By April 1955, because of the students' efforts at Northwood, as well as those of Hicks and her group in downtown Baltimore, all of the Read's Drug Stores in Baltimore City opened their lunch counters to Blacks. According to Hicks, "Many Baltimore students at Morgan brought their ideals and activist inclination with them to college, noting that their activism wasn't limited to campus organized protests . . . there would be demonstrations around school during the school year but not in the summer or over break. Then you might do something downtown with the NAACP or somewhere else, not necessarily as a Morgan student."[16]

While the students made progress with the Read's Drug Store chain, protests at the other businesses at Northwood Shopping Center continued. Although the students received local publicity for their activities, the affiliation with the Baltimore NAACP and CORE also garnered them national acclaim in the civil rights communities. That acclaim prompted a visit in 1959 to the campus by Daisy Bates (Little Rock Nine). She spoke with students as they staged a sit-in at one of Northwood Shopping Center's establishments and told them "how proud she was of them because they were on the right track, and at an early age they get to decide what type of world they would live in."[17] Bates wanted the students to know she approved of their protest, but she also wanted to ensure they understood the gravity of their actions. The students were taking responsibility not only for their futures but also for the futures of their children. The students at the sit-down surrounded her, trying to get an autograph from the famed civil rights leader. The visit by Bates occurred prior to 1960, before the period of Black college student protests. A visit by a nationally recognized woman of the civil rights movement gave Morgan students needed encouragement and assured them that national civil rights leaders noticed and supported their efforts.[18]

National civil rights leaders were not the only women supporting the protest activities of Morgan students. Local high school girls were also recruited to join the protests. Mary Sue Welcome, the daughter of Senator Verda Welcome (the first African American woman to serve as a Maryland state senator) and prominent physician Henry C. Welcome, also took part in a protest at Hooper's Restaurant and was arrested. The sixteen-year-old was a member of the Civic Interest Group (CIG), whose stated purpose was "to dramatize our belief that human dignity is a God-given bequest and should be respected by everyone." She continued, "We are trying to do our bit to help release our country from the ugliness resulting from segregation and discrimination which ignores one's dignity."[19] In an article in the *Baltimore Afro-American* newspaper, Welcome recalled her June 30, 1960, arrest and the subsequent three hours spent at the Pine Street Jail. She said Hooper's son read the trespass law with a police officer present, and he promptly requested that she leave, which she refused to do, as she received no service. She was arrested after a two-hour wait at the site for the arrest warrant and was transported to the Pine Street Jail. Welcome was frisked by the female matron in the presence of male officers and expressed embarrassment at the condescending words of the lead matron, who called her "stupid" and stated that she should "act like a college student not an animal." In closing, she stated, "Can you imagine how I felt . . . just like a criminal; but I had really done nothing more than asked to be served food in a restaurant. That was my crime!"[20] Welcome was a member of the 1966 graduating class of Morgan State College. She, like many of the other protestors, earned a degree in political science. Later she became an attorney and gained national prominence.[21]

As a Student Nonviolent Coordinating Committee (SNCC) affiliate, the CIG sent female students to assist with protest efforts in other cities. In the summer of 1961, Morgan students Carole Johnson and Norma Collins traveled to Fisk University in Nashville, Tennessee, to attend a seminar on social change and integration. While at the seminar, the women joined a picket line at the H. G. Hill Supermarket. This chain had two stores located in the Black section of the city but employed no Blacks. The protest turned violent when whites attacked the nonviolent protestors. The women stated, "We suffered all weekend some of the most brutal treatment while the police stood by and watched." Johnson added, "Members of our group were mistreated by the police. Two had to go to the hospital."[22] Johnson and Collins were arrested when they went to police headquarters to make a plea for protection while protesting. Additionally, they made a jailhouse visit to Diane Nash, the coordinating secretary of Nashville's branch of SNCC, who was arrested in a separate incident while picketing at the supermarket.[23]

At the time, these women were breaking the racial barrier known as "Jane Crow," a term coined by Pauli Murray, a civil and gender rights activist. The term "Jane Crow" was a reference to the nature of the discrimination that African American women suffer.[24] They have had little time or energy for consideration of women's rights. As the civil rights struggle gathered momentum, women began to recognize the similarities between "paternalism and racial arrogance."[25] The following recollections speak to the power of the women within the larger context of the Black student movement.

The *Baltimore Sun* newspaper's commemoration of the fiftieth anniversary of the Northwood Shopping Center theater mass arrest included statements by participants, including Joyce Dennison, who said, "You say that you want to open a facility to the public—we are part of the public."[26] Dennison grew up in upstate Pennsylvania with Quakers as her neighbors. Therefore, she did not understand the "Jim Crow" laws and the discriminatory policies in Baltimore. "People were people and the color of their skin was not a factor." Dennison spent four days in jail during the Northwood theater mass arrest and said she "would do it again to affect a change."[27]

On February 20, 1963, Peggy Araya (then Peggy Wilson) put on her brown corduroy suit and announced to her parents that she "was going to school to get arrested. My mother begged me please don't because you will never get a job." Araya said, "Students were holding meetings in the auditorium every day and I wanted to be involved. I knew there were white students from Johns Hopkins University and Goucher College getting arrested and if they can do it I could too."[28] Being arrested was the goal of this protest. Their strategy was to fill the jails, shock the public, and cause a real disruption to public safety. How long could the authorities justify holding students versus actual criminals? "By the time I arrived," said Araya, "the warden was pulling out his hair. They told us not to give the prisoners anything, no cigarettes, no makeup, so of course we gave them everything we had, cigarettes, makeup, jewelry, whatever they asked for we gave them. We totally disrupted the jail."[29] Araya said that her parents were in New York City at the time of her arrest, and her mother saw her being arrested on national television. Her parents sent her aunt and uncle to bail her out. She refused bail as a show of solidarity. When she finally went home, she promptly threw away the corduroy suit that she had worn during her three days in jail.[30]

The students were determined to fill the Baltimore City Jail, and crowds of them continuously arrived at the Northwood Theater to protest. The police department was running out of transport vehicles. With mounting pressure from then-mayor Philip Goodman and the NAACP, the movie theater made the decision to desegregate. Many citizens celebrated the victory with the students. Hairdressers throughout the city offered shampoos and hairdos to the women protesters because they had been washing their hair with lye soap.[31] This was a gesture of admiration and support. Hairdressers and barbers were respected business leaders in the African American community, where their shops served as unofficial meeting places for news and information. These places gave African American citizens a safe haven to discuss issues essential to the community as well as gender-related issues.

Throughout this whole ordeal, the female students had an ally in Thelma Bando. Araya and Dennison spoke fondly of her. She brought their books and other necessities to the jail. Dennison was quoted as saying, "[Bando] did not accept being in jail as an excuse for not studying."[32] Bando cared not only for the needs of Morgan students but also for those of the Johns Hopkins and Goucher students as well. She ensured that even though the women were in jail, they were to be treated and act like "ladies." Bando brought linen napkins and tablecloths so the women could set a proper table for dinner.[33]

Bando was a member of the National Association of College Women and the National Association of Women's Deans and Advisors of Colored Schools. These organizations were founded by Lucy Diggs Slowe, the first dean of women at Howard University and cofounder of Alpha Kappa Alpha Sorority Inc., the premier authority on African American college female student affairs and Bando's professor and mentor. Slowe, a Baltimorean and graduate of Baltimore Colored High and Training School (now Frederick Douglass High School), earned her master's degree from Columbia University Teachers College.[34] Slowe urged Bando to study student personnel at Columbia as well, instead of English.[35]

August Meier, faculty member of Morgan's History Department and advisor of CIG, said, "Thelma Bando, Dean of Women, to our surprise forcefully backed the demonstrations, when other deans and faculty remained silent."[36] Bando always wore a hat and gloves and always impressed on the female students the importance of conducting themselves as "Morgan Women." The fact that she took books and table linens to the jails said to the white jailers that despite racial stereotypes, her students were women of class and dignity, not criminals. Additionally, it was a message of support for the jailed students and further reinforced her expectations of them, regardless of their surroundings.[37]

Bando also served as a model for her contemporaries, such as Dr. Willa Player, president of Bennett College. Player was a Columbia Teachers College graduate and member of the National Association of College Women and the National Association of Women's Deans and Advisors of Colored Schools. Player managed through the arrest of 40 percent of her students during a May 1963 protest in Greensboro, North Carolina. Faced with mounting pressure from Greensboro mayor David Schenck and city leaders "to stop the demonstrations and call her girls out of jail," she refused, visited the jail, and reassured the women of her continued support. She vowed "to organize assignments and coordinate lessons," and promised "to have final exams in jail if necessary."[38]

Bando, Slowe, Player, Mitchell, and Jackson epitomized the image of "political respectability," the term coined to describe the function of African American women in the Black Baptist Church during the Progressive Era. It specifically referred to an "insistence upon Blacks conforming to the dominant society's norms of manners and morals. The politics of respectability emphasized the reform of individual behavior and attitude both as a goal and as a strategy for reform of the entire structural system of American race relations."[39] Through the politics of respectability, African American women, especially those discussed in this chapter, emphasized "manners and morals while simultaneously participating in traditional forms of protest, such as petitions, boycotts and verbal appeals to justice."[40]

Another form of respectability demonstrated by the female students who participated in the Northwood Theater protest was "parental respectability." Many students chose to protest but, at the demands of their parents, avoided getting themselves arrested. Gloria Marrow was one of the students who made this choice. These women were just as important to the movement as those arrested. Marrow protested not only at Northwood but also in downtown Baltimore and the Eastern Shore. She spoke in an interview with pride of how the members of Delta Sigma Theta Sorority (Alpha Gamma Chapter) were quite active in the protest.[41]

Morgan student protestors received outside support from white students from nearby colleges. A young Jewish woman named Roslyn Garfeld Lang was one such student. She picketed segregated downtown restaurants with her fellow Goucher classmates. Interracial pairs of students would attempt services at different establishments. Every weekend, Garfeld Lang would protest while also avoiding arrest. During a visit from one of her friends from New York City the friend talked her into being arrested. She and five friends, including the one from New York, were arrested at Hooper's Restaurant and sent to the Pine Street Jail. A group that supported the students' efforts posted bail for Garfeld Lang (she was unsure of the source). During the interview Garfeld Lang stated, "The restaurants would take black citizens' money as payment for carryout food but would not allow them to eat inside the restaurant. . . . That was just wrong."⁴²

Women were instrumental in the Morgan student protests on the Eastern Shore of Maryland. The city of Cambridge in Dorchester County was a hotbed of racial unrest. Gloria Richardson was the catalyst for the Cambridge Movement after her high school daughter was arrested. The Cambridge Movement began with African American Cambridge residents sitting in at segregated movie theaters, bowling alleys, and restaurants, but this movement evolved into a struggle for the economic rights of Cambridge citizens, many of whom were burdened with low wages and unemployment. In June 1963, the Cambridge protests escalated into a major riot.⁴³ Morgan students had many supporters in their efforts on the Eastern Shore, some of whom were students at Maryland State College (now the University of Maryland Eastern Shore). One particular student was no stranger to the CIG and its strategies: Rosalie Cornish (Spence) joined the CIG as a fifteen-year-old junior at Baltimore's Forest Park Senior High School. Her father was a native of Cambridge, and her uncle was the Reverend Howard L. Cornish, the director of Morgan's Christian Center for forty-nine years. Rev. Cornish was an ally of the students, and they often used the Christian Center for organizational meetings.⁴⁴

In the spring of 1960, Cornish Spence attended the SNCC training at Shaw University in North Carolina. Within months of receiving the training, she began her protest activities. She was arrested at the Double T Diner on Route 40 West in Baltimore County and at Jimmy Wu's, a Chinese restaurant in Baltimore. According to Cornish Spence, "The arrests were an organized affair. The CIG always arranged legal support [attorneys and bail], which according to her was always provided or paid by the Baltimore NAACP." She also supported the CIG and NAACP 1960 (summer) voter registration drive and babysat children at the McCullough Homes housing project while their parents went to the polls in November 1960.⁴⁵

Cornish Spence spoke very highly of the Morgan students and never saw any divisiveness between the Morgan students and the leadership of the established civil rights organizations. In addition, she outlined an organizational chart of the civil rights movement in Maryland. She stated that in no uncertain terms, "Lillie Carroll Jackson was the at the top of chart, followed by NAACP attorney Juanita Jackson Mitchell."⁴⁶

During the summer of 1963, with the success achieved throughout Baltimore and the surrounding area, Morgan students and their supporters heightened their protests of the segregated practices at the Gwynn Oak Amusement Park in Baltimore County. Two Morgan alumni joined in the protest: Senator Verda Welcome (Morgan State class of 1939) and her mentee, Reva Lewie (Morgan State class of 1956), who had worked with her on several initiatives involving the rights of African Americans.[47] After several arrests of African American, white, and Jewish protesters, coupled with the negative publicity the park was receiving, management agreed to desegregate in the late summer of 1963. In keeping with the theme of this essay, it is only fitting that the "first African American child to ride the merry-go-round was an 11-month-old girl named Sharon Langley."[48]

Although women led successful and meaningful initiatives within the context of the long civil rights movement for decades prior to the 1960s, patriarchal era men like James Meredith of the University of Mississippi believed that women and children should not be involved with certain roles during the fight for civil rights. He said it was the responsibility of men to face peril and otherwise shield women and children. Meredith argued, "Ironically enough, the very presence of women and children in the demonstrations has at times minimized the violence and aroused the sympathies of the American public."[49]

This is true of the mass arrests during the Northwood Movie Theater protest in Baltimore, Maryland. A public outcry after photographs were published locally and nationally of 208 Morgan State women students in an unsafe overcrowded jail, with a capacity of only 140, coupled with pressure from public safety officials, the NAACP, and other activist organizations, resulted in the students being released. This mounting pressure and disruption to business led to the integration of the movie theater.[50]

Black women face a triple barrier of discrimination that includes race, class, and gender.[51] The discrimination the women of the civil rights movement suffered at the hands of their male counterparts was just as devastating as the segregationists' discrimination. The civil rights movement of the 1950s and early 1960s was largely a church-based affair. According to Barnett, "Women have traditionally performed roles and have been considered the backbone in the church; however, black women historically have not been allowed the opportunity to become ministers, deacons, trustees—the 'heads' and top decision-makers in the male-dominated hierarchy of the Black Baptist Church."[52] According to feminist and theologian Jacquelyn Grant, "The term backbone can give the appearance of a compliment; however, the most distinct portion of the word 'backbone' is back," which Grant said referred to location and not position, as in the back of the bus. Women were support workers, usually relegated to kitchen duties. Grant added that women rarely were in policy or decision-making positions. She concluded by stating, "It is by consideration of the distinction between the tribe support position and the policy making, leadership position that the oppression of African American women in the African American church can be seen more clearly."[53] This pattern of gender discrimination transitioned effortlessly into civil rights organizations given the close relationship between the church and movement. This practice was prevalent in both the old and new guard organizations.

Martin Luther King Jr. wrote in the preface to Septima Clark's autobiography, *Echo in My Soul*, that the work "epitomized the continuous struggle of the 'Southern Negro women' to realize her role as a mother while fulfilling her forced position as community teacher, intuitive fighter for human rights and leader of her unlettered and disillusioned people." Additionally, he believed that women were capable of leadership; however, they should not pursue this talent because women were innately able to rear children and be supportive wives.[54]

Ella Baker believed that the paternalistic nature of the Southern Christian Leadership Conference (SCLC) prohibited her from being considered for a leadership position. According to her,

> The combination of being a woman, and an older woman, presented some problems.... The combination of the basic attitude of men, and especially ministers, as to what the role of women in their church step-ups is—that of taking orders, not providing leadership—and the ego that is involved—the ego problems involved in having to feel that here is someone who had the capacity for a certain amount of leadership, and certainly, had more information about a lot of things than they possessed at that time—this would never had lent itself to my being a leader in the movement there.[55]

After being denied an appointment to a leadership role, Baker left the SCLC; to add insult to injury, her male replacement's salary surpassed hers tremendously.[56]

Maryland's women civil rights leaders did not conform to the paternalistic nature of the movement, and thus they dominated the leadership role throughout the state. Beginning in the 1930s, Lillie Carroll Jackson and Juanita Jackson Mitchell were directly involved in all matters involving civil rights. These women had achieved several court victories before Morgan students began to sit down in protest in the 1950.

Jackson and Mitchell were supported by the African American ministers; this was evident by this SCLC chapter's large membership numbers. Many members of the Baltimore NAACP had strong religious ties, and according to a 1976 interview, Rev. Marion Bascom stated, "Jackson was a 'go-getter' at our church [Douglas Memorial], which was right behind the NAACP office. And of course, it was one of the churches that had historically supported Jackson. So, my falling in line with Jackson was almost a must, as well as kind of the normal thing for me to do." According to Bascom, Jackson said that the "church was the bulwark of the NAACP and hardly ever was there a meeting held outside of some local church. She never went outside of the church. The church was 'it' as far as Mrs. Jackson was concerned."[57] Bascom also referred to Jackson's demeanor as "aggressive, arrogant, demanding, commanding, and insulting. I don't want you to think that Miss Lillie was just a quiet person. She'd holler at anybody."[58] These statements made by Bascom, coupled with the fact that she was offered the presidency of Baltimore's NAACP branch by Carl Murphy, owner of the *Afro-American* newspaper and one of the most influential men in Baltimore, are an indication of the public support Mrs. Jackson and her daughter Juanita received from ministers and the male leadership in the city.

However, the female Morgan students who were involved with the movement did not have prominent women student leaders as role models. Throughout the civil rights protest years, (1952–1963) there were several men who were considered "big men" on campus due to their protest activities; there was no female equivalent. In recent years, Helena Hicks has become the face and voice of Morgan's female students from the civil rights era. It must be noted that Hicks graduated in 1955, at the time that protests were just beginning. No student spokeswoman represented the women during the mass arrest of 1963. Women were the majority of the student population arrested, with Morgan Juanita M. Hansen being among the first. None of the male leaders of the CIG were arrested. The women felt as though they had been used by CIG's leadership, and seventy-four women signed bailout documents after being in jail for five days. However, leadership reiterated the importance of "jail-packing" and the disruption to public safety as negotiating tools; the women conceded that "a bail-out might have snapped the spine of the Goliath they had created."[59]

The male-dominated factions of SNCC also excluded women from its leadership. All of the chairs and all the members of the executive committee were men. A potential woman volunteer wrote a letter to SNCC, stating that "many of us are interested in the possibility of going to the South, but are hesitant because from the information we have received about SNCC, we could find only male students' name in accounts of students working there."[60] Julian Bond responded to the letter, saying that although SNCC had no women on the staff at present, it had had women on staff in the past and named former members such as Diane Nash Bevel, Ruby Doris Smith, and Doris Derby. However, he closed the letter with the following: "Let me say that if I were able to hire girls to type some of our correspondence, I wouldn't have made as many mistakes as I have."[61]

No affront was more egregious than the manner in which the women civil rights leaders were ignored and dismissed at the March on Washington for Jobs and Freedom in 1963. Dorothy Height, president of the National Council of Negro Women, said, "The women of the civil rights movement had been thoroughly rebuffed in seeking at least one speaking opportunity for the women; such sex-specific glory-seeking, they were repeatedly told, was anathema to the movement and the many women involved in its several organizations."[62] Though the organizers of the march decided late in the day to have a "Tribute to Women," A. Philip Randolph, host of the event, stumbled as he tried in vain to name the women leaders in attendance. According to Houck and Dixon, Randolph's "halting delivery, combined with a complete unawareness as to why the women were even assembled . . . turned what should have been a token gesture of solidarity into a spontaneous display of sexism."[63]

Unfortunately, this paternalistic attitude was common in the South and encompassed both Black and white women. The patriarchal system, which has historically controlled all women in American society, arrived with the Europeans who settled here. Women took subordinate roles to males, while men were praised for work the women performed.[64]

Gender exclusion within the civil rights movement was a manifestation of the era. "[Gender] also created a construct of exclusion that assisted in the development of a strong grassroots tier of leadership that served as a critical bridge between the formal organization, adherents and potential constiuents."[65] However, not all bridge leaders were women; bridging was the primary area of leadership available to women. The effect of gender exclusion prevented strong women leaders from becoming formal leaders while producing a remarkably capable tier of leadership that strengthened the movement.[66] Activism demonstrated by women of the CIG is indicative of what social scientist Belinda Robnett described as the work of bridge leaders. These women acted as a bridge between the ideals and strategies of the male leadership and their successful implementation.[67]

In most instances, the formal leaders of the movement did not mobilize the masses; it was the bridge leaders who created the mobilization. Baker's frustration with the ministers of the SCLC caused her to focus on the "development of a national student movement organization. She believed that student activists would benefit from contact with one another and she thought to create that bridge through the development of SNCC."[68] These types of bridges were essential to the development and success of the civil rights movement. The formation of SNCC allowed students to coordinate their efforts and to connect to one another. This connection allowed SNCC and its affiliates to reach broad-based populations.[69]

The protests and sit-ins in Baltimore and the surrounding areas demonstrated that women could be strong and courageous leaders who could stand on a foundation of successful endeavors and milestones against any man of the movement, while, by contrast, the CIG had no female leadership representation in its civil rights victories.

In "Invisible Southern African American Women Leaders in the Civil Rights Movement: The Triple Constraints of Gender, Race, and Class," Barnett states that "race, gender and class constraint prohibited women from being recognized as articulated spokesperson or media favorites. However, women did perform a multiplicity of significant leadership roles, such as the initiation and organization of action, the formation of tactic, and the provision of crucial resources such as money, communication channels and personnel necessary to sustain the movement."[70]

Black women's leadership, at its core, is a Black feminist movement that seeks to encompass the simultaneous realities of race, gender, and class, and to eradicate all forms of oppression that accompany multi-axis identities.[71] "The leadership that emerges from this Black feminist conceptualization carriers with four core tenets which include: bridging theory with practice, and informing each other, the group is proactive, not reactive, adopts a group center approach with group-ownership of the movement, and the utilization of traditional and non-traditional forms of activism."[72]

The production of intellectual work is not attributed to Black women artists or political activists. In institutions of higher education, these women are considered objects of study. However, this classification creates a false dichotomy between scholarship and activism, between thinking and doing. Analyzing the thoughts and activities of this omitted group must include their behavior, which is a necessary statement of philosophy or a part of the scholar-activist tradition in the African American intellectual tradition.[73]

These traditional objects of study created the intellectual tradition that changed the dynamics of the civil rights movement. Through the adoption of group-centered leadership and the incorporation collective actions, these women students continued to build on the intellectual foundation set by their predecessors and mentors while empowering the next generation of women intellectuals. Today, the ladies of Morgan State's movement, which began in the 1940s, are involved in helping to document their stories as a part of an important oral history initiative.

NOTES

1. Bay et al., introduction to *Toward an Intellectual History of Black Women*, 1.
2. Olson, *Freedom's Daughter*, 13.
3. Olson, *Freedom's Daughter*, 284.
4. Zinn, *SNCC*, 33; Carson, "Waveland Retreat," in *In the Struggle*, 147–48.
5. Meier, *A White Scholar and the Black Community*, 22.
6. Marbella, "Theater Will Integrate Today," 46.
7. Marbella, "Theater Will Integrate Today," 46.
8. NAACP—Part III Youth File, Schools and Colleges, Box III–E7, Folder 22, Morgan State College, Baltimore, Maryland, Membership Report—October, 1938, Library of Congress, Washington, DC.

9. Kane, "Students Share in Own Black History Book."
10. Elaine Blackwell, interview by author, March 7, 2013.
11. Marbella, "600 Morgan Student March."
12. Marbella, "Mrs. Adah Jenkins," 10.
13. Marbella, "Mrs. Adah Jenkins," 10.
14. Nathan, "A War of Words," in *Round and Round Together*, 189.
15. Helena Sorrell Hicks, PhD, interview by author, March 22, 2011.
16. Helena Hicks quoted by Cassie, "And Service for All."
17. Afro Magazine Section, *Baltimore Afro-American*, April 7, 1959, B-5.
18. Afro Magazine Section, *Baltimore Afro-American*, April 7, 1959, B-5.
19. Welcome, "Three Hours behind the Bars," 5.
20. Welcome, "Three Hours behind the Bars," 5.
21. Badger, "More than 700 Make Crystal Ball Another Big Success."
22. Marbella, "Baltimoreans on Picket Line," 8.
23. Marbella, "Baltimoreans on Picket Line," 8.
24. Houck and Dixon, "Pauli Murray," in *Women and the Civil Rights Movement*, 232.
25. Houck and Dixon, "Pauli Murray," 232.
26. Marbella, "Former Students Protesters Remember Civil Rights Battle."
27. Joyce Dennison, telephone interview by author, February 21, 2013.
28. Peggy Wilson Araya, in-person interview by author, April 13, 2013.
29. Araya interview.
30. Araya interview.
31. Ham, ". . . And Homage as We Sing," 9; Meier, "Case Study in Non-violent Direct Action," in *A White Scholar and the Black Community*, 141.
32. Marbella, "Former Students Protesters Remember Civil Rights Battle."
33. Garrett, "Dean Bando Was an Angel of Mercy," 1.
34. Perkins, "Lucy Diggs Slowe," 93.
35. Miller and Pruitt-Logan, *Faithful Task at Hand*, 412.
36. Meier, *A White Scholar in the Black Community*, 145.
37. Shirley N. Barrett, informal discussion with author, January 25, 2015.
38. Brown, "You Will Be Expected to Practice What You've Learned: Willa Player, Bennett College, and the Civil Rights Movement," in *The Long Walk*, 174–77.
39. Higginbotham, "The Politics of Respectability," in *Righteous Discontent*, 187.
40. Higginbotham, "The Politics of Respectability," 192.
41. National Society of Pershing Angels, http://www.pershingangels.org/history.
42. Roslyn Garfeld Lang, telephone interview by author, February 22, 2013.
43. Marbella, "17 Students Jailed in Cambridge Protest," 14.
44. Rosalie Cornish-Spence, interview by author, January 20, 2015.
45. Cornish-Spence interview.
46. Cornish-Spence interview.
47. Reva Lewie, telephone interview by author, March 26, 2013.
48. Nathan, *Round and Round Together*, 203.
49. Houck and Dixon, "Pauli Murray," 234.
50. Marbella, "74 Arrested, Crowd Grows," 50.
51. Gyant, "Passing the Torch," 629.

52. Barnett, "Invisible Southern Black Women Leaders," 170.
53. Barnett, "Invisible Southern Black Women Leaders," 170.
54. Rev. Dr. Martin Luther King Jr. quoted in Robnett, "African-American Women in the Civil Rights Movement," 1672.
55. Ella Baker quoted in Robnett, "African-American Women in the Civil Rights Movement," 1671.
56. Barnett, "Invisible Southern Black Women Leaders," 176.
57. Rev. Marion C. Bascom, oral interview, McKeldin-Jackson Project, 1969–1977, The Maryland Historical Society, June 18, 1976, Transcript—Cassette I Side:1, 9.
58. Bascom interview, Tape Index—Cassette I Side: 2, 6.
59. Meier, "Case Study in Nonviolent Direct Action," in *A White Scholar and the Black Community*, 141.
60. Julian Bond quoted in Robnett, "African-American Women in the Civil Rights Movement," 1673.
61. Robnett, "African-American Women in the Civil Rights Movement," 1673.
62. Dorothy Height quoted in Houck and Dixon, introduction to *Women and the Civil Rights Movement*, x.
63. Houck and Dixon, introduction to *Women and the Civil Rights Movement*, x.
64. Barnett, "Invisible Southern Black Women Leaders," 175.
65. Robnett, "African-American Women in the Civil Rights Movement," 1667.
66. Robnett, "African-American Women in the Civil Rights Movement," 1676.
67. Robnett, "African-American Women in the Civil Rights Movement," 1678.
68. Robnett, "African-American Women in the Civil Rights Movement," 1678.
69. Robnett, "African-American Women in the Civil Rights Movement," 1679.
70. Barnett, "Invisible Southern Black Women Leaders," 177.
71. Melina Abdullah, "The Emergence of Black Feminist Leadership Model: African-American Women and Political Activism in Nineteenth Century" in Abdullah and Collins, *Black Women's Intellectual Traditions*, 328–29.
72. Abdullah, "The Emergence of Black Feminist Leadership Model," 329
73. Patricia Hill Collins, "The Politics of Black Feminist Thought," in Abdullah and Collins, *Black Women's Intellectual Traditions*, 412.

REFERENCES

Abdullah, Melina, and Patricia Hill Collins. *Black Women's Intellectual Traditions: Speaking Their Minds*. Edited by Kristin Waters and Carol Conaway. Lebanon: University Press of New England and University of Vermont Press, 2007.

Badger, Sylvia. "More than 700 Make Crystal Ball Another Big Success." *Baltimore Sun*, March 19, 1991. http://articles.baltimoresun.com/1991103119/features/1991078185_1_crystal-ball maryland-senate-portrait.

Baltimore City Police History/African American Police. Accessed March 31, 2016. http://www.baltimorecitypolicehistory.com/index.php/baltimore-police-history/afr-amer-police.html.

Barnett, Bernice McNair. "Invisible Southern African American Women Leaders in the Civil Rights Movement: The Triple Constraints of Gender, Race, and Class," *Gender and Society* 7 (1993): 162–82.

Bay, Mia, Farah Griffin, Martha Jones, and Barbara D. Savage. *Toward an Intellectual History of Black Women*. Chapel Hill: University of North Carolina Press, 2015.

Bond, Julian. "SNCC: What We Did." *Monthly Review: An Independent Socialist Magazine* 52 (October 2000). https://monthlyreview.org/2000/10/01/sncc-what-we-did/.

Brown, Linda B. *The Long Walk: The Story of the Presidency of Willa Player at Bennett College*. Danville, VA: McCain Printing Company, 1998.

Carson, Clayborne. *In the Struggle: SNCC and the Black Awakening of the 1960s*. Cambridge, MA: Harvard University Press, 1995.

Cassie, Ron. "And Service for All: Sixty Years Ago, Morgan State College Staged the First Successful Lunch Counter Sit-in." *Baltimore Magazine*, January 2015. http://www.baltimoremagazine.com/2015/1/19/morgan-students-staged-reads-drugstore-sit-in-60-years-ago.

Cole, Eddie R. "African American Women at Historically African American Colleges during the Civil Rights Movement." *Journal of the Indiana University Student Personnel Association* (2009): 20–28.

Garrett, Lula Jones. "Dean Bando Was an Angel of Mercy." *Baltimore Afro-American*, March 2, 1963.

Gyant, LaVerne. "Passing the Torch: African American Women in the Civil Rights Movement." *Journal of African American Studies* 26 (1996): 629–47.

Ham, Debra Newman. ". . . And Homage as We Sing: Fair Morgan's Frontal on Segregation." *Morgan Magazine* 1 (2011): 4–10.

Higginbotham, Evelyn Brooks. *Righteous Discontent: The Women's Movement in the African American Baptist Church, 1880–1920*. Cambridge, MA: Harvard University Press, 1993.

Houck, Davis W., and David E. Dixon, eds. *Women and the Civil Rights Movement*. Jackson: University Press of Mississippi, 2009.

Kane, Gregory. "Students Share in Own Black History Book." *Baltimore Sun*, May 16, 2007. http://articles.baltimoresun.com/2007-05-16/news/0705160289_1_annapolis-warren-johnson-high.

Marbella, Jean. Afro Magazine Section, *Baltimore Afro-American*, April 7, 1959.

Marbella, Jean. "Baltimoreans on Picket Line in Nashville, Tenn." Special Edition, *Baltimore Afro-American*, August 19, 1961.

Marbella, Jean. "Former Students Protesters Remember Civil Rights Battle over the Northwood Theater." *Baltimore Sun*, February 16, 2003. http://articles.Baltimore Sun.com/2013-02-16/news/bs-md-Northwood-civil-rights.

Marbella, Jean. "Mrs. Adah Jenkins, 72, Was AFRO Music Critic." *Baltimore Afro-American*, May 19, 1973.

Marbella, Jean. "17 Students Jailed in Cambridge Protest." *Baltimore Afro-American*, April 6, 1963.

Marbella, Jean. "74 Arrested, Crowd Grows in Northwood: Protest of Segregation in 6th Day; Mayor in 2-Hour Talk." *Baltimore Sun*, February 21, 1963.

Marbella, Jean. "600 Morgan Student March on Capital to Demand Needed Funding for Education." *Baltimore Afro-American*, April 5, 1947.

Marbella, Jean. "Theater Will Integrate Today: All 343 Jailed Students Freed." *Baltimore Sun*, February 22, 1963.

Meier, August. *A White Scholar and the Black Community, 1945–1965: Essays and Reflections.* Amherst: University of Massachusetts Press, 1992.

Miller, Carol L. L., and Anne S. Pruitt-Logan. *Faithful Task at Hand: The Life of Lucy Diggs Slowe.* Albany: State University of New York Press, 2012.

Nathan, Amy. *Round and Round Together: Taking a Merry Go Round Ride into the Civil Rights Movement.* Philadelphia: Paul Dry Book, 2011.

"National Society of Pershing Angels." Accessed April 29, 2013, http://www.pershingangels.org/history.

Olson, Lynn. *Freedom's Daughter: Unsung Heroines of the Civil Rights Movement from 1830 to 1970.* New York: Simon and Schuster, 2002.

Perkins, Linda M. "Lucy Diggs Slowe: Champion of Self-Determination of African American Women in Higher Education." *Journal of Negro History* 81 (1996): 189–204.

Robnett, Belinda. "African-American Women in the Civil Rights Movement, 1954–1965: Gender, Leadership and Micromobilization." *American Journal of Sociology* 101 (1996): 1661–93.

Welcome, Mary. "Three Hours behind the Bars." *Baltimore Afro-American*, July 16, 1960.

Zinn, Howard. *SNCC: The New Abolitionist.* Cambridge, MA: South End Press, 2002.

Archives

US Library of Congress, 1938, NAACP-Part III Youth File, Schools and Colleges, Box III-E7, Folder 22, Morgan State College, Baltimore, Maryland, Membership Report, October, 1938.

Oral History Interviews

Araya, Peggy. Interviewed by Simone R. Barrett, April 12, 2013, Baltimore, MD.
Barrett, Shirley N. Interviewed by Simone R. Barrett, December 3, 2010, Baltimore, MD.
Bascom, Marion. Interviewed by Richard Richardson. *The McKeldin-Jackson Oral History Collection—Museum and Library of Maryland Historical Society, June 18, 1976,* Douglas Memorial Community Church, Baltimore, MD.
Blackwell, Elaine. Telephone interview by Simone R. Barrett, March 22, 2013, Baltimore, MD.
Cornish-Spence, Rosalie. Interviewed by Simone R. Barrett, January 20, 2015, Baltimore, MD.
Dennison, Joyce. Interviewed by Simone R. Barrett, February 22, 2013, Baltimore, MD.
Hicks, Helena S. Interviewed by Simone R. Barrett, March 22, 2011, Baltimore, MD.
Garfeld Lang, Roslyn. Interviewed by Simone R. Barrett, February 25, 2013, Baltimore, MD.
Lewie, Reva. Telephone interview by Simone R. Barrett, April 23, 2013.
Marrow, Gloria. Interviewed by Simone R. Barrett, April 13, 2014, Baltimore, MD.

Chapter 5

ELRETA MELTON ALEXANDER

A Theoretical Approach[1]

VIRGINIA L. SUMMEY

"Nobody is going to sleep under my roof without a college education." Those words, spoken by the Reverend J. C. Melton, left an indelible imprint on his youngest daughter, Elreta. Elreta Melton Alexander (1919–1998) went on to become a pioneering African American attorney from Greensboro, North Carolina. Coming of age in the Jim Crow South, she was the daughter of a Baptist minister and a teacher and grew up in a Black, middle-class community. Alexander was always able to sleep under her father's roof, as she earned her bachelor of arts from North Carolina Agricultural and Technical State University (A&T) at the age of eighteen before going on to become the first African American woman to graduate from Columbia Law School in 1945. After briefly practicing law in Harlem, Alexander returned to Greensboro in 1947, becoming the first African American woman to practice law in North Carolina. In 1968, Alexander became the first African American woman to become an elected district court judge. In 1974, she ran for North Carolina Supreme Court chief justice, losing in the Republican primary to a white fire-extinguisher salesman. Her loss changed North Carolina politics, as it prompted changes to judicial election requirements.

In spite of her many accomplishments, her story has gone largely overlooked in southern, intellectual, and civil rights history. While the work of other Black women attorneys, such as Sadie Tanner Mossell Alexander, Constance Baker Motley, and Florynce Kennedy, has been noted in books examining African American women's history, Elreta Alexander has been excluded. This chapter attempts to rectify that exclusion and examines Judge Alexander's contributions as a public intellectual as well as her place within existing theoretical frameworks.

Alexander's story offers a new perspective on civil rights leadership. During the civil rights movement, when the arc of Alexander's career occurred, her personal style and demeanor challenged traditional notions of "activism." She dedicated her career to civil rights and to challenging the status quo of the segregationist South through performative leadership, and she used her professional standing to advocate for marginalized individuals who lacked a voice in the southern legal system. Her civil rights activism was most evident in the way she conducted herself in the courtroom and on the campaign trail. Alexander developed her own political and intellectual influence, but she also embodied other theoretical frameworks. Three theoretical frameworks Alexander represented were Black Marxism, performance theory, and theories of intersectionality and assemblage. She took these frameworks and made them her own. This chapter is not an analysis of Alexander's legal career; instead, it establishes her as a public intellectual and examines her identity as an educated, African American woman attorney through these frameworks, examining how they interweave to form a holistic view of her life, thought, and career.

An analysis of several books examining the intellectual history of Black women strengthens the case for Elreta Alexander's inclusion in Black women's intellectual history. Stephanie Y. Evans's *Black Women in the Ivory Tower, 1850–1954: An Intellectual History* examines the struggle of Black women to gain entry into academe, a concept Alexander was all too familiar with. The authors of *Toward an Intellectual History of Black Women* examine a wide swath of Black women intellectuals, including Florynce Kennedy and her fight in the greater reproductive rights battle.[2] Alexander did not participate in the same level of political agitation outside the courtroom as Kennedy, but she employed performance activism to agitate white attitudes in the courthouse. Also included is writer Amelia E. Johnson, whose writings used "the lash of criticism" and challenged white attitudes toward race.[3] Alexander was not as prolific a writer as Johnson, but her poetry employed both Christian ideology and her own views on racial injustice. Finally, Sadie Tanner Mossell Alexander was an attorney and economist (the first Black woman to receive her PhD in economics in the United States) who has been written about many times in the realm of intellectual history, including in *Segregated Scholars: Black Social Scientists and the Creation of Black Labor Studies, 1890–1950*. Sadie T. M. Alexander's career predates that of Elreta Alexander, and her work as a public intellectual helped make Elreta's possible. Francille Rusan Wilson, the author of *Segregated Scholars*, states that the works of many notable Black women have been "twice silenced . . . first in their own time by race and gender discrimination that limited their access to advanced degrees and circumscribed their careers, and, second, in the historical record that has all but erased their intellectual work."[4] Sadie T. M. Alexander's work is increasingly being given a voice, opening the doors for the intellectual work of other Black women to be recognized. Elreta Alexander is one of these women whose intellectual contributions should be recognized as historians revive their voices and intellectual work.

Alexander's background is critical to understanding her career. Elreta Narcissis Melton was born in 1919 in Smithfield, North Carolina. Her father, J. C. Melton, was a Baptist minister, and her mother, Alain Reynolds Melton, a teacher. Elreta Melton grew up the youngest child in a biracial, educated, middle-class family. After the family settled in Greensboro, North Carolina, she attended Dudley High School. In interviews, she recalled being called "high yellow" by her classmates and singled out by teachers based on her class and parents' education. From an early age, Elreta Melton was acutely aware of how issues of class and race affected her community.

Education was paramount in the Melton household, and Alexander's early exposure to intellectual activity started in the home. She recalled that after school her father would give her and her siblings additional lessons to supplement the underfunded education his children received at segregated, southern schools. "[We] had to do three things: read Latin fluently . . . , be proficient in mathematics, and read with understanding. My father held class in his house every night, until we got up in high school, to be sure you got the fundamentals." For the rest of her life, Alexander never lacked the confidence or ability to engage in intellectual discourse.

After Dudley High, Elreta attended North Carolina A&T State University in Greensboro, and after graduation, she taught school in South Carolina. In 1938 she married her college sweetheart, medical student Girardeau "Tony" Alexander. The couple returned to Greensboro for the sake of Tony's career, while Elreta worked part-time. Bored with her new role of housewife and part-time worker, Alexander decided to pursue a career in law. In 1943, she was accepted to the law program at Columbia University in New York. Upon her arrival at Columbia, the dean of the law school warmly greeted Alexander, saying, "We welcome you, Ms. Alexander. You know, you're the first woman of your race we've ever accepted in this school. We've had women here since 1927." That greeting unnerved Alexander. She later said, "They put the weight of a whole race of people on me" and commented that she could not even hear the lectures the first six weeks of class.[5]

Despite a frustrating start, Alexander went on to thrive at Columbia and graduated in 1945. That same year, Alexander made her first attempt to take the North Carolina bar exam. However, she was not allowed to take the North Carolina exam until 1947, after proving herself "exceptional and meritorious" through the affidavits of her law professors. This was the only way for African American attorneys to become licensed in the state of North Carolina during the Jim Crow period.[6] Alexander went on to become the first Black woman to practice law in North Carolina, establishing her practice in Greensboro, where her husband was a surgeon at the all-Black L. Richardson Hospital. After establishing her career, Alexander became a prominent and successful attorney, joining the ranks of the elite, Black professional class while integrating previously all-white spaces and altering the image of what a successful lawyer can look like.

In the introduction of *Toward an Intellectual History of Black Women*, the editors state that Black women have not received their due credit for being producers of knowledge.[7] Elreta Alexander was not just a courtroom activist, but a producer of scholarship, poetry, and legal ideas. Before her first courtroom appearance, Alexander established herself as an intellectual. In an international labor law class at Columbia, Alexander wrote a paper entitled "A Student's Plan for Peace," which shows that she was a future attorney dedicated to human and civil rights. Written in April 1944, the plan was built on the assumption that the Allied nations would establish some sort of international organization and utilize the International Labour Organization in international labor relations.[8] Alexander's proposed world organization consisted of three major divisions: an assembly, a security council, and a world court, all designed to "increase men's happiness in socio-economic fields . . . [and] to aid in the preservation of peace." Alexander also addressed the plight of oppressed peoples in the United States and throughout the world, saying, "The exploitation of racial, religious and minority groups is another dark spot in our national and international history. The thirst for economic power which has made the peoples of the world half slave and half free has sought its justification in the *a priori* development of a psychology of innate superiority, or condescending benevolence, or what have you."[9] Alexander carried these ideals with her throughout her career as an attorney and judge.

Over twenty years later, in 1967, Alexander published her book of poetry, titled *When Is a Man Free?* Her poetry contains fiery rhetoric directed at whites, which was different from her rhetoric in white, male-dominated courtrooms. She writes: "You say we are lazy, ill-mannered, half-crazy / Ungrateful, immoral, unprepared; / Yet we have climbed your ladders round by round, / In spite of your attempts to push us down. / Your statistics show we commit more crimes— / Oh, I wish I had the dimes / For the cases I have tried: / Verdict— 'guilty'—when simply justice was denied."[10] Her words reflected not only her own personal frustration but also the frustration of many African Americans in the twentieth century who struggled because of the racism they experienced in institutional and social structures.

Alexander's poetry also displayed her extensive knowledge of history and religion. Her words highlighted the entrenched racism in the United States, discussing American history from the Atlantic slave trade to the Revolutionary

War, the Hayes-Tilden Compromise to urban redevelopment and the Federal Housing Administration. From Phillis Wheatley to Pauli Murray to Audre Lorde, poetry has often been used as a method of activism and as an example of Black women's intellectual contributions. Black women have used poetry as a creative outlet to respond to systemic racism and injustice. Alexander could not give judges and juries lectures on oppression throughout American history, so she found another way to express her anger, as well as display her education and intelligence.

Alexander also changed how legal theory and the application of sentencing is approached. In the legal realm, as in so many other areas, Black women thinkers are largely overlooked. In the case of Judge Alexander, her revolutionary juvenile deferred sentencing program, Judgement Day, became a forerunner for contemporary deferred sentencing programs. The Judgment Day program was established specifically for young, first-time offenders. In the Judgment Day program, after pleading guilty, the judge would refrain from entering judgment and instead give the young offenders various tasks to perform. The tasks generally consisted of community service, writing reports on the dangers of their crime, and subsequent actions they took to rehabilitate themselves. The reports had to be presented before churches, schools, youth-based societies, and to the judge.[11] On a preset date, offenders would read their reports and make their case for rehabilitation to the court. If the report met the judge's satisfaction, then the conviction would be dropped from the offender's record. Judge Alexander's favorite quote—and her primary judicial philosophy—was "the truth shall set you free."[12] She built the Judgment Day program on that philosophy. If a young person committed a crime, told the truth, plus worked toward their own rehabilitation and self-improvement, they were free.

Alexander's Judgement Day program coincided with the rise in heavy policing tactics, which concerned many African Americans, as the incarceration rates for men of color skyrocketed. Alexander's philosophy was that the bench should be used for something other than punishment. The idea that courts could treat rather than punish, also known as rehabilitative justice, came from the progressive movement of the early twentieth century. The goal of rehabilitative justice was to find the cause of the crime and treat the accused accordingly. From this idea came juvenile courts, probation programs, parole programs, and reformatories. It widened judicial discretion and created options within the existing penal process.[13]

While Alexander contributed her own ideas and exhibits many of the same traits as other intellectual Black women, she also embodies theoretical frameworks that help contextualize her intellectual contributions. In addition to her contributions to the intellectual discourse around activism and legal thought, Alexander is also the personification of intellectual theory. As a successful attorney and the wife of a surgeon, Alexander and her husband were among a small group of upper-class African Americans. Cedric Robinson's *Black Marxism* helps contextualize the class component of Alexander's life. Alexander was the product of educated, middle-class parenting—the "Black bourgeoisie." Karl Marx argued that "politics was the concentrated expression of economics.... The propertied and the property-less were locked in an irreconcilable struggle, in which those who worked the means of production would eventually control them."[14] Robinson took Marx's Eurocentric analysis and applied it to the economic and cultural repression of African Americans. He theorized that the white intelligentsia wrote history in a manner that "accommodated" the exploitation of the laboring classes by the ruling class. The Black petit bourgeoisie felt they needed to incorporate their history into the broader American narrative. Robinson states that the "aspirations of the Black middle class required a history that would ... lend historical weight to the dignity they claimed as a class, and suggest their potential as participants in the country's future. They required a black historiography that would challenge their exclusion from the nation's racial parochialisms while settling for those very values."[15] In order to fight for inclusion, the Black middle class had to embrace the principles of those who determined economic and cultural norms. In the case of the Alexander family, this involved overcoming the educational restrictions placed on them by Jim Crow society. Local and state governments in the South dedicated little funding for all-Black schools, resulting in inadequate facilities, overcrowding, and out-of-date textbooks. To remedy this inequity, Alexander's parents enrolled their children in music lessons, requiring each child to learn how to play a musical instrument. Reverend Melton also continued his children's schooling after their formal classes, reiterating the basics, such as reading and mathematics, and also teaching them Greek and Latin.[16] While this helped with assimilating into white cultural norms, it also prepared Alexander for her future Ivy League education.

When Carter G. Woodson wrote *The Mis-Education of the Negro* in 1933, higher education was dominated by white males who espoused racist ideas and rhetoric. Woodson, who earned his PhD in history at Harvard University in 1912, rose through the academic ranks when the philosophy of the Dunning School dominated historiographical thought. In *The Mis-Education of the Negro*, he criticizes the Black intelligentsia who came up through the same system, accusing them of failing to uplift the race and for seeking to assimilate in white society.[17] Asserting that Eurocentrism and racism permeated the academy, Woodson contends the Black intelligentsia had to embrace a racially conservative ideology in American institutions of higher learning. In the early twentieth century, however, a certain degree of assimilation was necessary to achieve a high level of education.

In 1945, when Elreta Melton Alexander became the first African American woman to graduate from Columbia Law School, she had just completed a rigorous course of study on American law based on a legal system that discriminated against African Americans, and particularly African American men. In order to achieve this, she had to act—and look—the part. Speaking of her time at Columbia, Alexander said, "My sister made me some beautiful clothes so I could be decent going to Columbia Law School."[18] Part of the challenge of attending Columbia was fitting in with her rich classmates who the professors "expected to become Senators."[19] Perhaps it was because of the lightness of Alexander's skin, or perhaps it was because of her status as a Columbia Law student, but Alexander was accepted by the white establishment at Columbia University.

Despite acceptance from her white peers, Alexander still found her skin color, not gender or class, to be the primary demarcation that separated her from her other classmates. In Greensboro Alexander had primarily interacted with other African Americans. But at Columbia she found her light complexion more acceptable to her fellow white classmates than that of her darker-skinned classmate Herman Taylor. "The white students would invite me to all their parties; I was invisible and didn't shock their mores . . . I always took Herman with me when I'd go with my white friends, and sometimes sitting on the subway, Herman would be the only dark person in the group." Having attended all Black schools until Columbia, Alexander became acutely aware that her light complexion afforded her opportunities not received by Taylor. It was when walking down Broadway with white friends that Alexander realized she could "pass" without trying.[20]

Many African Americans with light complexions can "pass" as white. In the antebellum South, those who could pass sometimes did so to evade the confines of slavery. After emancipation, passing could help some African Americans avoid the horrors the Jim Crow era, but it could also be seen as a betrayal of one's own race, and often meant denying one's family and community.[21] As Alexander increasingly became a part of a predominately white legal community, her ability to pass as white taught her about the power of racial privilege.

While for some passing might have been a form of reinvention, for Alexander it was an unexpected foray outside of the segregated South she grew up in. She stated, "In New York, my Negro blood was hidden. . . . I was thrown into this white world, but I did have two sets of friends. Some weekends I'd be with the black lawyers and their friends. . . . But most of the time it was in a white world."[22] It was at Columbia Law that Elreta Alexander chose to embrace identity as a Black woman by confronting her white friends about her race. In one instance Alexander confronted her white friend Mildred Preen about race. She said, "You love me in spite of the fact that I am a Negro. But I want you to know that I will be a Negro all of my life, and I will never disclaim this. You must see me as I am.... I'm not going to live on the other side." Alexander said her white friends, who had very little experience with African Americans, "just couldn't seem to understand how this girl with so many talents and with such fair skin, how she could be identified with Negros."[23] Alexander was determined to show her new white friends just how talented a Negro could be and to use her professional standing to advocate for other African Americans.

The Black Marxist critique lies in whether or not Alexander used her bourgeois education, complexion, and class status to challenge white, capitalistic structures. She used her ability to pass as an effective weapon against racial discrimination and as a method of exposing the hypocrisy of racial thinking on the part of most whites. In one instance after becoming a judge, a white woman complained that her daughter was "runnin' around with colored boys." Alexander peered down from the bench and said, "Darlin, have you looked at your judge?"[24] But as an attorney, she used her position and wealth to aid the Black proletariat in Greensboro. She stated that "I would haul three or four loads of clients to court, just so they could ride in the Cadillac or Lincoln; that's how much it meant to them to be able to ride in a car, to have something of material value that they could be associated with."[25] While Marxists could easily accuse Alexander of perpetuating white ideals of class and status, for her and for her clients, this same perpetuation was a challenge to racial structures of class that defined social status in the South.

How extensively Alexander reproduced "African" culture in her life or the extent to which she assimilated into and reproduced white society is debatable.[26] While Alexander was an active member of Greensboro chapter of The Links, an organization for professional women of color, it is unlikely that she could embrace many of the aspects of Black American culture and still assimilate into the legal community of the 1950s and 1960s South. According to E. Patrick Johnson, the "black who has been accepted into the elite circle of whiteness is expected to bracket the blackness that proffered his or her (temporary) invitation to the welcome table of whiteness." In other words, for African Americans to make it into elite establishments, there is a requirement that they "check their blackness at the door."[27] In order to do this, a certain amount of "performance" is required.

Whether consciously or unconsciously, we all engage in performance to adapt to certain circumstances. Individuals adjust their behaviors in order to "fit in" as circumstances dictates. Poor African American children sometimes fail to assimilate or "fit in" with "mainstream" America because they do not adopt and conform to middle-class, "white" values. Conversely, members of the Black leadership who have been accepted into the American mainstream have been accused of losing the ability to understand what it would take to connect the African American community to the rest of society.[28] Alexander grew up in an educated, middle-class household, which paved the way for her assimilation into mainstream America. However, for Alexander to establish a career in the segregationist South, a certain amount of performance was necessary.

There is little question among those who knew her that Elreta Alexander had performance down to a fine art. She used performance to highlight the contradictions inherent in a segregated society. In the 1950s, many of the courtrooms where Alexander tried her cases were segregated. On the days when she appeared in a segregated courtroom, Alexander stated she would "wear a mink coat into the courtroom and instead of sitting with whites, I would sit behind the bar next to the dirtiest, blackest, Negro working man . . . it would upset the court." After being told several times by the judges to sit inside the bar with the other attorneys, Alexander responded, "If my people have to sit on one side, I want to be with my people." Alexander's "performance" extended to water fountains as well. She would approach white judges saying she wanted to "see what the difference is in this white water and this colored water" before boldly approaching the white water fountain and taking a drink.[29] In addition to employing no small amount of bravado, Alexander used performance to not-so-subtly point out the hypocrisy and injustice of segregation.

Alexander used performance intentionally to prove a point. I argue that her performance was actually her unique brand of activism. Alexander always considered herself a "showman," and stated that "it always seemed kind of stupid to me for people to treat people as second-class citizens and expect a first-class performance."[30] Musically trained as a child, Alexander was also familiar with the stage. In her legal career, she often used courtrooms and meeting rooms as her stage. Alexander frequently used performance to change the attitudes of individuals in North Carolina.

Alexander's performance particularly called attention to the attitudes and behaviors of white, male attorneys in North Carolina. While male lawyers respectfully referred to each other as "Mr." or "Attorney," most male colleagues simply referred to Alexander as "Elreta." When trying a case once in Eastern North Carolina, the other attorney simply referred to her as "Alexander." She responded by saying "If you want to communicate with me, sir, if you'll just write it on a piece of paper, I'll answer you on a piece of paper. . . . Other than that, if you'll just grunt like a pig, then I'll respond. But if you call me anything, you call me '*Mrs.* Alexander' or 'Lawyer Alexander.'"[31] Alexander turned demanding respect into a creatively articulated performance.

Alexander's performance extended into her wardrobe, making use of accessories props that demanded attention. She became known for her flashy jewelry, expensive wardrobe, blonde wigs, dramatic makeup, and fleet of Cadillacs.[32] Upon her death, the *Greensboro News and Record* headline read "'Judge A' Paved Way—With Style."[33] Viewing this from a Black Marxist perspective, one could assert that Alexander's style and lavish tastes were an attempt to incorporate herself into a capitalist, white-dominated bourgeoisie. Viewing her style from a performance theory standpoint, however, one sees Alexander's use of accessories as memorable props that brought attention to her skill as a litigator and judge. Historian Blain Roberts argues that for Black women, beauty serves as a form of empowerment, which is certainly the case for Alexander. She used her ability to afford high fashion as a power statement in the courtroom but also as a means of empowering some of her poor, Black clients before they entered a courtroom. Alexander sent her clients to court in luxury cars to give them a sense of confidence when entering a courtroom where the justice system was already skewed against them.[34]

Gender and race, in addition to class, are two important frameworks in which to analyze Alexander's life and career. Black women wield a "multiple consciousness," dealing with issues of race and gender in their daily lives. According to Patricia Hill Collins, "On certain dimensions, black women may more closely resemble black men, on other, white women, and still on others, black women may stand apart from both groups."[35] Postmodernist theories of intersectionality and assemblage examine how these multiple characteristics inform our understanding of women like Alexander.

The theory of intersectionality examines the different aspects of an individual, such as race, gender, and class, as separate units of analysis. When these different aspects of an individual meet, intersectionality takes, in the case of Alexander, their status as African Americans and their status as women as disassembled parts of their lives. The theory of intersectionality, however, can be problematic, as it separates dimensions of one's holistic self into single categorical axes. Kimberlé Crenshaw argues that Black women are "sometimes excluded from feminist theory and antiracist policy discourse because both are predicated on a discrete set of experiences that often does not accurately reflect the interaction of race and gender."[36] The experiences of Black women are at times influenced by their race, at times influenced by their gender, and at times both.

While specific experiences might be influenced by race or gender, the two can never be separated within an individual. For a Black woman, race and gender are interconnected. Jasbir K. Puar argues that the theory of assemblage is a more apt way to describe the experiences of those with multifaceted identities. Assemblages take the different social statuses of individuals and place them together in an overlapping network of class, gender, race, and sexuality. Puar states that "an assemblage is more attuned to interwoven forces that merge and dissipate time, space, and body against linearity, coherency, and permanency."[37] Assemblage allows for a fluidity of multiple characteristics to merge and interact as necessary, while intersectionality places the same characteristics on a linear path. If we apply the assemblage concept to the life of Alexander, we can examine how her multiple identities as an educated, African American female attorney from Greensboro at times intersect and at other times are indistinguishable from each other.

As Alexander moved forward in her education and career, her understandings of race and gender began to become more intertwined. The intersection of race and gender in Alexander's career collided in the fall of 1964, when she served as the defense attorney for Charles Yoes, a young Black man convicted, along with three of his friends, of raping a white woman. Alexander vigorously defended Yoes in a rape trial during a time when heightened racial tensions brought out the worst intentions of white people in town. Just three years after the 1961 Woolworths sit-in, Greensboro was ground zero in the North Carolina civil rights movement, a movement further fueled by the Civil Rights Act of 1964, signed in early July by President Lyndon B. Johnson.

The act, which banned segregation in public places and instituted equal employment opportunity measures, not only handed the South to the Republican Party for generations to come, but led to increased violence and demonstrations during the period when Alexander was preparing for trial.[38] According to Alexander, "The papers were full of racial news. . . . People could see every Negro jumping into every white woman's bedroom."[39] For many in the South, the old trope of the ravenous Black man preying on white women held strong throughout the twentieth century.

In recognition of the historical and social odds stacked against her client, Alexander attacked the jury selection process in Guilford County. She uncovered the racially biased jury selection procedures in the county and ultimately succeeded in getting one African American man on the jury.[40] While identifying with, and fighting against, the racial biases against her client, she ultimately had to adopt a harsh approach with the woman allegedly raped. In her cross-examination of the woman, Alexander poked holes in her story, employed rapid-fire questioning, and capitalized on previous rumors regarding the woman's possible background as a prostitute. Alexander's tough questioning led the woman to break down crying on the stand.[41] While her defendant was ultimately found guilty, he avoided the death penalty. The lone Black juror recommended life in prison, which saved her client's life.

Sexual stereotypes have been stacked against African Americans for centuries. After slavery the traditional southern class hierarchy weakened. While some white women were still thought to be more worthy of protection than others, white men increasingly felt the need to protect all white women.[42] The rape of Black women by white men after slavery was simply considered a "moral lapse" and better ignored, while the rape of a white woman by a Black man was a "hideous crime punishable with death by law or lynching."[43] After slavery Black women occupied the lowest rung in the social hierarchy. Even if they made it clear they were no longer under any obligation to fulfill the white man's sexual desires, they were still violently raped and cast as loose women.[44] The rape of a white woman by an African American man, however, was viewed as an affront to white superiority and masculinity, and the issue served as a rallying cry for conservative, male southerners as yet another reason to deny suffrage and equal rights to Black men.[45] Alexander expressed that she felt some sympathy for the woman allegedly raped, but in this case, where the intersection of her race and gender met, she stood on the side against racial oppression.

For Alexander, the multiple identities of race and gender are again apparent in her political races for judgeships, and in particular the 1974 race for North Carolina Supreme Court chief justice. The slogan of Alexander's campaign was "The Symbol of Justice Is a Woman." Her campaign literature contained that slogan, along with a picture of the symbol of justice with the scales in her hand, and a headshot of Alexander. Alexander had maintained her political affiliation with the Republican Party, and her primary competition was James Newcomb, a white, fire-extinguisher salesman with little more than a high school diploma. At the time, the State of North Carolina had no requirements establishing educational or career requirements for judges. In her campaign literature Alexander highlighted Newcomb's lack of qualifications versus her own extensive record. Newcomb's lack of record did not bother Republican voters though, who were likely influenced in the same election by Richard Nixon's "Southern Strategy." Judge Alexander lost the Republican nomination by a vote of 53 percent to 27 percent.[46]

Had Newcomb not entered the race, the general election would have pitted Judge Alexander against Susie Sharp, a white female attorney. Sharp, who ultimately won the general election and became North Carolina's first female Supreme Court chief justice, speculated that it all came down to gender. She said, "People hadn't heard of either one but they knew one was a man and the other a woman so they voted for the man."[47] While it is true that many voters throughout North Carolina did not know who Judge Alexander was, even fewer knew who James Newcomb was. Throughout her career, Alexander had received statewide press, especially six years earlier, when she became the first African American woman in the nation to become an elected district court judge. Regardless, it was impossible to separate Alexander's race from her gender, as the theory of assemblage explains.

As far as how Alexander identified herself, she stated that "I've always considered my mission that of inter-racial harmony.... Mine is open to people's hearts without lecturing to them, just by being me, and the race becomes secondary.... I learned a long time ago that if I see the Queen of England or anybody else, no matter how much I wanted to, I can't be two or three different personalities. Just be yourself."[48] Theories of intersectionality or assemblage might help explain how society views multiple positionalities, but according to Alexander, those are secondary to being true to oneself.

The editors of *Toward an Intellectual History of Black Women* state that "most scholarship on black women focused on their work as activists, or discussed them as the objects of intellectual activity, but they rarely received attention as producers of knowledge." This work aims to complete all three. Elreta Alexander was an activist, intellectual, and "producer of knowledge."[49] An examination of her intellectual contributions demonstrates that she changed the way we approach justice as well as activism. Existing theoretical frameworks also contextualize her contributions. Black Marxism, performance theory, and postmodern theories of intersectionality and assemblage can all be applied to examine the life of Elreta Alexander as an examination of her contribution to Black women's intellectual history. As a part of the Black bourgeoisie, she went into a career requiring performance and found herself in political situations where her multiple positionalities were placed under a microscope. While theoretical perspectives might not have dominated her daily thoughts, she was conscious of how her actions were perceived by the multiple communities in which she resided. In a world dominated by white men, at times Alexander had to "check her blackness at the door" or was called "a credit to their race." These theoretical perspectives help us to analyze how Alexander reacted to such situations, and also how these theoretical and intellectual perspectives played out in the civil rights era South.

NOTES

1. A version of this paper was originally presented at the Southeastern Women's Studies Association Conference at Winthrop University in Rock Hill, South Carolina, on April 2, 2016.

2. Randolph, "Not to Rely Completely on the Courts," 233–51.

3. Alexandra Cornelius, "A Taste of the Lash of Criticism: Racial Progress, Self Defense, and Christian Intellectual Thought in the Work of Amelia E. Johnson," in Bay et al., *Toward an Intellectual History of Black Women*, 93–109.

4. Wilson, *The Segregated Scholars*, ix.

5. Interview with Judge Elreta Alexander Ralston by Anna Barbara Perez.

6. Alexander interview, June 16, 1977, Box 5, Folder 10, Alexander Collection. Alexander claims in interviews that the State of North Carolina would pay for African Americans to attend law school out of state. At this time, however, I have not found the specific statute stating African Americans must be exceptionally meritorious. Also see Alexander Interview, 25, Southern Historical Collection.

7. Bay et al., introduction to *Toward an Intellectual History of Black Women*, 4.

8. Alexander, "A Student's Plan for Peace." The United Nations was formally established on October 24, 1945, one year and six months after Alexander's paper was written. The International Labour Organization is now a United Nations agency.

9. Alexander, "A Student's Plan for Peace."

10. Alexander, *When Is a Man Free?*, 13.

11. John Lowe, "Judgment Day in High Point Gives Young Another Chance," *High Point Enterprise*, December 29, 1977, 1B, 2B.

12. Alexander interview, 3, Southern Historical Collection.

13. Thomas G. Blomberg and Karol Lucken, *American Penology: A History of Control* (New York: Aldine De Gruyter, 2000), 63.

14. Watkins, "Chapter Five."

15. Robinson, *Black Marxism*, 189–90.

16. The conditions of schools for Black students in the Jim Crow South are well documented. See Stephanie Shaw, *What a Woman Ought to Be and to Do* (Chicago: University of Chicago Press, 1996); Adam Faircloth, *Teaching Equality: Black Schools in the Age of Jim Crow* (Athens: University of Georgia Press, 2001); Alexander interview, 8, Southern Historical Collection.

17. Dagbovie, "Among the Vitalizing Tools."

18. Elreta Alexander Collection, MSS 223, Box 5, Folder 7, Martha Blakeney Hodges Special Collections and University Archives, University Libraries, University of North Carolina at Greensboro.

19. Alexander Collection, MSS 223, Box 5, Folder 9.

20. Alexander interview, May 20, 1977, Box 5, Folder 9, Alexander Collection.

21. See Hobbs, *A Chosen Exile*.

22. Alexander interview, July 13, 1977, Box 5, Folder 11, Alexander Collection.

23. Alexander interview, July 13, 1977, Box 5, Folder 11, Alexander Collection.

24. Jackson, *Judges*, 134.

25. Alexander Papers, MSS 223, Box 5, Folder 11.

26. Robin D. G. Kelley, preface to Robinson, *Black Marxism*, xx.

27. Johnson, *Appropriating Blackness*, 9.

28. Fulani, "The Development Line."

29. Alexander Collection, MSS 223, Box 5, Folder 11.

30. Summey, "Redefining Activism."

31. Summey, "Redefining Activism."

32. Summey, "Redefining Activism."

33. Jim Schlosser, "'Judge A' Paved Way—With Style," *Greensboro News and Record*, March 16, 1998, A1.

34. Roberts, *Pageants, Parlors, and Pretty Women*.

35. Collins, "The Social Construction of Black Feminist Thought," 191.

36. Crenshaw, "Demarginalizing the Intersection of Race and Sex," 209.

37. Puar, *Terrorist Assemblages*, 212.

38. Loevy, *The Civil Rights Act of 1964*.

39. Alexander interview, November 6, 1977, Box 5, Folder 13, Alexander Collection.

40. Superior Court Transcript, Supreme Court Original Cases, Fall 1967, Cases # 613–59, Box 15.

41. Alexander interview, November, 6, 1977, Box 5, Folder 13, Alexander Collection.
42. Dorr, *White Women, Rape, and the Power of Race in Virginia*, 7.
43. Hall, "The Mind That Burns in Each Body."
44. Rosen, *Terror in the Heart of Freedom*, 72.
45. Rosen, *Terror in the Heart of Freedom*, 173.
46. Summey, "Redefining Activism."
47. Summey, "Redefining Activism," 354.
48. Alexander Papers, MSS 223, Box 5, Folder 11.
49. Bay et al., introduction to *Toward an Intellectual History of Black Women*, 2.

REFERENCES

Alexander, Elreta. "A Student's Plan for Peace." April 1944. Arthur W. Diamond Law Library, Columbia University, New York, NY.

Alexander, Elreta Melton. *When Is a Man Free?* Philadelphia: Dorrance and Company, 1967.

Bay, Mia, Farrah J. Griffin, Martha S. Jones, and Barbara D. Savage, eds. *Toward an Intellectual History of Black Women*. Chapel Hill: University of North Carolina Press, 2015.

Collins, Patricia Hill. "The Social Construction of Black Feminist Thought." In *The Black Feminist Reader*, edited by Joy James and T. Denean Sharpley-Whiting. Malden, MA: Blackwell, 2000.

Crenshaw, Kimberlé. "Demarginalizing the Intersection of Race and Sex: A Black Feminist Critique of Antidiscrimination Doctrine, Feminist Theory and Antiracist Politics." In *The Black Feminist Reader*, edited by Joy James and T. Denean Sharpley-Whiting. Malden, MA: Blackwell, 2000.

Dagbovie, Pero Gaglo. "Among the Vitalizing Tools of the Radical Intelligentsia, of Course the Most Crucial was Words." *Journal for the Study of Radicalism* 3, no. 2 (Fall 2009): 81–112.

Dorr, Lisa Lindquist. *White Women, Rape, and the Power of Race in Virginia, 1900–1960*. Chapel Hill: University of North Carolina Press, 2004.

Evans, Stephanie Y. *Black Women in the Ivory Tower, 1850–1954: An Intellectual History*. Gainesville: University Press of Florida, 2007.

Fulani, Lenora B. "The Development Line: Helping the Poor to Grow, A Special Report on Solving the Poverty Crisis in America." All Starts Project, Inc., April 2013.

Hall, Jacquelyn Dowd. "The Mind That Burns in Each Body: Women, Rape, and Racial Violence." *Southern Exposure* 12, no. 6 (Nov.–Dec. 1984): 61–71.

Hobbs, Allison Vanessa. *A Chosen Exile: A History of Racial Passing in American Life*. Cambridge, MA: Harvard University Press, 2016.

Jackson, Donald Dale. *Judges: An Inside View of the Agonies and Excesses of an American Elite*. New York: Atheneum, 1974.

Johnson, E. Patrick. *Appropriating Blackness: Performance and the Politics of Authenticity*. Durham, NC: Duke University Press, 2003.

Loevy, Robert D., ed. *The Civil Rights Act of 1964: The Passage of the Law That Ended Racial Segregation*. Albany: State University of New York Press, 1997.

Puar, Jasbir K. *Terrorist Assemblages: Homonationalism in Queer Times*. Durham, NC: Duke University Press, 2007.

Randolph, Sherie M. "Not to Rely Completely on the Courts: Florynce Kennedy and Black Feminist Leadership in the Reproductive Rights Battle." In Bay et al., *Toward an Intellectual History of Black Women*.

Roberts, Blain. *Pageants, Parlors, and Pretty Women: Race and Beauty in the Twentieth-Century South*. Chapel Hill: University of North Carolina Press, 2014.

Robinson, Cedric J. *Black Marxism: The Making of the Black Radical Tradition*. Preface by Robin D. G. Kelley. Chapel Hill: University of North Carolina Press, 2000.

Rosen, Hannah. *Terror in the Heart of Freedom: Citizenship, Sexual Violence, and the Meaning of Race in the Post-Emancipation South*. Chapel Hill: University of North Carolina Press, 2009.

Summey, Virginia L. "Redefining Activism: Judge Elreta Alexander Ralston and Civil Rights Advocacy in the New South." *North Carolina Historical Review* 90, no. 3 (July 2013): 237–58.

Watkins, William H. "Chapter Five: A Marxian and Radical Reconstructionist Critique of American Education: Searching out Black Voices." *Counterpoints* 237 (2005): 107–35.

Wilson, Francille Rusan. *The Segregated Scholars: Black Social Scientists and the Creation of Black Labor Studies, 1890–1950*. Charlottesville: University of Virginia Press, 2006.

Archives

Elreta Alexander Collection, MSS 223. Martha Blakeney Hodges Special Collections and University Archives, University Libraries, University of North Carolina at Greensboro.

Supreme Court Original Cases, Fall 1967. State Archives of North Carolina, North Carolina Department of Natural and Cultural Resources.

Oral History Interviews

Alexander Ralston, Judge Elreta. Interview by Anna Barbara Perez, February 18, 1993, and March 4, 1993. Interview number J-0018 in the Southern Oral History Program Collection #4007, Southern Historical Collection, Wilson Library, University of North Carolina at Chapel Hill. http://dc.lib.unc.edu/u?/sohp,1262.

Chapter 6

MORE THAN AN ICON

Taking Shirley Chisholm at Her Word

MARISSA JACKSON SOW

Shirley Anita St. Hill Chisholm is an American hero, one whose legacy and likeness have achieved iconic status within popular political culture, particularly as women have increasingly sought elected office.[1] In 2019 in her home state of New York, Governor Andrew Cuomo created a state park in her honor.[2] Several months earlier, New York City mayor Bill de Blasio's administration had announced the creation of a monument in Chisholm's honor in Brooklyn's Prospect Park.[3] Both sites incorporate and rely on both the visual depictions of Chisholm that have become political iconography—the Congresswoman's dark brown face and glasses centered by a big black halo of hair that belied her slight frame[4]—and her legacy as a "trailblazer."[5] These sites were constructed in her honor as gestures of commitment to progressive values. The park monument was in response to national dialogue concerning who is honored and memorialized, who is not, and why.[6]

Chisholm was proud of her accomplishments and her reputation as a fiercely independent elected official. She would have been proud of the monuments constructed in her honor and of the popularization of her physical likeness. Visual depictions of Chisholm as a larger-than-life elected official dominate her iconography despite the fact that she was a petite, even frail, woman. Much like her campaign slogan, "Unbought and Unbossed," popular visual depictions of Chisholm are easily recognizable to those familiar with American politics—partly because of Chisholm's distinctive appearance, but mostly because a select few photos of Chisholm have become as closely associated with her legacy as her most popular catchphrases. For those who are familiar with Chisholm, perhaps those images will immediately come to mind: speaking forcefully at a podium while announcing her presidential candidacy in 1972; throwing her hands up to make the victory sign with her forefinger and middle finger; or seated, smiling, with her head resting on one fist.

Chisholm was also incredibly proud of her intellectual acumen, and while visual depictions of her have informed the prevailing narrative of her as a woman with political power, they do not speak to her formidable authority as a public intellectual. As a result, Chisholm remains poorly known and even less well understood;[7] she would not have approved of this at all. That so little is actually known—by the average American and even many elite Americans—about the nation's first Black congresswoman is inexcusable. Not only did Chisholm offer many an interview and give public speeches throughout her life, she was the author of two autobiographical works, *Unbought and Unbossed*[8] and *The Good Fight*.[9] As this chapter details, Chisholm used her written works to set forth her vision for the United States and to articulate her philosophies concerning racial and gender justice. She further expanded on her thinking in her interviews with the press and archivists at various stages of her life. Shockingly, even a cursory engagement with her work reveals that Chisholm would have objected to the use of her likeness and legacy. Indeed, Chisholm's image, memory, and catchphrases have primarily been co-opted by white liberal and white feminist movements from whom she felt alienated during her lifetime.[10]

The misappropriation of Chisholm's likeness, words, and legacy is not unique to her—other human rights and civil rights icons, from Dr. Martin Luther King Jr. to Nelson Mandela—have suffered similar fates. In each case, their very clear condemnations of structural and systemic oppression of people of African descent, of poor people—and in Chisholm's case, of women—and corresponding articulations of radical visions for liberation have been co-opted by people and movements purporting to share their values while intentionally distorting and diluting their messages and legacies.[11] In each case, this has resulted in the creation of an iconic, almost-mythical figure who represents a perversely sanitized version of a person who polite white society reviled during their most active years.[12] Worse still, and particularly evident in Chisholm's case, is the promulgation of a distorted narrative and branding of the congresswoman by those who purport to be progressive allies of Black America and feminists. These groups, who should be invested in ensuring that Chisholm's truth is told on her own terms, instead insist on re-creating her in their own image because of the paternalism and white supremacy so endemic to their own movements. This irony is particularly cruel because Chisholm singled out these people for condemnation in *Unbought*, labeling them "civil rights crusaders" who were "racist, in a subtle but no less destructive way."[13]

Chisholm's word-work deserves serious engagement, and such an engagement reveals to the reader that her accomplishments are as multilayered as her thinking is complex and, at times, complicated. Chisholm's strengths lie in much more than her ability to shatter race and gender barriers in her election to political office. Indeed, as much as she made history as a Black woman first on multiple occasions, Shirley Chisholm's vision for racial and gender justice make her trailblazing an indictment of American society, not a cause for celebration.[14] Chisholm was much prouder of, and much more insistent on, her use of community organizing strategies, political acumen, and sheer will to outsmart, outstep, and outlast the forces of oppression in her neighborhood, the Democratic Party, and American society as a whole.

Shirley Chisholm had, to use her own words, "a brain," and she put her genius to work as a race and gender theorist, of the people and for the people, as a public intellectual.[15] As detailed in this chapter, Chisholm highlighted her own approach to public intellectualism by expounding on her desire to be remembered for her social and political impact; her adoption of a liberal feminism that would become increasingly intersectional over time, placing her at odds with white feminists and Black and white men alike; her bold-but-nuanced incarnation of Black womanhood and her rage over the impact of racism and sexism on her life; and what it really means to be "unbought and unbossed." Serious analysis of Chisholm's thought reveals her to be much more than an icon for a political Left that intentionally misunderstood her and misappropriated both the life and depth of her work and reduced her to an inspirational figure because of her electoral achievements.

In her afterword to the 2010 edition of *Unbought*, Shola Lynch wrote of the erasure of Chisholm from history's annals, despite her political achievements, and the distortion of her character, "from a vibrant, challenging figure with daring, guts, and a tremendous sense of humor" to a "flattened, scolding teacher who wagged her finger and forced us to confront what we preferred to ignore."[16] This chapter unflattens Chisholm's legacy and reimagines it in the Black feminist tradition, using the congresswoman's own words and wishes to locate her rightful place in the history of ideas, with particular emphasis on her contributions to Black women's intellectual history. Primarily relying on *Unbought and Unbossed*, but also using interviews and access that Chisholm granted the press and documentarians, I look beyond popular iconography and mythology *about* Chisholm and *to* Chisholm's intellectual labor—her *word-work*—to provide dimension to her legacy. This chapter will delineate major themes in Chisholm's unique and deeply complex views on race, gender, and politics and provide context to the catchphrases for which she is most widely known and yet misunderstood.

Exploring prominent themes in *Unbought*, the essay presents Chisholm's word-work both as an intentional communication of political ideas to the American public and as a form of labor worth engagement by scholars, progressive politicians, and everyday readers alike. The author unpacks the catchphrases associated with Chisholm's legacy, reconstructing their meaning in a manner consonant with Chisholm's feminism and lifelong passion for racial justice and democratic political transformation. I examine, in turn, Chisholm's feminism and her vision for gender and racial justice; her exploration of rage as a militant Black woman frustrated with American government and American oppression; her pride in her intellectualism; and the persistent, prophetic value of her work decades after her retirement from Congress.

Shirley Chisholm's posthumous iconic status is largely tied to her symbolic value to center-left and progressive politics, and to feminist politics in particular: she is a diverse hero white-led liberal movements can rally around, especially when such movements are uninterested in a serious examination of their racial politics, preferring instead to focus on the race-neutral feminism Chisholm advanced early on in her political career.[17] Within those spaces, the narrative around her is straightforward—the congresswoman was a trailblazer who shattered barriers and put dents in glass ceilings. Unfortunately, this narrative—laudatory as it may be—is also reductive, and reflective of limits placed on Black heroism and achievement, even in the realm of progressive politics and social justice. As with most discourse concerning "Black firsts," the refusal to derogate from a narrative that singularly celebrates Chisholm's status as the first Black woman to be elected to Congress or seek the presidency is undergirded by a belief that Black people's worth is located only within American whiteness, and their ability to access it via assimilation, integration, and barrier-breaking.[18]

Chisholm wrote persuasively regarding the failures—and the racism[19]—of the very white liberals and progressives who lauded her, a decade and a half after her death, and serious engagement of her work reveals her to not only have been profoundly incisive in 1970 but prophetic as well. In *Unbought*, Chisholm excoriates "white middle-class intellectual" lawmakers and policymakers who came to conclusions about Black and Brown people and designed policies impacting their lives despite having no "experience of being poor, despised, and discriminated against."[20] Chisholm continued: "There was no way that the antipoverty strategists could see the importance of this factor. They knew about it theoretically, but they had not been there themselves. . . . If they had gotten together with their 'clients' in the poor communities from the start, things might have been different."[21] The congresswoman was acutely critical of liberal white politicians and advocates who exhibited the audacity to design policies impacting Black people without Black people's input, and she would have been incensed by the brazen misappropriation of her legacy in the service of politicians who still failed to center the voices and interests of Black and Brown communities, despite the explicit demands she sets forth in *Unbought*.

Chisholm's body of work reveals a woman who would evolve over time from a race and gender analysis that was radical for its day, but often explicitly lacking intersectionality,[22] to an analysis that was both intersectional and transformational for Black women in particular.[23] The Shirley Chisholm who proclaimed that her gender was a greater obstacle for her than her race is the Chisholm popular among white feminists and their fellow white liberal and progressive counterparts, and she is therefore the Chisholm who is celebrated and promoted.[24] This abbreviated Chisholm brand is not the Chisholm who is respected and beloved by Black women, who have long been mistrustful of mainstream feminism. Because of Chisholm's unequivocal embrace of feminist politics and advocacy, Black observers—many of whom are understandably unfamiliar with the totality of Chisholm's history—have largely ceded her legacy to the liberal white feminist imagination, even though Chisholm also fiercely advocated for Black liberation and power, both in *Unbought* and throughout the entirety of her adult life.[25]

Chisholm is certainly not the first African American women whose wordwork has been left ignored, but the prevailing refusal to take Chisholm at her word is particularly egregious during the age of information. Chisholm's autobiographical works are readily available for purchase and online access, as are interviews and documentaries about her life. Still, her service to the country is given more value than contributions to progressive and radical American thought because of long-held notions that Black people are laborers, not thinkers—notions that persist even in the face of mountains of evidence to the contrary—and because of liberal white resistance to Black education and power cultivation that is the subject of Chisholm's searing critique in *Unbought*.[26]

The misappropriation of Chisholm's legacy is but a microcosm of how Black women's contributions and achievements are used and misused, even by those whom Black women would hope to rely on as allies in the struggle for racial and gender justice. The liberals Chisholm excoriates for engaging in making policy about Black lives without consulting Black voices continue to silence and erase Black women's intellectualism, preferring instead to extract labor and service from Black women's bodies.[27] Therefore, Chisholm's accomplishments as a public servant are more digestible, and certainly more marketable, when they are branded as sacrifice for the country, and as service to a feminist movement that uses the likeness of a Black woman as a battle cry for the entry of more (mostly) white women into the political arena. There seems to have been little place within the movement for a serious engagement of her written work beyond use—with little context considered—of the slogans for which Chisholm is most widely known.

Chisholm expressly recommended that more women seek elected office in *Unbought*;[28] therefore, it is fitting that she serves as an inspiration for generations of women for whom she made political careers possible. But which Chisholm is serving in this posthumous role? Is it the mythical Shirley Chisholm created in the image of a liberal political establishment she sought to topple? Or is it the relatively unknown Chisholm, who continues to speak to her readers, listeners, and acolytes from the grave with prophetic clarity? Moreover, is it a justice to Chisholm's legacy that she only be admired and emulated because of her political accomplishments, when her accomplishments as a public intellectual—a feminist theorist and a race woman—were also formidable?

Black women politicians, in particular, have looked to Chisholm for inspiration and have used her accomplishments as justification for their political aspirations in a country that still does not desire Black women's political leadership. The use of Chisholm's iconography by these women is strategic, as they wish to convey to the American public that they can win because Chisholm already won, and that they are capable of holding elected office because Chisholm already proved to the nation that Black women were competent.

Yvette Clarke currently represents the congressional district Chisholm represented, and she often pays tribute to her predecessor.[29] On February 1, 2020, Clarke tweeted about Chisholm, calling her a "trailblazer" whose "life and legacy left a profound impact" on her life.[30] Perhaps more poignant still, however, was the social media post of first-term congresswoman Ayanna Pressley, who is the first Black woman to ever represent Massachusetts's Seventh Congressional District, after Pressley moved into Chisholm's former congressional office.[31] Pressley has referred to Chisholm as her "shero" and noted that political aspirants around the country were traveling a road Chisholm had paved for them.[32]

Chisholm publicly expressed ambivalence about being the first Black woman elected to the House of Representatives in *Unbought*, noting that that her election to Congress was an accomplishment for the United States that was overdue. Said Chisholm, "That I am a national figure because I was the first person in 192 years to be at once a congressman, black, and a woman proves, I would think, that our society is not yet either just or free."[33] Chisholm also purposely limited the number of terms she served in the House of Representatives, and her legacy is more expansive than her time in public office. While Chisholm's legacy of political accomplishment remains a valid and powerful source of inspiration for women—including Black women such as Congresswomen Clarke and Pressley—any narrative that emphasizes seeking office and other leadership opportunities within the political realm and excludes Chisholm's contributions as a public intellectual is incomplete and, accordingly, unjust.[34] Chisholm, like so many high-achieving Black women, contained multitudes and demonstrated excellence across a number of spheres during her lifetime. Chisholm's posthumous fame must account for the totality of her work, including her work as an educator, a community organizer, an activist, an author, and a brilliant political and social commentator.

When Black women such as Yvette Clarke and Ayanna Pressley speak of Chisholm as an inspiration, they attempt to reclaim her legacy of political achievement and place it within the context of African American women's history. For them, Chisholm's persistence and resilience when battling local opposition does provide an actual blueprint for their own success. As with Chisholm and most Black women in politics, raising money and achieving broad, multiracial support as a political candidate is much tougher for Black women than it is for men or white women. In a story not unlike Chisholm's, shared with the American public, Congresswoman Pressley did not enjoy the support of the Congressional Black Caucus during her historic 2018 congressional race, as the caucus decided to back her white male rival instead.[35] When Pressley points to Chisholm as a personal hero, it is because she can relate to Chisholm's own battles for political support in a way that is simply not possible for a similarly situated Black man or white woman.

What remains missing from the congresswomen's heartfelt tributes to Chisholm, however, is engagement with her work as a public intellectual. Even as Black women fight for more value to be attached to their physical labor and continue to seek access to spaces and spheres previously inaccessible to them, they must simultaneously fight for recognition of their intellectual labor, production, and impact. And they must be the guardians of each other's legacies. As has always been the case in the United States, the burden of creating and, when necessary, correcting the record with respect to Black women's histories and contributions lies with Black women themselves. The recognition of Chisholm's intellect and her intellectual contributions is feminist work, and it is racial justice work, and it is therefore incumbent on all who engage with Chisholm's memory and legacy—inclusive of visual depictions of her—to center her wishes for her legacy by highlighting her words and the thoughts behind them. Chisholm was proud of her intellectual acumen, which was described by NBC News as "near genius," and she was categorical in her expression of this pride, not just because of what she had done, but rather for her impact. This essay reclaims Chisholm's history and legacy using a lens that prioritizes Chisholm's radical, unsanitized political *and* intellectual work in service of liberation for women, Black and Brown communities, and the poor.

When asked about her wish for her legacy, Congresswoman Chisholm responded that she wanted to be remembered as a catalyst for change,[36] declaring that she wanted to be remembered for what she had done and not who she was. As has too often been the case for Black American women throughout history, society has firmly ignored Chisholm's wishes and, in advancing a one-dimensional narrative about her that contradicts the body of her work, has effectively silenced her. That Chisholm put her thoughts to print is sufficient proof of her desire to contribute to public intellectual thought. That Chisholm left the public with her personal narrative, her theory of governance, and her own brand of critical race and feminist theory, as she did in *Unbought*,[37] is at least of equal importance to her electoral victories and defeats. Her writings are a palpable demonstration of what she did and what she hoped to accomplish, and they give the public a clear and multidimensional picture of who she was, what and how she thought, and how she—an American hero, leader, and icon—wished to be remembered. Moreover, a close reading of *Unbought* reveals that the congresswoman, who lays forth her vision for feminist and antiracist liberation in sections of the book titled "Speaking Out" and "Looking Ahead," wished to be a catalyst of discursive and ideological change just as much as she wished to destroy obstacles to race and gender equity.[38]

Chisholm spoke plainly and bravely about sexism within the African American community, the personal costs and challenges of her public life, American racism, and her vision for racial and gender justice. Chisholm also made mention of her training and work as an educator, and while her written work has been styled as a memoir, it is also the work of someone who was both an astute political strategist and a passionate thinker who had meaningful work experience. The versatility of Chisholm's autobiographical work is emblematic of her desired legacy as a woman who was a master of all to which she put her hands, her mind, and her will. Chisholm had little desire to maintain a status quo that had no room for her, and this manifests itself as a philosophy—as a path to intellectual and political liberation for African Americans, women, and particularly Black women looking to Chisholm as a blueprint. The opening pages of Bay, Griffin, Jones, and Savage's groundbreaking volume on Black women's intellectual history, *Toward an Intellectual History of Black Women*, summarizes the plight of Black women "artists, activists, and intellectuals" in a world that devalues their bodies, lives, labor, and thought.[39] Despite the value of their ideas, which have been "shaped by lives lived at the crossroads of race, gender, and justice," they have largely been ignored.[40] The ideas of nontraditional intellectuals have been particularly neglected, though their lived experiences have tended to lend particular relevance to their theories concerning race, gender, class, and politics.[41]

Shirley Chisholm was one such public intellectual, one whose thought flowed from her "public work rather than . . . traditional academic theorizing."[42] Though scholarly all her life and highly educated, the congresswoman was not arrogant—she was a working woman and a worker's woman, and she branded herself accordingly throughout her political career—a timely and strategic move in the 1960s and 1970s, when Black women intellectuals were choosing to "professionalize public intellectual work" and renegotiate gender norms in race leadership.[43] Chisholm's thought was informed by her rich experiences as the child of immigrants and one-time expat, as a college student leader, as an organizer in Brooklyn seeking racial justice, and as a Black woman seeking respect, voice, and place within a male-dominated political scene. Chisholm wrote her autobiographical work with the common American voter in mind, in their shared language, with the goal of informing her readers and inspiring a revolution that would have to take place in the mind of the reader before coming to pass in the streets of Brooklyn or Washington, DC.

The neglect and erasure of Black women intellectuals and their output has also been compounded by extremely harsh critique of their work, and Chisholm was no exception. In her 1970 *New York Times* review of *Unbought*, African American journalist Charlayne Hunter-Gault concludes that "Shirley Chisholm's book is not a literary masterpiece" and goes so far as to note that "sometimes it reads like a school primer." Hunter-Gault praises Chisholm's "plain talk" and admits that the book is "important," but not without insinuating that Chisholm thought too highly of herself when she criticizes Chisholm for describing her "speaking abilities as 'Messianic' without smiling just a little bit about it."[44] When Hunter-Gault posited that "it is possible that her most significant contribution since her arrival in Washington is this book,"[45] it is difficult to know if she was paying a compliment to the new congresswoman or insulting her.

While Hunter-Gault's review was harsh, it still did some justice to Chisholm's writing and the value of the ideas therein. Chisholm was not Toni Morrison, but the fact that her writing was written by a proletarian for the proletariat is what counts it among the "unique intellectual labors of women of Africa and its diaspora"[46] deserving of "a more distinct place in the history of ideas." Like Morrison's, Chisholm's ideas were "produced in dialogue with lived experience and always inflected by the social facts of race, class, and gender."[47] Chisholm did not seek to write beautiful prose; rather, in *Unbought*, she lay forth the manifesto of a politician who was both a visionary and a militant.[48]

In *Intellectual History*, the editors ask, "Can we recover the intellectual traditions of thinkers who were often organic intellectuals and whose lives and thought are modestly documented?"[49] This question is of particular pertinence where Chisholm's work is concerned. The congresswoman's political and electoral achievements are very well-documented, and her own thought is captured in her autobiographical work; conversely, however, Chisholm would have been the first to complain that her intellectual work has never received the analysis due, or even adequate documentation in the first instance. In order to recover and reconstruct Chisholm's collective intellectual contribution, we must measure her documented thought against her biography and her physical work.

Among the central ideas that Chisholm advanced in *Unbought*—and of which she was most well known by her admirers and detractors alike—was that sexism was a much more pernicious form of oppression than racism.[50]

Chisholm declares that she had faced more discrimination on account of her sex and gender than she had on account of her race.[51] To make such a statement, particularly just after the apex of the southern civil rights movement, was a bold choice that would forever mark Chisholm as being more aligned with the mainstream feminist movements of the 1970s than with the African American civil rights struggle. This casting of Chisholm, however, is unfair, and the choice it attempts to force is unjust. By pitting Chisholm between the interests of white women and Black men, one erases the intersectionality of her existence as a Black woman—an erasure that Chisholm even inflicts on herself at certain points in the book. At the time Chisholm wrote *Unbought*, she did not grasp intersectionality as well as she did in subsequent years, as the concept of intersectionality began to enter feminist discourse. Nevertheless, even as Chisholm does not always explicitly articulate her oppression from the specific standpoint of Black womanhood in *Unbought*, she articulates Black feminist thought throughout.

Chisholm's leadership within the mainstream feminist movement is incontrovertible. She built alliances with white feminist icons Gloria Steinem and Betty Friedan, among others,[52] and her universalist approach to feminism reflected her investment in second-wave feminist thought.[53] Chisholm wrote *Unbought* more than a decade before bell hooks and Kimberlé Crenshaw articulated the theory of intersectionality.[54] Accordingly, reading *Unbought* with an intersectional lens can be frustrating because it relies on a clear bifurcation between race and gender at various points, and Chisholm maintained throughout that sexism was a bigger burden to bear than was racism. At the same time, however, Chisholm made clear to the reader that she was living her life as a Black woman—as a Black person and as a woman all at the same time. Chisholm conceived of the double burden she bore—of Blackness and womanhood—as oppressions that weren't so much intersecting as they were compounded, and this understanding evolved into a clearer theory of intersectionality within a few years' time.

Chisholm's feminism is the feminism of a militant race woman.[55] Present-day iconography and narratives concerning Chisholm have ignored her deep investment in racial justice, instead painting the congresswoman as a spunky mainstream feminist who transcended race. In actuality, Chisholm's feminism—including her calls for women's revolution and liberation, as opposed to accommodationism—was informed by her critical race theory, and not vice versa. Chisholm admitted in *Unbought* that she had been a political moderate at first,[56] and the reader gets a clear glimpse into her desire to build coalitions across racial lines based on her belief that solidarity among all woman would beget political transformation. Indeed, a multiracial coalition of women helped her win election to the New York State Assembly, but

Chisholm notes that Black men formed part of her base, too, even as many sought to stifle and silence her. Chisholm's evolution into an intentionally intersectional feminist devoted to Black women's liberation in particular became most evident by 1974, in a speech Chisholm delivered at the University of Missouri,[57] but her simultaneous commitments to both racial and gender justice are on display in *Unbought*, and both flow from her lived experiences with burdens that she did not fully understand as being intersecting, but instead felt was compounded.

Bay, Griffin, Jones, and Savage assert that "black women have always worked through complexities produced by the intersection of race and gender, though not always in the same ways."[58] According to them, "some black women thinkers developed sophisticated theories of how race and gender work together to produce both power and inequality, while others privileged one thread of analysis over another, helping us to understand the changing and historically contingent nature of these social constructs."[59] They continue to assert that "through the lives of black women intellectuals, we see the fragile and sometimes false nature of analytic categories. Binaries between race and gender, politics and ideas, social sciences and the arts, and public and private all prove to be false as black women thinkers move through space, time, and many spheres of ideas and action."[60]

Chisholm is not easily categorized now, nor was she during her lifetime; this has lent to her mystique while also proving a burden as various communities and movements fight over her legacy without a thorough, nuanced understanding of her vision and ethos. The difficulty of categorizing Chisholm's theories on race and gender has contributed to the academy's failure to take them under serious consideration, and it has also contributed to her enigmatic and even strained positioning within Black Americana, and among Black men in particular. Chisholm's intellectual output, however, puts to shame the insistence by some on forcing Black women into categories they have had no say in creating. *Unbought* reveals that Chisholm's investment in the mainstream second-wave feminist movement did not detract from her commitment to racial justice. Indeed, in *Unbought*, Chisholm called on those invested in women's liberation to take pages out of the playbook of antiracist liberation—the movement she knew first and, arguably, knew best.

Shirley Chisholm was an unabashed Black feminist, and she lived, worked, and wrote accordingly. Her passion for antiracist revolution *and* gender justice catapulted her into political activism in Brooklyn. Chisholm joined the NAACP while in college,[61] founded the National Congress of Black Women, and years beforehand, had founded a sorority-like organization for Black women while a student at her alma mater, Brooklyn College.[62] Chisholm would ultimately also join a sorority for Black women, Delta Sigma Theta, Incorporated.[63] Each of these organizations required a commitment to activism by and for Black women as a central and unifying cause, and each provided Chisholm with an outlet for her Black feminist civic and political activism. Chisholm's indictments of sexism and racism left her with the unstated, yet apparent, belief that only other Black women held Black women's best interests at heart on a consistent and fervent basis. Ipothia, the student group she formed at Brooklyn College, was formed in resistance to racism on campus because campus social clubs did not allow for Black student membership. The group ultimately disbanded once the white social clubs began admitting Black members,[64] revealing that Chisholm maintained integration by Black Americans into American society as a goal and that she was not a separatist. However, Chisholm's membership in Delta Sigma Theta, and her founding role at the National Congress for Black Women, does indicate that she was certain that Black womanhood was, and would always be, both her identity and refuge.

Chisholm recounted an interaction with one of her professors at Brooklyn College that was both annoying and encouraging to her, as are such interactions with white allies who do not—who cannot—deeply understand the realities and the weight of living under the yoke of American racism and sexism on a daily basis. When "Proffy," as Chisholm affectionately called him, told her that she should consider a political career, she reminded him that she was both Black and a woman. He responded, "You really have deep feelings about that, haven't you?" Chisholm noted that she was "astonished at his naivete."[65] The interaction with Proffy would eventually push Chisholm toward politics. Though Professor Warsoff's question intimated that Chisholm's feelings about her Black womanhood were too deep, Chisholm embraced the profoundness of her feelings, using them as fuel for her political ambitions. In so doing, Chisholm further identified herself with Black feminist tradition, which prioritizes the fullness of Black women's humanity and the dismantling of oppression of Black women by shining a light on the sources of that oppression—which unfortunately, often are the men closest to Black women.

Chisholm's Black feminism and her wider feminist theory were evident as she recounted her journeys to the New York State Assembly and then to the United States House of Representatives. Chisholm wrote matter-of-factly about not wanting to have children because of her political ambitions.[66] And while Chisholm wrote in celebration of her husband Conrad's steadfast support of her ambitions,[67] she also expressed dismay and frustration over her political rivals' insinuations that she dominated her husband because she was active in public life and their use of those insinuations as dog whistles to Black male voters unwilling to support a Black woman for election to political office.[68] Chisholm described the misogynistic campaign tactics that James Farmer used against her during their race for New York's Twelfth Congressional District: "Farmer and his people were using my sex against me," Chisholm wrote, noting that "to the black men . . . sensitive about female domination, they were running me down as a bossy female."[69] Chisholm also recounted how an elderly Black man lashed out at her on the street when she asked him to sign her nominating petition, asking her, "Did you get your husband's breakfast this morning? Did you straighten up your house? What are you doing running for office? That is something for men." Ultimately, he signed her petition, and Chisholm noted that "I understood too well their reasons for lashing out at black women; in a society that denied them real manhood, I was threatening their shaky self-esteem still more."[70] Chisholm's sympathetic approach to a Black man's aggressive sexism is reflective of her status as both feminist and race woman. Chisholm ultimately won the assembly and congressional seats by simultaneously chipping away at racism and sexism while building—and never taking for granted—a multiracial coalition of voters buoyed by a multiracial coalition of women with whom she had been organizing for well over a decade, writing with no small amount of satisfaction:

> It is true that women are second-class citizens, just as black people are . . . and I want the time to come when we can be as blind to sex as we are to color. But that time is not here, and when someone tries to use my sex against me, I delight in being able to turn the tables on him, as I did in my congressional campaign.[71]

Shirley Chisholm lived out her Black feminism on a daily basis, rejecting the double burdens of racism and sexism while shouldering them all the same. Ever strategic, in *Unbought*, Chisholm recounted her personal narrative first, before setting forth her prescriptions for liberation of women, Black people, and the poor and working class, using her own lived experiences as evidence of her subject-matter expertise. To invert the popular proverb, Chisholm used *Unbought* to preach what she practiced, "black woman–style."[72]

Chisholm was clear, as she wanted her readers to be, that her fidelity to her own convictions and her maverick politics were the key to her political victories and defeats, and not ties to any political boss or machine.[73] Chisholm had not so much broken the mold for American politics as she had created an entirely different mold that had been, theretofore, *du jamais vu*. She was Black, she was a woman, and she was not grateful to the system for allowing her to survive and transcend it. Neither did Chisholm feel any obligation to anyone or anything aside from her constituents and her convictions concerning how government should serve common citizens—in a society that had told her early on that she had nothing to gain,[74] Chisholm felt rather strongly that she also had nothing to lose.

In *Unbought*, Chisholm advanced the idea that having little to lose in the United States can be a liberating element that allows for women and Black Americans to excel in politics and public life.[75] Even—perhaps especially—after the Obama presidency, Chisholm's wisdom remains prophetic in a new era of activism and political engagement by Black American women. Chisholm discussed this idea in two ways, first acknowledging the burden she felt as a young Black woman because of her lack of social capital, political capital, networks, money, and power. She wrote frankly about a lack of career options, even as a college-educated woman, precisely because of her Black womanhood.[76] But she then also credited her limited options and her simple living conditions with keeping her free to work as she pleased and with forcing her to fight for every single chance, opportunity, and eventual victory.[77]

Chisholm offered the cautionary counterexample of her African American community in New York City. After sharing with the readers a bit about her struggle to find work upon graduation from college, she noted that for some, having a job—while absolutely necessary—undermined their ability to achieve freedom, and that pressure to retain employment had hindered the entire African American community from combatting the forces of white supremacy.[78] Because of the never-ending work involved in trying to assimilate into, and prosper within, a racist society, it was normal, and remains normal, for African Americans who were fortunate enough to be hired for a job to be overcome by the fear of losing it. The obsession with safeguarding one's employment resulted in an obsession with one's individual well-being that overcame the interest in collective solidarity. Said Chisholm:

> The black community had less sense of brotherhood in those days and . . . black people were almost all afraid. They feared, and justly, the power the white man had over their lives . . . The few black people who had jobs through city appointments were the worst of all. If they showed the slightest sign of opposing the system, they were warned . . . "Don't bite the hand that's feeding you." Man, black men who could have become leaders were neutralized that way.[79]

If these workers' jobs were the most important thing to them, this was not the case for Chisholm. "I didn't have that worry. I had my job as a nursery school teacher and I had no family to support. Nobody could touch me."[80]

Whether or not Chisholm was untouchable in reality, that she felt untouchable gave her the confidence and courage to become politically active and fight her way to power.[81] Chisholm transformed feelings of resignation over the oppression she lived under in American society into a source of mental, and then tangible, freedom. As a Black woman, as a child of immigrants, and as a one-time expatriate, Chisholm did not have high expectations for a country that did not have high expectations for her—but rather than resigning herself to a miserable fate or desperately clinging to the ever-elusive promises of American capitalism, Chisholm decided to wear America like a loose garment. For Chisholm, traveling light—both physically and mentally—allowed her to commit herself to fighting for justice and power for Black and Brown communities, and for the nation's women. By not selling her soul or even too much of her time to a political party, party boss, or even an ordinary boss at work, Chisholm had nothing to lose or fear in her fight for racial and gender justice; she was, quite literally, unbossed and unbought.

In *Toward an Intellectual History*, the editors discuss the "centrality of black women to the construction of freedom, democracy, and citizenship."[82] Chisholm is a critical participant in that tradition. In *Unbought*, she noted that had she attended a fancier, more elite university, she would have likely met an alternative destiny in life.[83] Ultimately, however, her Brooklyn College education would train her as a revolutionary politician, permanently devoted to and aligned with America's working class, and this alignment shaped her politics, her political engagement, and her worldview.[84] By reproaching the Black community's reliance on city jobs, which they prioritized over an opportunity to achieve municipal, state-level, or federal political power, Chisholm intentionally promulgated her theory of Black liberation—emphasizing intracommunity solidarity, abandonment of Black patriarchy, and concerted political activism by Black men and women alike. Here, Chisholm's intellectual contributions to critical race theory, feminism, and a theory of governance converged, forming a prevalent theme of her written work and reflecting her lived experiences.

Shirley Chisholm's thought cannot be separated from her life—her personal was, quite literally, political,[85] as a Black woman experiencing the burdens of racism and sexism both before and after her election to Congress. One of the most revolutionary aspects of the congresswoman's written work was, and still is, her embrace of her personal rage. Chisholm, who was a physically petite woman, had no reservations about taking up space and filling it with her discontent when necessary to break down illegitimate barriers between her and her goals. While interviews with the late congresswoman[86] and secondhand accounts[87] reveal a warm, humorous, and gracious persona, Chisholm was not afraid to become angry and make her anger count.

Unsurprisingly, commentators attributed a number of unflattering stereotypes to Chisholm—assuming her to be "a noisy, hostile, anti-white type,"[88] a "would-be matriarch,"[89] and "hard to handle."[90] In her review of *Unbought*, Charlayne Hunter-Gault wrote of Chisholm: "Mrs. Chisholm is known as a fiery speaker, and her portrait is usually recorded by photographers during her most formidable looking moments. There are consequently those who, as a result of her public image, are apprehensive about getting close enough to find out what she has to say even if they have missed it."[91] Chisholm embraced each of these stereotypes in her own subversive way, never attempting to quash her confidence, her independence, her feminism, her zeal, or her anger at an unjust society and ineffective government.

James Baldwin famously said that "to be a Negro in this country and to be relatively conscious is to be in a rage almost all the time."[92] This rage can be explosive sometimes, and a mere simmer at other times, and expressed as fatigue, sadness, resignation, or dismay otherwise. Chisholm's experience with all of these emotions relating to her weariness in the face of racist and sexist oppression is evident in *Unbought*. Chisholm's keen awareness of the limits society placed on her potential because of her race and gender is so clearly articulated in *Unbought* that it is, at times, excruciating to read, especially when Chisholm did not provide rage to the readers as a form of catharsis:

> If I had other ideas about what I might do, I dismissed them. My youth may have been sheltered from boys and some other realities, but I was black, and nobody needed to draw me a diagram. No matter how well I prepared myself, society wasn't going to give me a chance to do much of anything else.[93]

Upon graduation from college, cum laude, her earlier decision to become a teacher did not make it any easier for her to actually find any work—a problem Chisholm attributed to her slight, youthful appearance.

Chisholm wrote, "School after school turned me down, even as a teacher's aide.... Finally I blew up at one nursery school director. 'At least you could try me!' I exploded."[94] Her expression of anger had the desired effect; Chisholm got the job and worked at the nursery school for seven years.[95] Several years later, after Chisholm had overcome a number of obstacles and was serving as a congresswoman, she continued to express her rage in three main directions: at a government that intentionally structured society in a way that reserved political and economic power for white men; at a deeply racist American society that did not recognize the humanity of African Americans or accept that such humanity should translate to basic human rights or economic and political empowerment; and at sexism that was so pervasive in American society that most Americans did not even notice its presence.[96]

Despite her insistence that sexism was much more deleterious a force than racism in American society, Chisholm wrote most passionately about her anger with respect to anti-Black racism in *Unbought*. In an early chapter, Chisholm wrote of the anger she felt as a young woman at the arrogance and ironies of white supremacy, largely on behalf of Black men:

> It grew on me that we, black men especially, were expected to be subservient even in groups where ostensibly everyone was equal.... When I looked at the white people who were doing this ... it made me angry because so many of them were baser, less intelligent, less talented than the people they were lording it over.[97]

Chisholm's anger concerning racism evolved into fury as time passed. She recounted, just after telling the heartbreaking story of redcaps with whom she met in New York City, who "spent their lives growing gnarled and bent carrying white travelers' baggage for nickels and dimes," an encounter with a white audience member in St. Louis, where she gave a speech in 1969:

> A white member of the audience asked me a question that I have heard repeatedly. It makes me more furious each time I hear it, until I think it's a good thing I don't have a gun, or I would use it. "What do you Negroes want now?" he asked me. "You all aren't doing too bad. As a matter of fact, you're doing a lot better than some of the white people." My God, what do we want? What does any human being want?[98]

Toward the end of *Unbought*, as Chisholm set forth her vision for racial justice, she transforms a burning fury concerning the profound subjugation of Black lives in the United States into a prophetic vision for Black uprising and Black liberation:

> There is no longer any alternative for black Americans but to unite and fight together for their own advancement as a group.... How shall that fight be waged? Must it be with bullets, bombs, and guerilla armies? ... I can feel in myself sometimes an anger that wants only to destroy everything in its path. There is a point at which passions as great as those that burn in the hearts of black Americans will not be frustrated any longer.[99]

Chisholm's openness about her capacity for explosive anger is yet another explicitly Black feminist statement. She embraced being an angry Black woman not just because it was an expression of the fullness of her humanity but also because her anger either was strategically employed or was going to propel her to success in one form or another. In short, being angry worked for Shirley Chisholm, and her anger coexisted easily with her wit, her sense of humor, and her passion for her work.

Throughout *Unbought*, Chisholm complained about the complacency and resignation of Black people and women with respect to their oppression before expressly calling for both groups to revolt—and Chisholm knew that each group had to first become angry at their unjust subordination in American society before it would be possible for them to adopt the militancy necessary to topple oppressive forces.[100] True to form, Chisholm decided to be angry—and effective—on their respective behalf, leading, as always, by example and then committing her testimony and prescription to print.

Chisholm's famous call to action, "if they don't give you a seat at the table, bring a folding chair"[101] is also best analyzed in the context of her own storytelling and with a Black feminist lens. Chisholm had much to say about tables and how to engage them. In an interview with the Visionary Project, Chisholm recounted how upon being elected to the House of Representatives, her fellow representatives regularly refused to eat lunch with her because of her race and gender.[102] She recounted an incident when she mistakenly sat at the table reserved for the Georgia delegation one day and was instructed to move by a member of the Georgia delegation. She refused and instead directed the gentleman to sit at the New York table. Congresswoman Chisholm would sit at the table of her choosing; more importantly, there was no protocol so serious that she had to respect, especially in a setting where her peers refused to respect her presence.[103]

Placed in this context, and in the context of *Unbought*, a simple trailblazer narrative involving a woman creating political or social equality for herself by crashing a table with a folding chair is hollow. Chisholm was subversive and acutely aware of the gaps between her understanding of her value and America's understanding of the same. By bringing a folding chair to a table to which she was not invited, Chisholm meant to decolonize the table, to disrespect it and the racist, sexist etiquette attached thereto, and to seize control of the table for herself. Her folding chair obviously did not match the mahogany wood of the other chairs for the invited guests, and she meant to create an obviously awkward mismatch, just as she meant to pick up her folding chair and leave whenever she was done engaging the table on her terms, likely speaking out of turn all the while. It would be appropriately termed rebellion if she were, at any point, willing to acknowledge the table rules that she meant to disrespect—but she was not so willing. The table represents white supremacy, patriarchy, and machine politics all at once, forces with which she contended but never felt pressure to accept.[104] The table was not created with her in mind, and so its only utility to her was what she would do at the table once she occupied it by sheer force. Recognizing that "power concedes nothing,"[105] Chisholm also refused to concede her own power, and this imposition of her power is the central theme of *Unbought* and of Chisholm's entire political career. Chisholm did not seek inclusion or integration into a broken society; rather, she sought disruption and transformation, and she invited all women and African Americans to do the same: resist, perhaps, but by all means, insist.

While Chisholm could not ultimately surmount every political barrier, she remains remarkable, if not wholly unique, for her transcendence over and beyond labels and categories in mid-twentieth-century America. Chisholm recognized and relished this, and she boasts accordingly about this at several points in *Unbought* in ways that offer refreshing insights into how African Americans might achieve liberation, instead of mere equality, within a system she considered to be thoroughly corrupted and broken by patriarchy and white supremacy. Chisholm's intellectual labor is, therefore, best analyzed with an eye that does not faithfully subscribe to the white gaze or adhere to the belief that equality between Black and white Americans within a broken political system is the cause for which elected officials should be fighting. Chisholm speaks openly about wanting to overhaul and transform politics in *Unbought*, and if she were considered to be an agitator by white and Black men alike, it was for that reason: she could not follow the rules because she was bent on nullifying them in favor of new norms.

Chisholm's insistence on living a life that was unbought and unbossed was not only in respect to her thorough disregard for the rules of machine politics. A close reading of *Unbought* through a radical Black feminist lens reveals that Chisholm is celebrating the fullness of her Black womanhood in a way that leaves no room for consideration of any establishments, rules, or constructs that did not consider her or leave her space to create power. Indeed, her contempt for racism, sexism, and the brutality of capitalism was unbought and unbossed as well—it would not be controlled, neither would it be quieted, and it would fuel her activism and the effectiveness thereof. She, Shirley Ann St. Hill Chisholm, is a woman who contains multitudes—multitudes inherent to her, and not gifted her by any political boss, donor, or voter. Indeed, she is the gift, and she generously shares of that gift in *Unbought*, as in the halls of Congress, in the manner and tone of her choosing.

At present, two versions of Shirley Chisholm exist: the brainy educator and community organizer-turned-politician from Brooklyn who had a lot to say in her memoirs, speeches, and interviews about her visions for race, gender, and American government; and the Shirley Chisholm imagined by liberal interest groups whose condescension, arrogance, and stubborn white supremacy would have attracted Chisholm's ire were she still alive. Because the congresswoman left a clear record concerning her worldview and her vision for good governance and for racial and gender justice in America, which Shirley Chisholm we choose to acknowledge and hail is up to our individual and collective choosing. Our choices will reveal much more about us—how we regard Black women and their formidable intellectual contributions to American society—than they can reveal to us about the late former congresswoman. After all, she stated her case and made it plain. We must only decide whether or not we believe her.

NOTES

1. Steinhauer, "2019 Belongs to Shirley Chisholm."
2. New York State Department of Parks, Recreation, and Historic Preservation, "Shirley Chisholm State Park."
3. Prospect Park Alliance, "A Monument to a Trailblazer."
4. See Steinhauer, "2019 Belongs to Shirley Chisholm."
5. The New York State Department of Parks, Recreation, and Historic Preservation's website refers to Chisholm as a trailblazer and notes that she was the first African American woman to be elected to Congress and run for president of the United States. See New York State Department of Parks, Recreation, and Historic Preservation, "Shirley Chisholm State Park." See also Prospect Park Alliance website.
6. New York City's She Built NYC initiative sought to rectify the gender imbalance in New York City monuments, as part of a larger initiative to bring more racial and gender equity to public art, following a national conversation over Confederate monuments. New York City Economic Development Corporation, "She Built NYC."
7. See Cooper, *Beyond Respectability*, 115 (quoting Ponchitta Pierce, "Problems of the Negro Intellectual, *Ebony Magazine*, August 1966, 149). "The Negro woman intellectual is easily one of the most misunderstood, unappreciated, and problem-ridden of all God's creatures."
8. Chisholm, *Unbought*.
9. Chisholm, *The Good Fight*.
10. Steinhauer, "2019 Belongs to Shirley Chisholm."
11. Lockhart, "The Sanctification—and Sanitization"; Scahill, "The Sanitizing of Martin Luther King and Rosa Parks."
12. In the days after Nelson Mandela's 2013 death, Seumas Milne wrote about how the West had sanitized Mandela's image and legacy after persecuting him during his lifetime. Milne, "Mandela Has Been Sanitised."
13. Chisholm, *Unbought*, 151.
14. Chisholm, *Unbought*, 19–20.
15. The Visionary Project, "Shirley Chisholm."
16. Lynch, afterword, 193–94.
17. See Steinhauer, "2019 Belongs to Shirley Chisholm."
18. According to Shola Lynch, "Chisholm doesn't want to be remembered as a 'first.' It minimizes her humanness." Lynch, afterword, 198.
19. Chisholm, *Unbought*, 151.
20. Chisholm, *Unbought*, 168.
21. Chisholm, *Unbought*, 168.
22. In *Unbought*, Chisholm often compares Black people to women, failing to account for the existence of Black women and other demographics who are neither male nor white. Chisholm also often discusses women's liberation without disaggregating women of color, or women of different socioeconomic strata, ethnicities, faiths, etc. See Chisholm, *Unbought*, 175–81.
23. See Chisholm, "The Black Woman in Contemporary America."
24. Chisholm, *Unbought*, 20, 176–77.

25. Chisholm, *Unbought*, 147–74.
26. Chisholm, *Unbought*, 167–68.
27. Chisholm, *Unbought*, 167–69.
28. Chisholm, *Unbought*, 179–80.
29. For example, Rep. Clarke and Sen. Harris reintroduced legislation in 2019, which had been introduced by Rep. Clarke in 2019, to commission a statue of Chisholm for placement in the Capitol. See Kamala Harris for US Senate, "Harris, Clarke Reintroduce Legislation."
30. Rep. Yvette D. Clarke (@RepYvetteClarke), "On this first day of #BlackHistoryMonth, I would like to take a moment to recognize a Black woman whose life and legacy have left a profound impact on my own life. #ShirleyChisolm, whose seat I now have the honor of holding, was a political trailblazer." Twitter, February 1, 2020, https://twitter.com/RepYvetteClarke/status/1223613311830364161.
31. Rep. Ayanna Pressley (@ayannapressley), ". . . We just learned my Congressional Office designation will be #ShirleyChisholm's former office. How's that for divine intervention, AND the selflessness of my colleague @KatieHill4CA who drew a better lottery# but still wanted me to have it." Twitter, December 17, 2018, https://twitter.com/AyannaPressley/status/1074776839598563328?
32. Rep. Ayanna Pressley (@ayannapressley), "My #shero Shirley Chisholm said, 'if they don't give you a seat at the table, bring a folding chair.' Across the country, thousands of activist leaders refused to wait to their turn . . ." Instagram, November 5, 2018, https://www.instagram.com/p/BpoLaAPnZnB/.
33. Chisholm, *Unbought*, 1.
34. In support of a correction of Chisholm's record through a Black feminist lens, Shola Lynch wrote that "the seemingly harmless way, in which Chisholm could be rendered invisible and subsequently overlooked, despite her political victories, had consequences. It seeped into history, and our collective memory." Lynch, afterword, 193.
35. Dezenski, "CBC Endorses Capuano."
36. Brazile, foreword.
37. Chisholm structured *Unbought and Unbossed* as part memoir, part manifesto, telling the story of her childhood, adolescence, and early adult years, tracing her journey to and through local and state politics, before laying forth her views on, and vision for, American government, women's liberation, and racial justice for Black and Brown communities. See table of contents in *Unbought*.
38. Chisholm, *Unbought*, table of contents.
39. Bay et al., introduction to *Toward an Intellectual History of Black Women*, 1.
40. Bay et al., introduction, 1.
41. Bay et al., introduction, 1–3.
42. Bay et al., introduction, 3; see also Cooper, *Beyond Respectability*, 117.
43. Cooper, *Beyond Respectability*, 117.
44. Hunter-Gault, Review of *Unbought and Unbossed*.
45. Hunter-Gault, Review.
46. Bay et al. introduction, 3.
47. Bay et al., introduction, 4.
48. Chisholm, *Unbought*, 158.
49. Bay et al., introduction, 3.

50. Chisholm, *Unbought*, 176–77.

51. Chisholm, *Unbought*, 20.

52. In 1971, Shirley Chisholm, Fannie Lou Hamer, Gloria Steinem, Bella Abzug, Mildred Jeffrey, Dorothy Height, Liz Carpenter, LaDonna Harris, Eleanor Holmes Norton, Betty Friedan, and other prominent women cofounded the National Women's Political Caucus. National Women's Political Caucus, "About the Caucus."

53. See Chisholm, *Unbought*, 20.

54. Feminist scholars bell hooks and Kimberlé Crenshaw articulated their theories of intersectionality, with Crenshaw coining the term, in 1984 and 1989, respectively. See hooks, *From Margin to Center*, and Crenshaw, "Demarginalizing the Intersection of Race and Sex."

55. Chisholm, *Unbought*, 158. "Today I am a militant."

56. Chisholm, *Unbought*, 158. "I used to be a moderate. I spent twenty years going to all kinds of meetings, trying to find ways all of us, black and white, could work together."

57. See Chisholm, "The Black Woman in Contemporary America."

58. Bay et al., introduction, 5.

59. Bay et al., introduction, 5.

60. Bay et al., introduction, 5.

61. Chisholm, *Unbought*, 42.

62. Chisholm, *Unbought*, 43–44.

63. Delta Sigma Theta Sorority Inc., "Notable Members."

64. Chisholm, *Unbought*, 44.

65. Chisholm, *Unbought*, 43.

66. Chisholm, *Unbought*, 88. When Chisholm fell ill and went to see a doctor, the doctor informed her that she was either pregnant or hosting a tumor. "'Doc, you'd better know what you're talking about,' I told him, 'because I am running for Congress and I am not going to have a baby.'"

67. Chisholm, *Unbought*, 63–64.

68. Chisholm, *Unbought*, 63–64.

69. Chisholm, *Unbought*, 91.

70. Chisholm, *Unbought*, 70–71.

71. Chisholm, *Unbought*, 92.

72. Bay et al., introduction, 4.

73. Chisholm wrote at length about her refusal to play by the rules of the Democratic Party establishment before her election to the New York State Assembly while in the assembly and after her election to Congress. Regarding her reputation as a maverick in the assembly, Chisholm wrote the following: "I don't [play the rules of the game], because I don't choose to. It is not because I don't know what the rules are." Chisholm, *Unbought*, 75.

74. See Chisholm, *Unbought*, 20, 41.

75. Chisholm, *Unbought*, 48.

76. Chisholm, *Unbought*, 41, 45. Chisholm also wrote about how racism and sexism limited the career options of Black, Brown, and female Americans in general. Chisholm, *Unbought*, 175, 177.

77. Chisholm, *Unbought*, 48.

78. Chisholm, *Unbought*, 45.

79. Chisholm, *Unbought*, 48.

80. Chisholm, *Unbought*, 48.
81. Chisholm, *Unbought*, 46–57.
82. Bay et al., introduction, 3.
83. Chisholm, *Unbought*, 40.
84. Chisholm, *Unbought*, 43. Chisholm described the environment and activities at Brooklyn College as "politically oriented," "ultra-progressive," and "radical" before describing her own hyper-involvement on campus.
85. The use of this phrase, which has informed Black feminism, refers to Carol Hanisch's essay on feminist theory, the title of which became a slogan widely associated with second-wave feminism. Hanisch denies authoring the phrase, and she instead credits the editors of *Notes from the Second Year: Women's Liberation*, Shulie Firestone and Anne Koedt. See Carol Hanisch, "The Personal Is Political," in *Notes from the Second Year: Women's Liberation* (New York: Radical Feminism, 1970). See also Combahee River Collective, "The Combahee River Collective Statement" (Kitchen Table: Women of Color Press, 1986), http://circuitous.org/scraps/combahee.html.
86. The Visionary Project, "Shirley Chisholm."
87. Lynch, afterword, 193.
88. Chisholm, *Unbought*, 96. Chisholm wrote that weeks after arriving at Capitol Hill, "I realized that everyone had been expecting someone else, a noisy hostile, anti-white type. Some of my new colleagues admitted it frankly. 'You're not the way we thought you'd be,' one said. 'You're actually charming.'"
89. Chisholm, *Unbought*, 91.
90. Chisholm, *Unbought*, 84.
91. Hunter-Gault, Review.
92. Baldwin, "The Negro in American Culture," 205.
93. Chisholm, *Unbought*, 41.
94. Chisholm, *Unbought*, 45.
95. Chisholm, *Unbought*, 45.
96. Chisholm, *Unbought*, 175.
97. Chisholm, *Unbought*, 42.
98. Chisholm, *Unbought*, 148.
99. Chisholm, *Unbought*, 156–57.
100. Chisholm, *Unbought*, 181. "While most of us are not yet revolutionaries, the time is coming when we will be . . . to use the words of Women's Liberation activist Robin Morgan, 'Women are not inherently passive or peaceful. We're not inherently anything but human. And like every other oppressed people rising up today, we're out for our freedom by any means necessary.'"
101. Donna Brazile has quoted Shirley Chisholm as having given her that advice. See People Staff, "Chirley Chisholm, 1924–2005," *People* magazine, January 17, 2005, https://people.com/archive/1924-2005-shirley-chisholm-vol-63-no-2/.
102. The Visionary Project, "Shirley Chisholm."
103. The Visionary Project, "Shirley Chisholm."
104. See Chisholm, *Unbought*, 75–76.
105. Chisholm, *Unbought*, 76 (quoting Frederick Douglass, "The Significance of Emancipation in the West Indies").

REFERENCES

Baldwin, James. "The Negro in American Culture." *Cross Currents* 11 (1961).

Bay, Mia., Farah J. Griffin, Martha S. Jones, and Barbara D. Savage, eds. *Toward an Intellectual History of Black Women*. Chapel Hill: University of North Carolina Press, 2015.

Brazile, Donna. Foreword to *Unbought and Unbossed* by Shirley Chisholm, edited by Scott Simpson, xiii–xvii. Charlotte, NC: Take Root Media, 2010.

Chisholm, Shirley. "The Black Woman in Contemporary America." Speech, University of Missouri, Kansas City, June 17, 1974.

Chisholm, Shirley. *The Good Fight*. New York: Harper and Row, 1973.

Chisholm, Shirley. *Unbought and Unbossed*, edited by Scott Simpson. Charlotte, NC: Take Root Media, 2010.

Clarke, Yvette D. (@RepYvetteClarke). Twitter, February 1, 2020. https://twitter.com/RepYvetteClarke/status/1223613311830364161.

Cooper, Brittney C. *Beyond Respectability: The Intellectual Thought of Race Women*. Champaign: University of Illinois Press, 2017.

Crenshaw, Kimberlé. "Demarginalizing the Intersection of Race and Sex: A Black Feminist Critique of Antidiscrimination Doctrine, Feminist Theory and Antiracist Politics." *University of Chicago Legal Forum* 1989, no. 8 (1989).

Delta Sigma Theta Sorority Inc., "Notable Members." Accessed February 17, 2020. https://www.deltasigmatheta.org/notable-members.

Dezenski, Lauren. "CBC Endorses Capuano in Massachusetts Democratic Primary." Politico. May 18, 2018. https://www.politico.com/story/2018/05/18/michael-capuano-endorsed-cbc-597659.

Douglass, Frederick. "The Significance of Emancipation in the West Indies." Speech, Canandaigua, New York, August 3, 1857.

Farmer, Ashley D. *Remaking Black Power: How Black Women Transformed an Era*. Chapel Hill: University of North Carolina Press, 2017.

Kamala Harris for US Senate. "Harris, Clarke Reintroduce Legislation to Commission Statue Honoring US Representative Shirley Chisholm." United States Senate, March 7, 2019. https://www.harris.senate.gov/news/press-releases/harris-clarke-reintroduce-legislation-to-commission-statue-honoring-us-representative-shirley-chisholm.

hooks, bell. *From Margin to Center*. London: Pluto Press, 1984.

Hunter-Gault, Charlayne. Review of *Unbought and Unbossed*. *New York Times*, November 1, 1970.

Lockhart, P. R. "The Sanctification—and Sanitization—of Martin Luther King Jr." Vox, January 21, 2019. https://www.vox.com/identities/2018/4/4/17193286/martin-luther-king-assassination-50th-anniversary-jeanne-theoharis.

Lynch, Shola. Afterword to *Unbought and Unbossed* by Shirley Chisholm, edited by Scott Simpson, 191–99. Charlotte, NC: Take Root Media, 2010.

Milne, Seumas. "Mandela Has Been Sanitised by Hypocrites and Apologists." *The Guardian*, December 11, 2013. https://www.theguardian.com/commentisfree/2013/dec/11/mandela-sanitised-hypocrites-apologists-apartheid.

National Women's Political Caucus. "About the Caucus." Accessed February 17, 2020. www.NWPC.org/about/.

New York City Economic Development Corporation. "She Built NYC." Accessed February 17, 2020. https://women.nyc/she-built-nyc/.

New York State Department of Parks, Recreation, and Historic Preservation. "Shirley Chisholm State Park." Accessed February 9, 2020. https://parks.ny.gov/parks/200/details.aspx.

Pierce, Ponchitta. "Problems of the Negro Intellectual." *Ebony Magazine*, August 1966.

Pressley, Ayanna (@ayannapressley). Twitter, December 17, 2018. https://twitter.com/AyannaPressley/status/1074776839598563328?.

Prospect Park Alliance. "A Monument to a Trailblazer Comes to Prospect Park." November 30, 2018. https://www.prospectpark.org/news-events/news/chisholm-monument-prospect-park/.

Scahill, Jeremy. "The Sanitizing of Martin Luther King and Rosa Parks." *Intercept*, October 8, 2017. https://theintercept.com/2017/10/08/the-sanitizing-of-martin-luther-king-and-rosa-parks/.

Steinhauer, Jennifer. "2019 Belongs to Shirley Chisholm." July 8, 2019, *New York Times*. https://www.nytimes.com/2019/07/06/sunday-review/shirley-chisholm-monument-film.html.

The Visionary Project. "Shirley Chisholm: The First Black Congresswoman." Accessed February 10, 2020. https://www.youtube.com/watch?v=Ia2ngZgo17U&t=36s.

Chapter 7

LENORA B. FULANI

Distinguished Postmodern Revolutionary

OMAR H. ALI AND TIERA C. MOORE

It would take nearly three-quarters of a century after the ratification of the 1920 US Constitution's Nineteenth Amendment, which gave women the right to vote nationally, before the first woman was able to get on the ballot in all fifty states, running for US president.[1] In 1988, developmental psychologist Dr. Lenora B. Fulani, a Black, working-class woman, achieved this. This accomplishment was attained only after gathering upward of 1.2 million signatures and winning over one dozen legal battles against largely Democratic and Republican Party–affiliated officials trying to keep her off the ballot. She ran as a political independent in order to challenge bipartisan control of the electoral process, bring out the voices of ordinary citizens, and bring innovation into policy making. Remarkably, not only was she the first woman in US history to get on the ballot in all fifty states in 1988, she was also the first African American to do so.[2]

A bold and courageous independent political leader, an innovator in the psychological field of human development, and an exceptionally effective educator and community organizer, Fulani has spent her life creating with others activities, organizations, and approaches, helping to develop and empower ordinary people, with particular attention to the poor. Her developmental/empowering practice of building new ways of being with others is inspired by the Black Power movement and grounded in the work and methodological insights of Frantz Fanon, Lev Vygotsky, Lois Holzman, and Fred Newman, while her practical-critical activity is simultaneously postmodern (challenging the tenets of modernism, and its overdetermining categories and epistemological modes of being) and revolutionary (the building of environments that are developmental, where people do things ahead of knowing how to do them). These two factors distinguish her as a postmodern revolutionary whose revolutionary activity is organizing masses of people who create their own development in our postmodern world.[3] This is her story.[4]

Born Lenora Branch on April 25, 1950 in Chester, Pennsylvania, Fulani grew up in the poor and working-class Black community of her birth, located to the southwest of Philadelphia. Her mother, Pearl Branch, was a domestic worker before becoming a nurse; her father, Charles Lee, was a baggage carrier on the Pennsylvania Railroad. As a child, Fulani briefly participated in the public-school desegregation process following the *Brown v. Board of Education* decision in 1954. Northern forms of institutional racial discrimination, whether in public schools or other public services, mirrored aspects of southern Jim Crow, often with tragic results: the ambulance service that was called when Fulani's father had a heart attack when she was twelve years old refused to come into her Black neighborhood. Neighbors scrambled to carry her father to the hospital on a makeshift stretcher, but he died on the way. Fulani's response to such fatal consequences of poverty and racism was to become active in her community. A youth leader in the Black Baptist Church, she decided in her teens that she wanted to become a psychologist to help those in her community deal with their emotional pain—"the humiliation, the anguish, and the self-destructive rage that went with being black and poor and powerless in white America."[5] Fulani was driven to figure out a path out of the emotional destruction she saw around her. In her autobiographical account *The Making of a Fringe Candidate*, she recounts the challenges she faced growing up and discusses the women who supported her development. One such woman was Phyllis Bolding, about whom Fulani wrote, "One of my great teachers [was] a brilliant working-class black woman who died of racism and poverty long before her time . . . when I first met Phyllis, I was as yet unable to demand that middle-class black people not disdain the black poor, or to demand that poor black people provide leadership despite their humiliation. In knowing Phyllis I learned what I needed to do. I will always be deeply thankful to her for that lesson."[6]

Reflecting on her own history, Fulani wrote about how in 1967 she went to Hofstra University in New York on a scholarship. She entered "with high hopes, expecting that in psychology I would find a tool for dealing with and transforming the violence, the family disintegration, the drug and alcohol abuse and the insanity that had destroyed so many people I knew and loved."[7] But what she found in college were tools and methods that were limited and out of sync with who she was and where she came from. "The institution of traditional psychology," Fulani notes, "which did contain a strong liberal and humane tradition, nevertheless embodied all the biases of the rest of our Euro-centric, patriarchal, capitalist society: it was racist, it was sexist, it was anti-poor—not merely in its content but *in its method*, in its very mode of comprehending who human beings are" (emphasis added).[8]

In 1979, the Black feminist Audre Lorde spoke to the question of method when she offered a critique of white feminists for using what she called "the master's tools." Lorde argued that whether self-consciously or not, white feminists were reproducing patriarchal forms of oppression by using old conceptual tools, now directed toward women "who stand outside the circle of this society's definition of acceptable women ... those of us who are poor, who are lesbians, who are Black, who are older."[9] Several years later, the poet and author Alice Walker spoke of making "a world in which we could all flourish."[10] So, if the master's tools can't be used to dismantle the master's house, what tools are needed to build a world in which we can all flourish? Fulani would answer this over the coming decades through the intellectual and political journey she forged, starting with the Black Power movement in the late 1960s and into her college years.

Fulani would draw similar conclusions to Lorde's about the limits of the available tools: "With growing dismay," Fulani writes, "I began to understand that psychology, while purporting to be for and about human beings, actually reflected and validated the values, concerns, and point of view of particular human beings: white, middle class men."[11] In contrast to some Black feminist discussions about the largely exclusive leadership role of Black women in the making of a new world, Fulani began to see that no one group of people was necessarily in the best position to end oppression or promote the development of all people, but ending oppression required the development of all people. Even poor Black women had particular experiences and insights to offer. The path she pursued was not academic but practical-critical: building programs to facilitate human development using the most advanced approaches, practices, and breakthroughs in organizing and empowering diverse poor, working-class, and middle-class communities.[12]

As a teenager, Fulani became swept up in the cultural current of the Black Power movement, which captured the hearts, minds, and energies of young Black men and women across the nation. In particular, she was inspired by the writings of Frantz Fanon. Fanon, the Martinican psychiatrist and revolutionary who treated French soldiers and Algerian rebels while directing the mental ward of a hospital during Algeria's bloody war for independence, later wrote about the "psychology of the oppressed."[13] As Fulani describes, "Here was a black psychiatrist—obviously brilliant, obviously 'political'—who was actually talking about black people! And it seemed to me that he was talking about us as who we really are: the colonized, the oppressed, wretched of the earth who had nothing to lose but our chains. Eagerly, I read everything Fanon had written."[14] After graduation—and changing her last name to Fulani, the name of a nomadic people in West Africa, in order to reflect her sense of Black pride—she continued her studies at Columbia University's Teachers

College, where she wrote her master's thesis on Fanon and his psychology of the oppressed.

Fulani was particularly interested in Fanon's description in *Black Skin, White Masks* and the ways in which "colonized people internalize their oppression, turning the oppressor's contempt and scorn into self-hatred." She was also interested in his insights in *The Wretched of the Earth*, about how "European psychological concepts and categories could not help the colonized psychotic . . . nor, for that matter, the 'theoretically' emotionally healthy person living under colonial domination."[15] Fanon's clinically based insights were critical for Fulani in that they spoke about the oppression of *all* people. However, over the course of a number of years, she came to see Fanon's limits. "Fanon's books, in which his passionately held views are set forth in eloquent language burning with righteous anger toward the slave master and compassion for the slave, are among the most persuasive political indictments of racism ever written," writes Fulani. "Yet I [eventually came] to believe that Fanon—who continues to be an inspiration for me . . . was profoundly mistaken in many of his ideas about psychology." She explains: "Although he deeply desired to create a genuine psychology of the oppressed, Fanon himself was unable to produce one. [Ultimately,] his practice was carried out within the confines of . . . the institution of psychology/psychiatry—which did not allow him to go beyond it."[16] Fulani had spent several years working within traditional academic institutions and research centers, holding on to Fanon (quite literally carrying his books). But it was not until she had begun to work outside of the institution of psychology, building nontraditional community-based programs, that she arrived at her understanding of Fanon's limits. It was an understanding that would emerge over time while pursuing a more traditional research path.[17]

She continued with her studies, completing a master's degree at Columbia University Teachers College and then pursuing a doctorate. In 1984 she received her PhD in developmental psychology at the Graduate Center of the City University of New York. Her dissertation, "Children's Understanding of Number Symbols in Formal and Informal Contexts," was an exploration of the ways in which poor Black children learn mathematics inside and outside of school. It reflected her growing interest in the discoveries of the early twentieth-century Russian methodologist Lev Vygotsky, whose work in education and psychology she had been introduced to as a researcher at Rockefeller University during the mid-1970s. At Rockefeller, Fulani specialized in the interplay between social environments and learning, with a particular focus on African Americans. Increasingly she questioned the value of efforts to reform traditional psychology—including Black, feminist, and gay psychologies—when those very reform efforts perpetuated key features of it, such as labeling and identities.[18] Nevertheless, the Rockefeller laboratory appeared to be a promising site for the study of nontraditional approaches to human development. Michael Cole, the lab's director, had created a research method based on his studies in West Africa and Central America in which the learning skills of nonliterate people could be identified in the context of their everyday lives. In the US, Cole was seeking to apply this principal of "ecological validity" to people who were "not assimilated into the mainstream of middle class American cultural, economic, and social life." Applying this theory, Fulani's job was to study Black children in out-of-school contexts, specifically city playgrounds. She notes, "[At the time] I was convinced that in this cross-cultural approach there was at least the potential for creating a black psychology."[19] Her hope for a new psychology that could be relevant—that is, of developmental value—to poor and working-class African Americans was short-lived. Soon, she would learn of the nonpsychological (indeed, antipsychological, nonindividual, and truly socially based) approach to human development that was being pioneered by Fred Newman and the person who would become his chief intellectual collaborator, Lois Holzman.[20]

At Rockefeller, Fulani met Holzman, who had recently received her PhD in developmental psychology from Columbia University and was hired by Cole as part of a team of talented young researchers to do innovative context- and culture-specific research in the United States based on the premise that cognitive processes are cultural and social. Cole had been responsible for having Vygotsky's work translated into English, which was then published by Harvard University Press.[21] Holzman would be significantly influenced by the work of Vygotsky through Cole, her mentor at the time. Vygotsky created several developmental concepts based on his work in the Soviet Union in the late 1920s and 1930s—in the tumultuous years following that nation's civil war, in which hundreds of thousands of children were orphaned. Today, Vygotsky's best-known and taught concept in graduate programs in education and psychology in the United States is "the zone of proximal development," in which he describes the social processes through which children develop. His understanding of how development takes place was in sharp contrast to psychologist Jean Piaget's view of development as taking place in necessary and fixed stages—the view that dominates much of clinical psychology and education today.[22]

Born a generation before Fanon, and in a very different part of the world, Vygotsky nevertheless bore certain similarities to the Martinican: both were Marxists whose lives were steeped in the revolutionary politics of their respective times and places—Vygotsky in the wake of the Bolshevik Revolution, Fanon in the midst of Martinique's colonial French hold and Algeria's war for independence. Vygotsky, like Fanon, was equally driven to create a new and relevant psychology, not for "the wretched of the earth," but the "new human being," as part of building a humanistic socialist society. However, unlike Fanon's humanistic reforms (including desegregating the psychiatric ward he directed and prohibiting the use of straightjackets, helping to transform the authoritarian structure of his hospital into a therapeutic community), Vygotsky's work took place at a time when the institution of psychology had not yet been fully consolidated.

Vygotsky, whose work was largely suppressed in the Soviet Union after his death, identified the task of creating a new developmental psychology, not simply adding new content into existing categories, but searching for an appropriate method to study human life. Fulani would write, "Human beings, Vygotsky pointed out, cannot study ourselves in the same way that we study stars and mountains, atoms and quanta, bacteria and dolphins.... For [as Karl Marx points out] we are not only shaped by our environments; we are unique in that we also create and recreate the environments that shape us."[23] Marx's dialectical approach would shape Vygotsky, as it would Fulani, through Holzman and Newman. As Vygotsky writes in *Mind and Society*, "The search for method becomes one of the most important problems of the entire enterprise of understanding the uniquely human forms of psychological activity. In this case, the method is simultaneously prerequisite and product, *the tool and the result* of the study" (emphasis added).[24] For Newman and Holzman, nothing short of a developmental method that is both "a tool and result" can be properly applied to the study of human beings and our development.

Holzman and Fulani, coming of age a generation after Fanon, and each influenced by the progressive politics of the 1960s, were also looking for a radically humane and relevant psychology. Vygotsky offered a methodological direction. But it was not until Holzman introduced Vygotsky to Newman, the Stanford University–trained philosopher of science, writes Fulani, that Vygotsky's methodological insights were qualitatively advanced. This would be done through years of work creating on-the-ground programs in poor and working-class communities—that is, among "the wretched of the earth," about whom Fanon so poetically, passionately, and powerfully wrote.

Following the completion of her PhD, Fulani decided to work with Newman and Holzman in creating their approach to human development. This work, grounded in the ideas of Marx and Vygotsky and significantly advanced by Newman's insights on both, would transform over time into a "cultural-performatory" approach to human development. In the areas of psychology and education, Fulani worked with Newman, Holzman, and others to create a performance-based clinical approach to curing emotional pain, which they called social therapy.[25] Holzman, building on Newman's unique understanding of Vygotsky as well as his appreciation of the Austrian-British philosopher Ludwig Wittgenstein's contributions on language play, and, later, the use of performance and theater, would help shape Fulani's therapeutic and supplementary education programs.

Fulani's intellectual growth and development over the course of three decades may be seen in the transformation of the ways in which she articulated her work. In the mid-1980s, she offered a politically progressive critique of psychology, with echoes of Fanon, infused with a Black cultural nationalism, and combined with a socialist collectivist orientation; two and a half decades later, she expressed a postmodern revolutionary approach to human development, drawing on a range of methodological advancements *and* a quarter century of creating on-the-ground programs with tens of thousands of people. An example of her earlier articulation may be seen in her article "Poor Women of Color Do Great Therapy," published in 1988 (the same year she became the first woman and the first African American to get on the ballot in all fifty states running for president). In the piece, Fulani describes her therapy practice among mostly poor and working-class women. She writes:

> The Harlem Institute for Social Therapy and Research, located on 125th Street . . . serves, in my opinion, as a model of how to build among the black, Latino, Jewish, lesbian and gay, and other oppressed populations of this country a deeply needed . . . empowering sense of community based on the power of and love for the oppressed. The sense of community is not new to my ancestors. African American historians teach us of African communalism, the collective practice and spirit that dominated the work and lifestyles of our people . . . shaped into a critical tool in their respective fights for freedom and justice.[26]

After several years of operation, Fulani's Harlem Institute along with other therapy institutes she was affiliated with in poor and working-class communities were no longer sustainable.

The stigma of therapy was (and continues to be) too great in these communities. The failure of such efforts led Fulani and her colleagues to focus their developmental work on a larger scale, through the inner-city youth programs that they had already created and that were growing in response to great demand. The biggest of these programs, the New York City–based All Stars Talent Show Network, already involved thousands of Black and Latino youth each year. The All Star Talent Network's supplementary education program, which Fulani helped found in New York in 1981, was grounded in and informed by the early writings of Marx, Vygotsky, and Wittgenstein. Fulani also helped found the All Stars' sister program, the Development School for Youth, a leadership training school for young people based in New York, Newark, Chicago, and Los Angeles. Over the next years, the All Stars would expand into the largest developmental after-school program in the nation.[27]

Fulani, an organizer of people actively creating their own development (as opposed to development happening to people in a passive way), would neither let identity politics nor partisanship guide who she worked with and how. That is, her understanding of and commitment to people and their development was not limited to any particular grouping of people, as she was herself the product of various traditions and influences: early on, Black cultural nationalism and progressive politics; later, Marx, Vygotsky, and Wittgenstein, principally through Newman and Holzman.

Those involved in Fulani's various projects learned to practice an innovative performatory approach to human development pioneered by Newman.[28] This performatory approach rests on an understanding that participants (indeed, all people) relate to others and themselves as capable of doing things they do not yet know how to do. As Fulani describes, "It's in *performing as who we aren't* in a social environment—with other human beings who, surprisingly, support us by accepting that we are doing what we don't know how to do—that we make the ordinary and quite miraculous leap from baby talk to the real thing."[29] The developmental approach focuses on people self-consciously growing, instead of critiquing (or describing) people being insufficiently developed, as with the dominant practices in psychology and education of diagnosing/labeling people, young and old. Fulani and her colleagues' various projects—the All Stars Talent Show Network, along with the East Side Institute, the Development School for Youth, Youth Onstage!, and Operation Conversation: Cops and Kids, among others—are an integral part of her lifelong efforts to help people grow and develop. In these ways and in many respects she has—through her practice—come to redefine what it means to be a progressive in our postmodern world. And she would do this primarily with Holzman and Newman, among other close associates.

Holzman, a progressive middle-class Jewish woman, whose academic training included not only developmental psychology at Columbia but also linguistics at Brown University, kept one foot in academia for years. She taught at Empire State College in New York and was active in academic organizations, bringing in work for herself and Newman, while at the same time building programs outside of academia. For example, she served as director of the Barbara Taylor School, a Vygotskian-based elementary school, for twelve years. By the late 1990s she had left her teaching position at Empire to work full-time in advancing the developmental projects she and her colleagues had created, serving as an international ambassador for the developmental approach and helping to train and collaborate with hundreds of fellow developmental practitioners, including clinical psychologists, therapists, social workers, and artists around the world. Newman, on the other hand, a working-class Jew from the Bronx who had received his PhD in analytical philosophy from Stanford University in 1962, had long since left academia.[30]

As Fulani recounts, "In 1968 [Newman] gave up on a promising career as a professional philosopher. Academia had also given up on him, because he insisted on giving A's to all of his students, in order to help the men stay out of the war in Vietnam, and to protect his female students from discrimination. Newman became a community organizer, trying to create something that would be of value to people as a whole; in 1970, working as a counselor in a drug rehabilitation center, he observed that his clients were primarily being related to as prisoners who had committed a crime, not as people in emotional pain who were capable of creating their own growth.[31] Understanding the value of relating to all people as capable of creating their own growth, Newman partnered with Fulani to create a mass project impacting the lives of tens of thousands of people.

The All Stars, founded by Fulani and Newman in 1983, serves as a developmental youth program and is made possible by grassroots fundraising, mostly carried out by adult volunteers. This program involves tens of thousands of children and teenagers, as well as tens of thousands of others (parents, caretakers, and friends) who are directly or indirectly impacted by the activity of the young people. These young people, primarily from poor and working-class Black and Latino communities, produce talent shows in their neighborhoods. They not only dance, sing, and rap in these shows, but most critically, they take responsibility for producing all aspects of the shows. Everyone in the "auditions" makes it into the show, though not without certain kinds of demands placed on them. The young people work with adults from the All Stars, often veterans of the program, and from their own communities, and find locations for the shows, usually high school and junior high school auditoriums. They also sell the tickets, stage manage, usher, emcee, run the lighting and sound boards, and maintain security. Additionally, the young people build the audience for the shows and mentor younger children in the program—an important component of the developmental project. Fulani describes, "In the process [of these activities], these young people not only learn all sorts of technical skills, they also learn to relate to kids from other neighborhoods, to work with adults and to interact with their community's institutions (schools, churches, block associations, etc.). In short, they create an environment in which they can perform as leaders, and most of them, in fact, do."[32]

As the All Stars significantly took off in poor and working-class communities, social therapy was also practiced in less poor and working-class settings, always with the inclusion of a great range of people, in terms of gender, class, ethnicity, race, and sexual orientation. In many ways, social therapy groups, where a therapeutic conversation is carried out each week, are themselves a kind of "emotional performance, in which the group provides an environment for people to express their emotionality in new ways," as described by one participant.³³ According to Fulani, "The social therapy group is . . . an environment in which people who are more, and less, emotionally skilled participate together in the conjoint activity of creating an environment where they can get help with their emotional pain by creating a new emotionality. They don't create the environment for the purpose of getting help in a tool-for-result, means-to-an-end way; rather, the historical activity of building the group is what we take to be therapeutic."³⁴ Here, the radical nature of her work departs from identity-based therapeutic approaches and projects. She writes, "By analogy, we are not seeking to create a [therapy] for a class, however defined: working class people, black people, the wretched of the earth. In our view, to do so would be to capitulate to the existing societal power arrangement which determine identity, regardless of whether that identity is inferior (as in racist theories of intelligence) or superior (as some Black nationalists and some radical feminists suggest). This is the trap that ensnared even so brilliant and dedicated a revolutionary as [Fanon], who defined the oppressed solely in terms of their oppression and even idealized it."³⁵

Fulani created other projects infused with the methodology (a posture and practice) of relating to people as capable of creating their own growth. The Development School for Youth, founded in 1997, is a supplementary education program that offers social and internship experiences in different work settings. Unlike the All Stars, the Development School for Youth is a twelve-week program with two cycles each year. Smaller in size than the All Stars, it reaches several hundred young people each year. The program trains young people—using performance—to "enter the workforce, pursue educational opportunities, and face challenges in new ways." Both these and Fulani's other projects do not rely on government funding or foundation support, but on the contributions of thousands of people. They also, most critically, do not rely on participants knowing how to do things before doing them. The independent funding of these programs allows for their continuity and integrity in the community and, because of this, gives them their capacity to actively incorporate new ideas and practices—even as they inform the cultural-performatory, nonepistemological approach that guides them.³⁶

Fulani is also responsible for other programs, such as Operation Conversation: Cops and Kids, which was initiated in 2006 after the police shooting of a young Black man, Sean Bell, in Queens, New York. This program involves a series of dialogues and performance-based workshops with police and inner-city young people to improve and develop their relationship. In each of these programs, young people are related to as developmentally ahead of themselves. By relating (which is a type of self-conscious "performance") to the young people as capable of carrying out tasks in advance of knowing how to do them, the young people and the police grow and develop together.³⁷

By focusing on creating developmental environments by relating to people as developmentally ahead of themselves, Fulani questions "the common assumption that socially constructed identity and identity politics were and remain a 'natural' stage in the cultural-political process [of people's development]." She continues, "Coming as I do from a working-class African American family and having become a Marxist after I developed a strong black identity, I find Newman and Holzman's methodological challenges extremely helpful in understanding both the pulls of identity (especially racial identity) and how it is that, more often than not, I successfully resist them in my work, whether that is supporting black and Latino inner city youth to create new performances of themselves or working within the mostly white [independent political movement] to restructure the American political process."[38]

Fulani goes into a full discussion of race, identity, and epistemology: "Understood culturally rather than politically, the nationalism I embraced as a college student is the dominant tradition in the African American community. Nationalist political beliefs—such as the establishment of a separate Black state or a return to Africa [most widely expressed in the early twentieth century through Marcus Garvey's 'Back to Africa' movement]—are not widely held in the African American community, but a strong nationalist bias is apparent in the widespread belief that African American culture is of great importance and must be expressed in a multitude of ways in daily life." She continues by delving into the consequences of racism by noting that "racism, of course, historically forced the African American community to create its own institutions (e.g., Black colleges and Black churches) and foisted on it a constant awareness of racial identification."[39] The roots of the particular forms of racism that would develop in the US, born of the transatlantic slave trade, would be institutionalized through the racial codification of slavery in colonial America. This would be overthrown by the Civil War and the abolition of slavery but reinstituted in new forms under Jim Crow.

Despite this, Fulani describes the ways in which African Americans hold on to "race": "Since the post-integration 1960s, the African American community has purposefully perpetuated its over-identification with race. This kind of cultural nationalism goes beyond knowing one's history and taking pride in it. It entails a set of postures, attitudes and beliefs—for example, that the way to positively change institutions is to increase [the] Black presence in them—as well as language, gestures, dress, forms of music." As she states, these "have become identified as 'behaving Black' and, therefore, in this racially identified context, hip and cool. Parents implicitly and explicitly teach their children this nationalistic model as 'the way to be' in the world."[40]

Fulani speaks to this issue as a developmental psychologist, a Black woman, and a mother of two. She continues: "The problem with this model . . . is that it's culturally and politically naïve. [Such] postures, attitudes, and norms . . . are less than helpful in navigating the complex network of societal institutions in our multi-cultural society." Pivoting, Fulani points out that "ironically, while many black identified cultural postures and attitudes have been adopted by white Americans to enhance their hipness, and by major clothing manufacturers to market a cultivated hip/black image to both white and black consumers, the [poor and working-class] African American community, by virtue of the self-imposed narrowness of its cultural nationalism, has largely been unable to take advantage of this phenomenon." She concludes: "The contradiction between the cultural nationalism of the African American community and its desire to see its children educated and succeed in mainstream culture is something most parents have not yet come to terms with."[41]

Drawing on the work of the philosopher Kwame Anthony Appiah in addressing these questions, Fulani offers a poignant critique of our culturally held views about "race": "Like many scholars, Appiah argues that there is no such thing as race. Going beyond showing that there is no biological evidence for racial differences, he claims that race is not cultural either." She next states that "the move to identify racial differences as cultural, according to Appiah, falsely suggests that people in one cultural grouping are the same as each other and different from people in other cultural groupings. Racism is then understood as stemming from cultural misunderstandings."[42]

For Fulani, racism is not a matter of cultural differences or misunderstandings but of political power. Moreover, the problem with identity (racial and otherwise) is that it "becomes categorical, defining and rigid, signaling association with particular political or social agendas and particular beliefs." This is a pushback against modernist categorization and epistemology. She agrees with the psychologist Kenneth Gergen, who, like Appiah, writes persuasively of "the destructive effects of identity politics, as identity-identified interest groups compete with each other for legislative initiatives and social policy on the basis of presumed shared characteristics and on their own behalf." Appiah, writes Fulani, hints at "a different methodological foundation for human social life . . . a life where we are not so narrowly defined . . . but are rather simultaneously 'who we are' *and* 'who we are not.'"[43]

For Fulani, assuming an identity (different from a role, in the theatrical sense) is therefore a static, conservative form of life. Identities, in this respect, are tools *for* particular results, not tools *and* results, allowing for transformation—that is, development. The developmental approach focuses on people self-consciously growing instead of critiquing (or describing) people being insufficiently developed, as in the dominant practices in psychology and education of diagnosing and labeling people.

While Fulani's All Stars is well known and regarded in inner cities across New York and New Jersey and in many other parts of the country—with more demand for the program than organizers can meet—it is less known among academics, even in psychology and education. Over the years, however, a number of high-profile Black scholars in psychology, education, and African American studies have publicly discussed and praised the positive, developmental impact of the All Stars Project Inc. (the umbrella organization for Fulani's various supplementary education programs).

The eminent Black psychologist Edmund Gordon wrote an assessment of the All Stars for Columbia University's Institute for Urban and Minority Education, concluding, "While the goal of the programs is the development of young people, benefits accrue to those who are deliverers of services as well as to those who are the designated beneficiaries, creating a symbiotic relationship between the giver and the receiver."[44] After doing a survey of after-school programs across the nation, Harvard University's Henry Louis Gates Jr. called the All Stars, and specifically the Development School for Youth, the best supplementary education program he had observed firsthand: "Of all the projects that I have examined throughout this country . . . none has had better demonstrable results," reported Gates.[45] Finally, New York University's Derrick Bell discusses the success of the All Stars programs in his *Silent Covenant: Brown v. Board of Education and the Unfulfilled Hopes of Racial Reform*. In the book he notes, "Both [the All Stars and the Development School for Youth], supervised by Dr. Lenora Fulani, are privately funded supplementary-education ventures that serve tens of thousands of inner-city kids each year. . . . [H]er programs focus on issues of development. . . . They relate to people [as being able] to perform ahead of themselves. . . . [T]hey are taught how to create performances on stage as a way of learning to perform in life."[46]

Alongside Fulani's work in social therapeutics, the All Stars, the Development School for Youth, and Cops and Kids: Operation Conversation, she has worked to build a movement that challenges the bipartisan control of the electoral process, a system that stymies innovation in policy and suppresses the voices of millions of independents.

Fulani has long urged African Americas to diversify their political options as a way of both gaining greater leverage with elected officials and creating new alliances that could take the country in more developmental, democratic directions. At the core of her call was the need for political reform in the form of "fair elections." In 1988, running on the New Alliance Party ticket, Fulani campaigned under the slogan "Two Roads Are Better Than One." Defying convention, she ran with six vice presidential candidates, representing different constituencies, including Black, white, Latino, and Native American running mates. Fulani's "Two Roads" strategy encouraged voters to support Rev. Jesse Jackson in the Democratic primaries and then to support her in the general election in the event that Jackson did not receive the Democratic nomination.

During the fall of 1988, not only did Fulani get on the ballot in all fifty states (and the District of Columbia), but she also became the first African American woman to receive primary matching funds. She was beginning to peel away elements of key constituencies of the Democratic Party, which had (and continues to) assume the role of the sole electoral vehicle for progressive politics. The New Alliance Party emerged as the nation's fourth-largest party that year. Underscoring the purpose of her run for office was her officially registered name, "Lenora B. Fulani's Committee for Fair Elections," whereas the standard registered name for a presidential campaign is the candidate's name followed by "for President." Fulani's campaign made clear the purpose of what they were doing, which was focused on political reform.

The electoral playing field in the US is tilted heavily against third-party and independent candidates. Getting on the ballot in all fifty states had required Fulani's campaign to collect more than thirty times the number of nominating petition signatures than either of the major party presidential candidates. Moreover, Fulani was excluded from each of the presidential debates, and the media paid little attention to her campaign. Fulani and her associates in the New Alliance Party would lobby Congress and state assemblies, as well as file multiple lawsuits to challenge ballot access restrictions, among other electoral inequities. As *Ballot Access News* editor Richard Winger noted in 1992, "The New Alliance Party has done more for ballot access reform that anyone else."[47]

Instead of being supported by white liberals and Black Democrats for her work in communities of color, Fulani came under fire for challenging their party's claim as the party of the poor and working class—that is, the party of African Americans, the most loyal constituency of the Democratic Party. During the buildup to Fulani's 1988 presidential campaign, the Democratic Party took targeted measures to ostracize her and undermine her efforts to challenge Democratic authority in Black and Latino communities. Despite repeated attacks and accusations, Fulani continued to build avenues for independent politics, and within four years the nation would witness an independent voter revolt on a scale unprecedented in American history.[48]

Fulani would run with the New Alliance Party, among other progressive third parties, including the Peace and Freedom Party in California and the predominantly Black United Citizens Party in South Carolina. Approximately 250,000 people voted for her as a third-party or independent candidate that year. Other African Americans had launched presidential campaigns (from George Edwin Taylor in 1904 to civil rights leader Revered Jesse Jackson in 1984); other women had run for president (from women's suffragist Victoria Woodhull in 1872 to New York congresswoman Shirley Chisholm in 1972); none appeared on the ballot for president in every state of the nation. Fulani's 1988 campaign was therefore a milestone in terms of gender and race. But when asked whether it was more difficult running for president being Black or being a woman, Fulani responded by saying that it was more difficult running as an independent. Getting on the ballot across the country required extensive grassroots fundraising and logistical coordination, and only after gathering nearly 1.2 million nominating petition signatures and winning eleven lawsuits against election authorities did her campaign achieve the task.[49]

A pioneer in the creation of "Black and independent alliances" for political reform (largely disaffected Black Democrats working with white independents), Fulani forged the development of a postmodern independent Black leadership in the United States. This new leadership—most powerfully expressed in Senator Barack Obama during his 2008 presidential campaign in his reaching out to independents and Republicans, in addition to rank-and-file Democrats—is less identity based and ideologically driven than traditional Black politics, much of which had become tied to the Democratic Party since the mid-1960s. Instead, the postmodern Black leadership that Fulani developed two decades before Obama launched his presidential campaign was focused on reforming the electoral process itself. The creation of Black and independent alliances for political reform in 1988 took more discernable form during Fulani's second presidential campaign in 1992. Each of her campaigns was designed to spur the growth of independent politics nationally toward breaking up the bipartisan election monopoly of the Democratic and Republican Parties.

In 1992 Fulani launched her campaign by reaching out to white independents in New Hampshire; she would urge voters to also support Texan billionaire Ross Perot, who entered the race as an independent. He personally invested tens of millions of dollars to promote his candidacy (nearly $70 million in all). Fulani welcomed the opportunity presented by Perot's entrance into the race to build a movement of and for independent voters, even though she was politically progressive (on the left) and Perot was conservative (center-right). This campaign was "postmodern" in the sense that Fulani was willing to break ideological boundaries and create an on-the-ground pro-reform coalition between her multiracial progressive networks of support (many of which were Black) and the largely white and conservative networks of support that Perot had helped to inspire.

In the wake of the 1992 election, Fulani sought to build organizations that could carry on the desire for political independence and political reform that Perot had tapped into and helped to unleash. Over the next sixteen years she would build networks of independent activists around the country and promote independent and insurgent political reform–oriented candidates. In presidential campaigns, she supported Perot in 1996, John Hagelin (Natural Law Party) in 2000, Ralph Nader (Green Party) in 2004, and Barack Obama in 2008. Throughout the 1990s and into the 2000s, Fulani also spearheaded multiple campaigns to promote structural political reforms, including term limits, ballot access, initiatives and referendums, nonpartisan municipal elections, and open primaries, all designed to empower voters. Among the different political parties and organizations that she cofounded were the Patriot Party, the Reform Party, the Independence Party of New York, and the Committee for a Unified Independent Party—each of which was used to try to build networks and coalitions across a wide geographic, ideological, and demographic spectrum of Americans.[50]

In 2008 an unprecedented opportunity arose to try and secure political reforms with the insurgent presidential candidacy of then-senator Barack Obama. Commenting on the movement surrounding Obama, Fulani noted, "New political voices are emerging, searching for a new paradigm, new partnerships and a new way of doing politics." Black independents, particularly those allied with Fulani, were poised to support Obama. That year, Fulani's postmodern Black leadership-in-the-making was focused on gathering independent support for Obama's campaign in open primary and caucus states to advance political reform. Through a combination of African American and white independent support, Obama secured the Democratic Party nomination. He won over a dozen caucuses and open primary states, inclusion caucuses in Iowa, Minnesota, Texas, and Washington, DC, and open primaries in Alabama, Georgia, Mississippi, North Dakota, South Carolina, Vermont, Virginia, and Wisconsin. Independents, many of whom were prompted directly by Fulani and her associates across the country, laid the groundwork for Obama's victory; they had broken significantly in favor of him in the primaries and then in the general election (with an eight-point margin). Meanwhile, African Americans had overwhelmingly supported Obama in the general election (at rates of 95 percent and above).

Today, upward of 42 percent of Americans self-identify as politically independent (neither Democrat nor Republican) including a quarter of African Americans—despite the majority of Black voters remaining tied to the Democratic Party. In contrast to traditional Black politicians (focused on gaining liberal white support tied to the Democratic Party, to the exclusion of conservative white independents), Fulani had long been forging Black and independent alliances on the ground to push for political reform. Obama would adopt a similar approach in reaching out to Americans across the partisan, ideological, and racial divide.

Within the first decade of the new millennium, a contemporary Black and independent alliance had asserted itself. While Obama did not acknowledge Fulani for her pioneering work in either breaking the fifty-state ballot barrier as an African American, her creation of previous Black and independent alliances, or her role in the alliances that helped to produce his victories in the primaries, *New York Magazine* would go on to characterize Obama as the nation's first "Independent president"—that is, in addition to him being the nation's first African American president.

Fulani's postmodernization of Black politics through the development of Black and independent alliances has opened new possibilities—new ways for African Americans to engage in electoral politics. It was a process that developed over the course of twenty years, and it not only contributed to Obama wining the White House but pointed to future directions in American politics, with a steady increase of Black independence. A recent poll conducted by Tufts University reveals that upward of 44 percent of eighteen- to twenty-four-year-olds identify as independent; meanwhile, Pew Research Center surveys show that over one in four African Americans across all age groups are consistently declaring their independence.[51]

Although Fulani remains under-recognized for her work in the electoral arena, some Black leadership figures have acknowledged her and her accomplishments. In 2006, Rev. Al Sharpton—who remains a Democrat—spoke about Fulani's role in developing independent politics in the nation and challenging Black political orthodoxy:

> I've known Dr. Fulani for a long time. And she and I have agreed to disagree on any number of issues. But you know, there is a growing sense of independent voters in this country, any poll shows that. And one of the things that I think a lot of the media here misses, is Dr. Fulani rightfully is one of the pioneers of that, particularly in the African American community.... Twenty years ago, when [she] started talking about independence, most people in African American political circles thought they were crazy. Now there is a growing trend.[52]

To be sure, there are different ways of understanding Fulani and what she has done. One way of understanding her work in the electoral arena is—in the Vygotskyian formulation—as both a "tool and result" of her overall activities as a postmodernist. That is, her approach to building independent politics reflects her postmodern revolutionary practice, in that she seeks to create developmental, empowering environments where people can go (and grow) beyond themselves by bringing seemingly disparate individuals or constituencies together through shared activities. In politics, the shared activity she has focused on has been reforming the electoral process as opposed to simply promoting individual platform issues such as health care, defense, housing, education, and the like. Fulani has broken convention after convention as an

African American leader by pushing the boundaries of what is socially and politically acceptable, in the processes creating new political possibilities.

Fulani continues to build her supplementary education programs and advocate on behalf of independent voters. For her innovative educational work, she was featured in the documentary *America Behind the Color Line*, a PBS/BBS production by Harvard University's Henry Louis Gates Jr. Her programs have also received acclaim from some of the most powerful and diverse people in politics (including former congressman Charles Rangel, former president George H. W. Bush, former New York governor George Pataki, and former New York City mayor Michael Bloomberg). Most of the praise she receives, however, comes from the parents and family members of those who participate in her youth programs, seeing and experiencing the results more directly; business and community leaders concerned with the state of young people from inner cities have equally offered their praise and support over the years. Over the last two decades, Fulani has appeared as a guest on hundreds of radio, television, and cable news programs. Her social and political commentaries have also appeared in a range of daily newspapers as "This Way for Black Empowerment," or other op-ed columns. She is the author of the political autobiography *The Making of a Fringe Candidate*, the editor of *The Psychopathology of Everyday Racism and Sexism*, and a contributing author to *Postmodern Psychologies, Societal Practice, and Political Life*. But when it comes to African Americans and the US presidency, Fulani's most lasting contribution—beyond getting on the ballot in all fifty states—may very well be to have pioneered the creation of postmodern independent Black leadership. This new leadership includes hundreds of Black men and women whose names scarcely appear in print— people like David Cherry, Dr. Jessie Fields, Mariah Hunt, Stephanie Orosco, Brittany Rodman, Jamela Stevens, Cindy Little, Aliyah Ruffin, Lisa Linnen, Janet Harrel, Alan Cox, Michelle McCleary, and Alvaader Frazier. Notably, a recent University of Chicago–affiliated survey reported that upward of 38 percent of eighteen- to thirty-six-year-old African Americans do not identify with the two major parties.[53]

Moving away from "the master's tools" (race, identity, epistemology) and creating tools-and-results instead—namely, carrying out performances/improvisation/play (an ontological shift, as opposed to an epistemological shift)—Fulani's postmodern revolutionary activity has contributed to making a world in which we can all flourish. Practical-critically, she has done this by operationalizing some of the most valuable insights regarding human development and power, with particular attention to Black, poor, and working-class communities.

At an education panel hosted by the National Action Network in New York City, Fulani spoke to a mostly Black audience about the importance of learning about and using various powerful breakthroughs in human development: "[In] international circles the conversation among educators, social scientists, and intellectuals is not about the consequences of underdevelopment... it is about scientific breakthroughs in human development." Here, she is responding to endless analyses and discussion about the "achievement gap" and Black and poor kids' underdevelopment. Instead, she wants to focus on how young people (all people) can grow and develop. She continues, "It's about the work of radical psychologists, such as Lev Vygotsky, who championed the idea that relating to children as 'a head taller' than they are, allows them to grow and to learn. It is about the work of unorthodox philosophers, like Ludwig Wittgenstein, whose thoroughgoing re-examination of philosophical assumptions buried philosophy."[54]

Vygotsky's discoveries include the ways in which human development is socially created through play, and that it is by relating to children ahead of themselves that they learn and grow. Fulani, with Newman and Holzman, would build on these critical insights. Meanwhile, Wittgenstein's breakthrough in philosophy was to shift focus from what words and sentences *mean* to the *activity* of making language and connecting with others. Fulani goes on to say, "It is about the theory and practice of my mentor, Dr. Fred Newman, whose teachings about the developmental powers of performance and the idea that growth is collective, rather than individual, have revolutionized standard approaches to development and helped me and others to create the All Stars Project." She concludes: "Now, I know what many of my Black sisters and brothers are already thinking, 'Dr. Fulani—Vygotsky, Wittgenstein, Newman are all *white*. What do their thinking, what do their breakthroughs, what do their science have anything to do with Black people?'" Here she takes a breath before saying, "Well, let me give you my answer as a Black educator, and a damned good one! What I want for our kids is not *Black* thinking, I want the *best* thinking. I want the most sophisticated approaches. I want the most advanced theories with the most qualitative practice. That's what I want, and that's what you should want. And that's what I demand for our communities, whether in East New York, or Dakar, or Port-au-Prince, or Beijing, or Rio."[55]

Fulani, as the mother of two adult children, grandmother to one grandchild, and teacher, mentor, and source of inspiration for thousands of everyday people (each, in their own ways, having done extraordinary things, big and small) has spent nearly four decades as a practitioner and builder of independent programs, projects, and organizations that challenge conventional approaches to education, therapy, culture, and politics. She has done this by creating, and training others in, new and developmental ways for people to be in the world and with each other. Through this, her practical-critical work in communities across the nation, especially in these uncertain times, makes her a distinguished postmodern revolutionary.

NOTES

1. Jim Crow—the local and state-sanctioned legal disfranchisement and segregation of African Americans—would prevent Black women from voting until the Voting Rights Act was passed in 1965, providing federal enforcement of Black voting rights. See Omar H. Ali, *In the Balance of Power: Independent Black Politics and Third Party Movements in the United States* 2nd ed. (Athens: Ohio University Press, 2020). The present chapter synthesizes and updates Omar H. Ali's "Lenora Branch Fulani: Challenging the Rules of the Game," in *African Americans and the Presidency: The Road to the White House*, ed. Bruce Glasrud and Cary D. Wintz (New York: Routledge, 2010), 129–46, and "Fulani's Tools and Results: Development as Black Empowerment?" *Palimpsest: A Journal on Women, Gender, and the Black International* 1, no. 1 (2012), 31–51.

2. Dr. Lenora Fulani preceded President Barack Obama by twenty years in getting on the ballot in all fifty states. Obama got on the ballot as the Democratic Party nominee in 2008; Congresswoman Shirley Chisolm did not appear on the ballot for president, but she pioneered Black women seeking the nation's highest office. Fulani ran to build a movement against the two major parties. See Ali, *In the Balance of Power*.

3. The word "revolutionary" is usually associated with the narrow seizing of political power or an idea or discovery that is transformative, as in the history of science. Here we take revolutionary as an activity that is developmental—that is, practical-critical activity that shapes and reshapes environments where people create their own development. See interview with Lois Holzman by Omar H. Ali and Nadja Cech in which Holzman notes, "Practical critical is the creating of something . . . and that something is at the same time a critique of what exists." *Yes, and Café* podcast recorded on September 20, 2019, https://news.uncg.edu/wp-content/uploads/2020/03/Yes-And-Cafe-Episode-1-Transcript.pdf.

4. On October 24, 2018, Omar H. Ali introduced Lenora Fulani, who offered the annual distinguished lecture for Lloyd International Honors College at the University of North Carolina at Greensboro, which was followed by a conversation between the two about Fulani's life. Fulani had also recounted some of her own story in her acceptance remarks at the 18th Annual Anti-Corruption Awards of the New York Independence Party in New York City two weeks earlier (remarks sent to Ali on October 18, 2018, by Fulani's long-time assistant Lisa Linnen).

5. Ali, "Fulani's Tools and Results," 34.
6. Fulani, *The Making of a Fringe Candidate*, dedication.
7. Fulani, "Fanon, Newman, and Class Psychology," 1.
8. Fulani, "Fanon, Newman, and Class Psychology," 1.
9. Lorde, "The Master's Tools," 112. As Lorde notes, "What does it mean when the tools of a racist patriarchy are used to examine the fruits of that same patriarchy? It means that only the most narrow perimeters of change are possible and allowable." Lorde, "The Mater's Tools," 110–11.
10. Walker, *In Search of Our Mother's Gardens*, 112, quoted in Ali, "Fulani's Tools and Results," 31.
11. Fulani, "Fanon, Newman, and Class Psychology," 1.
12. Newman and Holzman, "The Practice of Method," 142–72.

13. For a biographical account of Fanon, see Bulhan, *Frantz Fanon and the Psychology of the Oppressed*, 15–36; and Gordon, Sharpley-Whiting, and White, *Fanon*, 1–10.

14. Fulani, "Fanon, Newman, and Class Psychology," 2.

15. Fanon, *Black Skin, White Masks*, and *The Wretched of the Earth*.

16. Fulani, "Fanon, Newman, and Class Psychology," 5.

17. Ali, "Fulani's Tools and Results," 31–51.

18. Ali, "Lenora Branch Fulani," 129–46.

19. Fulani, "Fanon, Newman, and Class Psychology," 6.

20. Fulani, "Race, Identity, and Epistemology," 152, 156. For a discussion on the roots of creating the approach to human development practiced by Fulani and her colleagues, see Holzman, *Vygotsky at Work and Play*, 21–44. Fulani's other closest collaborator in the realm of independent politics, Jacqueline Salit, has written extensively about her. See Salit's *Independents Rising*.

21. Vygotsky, *Mind and Society*.

22. For biographical information on Vygotsky and a detailed analysis of his developmental concept of the "ZPD," see Newman and Holzman, *Lev Vygotsky*, 5–9, 52–70. Newman and Holzman offer a radical reinterpretation of this concept, challenging the dominant ways in which it is written about and taught.

23. Fulani, "Fanon, Newman, and Class Psychology," 9; Marx articulates this concept in the opening of his *Eighteenth Brumaire of Louis Bonaparte* as "Men make their own history, but they do not make it as they please . . . but under circumstances existing already, given and transmitted from the past." See McLellan, *Karl Marx*.

24. Vygotsky, *Mind and Society*, 65.

25. Newman and Holzman, *Unscientific Psychology*, 157–205.

26. Fulani, "Poor Women of Color Do Great Therapy," 111.

27. Ali, "Lenora Branch Fulani," 129–46.

28. Newman passed away in 2011. For an example of one of their last collaborations and the cultural-performatory approach, see Newman and Fulani, "Let's Pretend," 1–9.

29. Fulani, "Fanon, Newman, and Class Psychology," 9.

30. Fulani, "Fanon, Newman, and Class Psychology," 39.

31. Fulani, "Fanon, Newman, and Class Psychology," 39.

32. Fulani, "Race, Identity, and Epistemology," 152.

33. This description comes from "The Origins of Social Therapy" (New York City Social Therapy Group, 2011).

34. Fulani, "Fanon, Newman, and Class Psychology," 14.

35. Ali, "Fulani's Tools and Results," 42.

36. Fulani, "Race, Identity, and Epistemology," 152.

37. Ali, "Lenora Branch Fulani."

38. Fulani, "Race, Identity, and Epistemology," 152. For an in-depth discussion of class identity in relation to revolutionary transformation, see Newman and Holzman, "All Power to the Developing!," 8–23.

39. Omar H. Ali, "Fulani's Tools and Results: Development as Black Empowerment?," *Palimpsest: A Journal on Women, Gender, and the Black International* 1, no. 1 (2012): 31–51.

40. Ali, "Fulani's Tools and Results," 45.

41. Ali, "Fulani's Tools and Results," 44–45.

42. Ali, "Fulani's Tools and Results," 45.
43. Ali, "Fulani's Tools and Results," 45.
44. Gordon et al., "Changing the Script for Youth Development," 16.
45. "Bloomberg, Schumer, Gates Turn Out for All Stars," *New York Amsterdam News* (April 29–May 5, 2004).
46. Bell, *Silent Covenants*, 177–79.
47. Ali, "Lenora Branch Fulani," 134.
48. Ali, "Lenora Branch Fulani," 133–36.
49. Ali, "Lenora Branch Fulani," 129–46.
50. Ali, "Lenora Branch Fulani," 129–46.
51. Center for Information and Research on Civic Learning and Engagement, Tufts University, https://circle.tufts.edu/latest-research/young-peoples-ambivalent-relationship-political-parties; Pew Research Center, US Politics and Policy https://www.people-press.org/2018/03/20/1-trends-in-party-affiliation-among-demographic-groups/.
52. Salit, "The Color of the Independent Movement," 6.
53. Ali, *In the Balance of Power*; Ali et al., "College Independents Poll," 3–36; Gen Forward May 2019, Politics Toplines (Race & PID) in association with the University of Chicago, 31. http://genforwardsurvey.com/assets/uploads/2019/06/2019-05-May-Toplines-Politics-by-Race-and-PID_nonembargoed.pdf.
54. Transcribed from Lenora B. Fulani presentation at National Action Network education panel (April 15, 2010, New York City), http://www.youtube.com/watch?v=VQg7SniidD8.
55. Fulani presentation.

REFERENCES

Ali, Omar H., Stephanie Orosco, Brittany Rodman, Mariah Hunt, and Rachel Cooley. "College Independents Poll: The Emergence of a Non-Partisan Politics?" Office of Research and Economic Development, University of North Carolina at Greensboro, 2013, 3–36.

Bell, Derrick. *Silent Covenants: Brown v. Board of Education and the Unfulfilled Hopes of Racial Reform*. New York: Oxford University Press, 2005.

Bulhan, Hussein Abdilahi. *Frantz Fanon and the Psychology of the Oppressed*. New York: Plenum Press, 1985.

Fanon, Frantz. *Black Skin, White Masks*. New York: Grove Press, 2008.

Fanon, Frantz. *The Wretched of the Earth*. New York: Grove Press, 1965.

Fulani, Lenora B. "Fanon, Newman, and Class Psychology." East Side Institute lecture, New York City, June 1996.

Fulani, Lenora B. *The Making of a Fringe Candidate, 1992*. New York: Castillo International, 1992.

Fulani, Lenora B. "Poor Women of Color Do Great Therapy." In *The Psychopathology of Everyday Racism and Sexism*. New York: Harrington Press, 1988.

Fulani, Lenora B. "Race, Identity, and Epistemology." In *Postmodern Psychologies, Societal Practice, and Political Life*, edited by Lois Holzman and John Morss. New York: Routledge, 2000.

Gordon, Edmund W. et al. "Changing the Script for Youth Development." Institute for Urban and Minority Education, Teacher's College, Columbia University, New York, June 2003.

Gordon, Lewis, T. Denean Sharpley-Whiting, and Renee T. White, eds. *Fanon: A Critical Reader*. Malden, MA: Blackwell, 2000.

Holzman, Lois. *Vygotsky at Work and Play*. New York: Routledge, 2009.

Lorde, Audre. "The Master's Tools Will Never Dismantle the Master's House." In *Sister Outsider: Essays and Speeches*. Berkeley, CA: Crossing Press, 1984.

McLellan, David, ed. *Karl Marx: Selected Writings*. New York: Oxford University Press, 1977.

Newman, Fred, and Lenora Fulani. "Let'sPretend: Solving the Educational Crisis in America." All Stars Project Inc. Special Report, New York (January 2011), 1–9.

Newman, Fred, and Lois Holzman. "All Power to the Developing!" *Annual Review of Critical Psychology* 3 (2003): 8–23.

Newman, Fred, and Lois Holzman. *Lev Vygotsky: Revolutionary Scientist*. London: Routledge, 1993.

Newman, Fred, and Lois Holzman. "The Practice of Method." In *History Is the Cure*, edited by Hugh Polk and Lois Holzman. New York: Practice Press, 1988.

Newman, Fred, and Lois Holzman. *Unscientific Psychology: A Cultural-Performatory Approach to Understanding Human Life*. Westport, CT: Praeger, 1996.

Polk, Hugh, and Lois Holzman, eds. *History Is the Cure*. New York: Practice Press, 1988.

Salit, Jacqueline. *Independents Rising: Outsider Movements, Third Parties, the Struggle for a Post-Partisan America*. New York: Palgrave Macmillan, 2012.

Salit, Jacqueline. "The Color of the Independent Movement." *The Neo-Independent. The Politics of Becoming* 3, no. 1 (Spring 2006): 5–8.

Vygotsky, Lev. *Mind and Society: The Development of Higher Psychological Processes*. Edited by Michael Cole et al. Cambridge, MA: Harvard University Press, 1978.

Walker, Alice. *In Search of Our Mother's Gardens: Womanist Prose*. New York: Harcourt Press, 1984.

Part III

Black Women's Public Intellectualism in Art, Media, and the Culture Wars

SUMMARY

Part III contains several pivotal chapters on Black women public intellectuals in journalism, art, media, and the culture wars. These open with "'Whoever Heard of a Woman Running a Newspaper?' The Public Life and Intellectual Odyssey of Charlotta Bass" by John Portlock. Bass was born in 1874 in South Carolina, the sixth of eleven children. She moved to Providence, Rhode Island, in 1894 to live with a brother; while there, she cut her teeth working for the *Providence Watchman*. In 1910, Bass relocated to California and took control of *The Eagle* amid a storm of criticism over her qualifications. She renamed the paper the *California Eagle* and used the paper to actively push for civil rights, civil liberties, and reform. Bass continued to serve as its publisher until she retired in 1951 and subsequently became more active in politics. While the general public might not know much about Bass, Portlock notes that scholars have begun to take "her measure as an activist, a journalist, and even as an antiwar woman." However, the author also laments that "despite the increasing number of ways in which scholars have examined and unearthed the life and legacy of Bass, none has yet to consider her primarily as an intellectual. This is strange; of all the things one imagines that Bass wished to be known for, primary among them was her deep intellect." He also notes that Bass was a woman "of the mind and devotedly so [which] is obvious for anyone familiar with her life. And yet, like so many other Black female leaders, Bass is cast most often as a 'doer.' . . . Bass the intellectual, it seems, hides in plain sight." Portlock has Bass the intellectual visible within the larger tradition of Black women's public intellectualism.

"'She Did It for the Culture': Black Women Visual Artists as Public Intellectuals in the New Negro Era," authored by Lauren T. Rorie, discusses visual artists such as Augusta Savage, Laura Waring, and Meta Warrick Fuller, women who "transformed the intellectual public sphere through their art and gave Black society a voice that was the embodiment of the Roaring Twenties." Using a variety of mediums, Rorie shows that these artists "improved the state of Black America, and initiated reforms" toward Black equality. Much of the work written on Black women intellectuals tends to focus on Black church women or educators, largely leaving visual artists out of this dialogue. Scholarly analyses of the New Negro Era also tend to focus not on visual artists but on the literary women active during the Harlem Renaissance. Rorie notes that Savage, Waring, and Warrick Fuller were indeed advancing the ideas of the New Negro era in their work. These women were also internationals who studied abroad and garnered international acclaim for their work as artists.

Black women public intellectuals are not a monolith. This is evident as we transition to a discussion of the culture wars from the perspective of Black women public intellectuals in areas such as the pro-life movement, public health, and entertainment. Hettie V. Williams's "Mildred Fay Jefferson and the Pro-Life Movement: A Conservative Black Woman Public Intellectual" is one of the first sustained scholarly assessments of Jefferson. In this chapter, Williams notes that Black women have been virtually ignored in the scholarly literature on the history of conservatism and the pro-life movement. Jefferson was the first African American woman to graduate from Harvard Medical School and the first woman to become a member of the Boston Surgical Society. She also served as the president of the National Right to Life Committee (NRLC). The NRLC is the largest and oldest right-to-life organization in the United States, with more than three thousand members and chapters or affiliates in all fifty states. Ronald Reagan once credited Jefferson with changing his views from pro-choice to pro-life. Jefferson eventually turned away from the academy to advance the pro-life cause as a Black woman public intellectual, during a time when many conservative intellectuals, such as Armstrong Williams, were doing the same.

Chapter 11 examines the life of Joycelyn Elders, the first African American woman surgeon general of the United States and a staunch supporter of a woman's right to choose. In "Naked Truths: Dr. Joycelyn Elders, Public Health, and Sex Education in the 1990s," Tedi A. Pascarella discusses the at-times controversial life of Elders. This chapter focuses specifically on her resignation as surgeon general under President Bill Clinton in 1994 and "the intersections of gender, class, race, and health." Pascarella also points to the impact that Elders had on sex education in America. She was fired at the height of the culture wars, as Americans began to more fervently debate abortion, sex, religion, and individual rights. There are few books that discuss African Americans and the culture wars and even fewer that situate women in the middle of this major moment in American history.

In "What She Knows for Sure: Oprah Winfrey and the Tradition of Black Spiritual but Not Religious Writing," Tejai Beulah centers Winfrey in the major conversations about race as a major purveyor of spiritual but not religious literature. Winfrey has authored more than half a dozen books and has a broad following. Although Winfrey does not have a long list of academic credentials, she is one of the most influential people in US history. Her influence extends beyond media to encompass literature (Oprah's Book Club), politics (her endorsement of Barack Obama), and religion (as a proponent of spiritual but not religious ideas).

By providing some of the first scholarly assessments of women such as Jefferson, Elders, and Winfrey, this section situates Black women into the histories of journalism, art, politics, and culture, and into the larger framework of the Black women's intellectual tradition.

Chapter 8

"WHOEVER HEARD OF A WOMAN RUNNING A NEWSPAPER?"

The Public Life and Intellectual Odyssey of Charlotta Bass

JOHN PORTLOCK

In the spring of 1912, Los Angeles's Central Avenue was abuzz. Word had it that a young woman would soon take over ownership of the city's oldest and most storied Black newspaper, *The Eagle*. She was an easterner and a two-year resident of LA whose only connection to the renowned paper was as a five-dollar-a-week subscriber and the paper's sometimes office manager. Few had heard of Charlotta A. Spears, and fewer still thought she had what it took to run a newspaper, let alone *The Eagle*. The job, critics noted, had taken founder and former editor John Neimore to an early grave—his death making necessary a new owner and editor of *The Eagle*—and the paper was mired in debt and facing stiff competition in an increasingly crowded news market. "She will not be able to go it alone," the naysayers intimated. If Neimore could not turn a profit, how, they asked, "did the young woman figure that she could?" Even those who didn't patronize Spears had to ask, so an older Charlotta Bass later suggested, "Who ever heard of a woman running a newspaper?"[1]

In 1912, of course, few had. Newspapering was largely a man's game in the second decade of the twentieth century, and it would remain so for decades to come. From New York to California, and from Chicago to New Orleans, men dominated the field of editing and publishing newspapers and magazines. If Black Angelenos had not heard of a woman running a newspaper, they likely had heard of, for example, Robert Abbott, the founder and editor of the *Chicago Defender*, or W. E. B. Du Bois, editor of the highly influential *Crisis*, the magazine publication of the National Association for the Advancement of Colored People. And these were only the best known. In contrast, the number of similarly positioned women was small, and the number of Black women who were editors, publishers, or proprietors of print publications was even smaller. One imagines that if Black Angelenos had ever heard of a woman running a newspaper, they would have heard of Ida B. Wells, the antilynching crusader of the late nineteenth and early twentieth centuries, who had a part-ownership stake in the Memphis-based *Free Speech and Headlight*. But beyond Wells, one has to wonder.

Spears, then, would be a revelation for at least a few reasons. First, unlike Wells, she would be the sole proprietor of a major newspaper. Second, Spears's paper would circulate in a major market, Los Angeles, which was well on its way to becoming the tenth-largest city in the union by 1920. And third, quite consciously, Bass would fashion herself as—and in turn truly become—not only an opinionmaker and influencer, but one of Black Los Angeles's and Black America's foremost public intellectuals.

For more than a decade now, historians have been sizing up the influence and impact of the twentieth century's "L.A. Race Woman."[2] She comes to us through history most often as a fellow-traveling radical who, in 1952, received the vice-presidential nomination of the Henry Wallace–inspired Progressive Party. But scholars have also taken her measure as an activist, a journalist, and an antiwar woman. Indeed, historian Douglas Flamming thought Bass's life was so multifaceted and consequential that he chose to use her biography as a framing device for his history of Black Los Angeles. But despite the increasing number of ways in which scholars have examined and unearthed the life and legacy of Bass, none has yet to consider her primarily as an intellectual. This is strange; of all the things one imagines that Bass wished to be known for, primary among them was her deep intellect. Her knowledge was vast and included deep historical understanding of her adopted California, her country, and an impressive grasp of world history, which she displayed during her run for the vice presidency. Bass revered institutions of higher learning, so much so that when on holiday from *The Eagle* offices, she made a habit of visiting local colleges and universities. On holiday to New York City in the late 1920s, for example, the editor enrolled herself in a journalism and public speaking course at Columbia University, seeking further knowledge of her tradecraft. The childless Bass also spent an inordinate amount of time and energy fighting school segregation schemes in LA, so as to ensure that Black schoolchildren had the best schools in the city open to them.

That Bass was a woman of the mind, and devotedly so, is obvious to anyone who is familiar with her life. And yet, like so many other Black female leaders, Bass is cast most often as a "doer." She is the one who fought racially restrictive residential covenants, the one who pried the LA County Hospital and Southern Telephone Company open to Blacks, and the first Black woman to run for vice president on a major party ticket. She is not generally remembered as a thinker, a race theorizer, or an intellectual, despite the fact that researchers have access to so many of Bass's thoughts and ideas. Almost the entirety of her papers remain intact and available to scholars; and the Progressive Party archive contains a full complement of her campaign speeches during the 1952 presidential run. Bass the intellectual, it seems, hides in plain sight.

It is not enough, however, to classify Bass as an intellectual, someone enamored of ideas merely for their own sake. While certainly a lover of learning, she pursued ideas in service of racial uplift. Bass "thought the struggle." Her ideas and their creation, be it her thoughts on unionization, Pan-Africanism, or integration, were always in service of Black freedom, broadly construed. Given this, and given the fact that Bass enjoyed a visibility and influence matched only by a very few of her race in the first half of the twentieth century, we must count her among a rarified group of Black public intellectuals whose thoughts and ideas have helped shape a people. Bass belongs, I contend, with names like Frederick Douglass, W. E. B. Du Bois, Martin Delany, and Marcus Garvey. More importantly, however, she belongs with names like Phillis Wheatley, Ida B. Wells, Louise Thompson Patterson, and Angela Davis, Black female public intellectuals who wielded influence and power in their own times and beyond. These women, like Bass, wrote and orated, opined and inquired, and in so doing fashioned an intellectual space and role for Black women in the movement for Black freedom.

The late professor Manning Marable, in his definition of the Black intellectual, accords him—for until only recently the Black intellectual has more often than not been classed male—three distinguishing characteristics[3] First, he is a "participant-observer" who offers thick description of Black life, made richer because he has jettisoned the notion of critical distance. He is, in short, a man of his people. Second, the Black intellectual determinedly challenges the stereotypical narrative of Blackness that has passed as truth for centuries in America. A shining example was the painstaking work of Ida B. Wells to show that white fear of Black male sexual predation, not actual predation, lay at the center of the lynching epidemic in the late nineteenth and early twentieth centuries. And third, Marable argues, the Black intellectual, beyond mere theorizing, proffers practical steps to racial uplift, whether that intellectual is a Martin Delany or Marcus Garvey, who counseled a return to Africa, a Booker T. Washington, who counseled industrial education, or a W. E. B. Du Bois, who spoke of the duties and responsibilities of a "talented tenth" of the Black race. Together, these characteristics fit men and women like Dr. Martin Luther King Jr., Cornel West, Mary Bethune, Ella Baker, and Charlotta Bass, who enmeshed herself in the life of Black Los Angeles, offered trenchant description of that life, and had the gumption, connections, and ideas to win material advancement for her community. Additionally, and here I offer an addendum to Marable's definition of the Black intellectual, Bass proved willing and able to speak uncomfortable truths to her race. She would rebuke her community for malaise in the face of urgency, and she would prod Black Angelenos to action when she sensed inertia.

Bass was an autodidact. She was self-educated from lived experience and her own reading of history, not by the academy per se. While in residence at Providence, Rhode Island, she gave the impression that she had attended the prestigious Brown University, but no evidence exists to corroborate her assertion. That she did not attend an institution of higher learning in youth, however, does not diminish her as an intellectual, neither does it diminish the ideational contributions she made to the movement. We recall that some of the most revered Black intellectuals of the American republic have been "organic intellectuals," to borrow the famed Antonio Gramsci appellation. Frederick Douglass did not know the ivy-draped walls of a college or university, nor did Phillis Wheatley or Malcolm X. What they had instead was as keen an understanding of the interplay between color and country, race and American democracy as any who studied in formal settings.

Thus, we miss much and risk much in not grappling with Bass as an intellectual. First, we risk absenting her from a long line of Black intellectuals, and in so doing, limit our collective understanding of the Black intellectual tradition. Second, we fail to attend to the way in which she regarded herself, which was as an intellectual. Third, we run the risk of glossing over the ideational odyssey she journeyed during her decades in the public eye. Hers was a journey that took her inside the Republican, Democratic, and Progressive political parties and the NAACP and the Universal Negro Improvement Association, two of the most diametrically opposed organizations of the early twentieth century, and took her from being a supporter of two world wars to one of the staunchest and loudest anti–Cold War voices at mid-century. And finally, in offering up Bass not only as an intellectual but as a public intellectual, we are reminded that Black women of the movement not only marched and sat in, organized and publicized, but also theorized and articulated, doing so on any number of subjects. And, indeed, for Bass theorizing and articulating began the moment she took the editor's chair at *The Eagle*. While some of her contemporaries characterized Bass as flighty, or a rank opportunist, we dare not write her off in this way. Rather, it is incumbent on us that we take her thinking and rethinking of her country and the globe seriously.

Any honest attempt at an intellectual history of Charlotta Bass has to confront the influence that her husband, Joseph Bass, had on her life and the life of *The Eagle*. (It goes without saying, of course, that any influence the husband had on the wife was equaled by the influence the wife had on the husband.) Arriving to Los Angeles from Montana in 1913, Joseph Bass soon found a wife and a new job as editor of *The Eagle*. Joseph Bass, among many things, was above all a newspaper man and a dyed-in-the-wool Republican. His last paper, which he had owned and edited, the *Montana Plaindealer*, had been a staunch supporter of Republican politics, in particular the progressive brand espoused by Theodore Roosevelt in his losing bid for the White House in 1912. Unsurprisingly, then, *The Eagle* became a Republican sheet, a foe of Wilsonian Democracy, which expressed a belief that government had a role to play in regulating business, and a skeptic of unions, racist as most of them were. Joe Bass also believed in peace through strength in foreign policy matters, in the self-help mantras of Booker T. Washington, and in the credo of Black economic nationalism. During his tenure at the *Plaindealer*, Bass had tidily bundled these ideas in the paper's motto "Peace! Prosperity! Union!," the same motto he gave to *The Eagle* soon after his arrival. His intellectual imprint, thus, was all over *The Eagle*. At the same time, he was not the brains behind *The Eagle* operation. Rather, the foregoing serves only to make clear that the paper and the woman were not necessarily one in the same; until his death in 1934, Joe Bass exercised significant editorial control. In her memoirs, published in 1960 under the title *Forty Years* to commemorate her four decades of service to the newspaper, Bass revealed that she "was not always in accord with [her husband's] political opinions," though she "respected his position."[4] Hence, it is problematic for any chronicler of Charlotta Bass to read all ideas and attitudes expressed in *The Eagle* as born of or even wholly representative of her thinking. That said, the paper is the place from which any unearthing of Bass as a public intellectual must begin.

Even during its early years, as the Basses tried to bring the business out of the red, the *California Eagle* did not want for strident opinion. As mentioned, the paper pushed Republicanism, waiting with bated breath for President Wilson to be turned out of office in 1916 and doing its mightiest to help pro-business Republicans at the local, state, and national levels win campaigns. The paper's editorial page, situated neatly in the middle of the eight-page *Eagle*, also counseled Black Angelenos to "organize" their money, a call for Blacks to patronize existing Black-owned business and to open new ones. In a January 1917 op-ed under the headline "Let's Organize Money," the editors declared that the "missing link to the success of the Negro [has been] his failure to successfully organize money," something they argued that the Japanese and other minority races inside Los Angeles had done far more effectively.[5]

If the Basses pushed Black nationalism in the realm of economics, they preached integration when it came to education. Early in Bass's tenure, segregation schemes at LA's public schools began to receive serious discussion in the paper. The notion of separating Black schoolchildren from white schoolchildren enticed not only white residents who had long been of the belief that their sons and daughters belonged with their own, but also some Black Angelenos who thought racial exclusion guaranteed jobs for Black teachers and the best education for Black children. The Basses couldn't have agreed less, making this abundantly clear in a September 1916 column that hit with all the flare and erudition readers had come to expect from *The Eagle*. "We realize that some of our best colored citizens . . . are advocating segregation," the piece read, "but we hold as we have always held that as long as scholastic association is good for the European peasants and other peoples who find their way across the briny Atlantic with the purpose of getting wealth for themselves and education for their children . . . then nothing shorter than this same conciliation in educational and other walks of life will [suit] the Negro." For those who wished segregation, the op-ed concluded, they might consider a move back to Dixie where "this sort of condition" was in full bloom. For all others, they were welcome to "stand straight up," along with their *Eagle*, to demand Black Angelenos' just claim to American citizenship.[6]

The Basses also spent a lot of time in their early years at the paper talking about country, about patriotism, and about loyalty. That they did so is not surprising. After all, a war was on, the first war that Americans had fought on the European continent. As all do, this war in particular inspired nationalist sentiment. The enemy, the Germans, were the hated Hun, determined to snuff out democracy in Europe and across the globe. Not only that, but they were among us, according to the American press: spies in our midst, preying on those whose loyalty to the flag, to capitalism, and to democracy itself wavered. Socialists came under heavy scrutiny, as did the foreign born. The federal government was also concerned that Blacks might turn fifth columnists or be duped into disloyalty by German spies. According to the War Department, evidence already abounded in the spring of 1917 that Blacks were turning on the war, which had been declared by Congress in April of that year. Like so many Black editors throughout the country, the Basses waded into the issue of war, its justifications, its possible consequences, and most importantly, Black Americans' place in it. From the beginning, they made clear a few things to their readers. First, they announced Blacks as unflinchingly loyal to the flag. Second, they pronounced the causes of war—German U-boat attacks on American shipping and indication that the Kaiser had tried to enlist the Mexican government to attack the US—to be "clean cut."[7] Third, the editors expected all draft-age Black men to fight in the war that President Wilson was claiming would "make the world safe for democracy."[8] In fact, *The Eagle* backed the formation of a California Negro Volunteer Regiment. And fourth, the Basses emphasized that a fight overseas did not in any way curtail Black Americans' fight for full citizenship rights at home. Charlotta Bass made this point clear when, in early fall 1917, she called for Black Americans to come together—where, she did not say—for a "grand silent parade" in protest of Jim Crow, lynching, and discriminatory employment practices.[9] Her idea, detailed in the October 6 run of *The Eagle*, was to replicate a July silent protest parade held in New York City with ten thousand participants.[10] Taken together, one can see that *The Eagle* during World War I pushed an agenda akin to the "Double Victory" campaign of the Second World War, in which Blacks pledged to fight fascism both abroad and at home.

Infamously, the war at home proved both bloody and intractable, not unlike the war abroad. More than 150 Black Americans were lynched between 1917 and 1919, and race riots tore apart cities from Chester, Pennsylvania, on the Delaware River to East Saint Louis, Illinois, on the Mississippi. In Texas, violence of an order and kind little known in American history took place in the late summer of 1917. Encamped Black soldiers made war on local whites in response to multiple incidents of police brutality and Jim Crow indignities. When the dust settled, sixteen whites and four Blacks had been killed, and more than a dozen Black soldiers waited execution. The story of the Houston riot was on the front page of every big-city Black newspaper, Los Angeles included. When the story hit on the front page of the *California Eagle*, Charlotta Bass had the byline. As luck would have it, Bass was able to be on the ground in Houston only days after the rioting. She had been away from *The Eagle* offices for a three-month sojourn to visit family and take the pulse of Black America on the other side of the Rocky Mountains. Upon her return Bass took two long columns to narrate the incidents at Houston. Her accounting of the event drew on interviews from residents, local newspaper accounts, and close observation of "the effect of the August 23rd riot not only upon the immediate vicinity of Houston" but also on the entire "state of Texas."[11]

Never interested in only providing narratives, Bass also used her columns to call her readers to action. To her mind, the racist indignities shown to the proud Black soldiers of the Twenty-Fourth Infantry division in Houston, Texas, were a slight to all Black Americans, and one that required a collective response. "What affects one Negro affects the entire race," she wrote in her last column on Houston. As such, it was her belief that "the colored people of the west must get busy, and with the race men and women of the east . . . demonstrate that as law abiding American citizens . . . we resent the present treatment of White America against Black America all over this country."[12]

Keen as she was to bring Black Angelenos together to "organize money," and keen as she was to bring Black Americans together to protest wrongs, Charlotta Bass was also keen to connect Blacks from around the world in order to ameliorate the problems that plagued the sons and daughters of Africa everywhere. That Pan-Africanism won Bass's heart is obvious given that this was a woman who at one time—the early 1920s—held high office in Marcus Garvey's Universal Negro Improvement Association, an explicitly Pan-African organization, or that she was chosen by the New York–based Women's Study Club of America as the western representative to the Second Pan-African Congress in London in 1921; or that she held membership in the Paul Robeson–led Council on African Affairs; or that she kept *Eagle* readers ever abreast of African efforts to throw off their colonial oppressors; and when we listen to her tell a South African anti-apartheid activist in 1952 that the "fight for freedom in the United States is inextricably linked to the struggle against tyranny . . . not only in South Africa but throughout the entire continent."[13] It would be a misread of this Black internationalist, though, to think she had eyes only for Africa. She didn't. Bass intuited ties of kinship tying Black Americans to all the world's oppressed: those under the thumb of colonialism, those under the thumb of czarist rule, and those under the thumb of transnational business interests. Her global take on oppression and uplift led her, during the throes of the Second World War, to write that "the struggles of the Negro people of America [are] inextricably bound to the struggles for freedom of the people of the world."[14]

And yet for all her talk and work to promote unity and uplift, protest and action, she was criticized by her readership for being too moderate, too conservative. In particular, these accusations plagued her during the Depression era, as Blacks fought tooth and nail to gain a foothold in the labor market. To know Charlotta Bass is to know her fight to integrate Southern California workforces, Southern California recreational spaces, and Southern California residential neighborhoods. In all of these ventures, she saw herself as a broker, uniquely positioned—if not uniquely powerful—to strike deals with employers or city officials and thus smooth the way for Blacks to enter previously segregated spaces. And to be sure, she had some definite thoughts about how this smoothing should happen. She preferred letter-writing campaigns, pledges not to buy where you can't work, and face-to-face meetings and discussions.

As the Depression gripped the country in the 1930s, Bass's decidedly middle-class tactics for uplift were questioned, most notably by Leon Washington, the editor of the upstart *Los Angeles Sentinel*. A Democrat and union champion, Washington mocked what he saw as Bass's weak-willed tactics and lambasted the editor's reluctance to back more aggressive ones. In 1937, the two clashed over how to secure Black employment gains at the local five-and-dime Kress department store. Two Black women were already in the employ of the store. Bass, a newly appointed member of the local Chamber of Commerce, counseled patience and "dispassion," assuring that "when the Negro employment situation is placed before the Kress company in the proper light, the Kress management . . . will bargain with those members of the race, who as true leaders are unselfishly interested in the eradication of the Negro's economic slavery."[15] Taking the opposite tack, Washington advocated a boycott of the store and a picket of its premises until more Blacks were hired. Though decried by Bass as well as Kress management as a provocative stance, Washington made no apology for his plan, nor did he second guess the involvement of the Congress of Industrial Organizations (CIO), whose ranks included a few communists. To Washington, the destiny of Black workers rested not on the good deeds of management—Kress did, in this instance, agree to hire additional Black women as "salesgirls" in the wake of picketing—but on the race's willingness to unionize. In response to Bass's aversion to the CIO and unionism generally, Washington wrote: "Whether the *Eagle* editor knows it or not, the vast majority of Negroes are workers; they cannot hope to get decent hours, wages, and working conditions unless and until they do organize into labor unions."[16] The day was fast approaching when Bass would believe the same.

By the time Charlotta Bass was debating Leon Washington over the relative merits of uplift stratagems for Black Los Angeles, she was a widow and the sole editor at the *California Eagle*, Joe Bass having died in 1934. With complete editorial control, it is from this point forward that the paper and the woman became one. However, it bears mention that *Eagle* readership had, for six years prior to 1934, already had a chance to hear directly from Bass in a column she wrote entitled "On the Sidewalk." It was here, every week on the paper's front page, that readers got a chance to read reflections from Bass on everything from local fare to geopolitical happenings. The column, whose title cast Bass in the role of street intellectual, a proletarian woman of the people, began in 1927 following one of her trips out East. In the fall of 1926, she began a journey that would take her back to Providence, Rhode Island, Chicago, Illinois, and Saint Louis, Missouri. Most of her time, however, was spent in New York, where she began coursework at Columbia University in journalism and public speaking. The impetus behind this decision was, she wrote in a missive back to *Eagle* offices that was later published in the paper, to "better prepare me for the work I hope to accomplish in California for the advancement of our people in that section."[17] It seemed what interested Bass most was investigative journalism, the drawing back of the curtain to expose truths both good and bad. She had tried her hand at this in Houston in 1917, and she did so once again while in residence at Columbia, writing an exposé of Harlem that appeared in installments in *The Eagle*. In her very first "Sidewalk" column, which appeared in the upper-righthand corner of *The Eagle* front page on July 1, 1927, Bass made it clear that the weekly piece would be "dedicated to happenings seen and heard on the sidewalk from time to time."[18]

The "Sidewalk" column lasted until 1951, the year Bass sold *The Eagle* and moved back East. Like Bass, the column was eclectic, a chance for her to discuss topics as varied as gender and faith, economics and politics, love and loss. It also fast became a chance for the editor to opine about things that, at first, appeared far distant from Los Angeles sidewalks. In her second rendering of "On the

Sidewalk," Bass delved into the topic of slavery and the fact that the trade in human beings "is still carried on in the Red Sea." Though this trade was half a world away, and hardly on the tips of the tongues of Black Angelenos, Bass brought this to readers' attention because, as she claimed in the same column, it "reminds us very tenderly of our own condition at this time—in shackles." "So long as one member of our black family is in the depth[s]," Bass assured, "all are stained with the dark [pain] that emanates therefrom."[19]

In retrospect, the column did a number of different things for Charlotta Bass. First, it gave her visibility and a platform, which she had not previously enjoyed. In the column, she had a byline each week, not just a credit as managing editor of a newspaper. Second, it allowed Bass the chance to put before readers ideas and musings that were her own, untouched and unfiltered by her husband or anyone else. Third, the column suggested authenticity and became a way for readers to connect in a more personal way to their editor. Finally, thanks to its title, the column helped Bass cast herself as a woman of the people, an everywoman with an abiding concern for her community and who had her ears and eyes out for the goings on therein. That she kept the column going for more than two decades suggests its popularity and effectiveness in communicating that which Bass hoped it would. Under the leadership of Bass, *The Eagle* became a distinguished chronicler of Black life and championed the interests of Black people with a quick wit and incisive prose.

For the life of the paper, which lasted until American entry into the Second World War, Bass continued to believe that the people's interest lay in Republican politics, in amenable relations between labor and management, in Black entrepreneurship, and in the free hand of the market. This showed itself most clearly in 1940 when Bass served as western regional director of the campaign of Wendell Willkie, the business magnate who promised to set the nation's commercial capacity free from the fetters of President Franklin Roosevelt's New Deal. But all of this began to change in the wake of Pearl Harbor. Increasingly at ease with the radicalism of the CIO, and increasingly less critical of communism, Bass would leave the Republican Party in 1942. She began to more readily see the world as bifurcated into haves and have-nots. Some have attributed this political turn, which saw her not only leave the Republican Party but join and leave the Democratic Party and finally land among the newly formed Progressive Party, as attributable to the influence of her nephew John Kinloch, a young liberal, who came to live and work with his aunt in 1937 and who, tragically, died eight years later at the Battle of the Bulge in Germany. They argue that Kinloch's idealism rubbed off on Bass, and when he died, she felt impelled to champion his youthful and quixotic radicalism. Others saw it as pure opportunism, a newspaper editor trying her mightiest to find relevance wherever and however she could. If the Republicans wouldn't have her, then she would be a Democrat. If the Democrats were not going to offer her a seat at the table, she would move on from them. If asked, Bass would have said she hadn't changed, that her ideas of racial justice, human equality, and freedom had necessitated moves across the political spectrum as one or another organ more fervently defended these ideals.

Be that is it may, by the postwar period Bass was well on her way to becoming "shocking pink," as Henry Luce's *Time* magazine would later put it.[20] She had warmed to the New Deal, which she had previously criticized as antibusiness and anti-Black. She was beginning to sound less an economic nationalist and more of a socialist who championed the interests of the underclass irrespective of race. Gone were the days when Bass might have seen the struggles of Los Angeles's Mexican or Japanese population as unconnected to those of Black Angelenos. Finally, Bass was also beginning to see Black freedom as bound up with world peace. As far back as the First World War Bass had intuited and believed in the liberalizing possibility of war, that a fight for democratic ideals abroad would help to flower those very same ideas at home. An *Eagle* editorial from the spring of 1917 had argued that "this great world's war may be God's way of making a real democracy both in spirit and in fact, whereby all Races and all nations shall come absolutely into their own."[21] Two years of race rioting, however, quickly put this notion to bed for Bass. A generation later, during the Second World War, there erupted race riots the likes of which had not been seen since the last world war. War seemed, then, antithetical to racial progress, or at the very least no panacea for racial animus. Neither did it appear the solution to ending colonialism, in Africa or elsewhere, which was a priority for Bass. At the conclusion of World War I the Allies merely transferred German overseas holdings to themselves, and at the conclusion of the Second World War, the Allies, in particular the British, resisted any talk of freeing colonial peoples.

This helps explain a bit of her turn left, if you will, but it does not present a complete picture. The role of religion in her life and her reading of history were also important factors in her ideological shift. Bass was a devout Christian, was a member of LA's famed Second Baptist Church, and spoke forthrightly with her readers about the ways in which her faith informed her worldview. She named faith as a reason she had long held deep skepticism and discomfort surrounding war even while she supported the fight against autocracy in the 1910s or fascism in the 1940s. In 1930, for example, Bass assured her *California Eagle* readers that "there is only one way by which lasting peace may come to the world, and that is by a recognition of God as the father of all [and] hence the brotherhood of man."[22] Ten years later, with Europe embroiled in bloody conflict and America doing its best to remain on the sidelines, Bass invoked the "Prince of Peace" during the 1940 Easter season in hope that all men would soon break the "enslaving chains of greed, hate, and violence [to] turn unashamed faces toward the stars in a world of peace."[23] During the postwar period, Bass continued to see peace as religiously prescribed. When the Korean War broke in late June 1950, one of her first moves was to call for the mobilization of "every minister and every [Black] church" to "act for peace."[24] A sense of the godly had Bass turning not only against war but also against the excesses of capitalism, which she saw as rampant in the wake of the Second World War. Weekly, it seemed, she opined about greed, avarice, despotism, and the hunger for land and treasure that drove imperialists. A people's war had just ended, one that was again to enshrine democracy from Beijing to London, and from Washington to Mumbai, and yet racism persisted, empires remained intact, and the "one world" Bass and others hoped would come to be in the wake of war was quickly being divided into three: the First, Second, and soon-to-be Third World. "Is religion being challenged today?" she asked in a December 1946 "Sidewalk" column. Yes, she answered time and again. "It seems that the great god of Greed occupies the upper chamber in the hearts and minds of a few in all the nations, and their doctrine is: Keep the people divided, and we shall rule." "Now," she went on in a 1947 piece, "the early teaching of Christ is lost in a maze of propaganda designed to turn the people's attention away from their real enemies," for example, racially motivated hate, disenfranchisement, and exploitation.

Much as Bass became disillusioned with American-style capitalism, and warmed to the anti-imperial and equality-laden rhetoric of the Soviet Union, which Stalin played up in the early Cold War, she never lost faith in her country or her reading of history. Time and again she told her readers that what America needed was not foreign ideology, however utopic socialism seemed, but rather "Americanism—the kind prescribed in the Constitution of the United States."[25] The ideas that would save the country, indeed the world, from exploitation, oppression, and colonial slavery, according to Bass, were native born, alive in the founding documents of the country. If she was enamored of the Soviet Union at all it was because the ideals of the October Revolution appeared, at least on their face, as liberal as those put down in 1789. Bass, who visited Moscow and the Caucuses in the summer of 1950 and remarked on the fact that she saw no color line, no talk of war, and women with "as many rights and opportunities as men," waited impatiently for America to reclaim its heritage. Notably, her wait—her call for America to remember its history—calls to mind the struggle of Dr. King, who in 1967, during the throes of the Vietnam War, urged America to "recapture [its] revolutionary spirit[,] declaring eternal hostility to poverty, racism, and militarism."[26]

Never one to wait patiently by, though, Bass quickly determined that the best way to revive the ideals of her nation was through politics, as both a candidate and a party operative. After an unsuccessful run for city council in 1945 as the

"People's Unity" candidate, Bass joined the nascent Progressive Party in 1948. Claiming the mantle of FDR's liberalism, as well as staunch antiracist positions and a gentler foreign policy toward the Russians, Progressives proved the far-left intellectual redoubt of American politics in the late 1940s. Bass gravitated immediately toward the party and its leader, former Roosevelt vice president Henry Wallace. In short order, *The Eagle* became the veritable Progressive Party mouthpiece in Southern California, with article upon article churned out weekly in praise of the party's policies. The paper's passionate support of the Progressive Party did not sit well with all *Eagle* readers. Indeed, Bass's declining subscription numbers suggest her endorsement of the Communist-backed Progressives did not sit well with a number of her readers. In a time when civil rights organizations such as the NAACP were ousting suspected communists from their ranks, and the White House was requiring a loyalty oath, few could stomach or risk backing a "red" agenda.

Some of *The Eagle* readership were confused by exactly how the "red" agenda, which by 1948 focused its rhetoric on the achievement of peace and the cooling of Cold War tensions, would translate into Black civil rights at home. Washington, predictably, regarded the Moscow "peace offensive," as Stalin's pacifistic talk was scornfully dubbed by Secretary of State Dean Acheson, little more than a cheap ploy to undermine the West's military readiness.[27] Bass heard from one frustrated reader who asked why the editor continued to "touch on the same things [i.e., peace and war] in that Sidewalk column every week."[28] The not-too-subtle suggestion was that Bass should spend less time on foreign matters and more on racial matters, spill more ink over Jim Crow and mob violence, and less on German rearmament and Truman's peacetime conscription order. Bass had none of this, spending an entire column explaining why she, an African American woman, kept an eye trained on Africa and Europe, Asia and Latin America, and why she fretted the maintenance of peace and the very real prospect of war. First there was the very real threat of nuclear war between the Russians and the Americans, due to the superpower's continued standoff over Berlin and the emergence of the North Atlantic Treaty Organization. Second, Bass harped on the "same things" because, in her mind, that which took place in Moscow, in Beijing, in Washington, and in London bore on what was happening—or not happening, as the case may have been—to Black Americans right there in LA. Tax dollars, wrote Bass in that same May 1949 column, which could have been used to build affordable housing or lessen the financial burden of medical expenses, were going to run down spies, establish loyalty tests, and staff un-American Activities Committees. Civil rights and civil rights leaders were being hemmed in on all sides by the constant contention that Black freedom was a Moscow-inspired plot. And finally, Bass—a member of the anticolonial and anti-imperial Council on African Affairs—reminded her readers that Africa remained in chains, that those in Washington concerned themselves with the "colonial question" only so far as it threatened American global hegemony, and that so long as Africa and others of the world's darker races remained a subjugated lot, Black Americans had little hope of realizing their freedom dreams on these shores.

Bass wasn't alone in these ideas, ideas which consisted of the notion that peace and civil rights were "indivisible."[29] A number of prominent Black women held the same position at the dawn of the Cold War, including Ada Jackson, Louise Thompson Patterson, Eslanda Robeson, and Lorraine Hansberry. To those gathered at Independence Hall in Philadelphia during the Progressive Party founding convention, Shirley Graham, in her keynote address, called forth a "nation of free and equal men and women" who would "lead the world into THE CENTURY OF PEACE!"[30] One among the thousands to hear Graham was Antioch College junior Coretta Scott, who some two decades later, with America embroiled in its then-longest war, would confidently assert: "You cannot separate peace and freedom; they are inextricably related."[31]

With her political turn to the left, Bass's intellectual circle grew, and she found herself part of an international left of intellectuals, pacifists, antiracists, and idealists, young and old. Ever the enthusiastic itinerant, Bass got her first chance to travel abroad in 1950 after years of attempts. In 1921 she had plans to attend the Second Pan-African Congress foiled on account of money, and in 1949, on her way to the Women's Asiatic Conference in Beijing, she could not procure the necessary documents. This opportunity was made possible because of an invitation to join fellow leftists in Prague, Czechoslovakia, at a Communist Party–backed international peace conference. Held less than two months after the beginning of the Korean War, the meeting of the World Committee of the Defenders of Peace took for its agenda the cessation of hostilities in East Asia and the complete outlawing of atomic weaponry. In recalling the event years later, an event that also drew fellow Progressive and antiwarrior W. E. B. Du Bois, Bass framed her purpose in crossing the Atlantic as follows: "I was on a mission in search of knowledge and a better understanding of the relationship between the peoples and the nations of the world. 'When I return,' I thought, 'I will be better prepared to help build peace in our country that will defy future wars.'"[32]

This mission did not end with the conference in Prague. Instead, Bass continued east, landing behind the Iron Curtain for a multiday tour of the Soviet state. The trip, oversaw by Stalin-approved handlers, took her to Moscow and the Caucasus and did nothing to diminish her faith in the promise of socialism. In recalling the journey years later in her memoirs, Bass still couldn't help but gush over what she witnessed. She recalled being amazed at the number of infrastructure projects, in particular the repair and construction of affordable housing units. She also remembered that she did not hear a word about war, nor did she detect a hint of racial animus. In the end, the trip fired a socialist vision in her that she determined to make real in the United States. Having left LA on a fact-finding mission and gathered her facts, Bass was determined to return to Southern California not only to share her facts and ideas with her readers, but to fashion a way to bring those ideas to life in her community and in her country.

From the fall of 1950 to the fall of 1952, she had myriad opportunities to do just this, including a congressional run in the fall of 1950 on the Progressive Party ticket, a presiding position over one of the most influential Black radical female organizations of the twentieth century, and her vice-presidential candidacy. During this time, Bass was the most influential and vital Black woman radical and one of the most crucial Black left public intellectuals. The evidence for this abounds, beginning with her campaign for Congress, which she set out on immediately following her return from Russia. Touting a platform that privileged "world peace, world-wide neighborliness, jobs for all, civil liberties, and security," she bested Progressive Party statewide averages, winning 13.8 percent of the vote in the Fourteenth District, including more than a quarter of the Black vote and nearly five thousand white votes.[33] The run was so impressive that party officials called it the "most outstanding campaign" in the state.[34]

She also adopted a leading role in what historian Erik McDuffie calls the most important organization of Black left feminism of the twentieth century.[35] The Sojourners for Truth and Justice (STJ), which came together in late summer 1951, months after Bass sold *The Eagle* and moved back east to Harlem, New York, was the brainchild of the renowned Black female community activist Louise Thompson Patterson and poet, actress, and activist Beah Richardson. Their mission was to bring Black women from all over the country to the nation's capital to demand from "this government . . . absolute, immediate and unconditional redress of grievances," including poverty, lynching, and the vain sacrifice of sons and husbands in foreign wars that had failed to make democracy a reality at home.[36] That Richardson and Patterson chose Bass to head up their new organization, as well as lead their march on Washington, hardly surprises given her obvious radical bona fides, her growing visibility, her decades of experience campaigning for civil rights, and the sharp tongue and even sharper prose she used as an editor and orator in Los Angeles. And though Bass balked at piloting an all-Black female organization, preferring at least initially that the "Sojourn" and the attendant organization be multiracial, she acquiesced, enunciating the antiracist, antiwar, and human rights agenda of the STJ for the duration of its one-year existence.

Finally, in 1952, Bass the public intellectual faced her greatest challenge as a public intellectual: a run for national office. After securing the nomination in March, the newly minted vice-presidential nominee of the Progressive Party began a tireless campaign to convince voters that (a) the Cold War had Americans chasing boogie men abroad and ignoring real threats to democracy at home such as segregation, wealth inequity, and the curtailment of civil liberties; (b) that the Korean War had to end immediately, "No Ifs, Ands Or Buts"; (c) that the arms race had to stop; and (d) that a peacetime economy, focused on full employment and a livable wage, must come to be.[37] What is most notable about Bass's run in 1952 is not the Progressive vote total in November; the party in the end was a nonfactor. Neither is it Black voter turnout; Bass convinced few to vote for a party widely regarded as "red." Rather, what is striking about her run is the visibility that she won, and the chance she had to alone articulate a vision for the nation's future. For half of the campaign, from April to August, Bass's running mate, Vincent Hallinan, sat in prison on a contempt of court charge. Hallinan was a labor lawyer, one who had the gall, in the eyes of some judges, to represent radical union leaders. Given the chance, one of these judges slapped Hallinan with a contempt citation just before the campaign got underway, landing the candidate in jail. And so, as one high-level Progressive aptly put it, Bass was literally the "standard-bearer of [the] party during the months of [Hallinan's] imprisonment."[38] Never before in the history of the republic had a Black woman been so placed, a fact Progressives were not shy about noting at the time.

Bass would live another decade and a half following the close of the 1952 campaign. She would continue to flex her might as an intellectual, speaking out against the war in Vietnam and against increasing Cold War tensions and lecturing on African American history. In her early life, she committed to articulating Black life in Los Angeles. Before long, she was articulating Black life in America. Two decades hence, in the context of the Second World War, and the ensuing Cold War, she became enamored of articulating the foreign to highlight its local implications. She observed, and she distilled. She thought, and she dared to express, even when certain expression contradicted previous thinking, earlier positions, or ideas. Such will always be the meandering journey of the intellectual, who accepts that ideas are of necessity contextual and subject always to change. If this is Bass, this is also Du Bois, King, and any number of other Black intellectuals. We dare not write off icons like Du Bois because of the changeable nature of his ideas—or his affinity for radical politics—and similarly we dare not write off Bass, who as surely as any deserves recognition as a leading intellectual in the history African Americans.

NOTES

1. Bass, *Forty Years: Memoirs from the Pages of a Newspaper*, 31.
2. Freer, "L.A. Race Woman."
3. Marable, "Black Studies and the Racial Mountain."
4. Bass, *Forty Years*, 42.

5. "Let's Organize Money," *California Eagle* (hereafter *CE*), January 6, 1917, 4.
6. "The Eagle's Attitude on Segregation," *CE*, September 9, 1916, 4.
7. "Ever Loyal," *CE*, April 21, 1917, 4.
8. "Woodrow Wilson, War Message to Congress, 1917," delivered April 2, 1917, US 65th Congress, 1st Session, Senate Document 5.
9. Charlotta Bass, "The Houston Riot," *CE*, October 6, 1917, 1.
10. For summary discussion of the New York City parade, see "The Negro Silent Protest Parade," in *The Making of African American Identity: Vol. II, 1865–1917*, accessed Jun 28, 2019, https://nationalhumanitiescenter.org/pds/maai2/forward/text4/silentprotest.pdf.
11. Bass, "The Houston Riot," 1.
12. Bass, "The Houston Riot," 1.
13. Charlotta Bass and Louise Thompson Patterson to Ms. Ray Alexander, April 5, 1952, Box 13, Folder 4, Louise Thompson Patterson Papers, Stuart A. Rose Manuscript, Archives, and Rare Book Library, Emory University.
14. "'A People's Victory Demands a People's Paper!'" *CE*, October 1, 1942, 8B.
15. Charlotta Bass, "On the Sidewalk," *CE*, September 30, 1937, 1.
16. "Go Ahead," *Los Angeles Sentinel*, May 13, 1937, 1.
17. Charlotta Bass, "In New York," *CE*, December 31, 1926, 1.
18. Bass, "On the Sidewalk," *CE*, July 1, 1927, 1.
19. Charlotta Bass, "On the Sidewalk: Dark Races Organize," *CE*, July 8, 1927, 1.
20. "Shocking Pink," *Time*, March 17, 1952, 22.
21. Editorial, *CE*, April 21, 1917, 4.
22. Charlotta Bass, "On the Sidewalk," *CE*, April 18, 1930, 1.
23. "Easter," *CE*, March 21, 1940, 1.
24. "California Eagle Asks Churches to Act for Peace," *CE*, July 7, 1950, 1.
25. Charlotta Bass, "On the Sidewalk," *CE*, May 2, 1946, 20.
26. Martin Luther King Jr., "A Time to Break the Silence," delivered April 4, 1967, in Washington, *A Testament of Hope*, 242.
27. For a summary discussion of the so-called Moscow "peace offensive," see Walker, "'No More Cold War.'"
28. Charlotta Bass, "The Sidewalk," *CE*, May 5, 1949, 1.
29. Charlotta Bass, "I Accept This Call," delivered April 1952, in Lerner, *Black Women in White America*, 344.
30. Shirley Graham, "Shirley Graham's Keynote Speech, 1948," Series 1: Correspondence, W. E. B. Du Bois Papers, accessed June 28, 2019, http://credo.library.umass.edu/view/full/mums312-b121-i315, 3.
31. King, *My Life with Martin Luther King, Jr.*, 273.
32. Bass, *Forty Years*, 157.
33. Bass, *Forty Years*, 173; Jack Berman, Executive Vice Chairman to All Clubs and Members, November 28, 1950, Box 13, Folder 51, Progressive Party Records, University of Iowa Special Collections and University Archives.
34. Berman to All Clubs and Members, Progressive Party Records.
35. McDuffie, *Sojourning for Freedom*, 173.
36. "A Call to Negro Women," 1951, Box 13, Folder 2, Louise Thompson Patterson Papers, Emory University.

37. "Progressive Party Platform," 1952, Box 10, Folder 23, American Left Ephemera Collection, University of Pittsburgh, accessed June 28, 2019, https://digital.library.pitt.edu/islandora/object/pitt:31735059397053.

38. Pat Richards, "1,200 at Chicago Peace Rally Hail Hallinan, Mrs. Bass," *Daily Worker*, September 23, 1952, 2.

REFERENCES

Bass, Charlotta. *Forty Years: Memoirs from the Pages of a Newspaper*. Los Angeles: Charlotta A. Bass, 1960.

Flamming, Douglas. *Bound for Freedom: Black Los Angeles in Jim Crow America*. Berkeley: University of California Press, 2005.

Freer, Regina. "L.A. Race Woman: Charlotta Bass and the Complexities of Black Political Development in Los Angeles." *American Quarterly* 56, no. 3 (September 2004): 607–32.

King, Coretta Scott. *My Life with Martin Luther King, Jr.* New York: Henry Holt, 1993.

Lerner, Gerda. *Black Women in White America: A Documentary History*. New York: Vintage, 1972.

Marable, Manning. "Black Studies and the Racial Mountain." In *Dispatches from the Ebony Tower: Intellectuals Confront the African American Experience*, ed. Manning Marable. New York: Columbia University Press, 2001, 1–30.

McDuffie, Erik S. *Sojourning for Freedom: Black Women, American Communism, and the Making of Black Left Feminism*. Durham, NC: Duke University Press, 2011.

Walker, Samuel J. "'No More Cold War': American Foreign Policy and the 1948 Soviet Peace Offensive." *Diplomatic History* 5, no. 1 (January 1981): 75–91.

Washington, James M., ed. *A Testament of Hope: The Essential Writings and Speeches of Martin Luther King, Jr.* New York: Harper, 1991.

Archives

American Left Ephemera Collection, University of Pittsburgh, Pittsburgh, Pennsylvania.

Louise Thompson Patterson Papers, Stuart A. Rose Manuscript Archives, and Rare Book Library, Emory University, Atlanta, Georgia.

Records of the Progressive Party Special Collections and University Archives, University of Iowa, Iowa City.

Chapter 9

"SHE DID IT FOR THE CULTURE"

Black Women Visual Artists as Public Intellectuals in the New Negro Era

LAUREN T. RORIE

Augusta Savage is among a host of Black women visual artists who concerned themselves with race reform during the Harlem Renaissance era and have been continuously overlooked by scholars of the African American experience. These women took bold stances by connecting ideas about race, gender, and space in their work to help awaken a strident race consciousness during the early twentieth century. Despite the valuable cultural, political, and social contributions to Black life these women made, their work continues to be overshadowed in the historical record by the political work of Black men active during the New Negro era. This is particularly noticeable in the area of intellectual history. Scholarship of Black women's ideas has yet to completely include Black women visual artists and their ideas about human liberation, though some scholars have begun the process by identifying the intellectual traditions of Black women. Mia Bay, Farah J. Griffin, Martha S. Jones, and Barbara D. Savage address the neglect of Black women's contributions and exclusion from American intellectual history in their text *Toward an Intellectual History of Black Women* while identifying a Black women's intellectual tradition.[1] *Toward an Intellectual History of Black Women* discusses Black women's intellectual history through analysis of race, class, gender, and their lived experiences.[2] This chapter inserts Black women visual artists more succinctly into this tradition.

Historian Keisha N. Blain offers a contemporary model for the Black intellectual tradition in the introduction to *New Perspectives on the Black Intellectual Tradition*, addressing the various approaches to intellectual history. Blain makes the claim that intellectual history is embedded within thoughts and methodologies deployed by critical actors. Understanding Black intellectual history in such a way allows us to deepen our understanding of how ideas influenced historical actors within cultural, social, and political spaces.³ I accept both of these arguments while examining the methodologies and intersectional dimensions within the work of visual artists Augusta Savage, Laura Wheeler Waring, and Meta Warrick Fuller. In an attempt to remedy the lack of inclusion of these visual artists in studies of American intellectual history, this chapter seeks to undo the marginalization of Black women within scholarship and solidify their status as coequals to their Black and white male counterparts.

Savage, Wheeler, and Fuller used visual art to make claims about racial uplift, social justice, and Black humanity during the height of the Harlem Renaissance in the United States and abroad. They used their artistry to transform the public sphere and gave Black society a voice, and they were concerned with all things race and dubbed by Du Bois as "race women." Several narratives on Black women public intellectuals tend to focus on political activists, educators, or Black churchwomen. Visual artists such as Savage, Waring, and Fuller responded to the racial climate of the early twentieth century through their art. The depth of their work spoke loudly as a radical plea to awaken nation consciousness as they redefined the term "intellectual" through gender and art inclusivity.⁴ Chernoh Sesay Jr. defines Black intellectuals as thought producers shaped by the changing contexts of slavery, race, and modernization as expressed in their ideas and experiences.⁵ These three women fit this definition well.

That Black women artists can be intellectuals is a perspective that is noticeably absent from African American history at the present. Kristin Waters and Carol B. Conaway's book *Black Women's Intellectual Traditions: Speaking Their Minds* offers an important historical intervention regarding Black women intellectuals, Black radicalism, and intellectual history. Waters and Conaway contend that "black women's intellectual traditions in North America span almost four centuries, traditions that have been transmitted through domestic arts and everyday activities."⁶ In her essay "What's in a Name? Womanism, Black Feminism, and Beyond," Patricia Hill Collins states, "Black women used their platforms to 'talk back' and as a result, African American women's ideas and experiences have achieved a visibility unthinkable in the past."⁷ Mia E. Bay and Farah J. Griffin discuss the plurality of Black women's roles as artists, activists, and intellectuals in their pivotal aforementioned text. In their edited volume, Bay and Griffin declare, "As we move forward into a new century, it's time to recognize black women's intellectual history as a distinct growing field of study."⁸ Since the late twentieth century, Black women's intellectual history has steadily flourished to include the voices of women involved in cultural work, such as the three artists discussed in this chapter.

For the past decade, scholarship on Black intellectual history has attempted to uncover the totality of Black women intellectuals, including Black women public intellectuals. Scholars have reconceptualized the meaning of the term "intellectual" to include artists and cultural workers. By exposing the voices amplified through the work of Savage, Waring, and Fuller, this chapter reclaims the territory of Black women's intellectual production while proving the necessary incorporation of these particular Black women into the Black women's intellectual tradition.[9] These women contributed to social, political, and cultural transformations during one of the most tumultuous eras for Black Americans while advancing ideas about gender and race in public spaces. They challenged political boundaries and carved out a space for visual art in conversations about race. Their art awoke a Black diasporic consciousness that encouraged national reform to systemic oppression and fostered a call for Black independence and a deeper understanding of Black identity. This study is essential to continue the Black women's intellectual tradition by analyzing ideas about race advanced by Black women visual artists during the New Negro era.

The Harlem Renaissance was a cultural movement that empowered Black voices. It inspired the flowering of Black art in Harlem from 1919 to 1934, and beyond, that was encouraged by social, political, and intellectual activism. This was a period of Black reclamation that supported the representation of Black life, Black cultural expression, and Black ideologies to combat deep-rooted stereotypes about Blackness. This era was revelatory in terms of revealing Black talent to its fullest artistic capacities.[10] Black artists such as Aaron Douglas captured the grace and beauty of Blackness and helped emancipate much of the race from feelings of inferiority. Art was a useful vehicle to transmit messages of Black freedom. It mobilized itself by resonating with the emotions of the Black community, with heartfelt meanings that circulated in newspapers, magazines, and literature. Behind all this creative activity, social activists and thinkers such as Charles S. Johnson and W. E. B. Du Bois gave their support to the arts.

The art of Augusta Savage, Laura Wheeler Waring, and Meta Warrick Fuller focused on ideas about race, gender, inequality, and the systemic oppression of Blacks advancing a New Negro agenda as defined by Du Bois. These women stepped into public spaces, used their art as a vehicle to advance the race, and provoked intellectual thought.[11] This was encouraged by Du Bois in his 1927 speech "Criteria for Negro Art." In this speech, he called for Black artists in America to create art as propaganda and the restoration and preservation of beauty. In order to fulfill this goal, truth, justice, honor, and goodness were crucial agents for art as propaganda. Du Bois stated in this speech: "I do not care a damn for any art that is not used as propaganda. But I do care when propaganda is confined to one side while the other is stripped silent. Thus, all art is propaganda and ever must be, despite the wailing of the purists."[12] Du Bois wanted Black artists to create racial art to record Black beauty and, at the

Anna Washington Derry by Laura Wheeler Waring. Smithsonian American Art Museum.

same time, generate cultural consciousness to speak to the racial climate faced by Blacks in America.

Langston Hughes was also an important proponent of racial art. In his essay "Black Art and the Racial Mountain," he contends:

> It is the intent of the Negro artist to express our individual dark-skinned selves without fear or shame. If white people are pleased, we are glad. If they are not, it doesn't matter . . . we build our temples for tomorrow,

strong as we know how, and we stand on top of the mountain, free within ourselves.[13]

Therefore, for Du Bois and Hughes, Black artists had an obligation to liberate themselves, uplift themselves, and empower themselves by stepping into public spaces. Du Bois labeled this group of leaders in the arts and beyond the "Talented Tenth."

Du Bois, as a leader of the artistic Renaissance in Harlem, also launched the first Pan-African Congress in Paris February 1919, in response to racial tensions across America and President Woodrow Wilson's embrace of Jim Crow ideologies. Du Bois initially believed Wilson was a "cultivated scholar of farsighted fairness, he has brains, and he will not seek further means of Jim Crow insult."[14] Wilson's campaign verbiage represented Black reform. He declared, "Blacks may count on me for absolute fair dealing. . . . My earnest wish is to see justice done."[15] However, upon Wilson taking office, he re-segregated Washington, DC, and removed Black employees from government positions. Du Bois was outraged by Wilson's deceit, regressive policies, and exclusion of African American representation in political public spaces. Du Bois, more determined than ever, successfully convened the Pan-African Congress and brought together Black elites such as Marcus Garvey, James Weldon Johnson, Blaise Diagne, John Hope, and Addie W. Hunton.[16] They all gathered to discuss issues concerning African diaspora communities and set a plan in motion. Du Bois, and other Black intellectuals at the conference, decided to push the mobilization of the arts. Thus, visual art became central to advancing the concerns of Black diaspora communities. Because racial uplift was the concern of this movement, Blacks no longer sought approval or tried to adhere to a nation that rested on racialist assumptions about Blackness.

The conference was merely one avenue Du Bois embarked on to achieve the elevation of Black humanity through Black art. Du Bois used *The Crisis* to bring an international awareness to the struggles Black artists faced in hopes of expanding viewership and value. He claimed, "Until the art of black folk compels recognitions they will not be rated as human. And when through art they compel recognition then let the world discover if it will that their art is as new as it is old and as old as is new."[17] In his magazine, Du Bois spoke of a Black woman artist whose clay work deserved a scholarship abroad and the opportunity to increase her knowledge and influence. Although Du Bois does not name this woman, Savage's, Waring's, and Fuller's struggles to secure scholarships abroad and overcome racism represent such a woman. Du Bois goes on to state, "There is in New York tonight a black woman molding clay by herself in a little bare room, because there is not a single school of sculpture in New York where she is welcome . . . this girl is working her hands off to

Laura Wheeler Waring painting of W. E. B. Du Bois. National Portrait Gallery, Smithsonian Institute.

get out of this country so that she can get some sort of training."[18] Achieving expatriate status became a key factor in the success of artists, including in the cases of Savage, Waring, and Fuller.

Du Bois not only possessed great intellectual stature, he was also an internationalist. He understood the value in obtaining education in Europe due to severe racial oppression in the United States. The early nineteenth century judicial system offered no protection for African Americans in the US and fundamentally contributed to the economic and social stagnancy of the Black community. Du Bois maintained close relationships with Savage, Waring, and Fuller by publicizing both their art and any discriminatory events they fought to overcome. These women all studied in Paris, mastering Western techniques, building an international network, and increasing their notoriety. They found ways to communicate to the larger Black community through art. Their time in Paris earned them critical acclaim that was accepted by the white world for its beauty and imagery. But their work also helped to alter perceptions about race, as illustrated with messages of Black reform and racial uplift.

Once Savage, Waring, and Fuller traveled back to the US, they hit the ground running by responding to national crises that erupted across America, and they created paintings and sculptures that exposed truths about Blackness. This artistry challenged white stereotypes that had long permeated American art. Art in all forms became the transformative tool for Black America, and visual art helped to alter persistent images of Black racial inferiority. These artists received international recognition that facilitated social reform. Savage's, Waring's, and Fuller's art acted as a form of intellectual activism and an expression of their ideas in public spaces, which helped usher in a "new democracy in American culture, with a new social understanding."[19]

Alain Locke's "New Negro" envisages the New Negro as a radical agent for Black reform, Black uplift, and race consciousness. Locke states that "with renewed self-respect and self-dependence, the life of the Negro community is bound to enter a new dynamic phase."[20] In public arts, Black artists created a platform to awaken Black consciousness transnationally and were a part of the Talented Tenth. According to David Levering Lewis:

> The talented tenth formulated and propagated a new ideology of racial assertiveness that was to be embraced by the physicians, dentists, educators, preachers, business people, lawyers, and morticians who comprised the bulk of the African American affluent influential—some 10,000 men and women out of a total population in 1920 of more than 10 million.[21]

Savage, Waring, and Fuller were members of this collective intelligentsia and established themselves as race women who asserted claims about Black life through public sculptures. As internationalists, these women generated international influence through racial linkages from "national concerns to global ones."[22] According to Keisha Blain and Tiffany Gill in their book *To Turn the Whole World Over: Black Women and Internationalism*, Black women internationals "maintained a global racial consciousness and employed a range of strategies and tactics to advance a black internationalist agenda." Through intersectional approaches to race, gender, and spatial, these women were able to re-create themselves in public spaces.²³

* * *

Augusta Savage was born in Green Cove Springs, Florida, in 1892. Savage, as a child, had undeniable talent that was apparent at an early age, when she began forming objects out of any material she could get her hands on. As she transitioned out of adolescence, she sharpened her technique and eventually applied these techniques in her studies, securing various scholarships to study abroad. By 1923, she was thrust into the spotlight after she was rejected from the Fontainebleau School of Fine Arts in Paris, France. Once the committee realized Savage was Black, they decided to no longer extend their offer.²⁴ This was a defining moment in Savage's career. Her response created an international awareness, and race became the underlying theme within her sculptures thereafter. Savage stated that this incident "only served to fire me with more determination than ever to succeed."²⁵ She immediately wrote the committee to express her dismay for their decision, stating:

> One of the reasons why more of my race do not go for higher education is that as soon as one of us gets his head above the crowd there are millions of feet ready to crush it back again to that dead level of commonplace thus creating a racial deadline of culture in our Republic. For how am I to compete with other American artists if I am not to be given the same opportunity?²⁶

Savage posed questions to the committee that highlighted the burden of white liberalism and advocated for Black inclusivity in art and educational sectors. The committee's nonacceptance perpetuated segregationist and xenophobic mandates against African Americans and preserved white womanhood at all costs. Savage's response was to fearlessly interrogate racism in academic settings and to voice her grievances during a time when Black Americans were to keep their heads down and remain voiceless, especially Black women. She used her global connections with the larger Black international community to advance the cause of Black equality.

This community included Du Bois, who rallied for the committee to reverse their decision. Du Bois, as one of the leaders of the New Negro Renaissance, followed up with a letter to the committee expressing his deepest disappointment. He also challenged the decision through publication in *The Crisis*, which stated:

I do not doubt that the ultimate art coming from black folk is going to be just as beautiful, and beautiful largely in the same ways, as the art that comes from white folk, or yellow, or red; but the point today is that until the art of the black folk compels recognition they will not be rated as human.[27]

Although the committee stood firm in its decision, this did create a buzz within the art world, leading to the Julius Rosenwald Fellowship in 1929 for the work *Gamin* (figure 3).[28] The word "*gamin*" is French for street urchin. The sculpture depicts a young boy with a wrinkled shirt looking outward. His expression appears much wiser than his years, suggesting he experienced oppressive societal norms within Black America. *Gamin* served as a rebuttal to years of false images of Blackness, such as represented with coons, minstrels, and sambos, and refuted stereotypes against Black boys as "primitive," "devious," or "dimwitted."

The realism captured within *Gamin* was inspired by Savage's nephew, who came to spend time with her over the summer. As she settled into her Parisian life, she won a scholarship for *Gamin*. The sculpture possesses a human essence that evokes a universal connective emotion of commiseration that Blacks identified with during this time. This three-dimensional sculpture creates a sense of ascension and prosperity over subjugation amid racial intolerance in its audience. Savage awoke a Black diasporic consciousness that emphasized the reality of exploitation against Blacks and the native resilience Blacks generationally possessed to come as far as they had in spite of racism. The eyes of the sculpture were a reflection of her own, suggesting the adjustments that she had to make to life in Paris. Savage desired to change her circumstances and the current and future circumstances of people of African diaspora communities. Reminiscent of Du Bois's "double consciousness," *Gamin* evoked a dual expression of internal hardship buried inside an assertive statue.

Savage worked every day to rise above racially discriminatory beliefs, and just like as represented in *Gamin*, her eyes told the story of hardship and internal strife. Savage stated, "Art is eternal. For example, The Gamin for instance, revolutions may come, and fascism may go but nothing could affect the smiling insouciance of the bust. The jaunty angle of his cap, the knowing twinkle in his eye, the scornful twist of his mouth, are all eternal equalities."[29] Savage recasts this time in a 1935 interview with F.A.C., in which she states, "They came, they saw,—I conquered."[30] She set off to Paris and spent the next three years enhancing her skills, finalizing a technique that gained international acclaim.

While abroad, Savage built a viable network that increased awareness of her exhibits. She created *The Laughing Boy*, resembling *Gamin* through her use of a Black boy. *Laughing Boy* gleamed with a joyful expression, looking up as freedom greets him. The bright smile highlights Black individuals' ability to

Gamin, a prize-winning sculpture by Augusta Savage. Arts & Artifacts Division, Schomburg Center for Research in Black Culture, the New York Public Library.

remain hopeful and jovial through deadly white supremacy. *Gamin* and *Laughing Boy* were a source of great pride for Savage and served as a reflection both of her inner sentiments and as a positive representation for African Americans. Savage exhibited both pieces in the American Art Association–Anderson Galleries Tenth Annual Spring Salon of American Art in 1932.[31] That same year, she opened Savage Studio of Arts and Crafts in Harlem, the growing capital

The Harp, a sculpture by Augusta Savage exhibited at the World's Fair in 1939. Arts & Artifacts Division, Schomburg Center for Research in Black Culture, the New York Public Library.

of Black nationhood.[32] This was an audacious move, made as it was during the height of the Great Depression. Savage was tenacious in her quest to develop a space for herself and her work. She possessed resilience and remained strong in adverse socioeconomic times. Her concern for race kept her driven, creating the school to provide a space for public intellectual thought in artistic forms. She taught and mentored William Artis, Ernest Crichlow, and Gwendolyn Knight.[33]

These students developed into notable artists in their own right, who used art to protest social inequalities and depict the uplift of the race.

While in Harlem, Savage coordinated with artist and Harlemite James Weldon Johnson. Their relationship influenced one of her most captivating works, *The Harp*. Inspired by Johnson's Black national anthem and poem "Lift Every Voice and Sing," *The Harp* was showcased in 1939 at the New York World's Fair.[34] The sixteen-foot sculpture was a strategic attack on the white narrative of the Negro. Johnson declared that "stereotypes of the Negro have been formed by such media as the stage. . . . Just as they were formed, they will be broken up in that way." *The Harp* displayed twelve figures arranged in ascending order to resemble the strings of a harp. All the figures were united by the "arm of God" supporting and bearing the burden of Black Americans, allowing them to look forward and sing. They didn't relish the existing racial state, but embraced the beauty in Blackness and Black voices that are empowered by God. This collaboration between Savage and Johnson awoke Black diasporic consciousness and acted as a physical realization of African Americans' faith that true equality would prevail in America.[35]

In a 1935 interview for *Metropolitan Magazine*, Savage stated, "I hope to create something which will not only add to the culture of my race but the culture of the world. . . . If I can inspire one of these youngsters to develop the talent I know they possess, then, my monument will be in their work. No one could ask for more than that."[36] Savage's artistic, racial provocations were retained through her students and allies as everlasting advancements within public art, public thought, and intellectual activism. She positioned herself as a political advocate for social reform for the Black community. Her strides in expanding Black consciousness solidified her purpose and created national change for Black America and Black culture. Through her work, Savage impacted race consciousness, as a Black woman international, and helped to perpetuate Black cultural awareness transnationally as a public intellectual and race woman.

* * *

Laura Wheeler Waring was born in 1887 in Hartford, Connecticut. From a young age, Waring's talent was clear, precise, and noticeably distinct. She graduated at the top of her class of 149 students. Through the A. William Emlen Cresson Memorial Travel Scholarship, Waring was selected to further her artistic studies across Western Europe after she graduated high school. In 1914, she arrived in Paris. However, upon the advent of the First World War, her studies were interrupted. She then traveled back home to resume a part-time teaching position that she had held since 1906 at the all-Black Cheyney Training School for Teachers near Philadelphia. Waring eventually became the head of the Art and Music Department. While teaching, she simultaneously continued to work on her own art and arranged several trips to Europe for further study. In 1924, Waring went back to Paris and, for the first time, she exhibited her paintings in Parisian art galleries and studied at the Académie de la Grande Chaumière in Paris.[37]

In 1925, Waring went to Algiers with Jessie Redmon Fauset and was stunned by the conditions she found. "The harbor was magnificent and crowded with poor dirty Arabs in the most nondescript garments you have ever seen."[38] This experience triggered Waring and Fauset to collaborate on an article for *The Crisis*. Fauset wrote the details and Waring provided the illustrations. In their published article, "Dark Algiers and White," this successful duo expressed their joint Black awareness and desire to portray accurate literature and visuals of the Africans they encountered while in Algiers. Unlike Garveyites, Waring felt a disconnect between Pan-African ideologies and Black America. In the article "Once More We Exchange Adieu," Waring drew an image that depicted a Black woman in modest dress and pumps holding a small suitcase or briefcase, gesturing to a white woman and child dressed in hats, scarves, and coats.[39] This image represented Waring and Fauset's discomfort with the way they were received. They experienced many unsettling stares from distant eyes.

Waring's art and success abroad won her international acclaim. Following their trip to Algiers, they toured across Europe, visiting several cities in Italy, including Genoa, Sarona, Rome, Florence, Venice, and Milan.[40] Waring was a part of the Black internationalist movement, documenting her global journey in a diary titled *My Trip Abroad*, sharing her ideas and experiences that struck her cultural interest.[41] Waring gained freedom and recognition that she could not tap into within the US and used her skills to influence social change in the art world.

In 1926, Waring, now an internationally prestigious artist, returned to the United States and served as an official in charge of the Negro Art section at the Sesquicentennial International Exposition in Philadelphia. She was the only African American chosen for the judges' panel of the Harmon Foundation during the first year the foundation gave awards.[42] Waring broke through racial and gender barriers with her panel presence, and was also awarded the foundation's highest award. She remains the only woman—Black or white—to be so honored. Waring was extremely modest and never proclaimed herself to be an activist. However, because of her success, international notoriety, and her experiences as a Black woman during a time when racism and inequality were explosive, her artwork nevertheless served as a political and intellectual basis for people of color to express their ideas about race in the public sphere.

Anna Washington Derry was one of Waring's most noteworthy works, celebrating the quintessential Black woman. Waring used a technique of painting the portrait over a poster with words to amplify the subject's white-washed achievements, symbolizing the years of degradation that Blacks endured. Waring remedied the harsh imagery of Blacks that was created through racial intolerance and produced *Anna Washington Derry* with an assertive and confident posture, with bright and sincere eyes. Most of Waring's paintings were of known societal figures, both Black and white, like W. E. B. Du Bois, James Weldon Johnson, James Hayes, and Mary White Ovington. She was primarily interested in capturing variations of Blackness. Along with *Anna Washington Derry*, her portraits *Velva, Frankie, Sunday Best,* and *Maria Cayetuna* showcased her versatility.[43] She became a trailblazer best known as a realist painter of portraits, landscapes, and still lifes, broadcasting respectable images of gendered Blackness, upheld in a dignified esteem. Racial uplift and Black identity were key themes that were projected throughout her work.

Waring painted a portrait of W. E. B. Du Bois to commemorate and to help popularize his achievements and success he created for Black America. Du Bois and Waring's relationship began with her cover illustrations for *Crisis* magazine, which helped to depict the political and social experience of Blacks, through a Pan-African lens. Waring's *W. E. B. Du Bois* offers a respectable representation of racial uplift and Black reformist sensibilities in America.

James Weldon Johnson was championed for his political and social activism for Black rights during the Harlem Renaissance. He was a successful Broadway lyricist, poet, novelist, and diplomat and an instrumental leader in the NAACP. In the 1920s, Johnson became known for his anthology *The Book of American Negro Poetry* and his works *African American Religion, God's Trombones,* and *Black Manhattan*, the first history of African Americans in New York City.[44] *The Book of American Negro Poetry* empowered Blacks across the world and served as a catalyst to his successful strategies to eliminate segregation laws in America. The background of Waring's *James Weldon Johnson* reproduced a visualization of "Creation," Johnson's best-known poem in *God's Trombones*, in which his tone mirrors church ministry to convey the beautiful beginnings of God's universe while using biblical metaphors such as Genesis. *James Weldon Johnson* toured nationwide from 1944 to 1954 and served as a visual rebuttal to racism. Waring captured Johnson's manner and air with vibrant colors surrounded in the message of change he expressed in his anthology. The piece promoted Black heroes during a time of racial turmoil and Black exclusion. *W. E. B. Du Bois* and *James Weldon Johnson* highlighted the respectability of Black men and elites.

In the late 1920s, several of Waring's paintings were displayed at the Harmon Foundation exhibit, which featured artwork from African American artists. Waring's art was highly sought after and displayed at several institutions, including the Smithsonian Institution and the Art Institute of Chicago. Her illustrations depicting prominent African American subjects appeared in several books and magazines, and in 1943 the Harmon Foundation commissioned Waring to paint the series "Portraits of Outstanding American Citizens of Negro Origin."[45]

Waring's time in Europe was crucial to her work, which developed during the 1920s and 1930s. Her time in France played a significant role in her development, and during her three different voyages, her interactions with renowned French, African, and African American intellectuals influenced her art, which attempted to capture Black life experiences.[46] These expatriate encounters gave her inspiration and the chance to experience liberties that were lost in Wilson's America. Waring illustrated everyday Black citizens and Black elites in her work and allowed her brushstrokes to champion them as heroes of both Black reform and Black culture. As a teacher with thirty years of experience, Waring saw the importance of visual historical imagery. She supported Du Bois and the cultural elevation movement to tear down white oratories and condemnations of the Black community and reinstitute an accurate account that represented all the talent and beauty that had been suppressed.

* * *

Meta Warrick Fuller was born in 1887 in Philadelphia, Pennsylvania, where she spent her adolescent years fine-tuning her freehand sketching and mechanical drawing skills at the Pennsylvania Museum School of Industrial Arts.[47] She graduated in 1899 and received a one-year scholarship to study in Paris at the American Girls' Art Club. It took Fuller over a year to make it abroad. However, upon her arrival in 1899, she faced severe racism and was immediately rejected by the Art Club's white attendees. Fuller was discouraged by this response, but she was determined to see it through. Fuller left the club and enrolled herself in the Académie Colarossi, where she mastered her sculpting in a naturalistic form. Things began to improve for Fuller abroad, and Paris offered her new opportunities. Of her experience abroad, she stated, "Women had the opportunity to direct their own lives in ways unavailable to them at home, where they were often tangled in household and familial duties."[48] What "home" meant to Fuller was persistent marginalization, inequality, and racial injustice. Garveyism, with its emphasis on Black male identity and nationhood, was also emerging in the US at this time, insisting on the importance of women taking their natural place as producers and supporting men from behind.[49] Fuller opposed the ideology espoused by Garveyites by focusing on gendered themes in her work while supporting the increased awareness of race.

Fuller's work received global recognition during the 1922 America's Making Expositions when she debuted *Ethiopia Awakening* in the heart of Harlem.[50] The forum was composed of thirty-three racial groups of immigrants who have settled in America from 1607 to the contemporary era. *Ethiopia Awakening* portrayed a shrouded female figure to suggest the awakening consciousness of race. Fuller raised awareness of Pan-African ideals and transracial connections to Africans across the diaspora. Adapting Egyptian form and the contemporary literary-religious tradition of "Ethiopianism," Fuller stated, "Here was a group (Negro) who had once made history and now after a long sleep was awaking, gradually unwinding the bandage of its mummied past and looking out on life again, expectant but afraid and with at least a graceful gesture."[51] Fuller intersected ideas of gender and race, conceiving the notion of duality. She uses an Egyptian queen with her breasts erect and feminine features, draped in a *nemes* (headdress), which was the traditional garb for Egyptian kings.[52] Fuller addressed contemporary Pan-Africanism through a feminist lens. She introduced the "New Black Woman," capable of leading, standing just as tall and possessing just as much prestige as men.[53] The exposition was a much-needed forum to promote cultural pluralism and cultural expression.[54]

Mary Turner: A Silent Protest against Mob Violence was a direct reply to racial violence in the United States. In 1918, the nineteen-year-old and eight months pregnant Mary Turner was killed when a mob of several hundred white people dragged her to Folsom Bridge, over the Little River, which separates Georgia's Brooks and Lowndes Counties. The mob tied her ankles, strung her upside down, doused her clothes in gasoline, and set her on fire. While she was still alive, someone split open her stomach and her unborn baby slid out and fell to the ground. The mob stomped and crushed the baby to death. Turner's body was riddled with hundreds of bullets. Later that night, the remains of Turner and her baby were buried a few feet away from where they were murdered. Fuller decided not only to pay homage to Turner but also use this vile and gruesome event as a testimony. Fuller stated, "I have pictured her clutching her child as she rises from the flames, she looks disdainfully back at her captors as she floats beyond their reach while they clutch after her in vain." The sculpture shows a beautified, soulful Mary Turner emerging from the flames, peacefully reuniting in eternity with her child. Turner is cradling her baby in her arms as she ascends to heaven. Fuller did not want to create a brutal and violent depiction of Turner, but wanted to maintain her spirit in a dignified and beautiful manner. Although she was murdered in the most heinous and egregious way possible, her soul and spirit will forever live on in Fuller's art.

Mary Turner's death began a series of anti-Black riots and killings led by white supremacists, thriving off Wilsonian ideas about race. Whites during this time felt empowered, and they were supported by racist policies that Wilson encouraged. The three most violent episodes occurred in Chicago, Washington, DC, and Arkansas. Jim Crow was a significant factor during these riots: it nullified Black rights and perpetuated the reality that Blacks were disposable and could be killed by whites without legal recourse. In Washington, DC, from July 19 to 23, four whites and two Blacks were killed; whites were astonished that Blacks dared to fight back, and in response to this, the attacks were especially brutal. The persistence of unpunished lynching contributed to the mob mentality among white men and fueled a new commitment to self-defense among Black men who had been emboldened by war service. James Weldon Johnson, as the executive director of the NAACP, organized peaceful protests to combat racial tensions, which ignited and mobilized African Americans to work collectively and nonviolently against racism and oppression. Because *Mary Turner* expressed the raw, brutal experiences of Blacks in America, it has been held sacred by the Black community. Fuller's art, then and now, has transcended time as a reference for future Black women intellectuals, utilizing their talents toward Black reform and racial uplift.[55]

Fuller was a "race artist" and a public sculptor of the early twentieth century. Her sculptures were visual representations of her ideas about negotiating race and gender. She sought to reclaim the dignity of African Americans and offered images to counter the negative ones often seen in fine art and the stereotypes prevalent in popular culture. Racial uplift was a recurrent theme in Fuller's work, just as it was ubiquitous in early twentieth-century racial discourse, cited in Black newspapers and monthly magazines and in studies of the "Negro Problem" and its solution. Race permeated the rhetoric of middle-class African Americans during the Progressive Era. Black men and women, following the lead of Du Bois, employed a range of strategies—discursive, cultural, and political—to convey a vision of uplift as racial progress, solidarity, self-improvement, respectability, Christian morality, and social mobility. Organizers of the America's Making Expositions in the early twentieth century believed that Fuller's sculptures, alongside displays of art, literature, statistical data, photographs, and inventions, would dispel the myth of the "Negro Problem." Fuller's sculptures remain an important symbol of Black achievement, Black consciousness, and Black identity. Themes of emancipation and Ethiopia have remained visible through exhibition in public venues. By 1921, Fuller had achieved a measure of success, but wide recognition still eluded her.

* * *

The history of Black women intellectuals has centered on politics, which omits a major movement inspired by visual art. Bonnie Claudia Harrison states the term "diasporada" "is a woman who transgresses national and political boundaries and is empowered by inserting black and female voices into a transnational Black public sphere."[56] Savage, Waring, and Fuller are deserving of the title diasporada. They advanced the discussion of Black identity and Black independence through the visual arts. Politics was no longer the sole outlet for legislative or social change within Black America, and art became the new intellectual milieu of the early twentieth century. Through the efforts of these women, art became a new form of universal activism that reached a broader network through imagery. It also assisted in helping to erase popular stereotypes of Blacks during this era. The work of these women was internationally recognized by whites and Blacks, which enhanced Black talent and showed that it stood alongside the art of their Black male counterparts. Their art renegotiated the value of Black lives and undercut the false narratives advanced by white critics.

The New Negro movement represented a new intellectualism in Black life and was in part led by African American women visual artists. Artistic expression allowed African descendants to work to dismantle racist rhetoric and oppressive social and cultural stigmas while improving the national Black experience and executing generational institutional reform. This international Black community included women such as Augusta Savage, Laura Wheeler Waring, and Meta Warrick Fuller. Through their visual representations, these women introduced modern ideas about race and gender that left a foundation for the Black Arts Movement that emerged in the mid-1960s. Savage, Waring, and Fuller are key figures in the history of Black women's intellectual traditions.

NOTES

1. Bay et al., *Toward an Intellectual History*.
2. Bay et al., *Toward an Intellectual History*.
3. Bay et al., *Toward an Intellectual History*, 3–4.
4. Dagbovie, *African American History Reconsidered*.
5. Chernoh Sesay Jr., "The Idea of the Black Intellectual," *Black Perspectives*, March 2015.
6. Waters and Conaway, *Black Women's Intellectual Traditions*, 2.
7. Collins, "What's in a Name?," 9.
8. Bay et al., *Toward an Intellectual History*, 3.
9. Bay et al., *Toward an Intellectual History*, 3.
10. Pearson, "Combatting Racism with Art."
11. Pearson, "Combatting Racism with Art," 122–25.
12. Lewis, *W. E. B. Du Bois*, 103.
13. Mitchell, *Within the Circle*.
14. Mitchell, *Within the Circle*, 117.
15. Mitchell, *Within the Circle*, 117.
16. Contee, "Du Bois, the NAACP, and the Pan-African Congress of 1919," 14.
17. Lewis, *W. E. B. Du Bois*, 104.
18. Lewis, *W. E. B. Du Bois*, 101.
19. Locke, *The New Negro*, 9.

20. Locke, *The New Negro*, 4.

21. David Levering Lewis, "The Intellectual Luminaries of the Harlem Renaissance," *Journal of Blacks in Higher Education* no. 7 (Spring 1995): 68, https://www.jstor.org/stable/2963433.

22. Blain, Gill, and West, *To Turn the Whole World Over*, 2.

23. Blain, Gill, and West, *To Turn the Whole World Over*, 6.

24. F.A.C., 1935, Augusta Savage Papers, Manuscripts, Archives and Rare Books Division, Schomburg Center for Research in Black Culture, New York Public Library.

25. F.A.C., 1935, Augusta Savage Papers, Manuscripts, Archives and Rare Books Division, Schomburg Center for Research in Black Culture, New York Public Library.

26. F.A.C., 1935, Augusta Savage Papers, Manuscripts, Archives and Rare Books Division, Schomburg Center for Research in Black Culture, New York Public Library.

27. F.A.C., 1935, Augusta Savage Papers, Manuscripts, Archives and Rare Books Division, Schomburg Center for Research in Black Culture, New York Public Library.

28. *Augusta Savage: Renaissance Woman* (Jacksonville, FL: Cummer Museum of Art and Gardens, 2018), 22.

29. T. R. Poston, *Metropolitan Magazine*, 1935, Augusta Savage Papers, Manuscripts, Archives and Rare Books Division, Schomburg Center for Research in Black Culture, New York Public Library.

30. F. A. C., 1935, Augusta Savage Papers, Manuscripts, Archives and Rare Books Division, Schomburg Center for Research in Black Culture, New York Public Library.

31. F. A. C., 1935, Augusta Savage Papers, Manuscripts, Archives and Rare Books Division, Schomburg Center for Research in Black Culture, New York Public Library.

32. *Augusta Savage: Renaissance Woman*, 22.

33. *Augusta Savage: Renaissance Woman*, 22.

34. *Augusta Savage: Renaissance Woman*, 25.

35. *Augusta Savage: Renaissance Woman*, 25.

36. T. R. Poston, *Metropolitan Magazine*, 1935, Augusta Savage Papers, Manuscripts, Archives and Rare Books Division, Schomburg Center for Research in Black Culture, New York Public Library.

37. Leininger-Miller, "'A Constant Stimulus and Inspiration.'"

38. James, "Art," 16.

39. James, "Art," 16.

40. Leininger-Miller, "'A Constant Stimulus and Inspiration.'"

41. Leininger-Miller, "'A Constant Stimulus and Inspiration.'"

42. Leininger-Miller, "'A Constant Stimulus and Inspiration.'"

43. Leininger-Miller, "'A Constant Stimulus and Inspiration.'"

44. Leininger-Miller, "'A Constant Stimulus and Inspiration.'"

45. Leininger-Miller, "'A Constant Stimulus and Inspiration.'"

46. National Portrait Gallery, "*James Weldon Johnson*," accessed April 26, 2019, https://npg.si.edu/object/npg_NPG.67.40.

47. Ater, *Remaking Race and History*, 17.

48. Ater, *Remaking Race and History*, 17.

49. Clare Corebould, *Becoming African Americans: Black Public Life in Harlem, 1919–1939* (Cambridge, MA: Harvard University Press, 2009).

50. The Negro in Literature and Art, Meta Warrick Fuller Papers, Manuscripts, Archives and Rare Books Division, Schomburg Center for Research in Black Culture, New York Public Library.

51. Ater, *Remaking Race and History*, 103.

52. Ater, *Remaking Race and History*, 103.

53. Ater, *Remaking Race and History*, 17.

54. Ater, *Remaking Race and History*, 116.

55. Armstrong, "Mary Turner's Blues," 214–15.

56. Harrison "Diasporadas." "Diasporada" is a word that I use from a hybrid of "diaspora" and "desperado." The word "diaspora" refers to the often-forced dispersal of a cultural, class, or racialized group; in this sense, I refer specifically to the temporal and geohistorical domain of the Black Atlantic. Diasporadas. The other half of diasporada, the word "desperado" was coined during an English passion for Spanish words in the sixteenth century. During this period the fashionable would add "-ado" to the end of regular English words: "ado" to "torn," and "bravado" was "ado" added to the word "brave." Desperado is an alternation of the word "desperate," meaning to be rash, extreme, or agitated. In honor of the subversive traditions of Black women transgressing boundaries to seek what was officially or surreptitiously denied them, such as recognition in transnational leadership or admission to white-only art schools, a feminized "ado" or "ada," is added to "desperado" to form "desperada." Desperada evokes the desperate and radical act of becoming invoked by women who have pushed beyond the limits imposed on their sex and race. Diaspora welded to desperada becomes "diaporada."

REFERENCES

Armstrong, Julie Buckner. "Mary Turner's Blues." *African American Review* 44, no. 1/2 (2011): 207–20.

Ater, Renée. *Remaking Race and History: The Sculpture of Meta Warrick Fuller*. Berkeley: University of California Press, 2011.

Bay, Mia E., Farah J. Griffin, Martha S. Jones, and Barbara D. Savage, eds. *Toward an Intellectual History of Black Women*. Chapel Hill: University of North Carolina Press, 2015.

Beardon, Romare, and Henderson, Harry. *6 Black Masters of American Art*. New York: Zenith Books, 1972.

Blain, Keisha N., Tiffany M. Gill, and Michael O. West. *To Turn the Whole World Over: Black Women and Internationalism*. Urbana: University of Illinois Press, 2019.

Chernev, Borislav. *Twilight of Empire: The Brest-Litovsk Conference and the Remaking of East Central Europe, 1917–1918*. Toronto: University of Toronto Press, 2017.

Collins, Patricia Hill. "What's in a Name?" *Black Scholar* 26, no. 1 (1996): 9–17.

Contee, Clarence G. "Du Bois, the NAACP, and the Pan-African Congress of 1919." *Journal of Negro History* 57, no. 1 (1972): 13–28.

Dagbovie, Pero Gaglo. *African American History Reconsidered*. Urbana: University of Illinois Press, 2010.

F. A. C. Augusta Savage Papers. Manuscripts. Archives and Rare Books Division. Schomburg Center for Research in Black Culture. New York Public Library, 1935.

Harrison, Bonnie Claudia. "Diasporadas: Black Women and the Fine Art of Activism." *Meridians* 2, no. 2 (January 2002): 163–84.

Hayes, Jeffreen M. *Augusta Savage: Renaissance Woman.* London: D. Giles Ltd., 2018.

James, Milton M. "Art." *Negro History Bulletin* 22, no. 1 (October 1958): 16.

James, Milton M. "Laura Wheeler Waring." *Negro History Bulletin* 19, no. 6 (March 1956): 126.

Leininger-Miller, Theresa. "'A Constant Stimulus and Inspiration': Laura Wheeler Waring in Paris in the 1910s and 1920s." *Source: Notes in the History of Art* 24, no. 4 (2005): 13–23.

Lewis, David Levering, ed. *Harlem Renaissance Reader.* New York: Penguin Books, 1994.

Lewis, David Levering, ed. *W. E. B. Du Bois: A Reader.* New York: Henry Holt, 1995.

Locke, Alain. *The New Negro: Voices of the Harlem Renaissance*, New York: Touchstone, 1997.

"Meta Vaux Warrick Fuller—Women's History Month." Black Media Mine, March 7, 2012. http://blackmediamine.blogspot.com/2012/03/meta-veaux-warrick-fuller-black-womens.html.

Milne, David. "Woodrow Wilson Was More Racist Than Wilsonianism." *Foreign Policy*, December 3, 2015. https://foreignpolicy.com/2015/12/03/woodrow-wilson-was-not-a-racist-in-foreign-policy/.

Mitchell, Angelyn. *Within the Circle: An Anthology of African American Literary Criticism from the Harlem Renaissance to the Present.* Durham, NC: Duke University Press, 1994.

The Negro in Literature and Art. Meta Warrick Fuller Papers. Manuscripts. Archives and Rare Books Division. Schomburg Center for Research in Black Culture. New York Public Library.

Nielsen, Euell A. "Mary Turner (1899–1918)." September 22, 2015. https://www.blackpast.org/african-american-history/mary-turner-1899-1918.

Norvell, Stanley B., and William M. Tuttle Jr. "Views of a Negro During 'The Red Summer' of 1919." *Journal of Negro History* 51, no. 3 (1966): 209–18.

Oreilly, Kenneth. "The Jim Crow Policies of Woodrow Wilson." *Journal of Blacks in Higher Education* no. 17 (1997): 117.

Pearson, Ralph I. "Combatting Racism with Art: Charles S. Johnson and the Harlem Renaissance." *American Studies* 18, no. 1 (1977): 123–34.

Poston, T. R. *Metropolitan Magazine*, 1935. Augusta Savage Papers. Manuscripts. Archives and Rare Books Division. Schomburg Center for Research in Black Culture. New York Public Library.

Smithsonian American Art Museum. "*Gamin.*" https://americanart.si.edu/artwork/gamin-21658.

Waters, Kristin, and Carol B. Conaway. *Black Women's Intellectual Traditions: Speaking Their Minds.* Burlington: University of Vermont Press, 2007.

White, Walter F. "The Work of a Mob." *The Crisis—A Record of the Darker Races* 16, no. 5 (September 1918), 221–23.

MILDRED FAY JEFFERSON AND THE PRO-LIFE MOVEMENT

A Conservative Black Woman Public Intellectual

HETTIE V. WILLIAMS

In the recent history of the United States, the antiabortion movement has primarily been a mass movement of mostly Catholic and Protestant doctors, lawyers, nurses, housewives, conservative politicians, and activists who came to view abortion as murder. These activists also came to see abortion as a moral sin as predicated on the idea of the personhood of the fetus. The idea of the personhood of the fetus was more firmly embraced by conservative Christians, some medical doctors, and far-right politicians in the mid-twentieth century. The antiabortion movement has largely been a movement of mostly conservative women since the mid-twentieth century—many of whom are associated with the Republican Party. Some of the notable women in this movement include Marjory Mecklenburg, Juli Loesch, Joan Andrews Bell, Shelley Shannon, Mildred Fay Jefferson, and Phyllis Schlafly. In *Women against Abortion: Inside the Largest Moral Reform Movement of the Twentieth Century*, Karissa Haugeberg describes the antiabortion movement as "the largest moral reform movement of the late twentieth century" and notes that the National Right to Life Committee (NRLC) had "millions of members and chapters in every state by the late 1970s."[1] Mildred Fay Jefferson was a cofounder of the NRLC and a Methodist. She became a prominent leader in the antiabortion movement during the period when organizations such as the NRLC began to make appeals beyond the Catholic community while at the same time making overtures to African Americans. This chapter is an examination of Mildred Fay Jefferson and her role in shaping the antiabortion movement as a public intellectual. First, an analysis of abortion in history is discussed; second, some necessary historiography on the antiabortion movement is covered; third, there is a discussion of Jefferson and her ideas as a major figure in the US antiabortion movement.

This chapter represents an important historical intervention in the history of the antiabortion movement because of its focus on Jefferson and her ideas about abortion. While there are many texts on the history of abortion, few of these works focus on the role of African American women in the antiabortion movement. There is currently no single text on Jefferson nor a scholarly work specifically focused on Black women, more generally, in the history of the pro-life cause. Jefferson is only mentioned in passing within much of the scholarship on the history of abortion. Jefferson was a leading voice in the history of pro-life activism, and she wrote extensively about her views on abortion and gave public talks on the subject on a regular basis. She was also instrumental in the development of key pro-life organizations at both the local and national levels. In many respects, she is a key architect of the idea of the personhood of the fetus. Jefferson used her knowledge as a physician to advance the pro-life agenda by using her position as a Black woman public intellectual to write about and deliver public lectures on abortion.

Abortion has been practiced in most societies. It is mentioned in "the literature of every period" as one of many methods of controlling pregnancy used by women.[2] Historical documents indicate that women have always found ways to manage their fertility or abort unwanted pregnancies. However, ideas about the legality and ethics of abortion, as a means to control human reproduction, have varied. There is a complex history of ideas surrounding the moral and legal aspects of abortion. It has not always been deemed disdainful or sinful or, in legal discourse, illegal. Some ancient texts actually provide advice on how to regulate fertility, including some information about abortion.

In ancient times, women used several techniques to abort pregnancies, including applying pressure to the abdomen, ingesting herbs with abortifacient properties, taking toxic chemicals, engaging in strenuous exercise, and using blunt instruments.[3] Descriptions of abortion as a practice and discussions of contraceptives appear in multiple ancient writings including in ancient Assyrian, Egyptian, and Sanskrit texts.[4] Judith Orr points out that the women of ancient Egypt used fermented animal feces or applied "honey to their vaginas" as contraceptives.[5] She further notes that the Egyptian work *Kahun Gynaecological Papyrus*, considered to be one of the oldest medical texts in history, mentions information about abortifacients including recipes for how to make these substances.[6]

Abortion took place in ancient societies to the rise of Christianity. Plato and Aristotle both discuss abortion in their writings.[7] Though the Hippocratic oath is often cited as an indication that the practice was frowned upon by medical practitioners in ancient Greece, and Hippocrates likely had followers who were hesitant to prescribe abortifacients, induced abortions took place in the Greco-Roman world. Roman records suggest that abortion was a common occurrence, though there are also prohibitions on the practice that can be found in the history of ancient Rome. The rise of Christianity in the first century of the Roman empire clearly had an impact on how westerners would come to view abortion, though the practice was not necessarily outlawed or banned outright in the Christian West until the early modern era. In spite of this lack of outright condemnation, early Christian texts were ambivalent about the practice. This is evident in first-century Christian writings, including the *Didache* (*The Lord's Teaching Through the Twelve Apostles to the Nations*), an anonymous work concerned with Christian ethics and morality; the *Epistle of Barnabas*, a treatise of instructions on living a Christian life; and the *Apocalypse of Peter*, a discourse on the rewards for Christian virtue and punishments for sin. Tertullian, Clement of Alexandria, and Augustine of Hippo also suggest a contempt for abortion in their writings. That said, there is also evidence that Christian clerics and churchmen such as Peter of Spain mentioned abortifacients in their writings during the late Middle Ages. By the nineteenth century, Catholic canon law came to more explicitly ban abortion. Thus, the antiabortion movement in Western societies and, more specifically, the US has had a connection to ideas about Christian ethics and sin.

There has been a perennial debate regarding the status of the fetus as a living thing or person, which is central to the development of ideas about the legality and morality of abortion in the history of Western societies such as the US. For early Christians, the existence of the soul (or "ensoulment") was a core concern. Until and throughout the early modern era, most early churchmen embraced the Aristotelian view that ensoulment took place only after several weeks into pregnancy. Thus, some argued that abortion was not considered murder (though others continued to argue it was a sin) until after the development of a soul. This concern with the emergence of a soul and the different phases of a pregnancy also reveals that the personhood of the fetus was not universally accepted, but rather that there was some debate about whether or not life begins at the point of conception. In other words, the idea of the personhood of the fetus emerged over time and has come to define the pro-life cause.

Until the mid-nineteenth century, the fetus was only considered a potential person in the American context before the quickening time (four to sixth months into the pregnancy or the point at which the mother can feel the fetus move), when legal restrictions against abortion were introduced in several US states.[8] There were laws in place against post-quickening abortions in Colonial America before the mid-nineteenth century, but the focus seems to have been on protecting the life of the mother while the punishment for such a crime was only a misdemeanor.[9] Scholars of colonial America have argued that "most forms of abortion were not illegal."[10] There were also few prosecutions for abortion before the late nineteenth century. Connecticut passed the first law in the US banning abortions after quickening in 1821.

In the nineteenth century, abortions were increasingly criminalized in the US, while the move toward decriminalization did not begin until the mid-twentieth century. By 1860, twenty states had laws prohibiting abortion. The Comstock Act of 1873 made it a federal offense to distribute birth control through the mail or across state lines, categorizing such material as illicit and immoral. By 1900, nearly every US state had a law prohibiting abortion at all stages of pregnancy. However, there were exceptions to these laws that allowed for therapeutic abortions, under the supervision of a physician, to save the life of the mother. That said, many women who could not afford to pay a medical doctor for the procedure were forced onto a dangerous black market to secure an abortion.

Margaret Sanger, who was prosecuted for her writings on birth control in 1914, opened the first birth control clinic in the US in 1916 in New York but was promptly arrested for violating the law. Due to the lack of access to safe birth control methods, countless women died as a result of unsafe abortions. With the rise of the women's liberation movement in the 1960s, these deaths led, in part, to calls for the relaxation of abortion laws. Several states, including Colorado, California, and New York, began to liberalize their abortion laws by 1967.

In the 1970s, amid this liberalization of abortion practices as well as the rise of the women's liberation movement in the 1970s, Linda Gordon authored one of the earliest analyses on the history of women's reproductive rights with her book 1976 *Woman's Body, Woman's Right: Birth Control in America*. This text shaped the historiography of women and reproduction in significant ways. Gordon contextualizes the history of birth control from the nineteenth century to the contemporary debates about abortion. She argues that the matter of choice for women had been sociopolitical rather than technological. She also advances this claim from a feminist perspective that has become central to much of the scholarship not only on abortion rights but also the history of women's liberation more generally.

Historians have largely neglected the antiabortion movement in their analyses of women in twentieth-century US history, having primarily focused on the rights and freedoms of women in relation reproductive choice from a left-leaning feminist perspective, despite the fact that by the mid-twentieth century, the movement was a women's movement that was advanced by primarily by women, be they grassroots activists, doctors, nurses, or lawyers. Histories of the twentieth-century women's movement are dominated by monographs and survey histories with a left-leaning interpretation of women that tend to focus on white radical or liberal feminists who embraced a pro-choice stance.

Some of the more standard surveys in this genre of books on the history of the women's liberation movement include classics such as *Personal Power: The Roots of Women's Liberation in the Civil Rights Movement & the New Left* by Sara Evans on the origins of the women's rights movement in the civil rights era and *Daring to Be Bad: Radical Feminism in America, 1967–1975*, a survey of radical feminists and their politics by Alice Echols. In the mid-1980s, as more texts began to appear that focused on women, abortion, and the antiabortion movement, the focus on the reproductive rights of women increased. Two of the more pivotal texts in this historiography include *Abortion and Women's Choice: The State, Sexuality, and Reproductive Freedom* by Rosalind Petchesky and *Reproductive Rights and Wrongs: The Global Politics of Population Control and Contraceptive Choice* by Betsy Hartmann.

In her groundbreaking text, Petchesky posits that abortion is both an individual and social event in that the choices we make as individuals are shaped by historical and social contexts. In her book, Hartmann emphasizes how global politics shape individual choice. These scholars made important contributions to our understanding of how state power informs behavior, while also demonstrating the impact of conservative politics on the freedoms of women.

In the late 1990s and early 2000s, the study of abortion in history became more expansive.[11] Abortion is a multifaceted subject in historical studies that includes a discussion of social movements, the history of ideas, science, politics, medicine, law, religion, and ethics. This is reflected in the series of scholarly texts that have been published on the topic from 1998 to the present, such as Monica J. Casper's *The Making of the Unborn Patient: A Social Anatomy of Fetal Surgery* on the history of the idea of the fetus as a person; Dorothy Roberts's *Killing the Black Body: Race, Reproduction, and the Meaning of Liberty*, one of the earlier scholarly discussions of race and the reproductive rights movement; Brian Stormer's *Articulating Life's Memory: U.S. Medical Rhetoric about Abortion in the Nineteenth Century*, concerning ideas about abortion in the medical profession during the nineteenth century as the practice became increasingly criminalized; and Ziad W. Munson's *The Making of Pro-Life Activists: How Social Movement Mobilization Works*, one of the earliest scholarly examinations of pro-life activism.

Scholarly analyses on abortion that include a discussion of race tend to approach the subject of abortion from an individual rights based analysis within a social justice framework such as in Roberts's *Killing the Black Body*, Jennifer Nelson's *Women of Color and the Reproductive Rights Movement*, and *Undivided Rights: Women of Color Organized for Reproductive Rights* by Jael Silliman, Marlene Gerber Fried, Loretta Ross, and Elena R. Gutiérrez.[12] Rickie Solinger also centers race and class in her expansive narrative *Pregnancy and Power: A History of Reproductive Politics in the United States* about the quest by US women to control their reproduction. These texts tend to focus on reproductive rights through a leftist lens centering individual rights, with an emphasis on abortion as an issue of equal rights for women. In texts that discuss race and abortion, the focus has been on women of color and the reproductive rights movement from a liberal perspective and on African American women as advocates for the pro-choice position. Scholars of the New Right have increasingly begun to fill this void in the scholarly discussion of abortion in history by incorporating some discussion of conservative women and their views on abortion.

More recently, histories of the New Right focused on religion and politics, and they are represented with a series of critical texts that discuss conservative women and their role in the antiabortion movement in greater detail.[13] These scholars have examined conservative women and the pro-life movement in depth, such as in Catherine Rymph's *Republican Women: Feminism and Conservatism from Suffrage through the Rise of the New Right* and *Phyllis Schlafly and Grassroots Conservatism: A Woman's Crusade* by Donald T. Critchlow. These texts have been followed by a growing number of books on the antiabortion movement and intellectual histories on antiabortion ideologies. Abortion features prominently in the larger political history of the New Right, and antiabortion activism is a common element of the culture wars.

In his book *Defenders of the Unborn: The Pro-Life Movement before Roe*, Daniel K. Williams details the early twentieth-century history of the pro-life movement before *Roe v. Wade*, illustrating how the antiabortion movement brought together a diverse contingent of activists who saw themselves as defenders of human rights. This suggests that scholars who have written about abortion focusing primarily on pro-choice ideologies and activists from a leftist-rights-based social justice analysis have neglected to realize that antiabortion advocates also saw themselves as the defenders of human rights. Before *Roe*, this category included liberal Democrats who participated in the civil rights movement. These liberal Democrats also began to link their cause to the Black freedom struggle.[14] Haugeberg focuses on the history of the antiabortion movement by detailing the rise of pregnancy crisis centers, the idea of postabortion syndrome, and the grassroots activism of pro-life women.

These two works are reflective of the most recent scholarship on the history of the abortion issue that have come to emphasize the antiabortion movement, as opposed to focusing primarily on pro-choice leftists within a social justice framework. Williams and Haugeberg both discuss the role of Jefferson in the early pro-life movement, but her part in advancing the intellectual development of the pro-life cause is largely muted in each text. In *Defenders of the Unborn*, Williams describes Jefferson as primarily concerned with personal responsibility and medical ethics in her antiabortion activism and as having "no religious reasons for opposing abortion."[15] However, Jefferson did in fact become increasingly far right in her thoughts concerning abortion while also adopting religious rhetoric in her public commentary on the subject. That said, Williams does further point out that Jefferson was not a "regular churchgoer" and tended to emphasize philosophical rather than religious reasons for her opposition to abortion.[16] Williams rightly notes that Jefferson was a key figure in the transition of the antiabortion movement from a cause largely dominated by Catholics into an "increasingly Protestant and female" movement. After the early 1970s, Jefferson's thinking about abortion gravitated further to the right.

In *Women against Abortion*, Haugeberg demonstrates that the antiabortion movement was one of the largest reform movements in US history to have women at the center. She describes Jefferson as a conservative who emphasized personal responsibility and rejected social entitlement programs such as affirmative action, who was "never considered" to be a serious candidate for public office, and as an activist who engaged in "secular antiabortion activism."[17] However, Jefferson's later writings clearly counter this claim that she was a secular activist. This view of Jefferson is inexact; Jefferson continued to make intellectual contributions to the pro-life movement through her speeches, writings, and continued grassroots activism, which engaged religious dogma and rhetoric to advance her argument.

Mildred Fay Jefferson, an only child, was born on April 4, 1926, in Pittsburg, Texas, to Millard, a Methodist minister, and Guthrie Jefferson, a public school teacher.[18] Jefferson was a child prodigy and completed her formal education in Texas at a young age. Though she graduated high school in 1941, at fifteen she was considered too young to enter medical school. She went on to earn a bachelor of arts degree (summa cum laude) from Texas College in Tyler, Texas, in 1944.[19] Texas College is a historically Black college associated with the Christian Methodist Episcopal Church. Jefferson's family relocated to Massachusetts after her graduation from college. She subsequently earned a master of science degree from Tufts University in Boston at the age of twenty.[20]

In 1947, she entered Harvard Medical School and earned a medical degree in 1951, becoming the first Black woman to secure a medical degree from that institution.[21] Jefferson also went on to become the first Black woman to earn a surgical internship at Boston City Hospital and the first woman doctor at Boston University Medical Center (now called Boston Medical Center), eventually becoming a professor of surgery at Boston University School of Medicine.[22] She is described by W. Victor R. Vieweg, a medical doctor and professor of psychiatry and internal medicine, as "the most qualified surgeon ever trained in the United States serving the equivalent of three complete general surgery residencies."[23] Her credentials show that she is an intellectual in the traditional sense of the word, as one who possesses a classical education and wrote her ideas down as a member of academe. However, she also turned to the public square to make her case against abortion as a medical doctor and an antiabortion activist.

Jefferson is a part of American women's history, and specifically African American women's intellectual history. The tradition identified by editors Mia Bay, Farah J. Griffin, Martha S. Jones, and Barbara D. Savage in their groundbreaking volume *Toward an Intellectual History of Black Women* does not include a sustained discussion of Black women conservatives such as Jefferson. Though these scholars reveal the intellectual tradition of Black women in US history by highlighting their intellectual approaches to empowerment, Black women conservatives are completely left out of this history.

African American women as public intellectuals who were at the center of the culture wars have been largely overlooked by most scholars who study this era in US history. Specifically, women such as Jefferson, Oprah Winfrey, and Joycelyn Elders, three women who were central to many of the key debates regarding religion, sex, and reproductive rights during this era, have been nearly erased in this history. That said, other conservative Black women intellectuals have also been left out of the larger discussion of Black women's intellectual traditions. Jefferson used some of the same tactics and approaches of Black women intellectuals more closely associated with this tradition. She was a noted orator and grassroots organizer who came to profoundly impact the antiabortion movement in the US. While Jefferson's conservatism goes against the grain of Black protest ideologies, nevertheless, she and women like Alveda King, niece of Martin Luther King Jr., are a part of Black women's intellectual history. She was among a contingent of Black intellectuals such as Armstrong Williams who turned away from the "liberal" university to advance her views on abortion by engaging a broader public outside of academia.

Many texts by the New Right that include some discussion of Jefferson or race and African Americans in the antiabortion movement more generally fail to incorporate a sustained discussion of the intellectual contributions that individuals like Jefferson made to the development of the antiabortion movement. She was not only pivotal in founding the modern antiabortion movement as a cofounder and president of the NRLC, but she also made significant intellectual contributions to the antiabortion cause. Jefferson adopted more strident religious rhetoric in her opposition to abortion, became noticeably antifeminist, and should be considered an important far-right culture warrior. Scholars of the New Right have noted that public policy debates, cultural contexts, and social movements show the ways in which antiabortion advocates were embroiled in the culture wars that began to play out in the 1960s.

Historians have typically referred the successive twentieth-century conflicts between traditionalist and modernist views over morality in the US as the "culture wars." This phrase is amorphous in terms of chronology and scope. There have been a series of culture wars in US history across the twentieth century involving political, cultural, and social conflicts over subjects such as creationism, school prayer, sex education, homosexuality, gay marriage, multiculturalism, and abortion, among other controversial topics. James Davison Hunter in his 1991 book *Culture Wars: The Struggle to Control the Family, Art, Education, Law, and Politics* defines the culture wars as "an ideological struggle to define America" as expressed in competing epistemologies about human morality.[24] This contestation between orthodox and more progressive views of human morality was reinvigorated during the 1960s in significant ways over the issue of abortion.

Historian Daniel K. Williams describes Jefferson as "a conservative who supported Richard Nixon" and "eventually joined the Republican Party."[25] She was a far-right Methodist and Republican Black woman conservative who was antiabortion, against affirmative action, and an outspoken critic of what she called the "radical feminist agenda."[26] Jefferson is most noted for being "the greatest orator" of the pro-life movement as so described by Darla St. Martin, an executive with the NRLC.[27] For Jefferson, American society was based on a "Judeo-Christian moral tradition" that shaped and determined laws about individual rights and freedoms.[28] Though she defined the right-to-life movement as a "people's movement" not bound by religious denomination, she discussed this cause with a noticeable religiosity that she joined with her understanding of medical and legal ethics: "The right-to-life movement is a people's movement. We belong to no one political party, no one religion, no one socio-economic group. We are united to preserve the Judeo-Christian sanctity-of-life ethic as the basis of our society and to defend the right to life as the foundation of our constitutional law."[29] She was one of the chief intellectual architects advancing the antiabortion argument from the mid-1970s until her death in 2010. Jefferson popularized many of the claims made by antiabortion activists during the height of the culture wars. She was to the antiabortion cause what Ella Baker was to the civil rights movement in terms of her grassroots activism and ideas about the personhood of the fetus. Jefferson considered questions of race, gender, and class in her development of ideas about abortion, but she did so from a conservative framework, informed by conservative philosophy, medical ethics, the law, and Christian ethics. She believed in self-empowerment and individual rights, but she approached these questions from an increasingly far-right perspective. Jefferson's beliefs represent one of the major competing epistemes that defined the culture wars—that of the far-right conservative Republican.

By the end of the 1960s, Jefferson had become a prominent opponent of abortion. Though many physicians increasingly opposed the liberalization of the practice, Jefferson did not. This was the same period in which antiabortion advocates came to see abortion as a moral sin. Jefferson, the daughter of a Methodist minister, eventually embraced this position, and as a medical doctor, she argued that the Hippocratic oath prevented her engaging in what she perceived to be preventing the natural growth of a human life. Historically, physicians have played an important role in the history of antiabortion as a social movement.[30] Their expertise as medical professionals helped to provide credibility to the pro-life cause. The legalization of abortion made this centrality more self-evident.

Jefferson cofounded the Massachusetts Citizens for Life in 1970, then was a founding member of the NRLC. The NRLC held its first national meeting for antiabortion leaders in 1970. In 1971, Jefferson became a member of the board of directors of the NRLC, and she was elevated to the position of vice president of the NRLC in 1973. The same year, she met Ronald Reagan. Reagan later credited Jefferson with changing his views on abortion. She also wrote extensively and spoke nationally on the subject of abortion.

Jefferson employed a holistic approach to understand and make arguments about the issue of abortion in her writings. She drew from several fields of thought to refine her case against abortion, including conservative philosophy, medical ethics, law, and Christian theology. This is evident in her public statements, speeches, interviews, and writings on the subject of abortion. Though she was not a regular churchgoer or an outwardly religious person, and she maintained membership in a "mainline Protestant denomination that was officially pro-choice," Jefferson nonetheless embraced Christian ethics as a part of her antiabortion rhetoric and protest epistemology. Her approach to the issue of abortion in US society always included Christian ethics from her overall pro-life rationale. She spoke of abortion in medical terms imbued with religious overtones, while also recognizing the moral implications of the practice in relation to her position as a medical doctor who was often called on to deliver expert opinions in legal cases.

Her holistic approach is evidenced early on in an article that she wrote titled "Abortion: Self-Defeat Solution," published in 1972 in *Centerscope* magazine. In this article, Jefferson defines abortion in medical terms but goes on to argue that the life process begins at the point of fertilization. She uses interdisciplinary logic to discuss abortion in this essay, but her Christian moralism is apparent. In that piece, Jefferson defines abortion: "Abortion, whether spontaneous or induced, may be defined as the premature expulsion or extraction of the developing mammalian organism from the uterus. The purpose of abortion in our sociobiologic scheme is to prevent the birth of a living human baby."[31] Jefferson goes on to contend that the procedure of abortion "settles" the question as to when life begins because it is a practice that is "carried out" with the "conviction" that if a pregnancy is not terminated a "living child will result."[32] Though she goes on to state that "clear evidence from modern embryology and perinatal physiology should have settled by now the centuries-old debate on when life begins," she does not state that a fetus is a living being. Instead, she argues that a living child will result if allowed to develop uninterrupted.[33] She employs a type of philosophical sleight of hand to make this claim and avoids stating explicitly that a fetus is a person that can survive outside of the womb. These are philosophical claims, not scientific conclusions. She argues that abortion disrupts the natural progression of a pregnancy without stating conclusively something that she knows to be medically impossible—that a fetus exists as a living person at conception:

> The strongest evidence of life before birth need not come from science or theology, but from the practice of abortion. If the developing organism were not considered to be alive, abortion would not be necessary; the end of gestation would not produce a living child. Abortion is carried out only with the conviction that if a given pregnancy is not interrupted, a living child will result.[34]

She speaks here about the disruption of the life process, suggesting that it begins at conception without explicitly stating that a fetus is a person. Jefferson then goes on to discuss the dangers of abortion in terms of maternal morbidity and mortality, as well as mortality of the child, arguing that these are subjects of "considerable debate in medicine." She refers to the fetus as a developing child or developing-organism-child in this essay on several occasions and asserts that "the life process" begins at conception. As a medical doctor, Jefferson lends her voice to the idea of the personhood of the fetus by noting such things as the fetal heartbeat twenty-five days after conception, physical development of the embryo at thirty days, and movement of the fetus at forty-five days. "Within one hour of fertilization, the nuclei of the germ cells have fused, determining a new being genetically different from its parents but perfectly ordained in its species destiny," states Jefferson.[35] Thus, for Jefferson, the fetus as a living being was deserving of equal protection of laws. This essay was published in the spring of 1972 when legal arguments were being advanced before the US Supreme Court in the matter of *Roe v. Wade*.

Jefferson's choice of words in this critical essay in support of the antiabortion cause, including such terms as conviction, applied to the medical practice of abortion, and "ordained species destiny" suggests how much Jefferson was influenced by her philosophical and religious stances. The essay is as much a sermon as it is a philosophical and medical treatise on the matter of abortion. Her Christian moralism ultimately intersects with her concern for rule of law and individual rights. In fact, her strident religious moralism is central to her claims that abortion is the "wanton destruction of human life" and that it should be rejected as "morally wrong."[36]

Jefferson's Christian moralism overrides any libertarian sensibilities she may have had earlier. In the essay, she states, "The physician who feels restricted by abortion laws should hesitate to replace the benevolent control of the state with the tyranny of individual dictation."[37] Here, the state is portrayed as benevolent and caring rather than as an overreaching entity that seeks to circumvent individual rights. For Jefferson, a woman's right to choose is understood as a type of tyranny. This is something anathema to the libertarian, at least the early 1970s iteration of libertarianism. She may have been more closely aligned with Republicans such as Richard Nixon before abortion became legal, but this changed following the legalization of abortion. Abortion pushed Jefferson to the extreme right, just as it did many Republican supporters of the antiabortion cause.

Jefferson's "Abortion: Self-Defeat Solution" essay provides the antiabortion movement with several key conclusions to help define the idea of the personhood of the fetus. Her claims that life begins at fertilization, that at this point the fetus is a living being "genetically different from its parents" and should have a right to life as protected by the due process clause in the US Constitution, served as the basis for arguments made by antiabortion advocates and politicians. "The practice of abortion takes life without allowing the victim due process of laws," states Jefferson. In her essay, the fetus is equivalent to a person deserving rights even though she does not state in medical terms that a fetus can survive as a person at conception. Though somewhat pseudoscientific on the matter of the fetus-as-person, the arguments made by antiabortion activists about the personhood of the fetus rested in part on the ideas and writings of medical doctors like Jefferson.

By defining the fetus as a living being, antiabortion activists drew on the social justice claims made by advocates for civil rights by linking the protection of the fetus to Black genocide. Jefferson proved to be a powerful figure in this cause as it evolved through the 1970s. In "Abortion: Self-Defeat Solution," she argued that not only does the "male parent" have an interest in protecting the rights of the "new being" but so too does the state. This suggests that abortion is a topic that extends beyond the private interests or individual rights of the mother. The majority opinion in *Roe v. Wade* also raises the concern of conflicting interests in the abortion debate.

Roe v. Wade, decided on January 22, 1973, might be seen as a measured or nuanced decision on the abortion issue and, in some ways, a split decision on the matter. In his majority opinion, US Supreme Court Justice Harry A. Blackmun states the following:

This right to privacy, whether it be founded in the Fourteenth Amendment's concept of personal liberty and restrictions upon state action, as we feel it is, or, as the District Court determined, in the Ninth Amendment's reservation of rights to the people, is broad enough to encompass a woman's decision whether or not to terminate a pregnancy.[38]

Thus, the court decided that under the due process clause of the Fourteenth Amendment, women have a right to privacy as citizens. This meant that the appellant's (Roe's) rights were violated and that a pregnant woman's decision to have an abortion is protected to an extent. Blackmun wrote, ". . . appellant and some *amici* argue that the woman's right is absolute and she is entitled to terminate her pregnancy at whatever time, in whatever way, and for whatever reason she alone chooses. With this we do not agree."[39] Blackmun in this majority opinion goes on to declare that pregnant women "cannot be isolated in their privacy" because they carry "an embryo and later a fetus."[40] According to the opinion, it is "reasonable and appropriate for a State" to consider the "health of the mother or that of potential human life" and that at some point a woman's right to privacy "must be measured accordingly."[41]

This decision did not include a conclusion by the court on the question of whether or not life begins at conception. The court found it unnecessary to do so given that the immediate question before the court had to do more specifically with a woman's right to privacy, though the court did find that the term "person or citizen," as it appeared in the Fourteenth Amendment, did not apply to the unborn. This decision was handed down using a trimester framework (later modified with the case of *Planned Parenthood v. Casey* in 1992), which suggests that the state has an interest in "measuring" a woman's right to privacy "accordingly" as counterbalanced with that of the potential human life.

Given this "split" decision by the court, right-to-life proponents sought to first define the personhood of the fetus, using the support of physicians like Jefferson, while eventually seeking a human life amendment to the US Constitution that would afford personhood and the equal protection of laws to the fetus. This approach was coupled with state laws that sought to circumvent or scale back the provisions of the *Roe* decision in states such as Texas, Mississippi, and more recently, Alabama.

The Supreme Court decision in *Roe v. Wade* in 1973 further galvanized antiabortion activists in the US such as Jefferson. It was at this time that Jefferson began to play a more recognized role in the pro-life movement, as both a physician and public intellectual. She served three terms as president of the NRLC, from 1975 to 1978. This was the most important national antiabortion association in the nation, with chapters across the country. Membership in the organization grew exponentially under her tenure, with, reportedly, more than ten million members by the end of her presidency.[42] In essence, for a time, Jefferson became the face of the national antiabortion movement and used her organizing skills to expand the organization while ensuring a more expansive appeal to African American community, including writing essays consumed by primarily Black audiences.

As an expert witness, grassroots organizer, and writer, Jefferson helped to make the NRLC a major force in American politics. In 1975, Jefferson provided expert testimony for the prosecution in the manslaughter case of Kenneth Edlin, who was on trial for performing an abortion in Boston City Hospital. Edlin was eventually convicted of manslaughter. Jefferson also authored a column in the NRLC newsletter and became a nationally known spokesperson for the pro-life cause. Through her work as NRLC president, public speaker, writer, and medical doctor, her ideas about abortion were audaciously expressed. Her grassroots organizational skills ensured that the NRLC became a robust national organization with chapters in nearly every US state and in Canada. This is significant, given that the organization was dominated by Catholics before Jefferson—a Methodist—became more heavily involved. Her presidency was likely in part a move to make the NRLC appear nonsectarian in order to ensure a more broad-based appeal across religious dominations.

While president of the NRLC, Jefferson was also invited to write columns in the *Bilalian News* (formerly known as *Muhammad Speaks*), the official newspaper of the Nation of Islam. Under Jefferson's leadership, the NRLC made appeals across lines of religion, race, and class. She framed the idea of abortion as a form of "class war against the poor" and a type of "genocide against Blacks," helping to shape the ideological foundation for a broad-based cross-racial and cross-class coalition to expand the antiabortion movement.[43]

Jefferson gave her support to pro-life candidates, and in 1980 she played a major role in the development of a political action committee for the NRLC called the Right to Life Crusade. Through her period of public activism, she moved within and between several pro-life associations at both the local and national levels. Jefferson first gave her support to Nixon, then Reagan, and she played a role in steering the party further right in the 1980s. President Reagan invited Jefferson to the White House in 1981. She eventually turned to politics herself in the mid-1980s because she came to see it as the best way to "get things done."[44] She never won her several bids for US Senate in the state of Massachusetts, but her endorsement of and support for pro-life candidates in local and national politics was critical to advancing the pro-life cause.

"Mildred Jefferson has been identified as the matriarch of the African American pro-life movement," states American Studies scholar Louis G. Prisock in his text *African Americans in Conservative Movements*.[45] African American women such as Jefferson emerged as grassroots organizers and leaders within the antiabortion movement, first in the 1970s, then as pivotal spokespersons and public intellectuals during the height of the culture wars in the 1980s and 1990s. These women such, as Ezola Foster, leader of a group in Los Angeles that focused on family values, and Annette Williams, an advocate in the school-choice movement, adopted the organizing practices and intersectional framework employed by Black women leftists, active within the larger Black freedom struggle, to help advance the pro-life cause.

By the 1980s, Jefferson's conservatism became noticeably more strident. Her writings and public statements show that she was gravitating to an extreme right-wing Republican worldview, particularly but not exclusively on the issue of abortion. She also began to embrace far-right talking points on a range of issues including economics, education, health care, and politics. In a piece entitled "Where Did All the Money Go?," Jefferson espouses the sentiments of fiscal conservatism, juxtaposed with concerns about personal responsibility, stating, "If money alone could solve the problem, there should not be a single hungry, homeless, ill-clothed or medically-neglected person in the country."[46] She then goes on to question the "inflated salaries" of planners and social welfare program administrators, illustrating her contempt for what she sees as bloated big government. Jefferson even attacks the political patronage system that she argued was in place and was used to "maintain party machinery."[47]

Jefferson maintained an intersectional approach to understanding the matter of abortion, as evidenced in the public statements and her writings on the subject. In several instances, she brought class, race, and gender into her pro-life polemics on abortion and, like many other Black women in the antiabortion movement, made race a critical element in her discussions about abortion. Louis Prisock has stated that a concern about race and racism has functioned as a major "tool in the organizing and mobilizing discourse of black pro-life activists."[48] Jefferson's comments, writings, and statements reflect this through her intersectional approach to understanding abortion. In a 1984 interview for the *Philadelphia Inquirer*, Jefferson described abortion as a "class war against the poor and genocide against blacks."[49] She went on to state that "for minorities in our population, we must remember that if we are fewer, we will disappear faster. The end result is not only genocide but national suicide."[50] Poor Black women were painted by Jefferson as the chief victims of this "black genocide."

Jefferson continues this line of reasoning in an article she wrote for *All About Issues* published in 1989 titled "Pro-Life Perspective." She describes the practice of abortion as "abortion-euthanasia killing" while promoting the idea of a human life amendment.[51] Jefferson was of a generation of Black women who came of age during the height of the Jim Crow era, when thousands of Black and poor women, such as noted civil rights activist Fannie Lou Hamer, were forcibly sterilized by the state without their consent. Some pro-life movement activists and intellectuals began to promote the idea that there was a link between the high rates of abortion among Black women and abortion as a form of Black genocide. Jefferson is one of the key architects of this idea. It is both an idea and organizing principle for mobilizing the Black community against the pro-choice cause.

Race as coupled with a pronounced Christian moralism seems to have featured more prominently in some of Jefferson's key writings in the 1990s. In the 1990s, Jefferson began to discuss the debate over abortion as part of a new civil war against Christianity while also supporting Clarence Thomas as a Supreme Court nominee, primarily because a conservative Supreme Court would more likely be willing to overturn *Roe*. It was also at this time that she spoke at a far-right Patriot Movement meeting.

With her essay "Faith on the Line in the New Civil War," published in 1990, Jefferson frames the pro-choice cause as part of a larger attack on Christianity, led in part by secular humanists.[52] According to Jefferson in this essay, these "secular humanists" have declared that their objective is to eliminate or remove "all traces" of Judeo-Christian "moral influence in the laws and customs" of the nation.[53] For Jefferson, what she framed as a "civil war" began not with the *Roe* decision but with the earlier Supreme Court decision that removed prayer in public schools.[54] In this essay, Jefferson frames the pro-life movement as part of a larger defense of Christian moral values in the US, and she is consistent with the far-right talking points of the early 1990s.

This language, describing the battle between pro-lifers and secular humanists, is further advanced by Jefferson in an article that appears in the May/June 1991 bimonthly magazine *Good News*, published by the United Methodist Church. In her essay "The Casualties of War," Jefferson uses strident religious moralism to characterize the battle over abortion, saying, "The real national war rages between those who would discard our Judeo-Christian moral tradition and the majority who would preserve the shared moral heritage that built our great nation."[55] She goes on to state that "the outcome of this battle will determine whether or not we can survive as a nation."[56] In the same essay, she excoriates modern feminism and attacks Margaret Sanger as a eugenicist, extending the idea of abortion as Black genocide. Conservative intellectuals such as Jefferson sought to discredit the pro-choice movement by advancing scathing critiques of "modern feminism," including attempts to discredit the work of Planned Parenthood and Sanger, one of its chief founders.

This view is further illustrated in Jefferson's 1991 essay "The Nature of the Race/Class Factor in Abortion." In it, Jefferson equates what she calls the population-control/social planner architects of *Roe* with Nazi eugenicists: "The post–*Roe v. Wade* population-control-driven public policy of abortion-on-demand lubricated by government funding of abortions for poor women neatly transplants the Nazi ideas into modern American life. The antiquated fascist model for social management is now called 'liberal.'"[57] She goes on to state that the "race/class factor in population-control/abortion-social-planning is inherent and inextricable."[58] Jefferson's intersectional approach to understanding the abortion issue from a conservative perspective is apparent here. Her critique of Sanger in this commentary on race/class describes Sanger's work as a "class war against the poor" while also indicting Sanger as a racist who promoted Black genocide. Race is central to her diatribes against abortion and critique of liberal feminism. These ideas became inculcated into conservative political ideology in part through the writings of Jefferson. Though she is often overlooked as a thinker and strategist within the larger history of the antiabortion movement, her ideas clearly shaped the development of rightist politics on this matter of abortion. Darla St. Martin, an executive with the NRLC, is quoted in the *New York Times* as stating that Jefferson was the "greatest orator" of the pro-life movement. Jefferson died in her Cambridge, Massachusetts, home of natural causes on October 15, 2010, at the age of eighty-four.

Mildred Fay Jefferson has been largely overlooked as a thinker in the African American intellectual tradition and in the history of the antiabortion movement. Her ideas have heavily shaped conservative politics. As a Black woman conservative intellectual, her life and thought go against the more commonly studied liberal Black women activists associated with the struggle for Black equality. This overproduction of studies on a singular view of Black society and culture feeds into the notion of a monolithic Black society that exists without contradictions. Though many might disagree with Jefferson's ideas about abortion, she was nonetheless one of the most important voices in the antiabortion movement and also contributed to the development of rightist ideologies through the twentieth century. It might be argued that these rightist ideologies have been mostly harmful to African Americans, but this does not mean that Jefferson and women like her should be left out of historical analyses of the Black experience or Black women's intellectual traditions. To the contrary, studying Black conservatives and their motives, strategies, and thoughts gives us greater insight into the complexities of African American life, including the ways that members of this community have shaped the development of US history, politics, society, and culture. A more humanistic portrait might emerge of African American life by including these alternative voices into the conversation.

NOTES

1. Haugeberg, *Women against Abortion*, 1.
2. Van de Walle, "Toward a Demographic History of Abortion," 115.
3. Bloomer, Pierson, and Estrada, "The Biomedicine of Abortion," 31–32.

4. Bloomer, Pierson, and Estrada, "The Biomedicine of Abortion," 31.

5. Orr, *Abortion Wars*, 41.

6. Orr, *Abortion Wars*, 42.

7. Pepe, "Abortion in Ancient Greece," 41.

8. Holland, "Abolishing Abortion," 3.

9. Holland, "Abolishing Abortion," 3.

10. Dudden, "Women's Rights Advocates and Abortion Laws," 103.

11. See the following texts for some of the more notable early scholarly works on abortion in US history: James C. Mohr, *Abortion in America: The Origins and Evolution of National Policy, 1800–1900* (New York: Oxford University Press, 1979) is one of the first major scholarly texts on the issue of abortion in history and public policy that focuses on the evolution of the criminalization of abortion in the nineteenth century; Kristen Luker, *Abortion and the Politics of Motherhood* (Berkley: University of California Press, 1984) is a survey history of the abortion debate including some discussion of both sides of the issue; Cynthia Gorney, *Articles of Faith: A Frontier History of the Abortion Wars* (New York: Simon and Schuster, 2000) draws on more than five hundred interviews and a wealth of archival sources to trace the history of abortion exploring both sides of the issue from 1973 to 1989. More recent texts that focus on the antiabortion movement include Ziad W. Munson, *The Making of Pro-Life Activists: How Social Movement Mobilization Works* (Chicago: University of Chicago Press, 2002), which focuses on the grassroots organizing efforts of pro-life activists; Williams, *Defenders of the Unborn* concerns the early pre-*Roe* history of antiabortion activism; and Haugeberg, *Women against Abortion* focuses on the women who galvanized and led the pro-life movement from the 1960s to the 1980s.

12. See Laura Briggs's *Reproducing Empire: Race, Sex, Science, and U.S. Imperialism in Puerto Rico* (Berkeley: University of California Press, 2002); Jennifer Nelson, *Women of Color and the Reproductive Rights Movement* (New York: New York University Press, 2003); and Jennifer Morgan, *Laboring Women: Reproduction and Gender in New World Slavery* (Philadelphia: University of Pennsylvania Press, 2004). For works that look at race and reproduction in relation to the eugenics movement, see Wendy Kline, *Building a Better Race: Gender, Sexuality, and Eugenics from the Turn of the Century to the Baby Boom* (Berkeley: University of California Press, 2005); Alexandra Minna Stern, *Eugenic Nation: Faults and Frontiers of Better Breeding in Modern America* (Berkeley: University of California Press, 2005); and Rebecca M. Kluchin, *Fit to Be Tied: Sterilization and Reproductive Rights in America, 1950–1980* (New Brunswick, NJ: Rutgers University Press, 2011). Some notable recent articles that focus on women of color and reproductive rights include Sherie M. Randolph, "Not to Rely Completely on the Courts: Florynce 'Flo' Kennedy and Black Feminist Leadership in the Reproductive Rights Battle, 1969–1971" *Journal of Women's History* 27, no. 1 (2015): 136–60, and Jennifer Nelson, "'All This That Has Happened to Me Shouldn't Happen to Nobody Else': Loretta Ross and the Women of Color Reproductive Freedom Movement in the 1980s" *Journal of Women's History* 22, no. 3 (2010): 136–60.

13. For texts representative of important studies of the New Right, see Alan Crawford, *Thunder on the Right: The New Right and the Politics of Resentment* (New York: Pantheon, 1980); Robert C. Liebman and Robert Wuthnow, eds., *The New Christian Right: Mobilization and Legitimation* (Piscataway, NJ: Transaction Books, 1983); Bruce J. Schulman and Julian E. Zelizer, eds., *Rightward Bound: Making America Conservative in the 1970s* (Cambridge,

MA: Harvard University Press, 2008); Clyde Wilcox and Carin Robinson, *Onward Christian Soldiers? The Religious Right in American Politics* (Boulder, CO: Westview Press, 2010); Darren Dochuk, *From Bible Belt to Sunbelt: Plain-Folk Religion, Grassroots Politics, and the Rise of Evangelical Conservatism* (New York: W. W. Norton, 2010); Daniel K. Williams, *God's Own Party: The Making of the Christian Right* (New York: Oxford University Press, 2012); and Kevin Kruse, *One Nation Under God: How Corporate America Invented Christian America* (New York: Basic Books, 2015).

14. Williams, *Defenders of the Unborn*, 170.
15. Williams, *Defenders of the Unborn*, 172.
16. Williams, *Defenders of the Unborn*, 173.
17. Haugeberg, *Women against Abortion*, 15–16.
18. Dennis Hevesi, "Mildred Jefferson, 84, Anti-abortion Activist," *New York Times*, October 19, 2010, B19.
19. Vieweg, "Review: *Against All Odds*."
20. Vieweg, "Review: *Against All Odds*."
21. Hevesi, "Mildred Jefferson," B19.
22. National Right to Life Committee, "National Right to Life Remembers Dr. Mildred Jefferson."
23. Vieweg, "Review: *Against All Odds*," 1307.
24. Manis, "Culture Wars," 177.
25. Williams, *Defenders of the Unborn*, 173.
26. Mildred Fay Jefferson, "Taking a Stand: Dr. Jefferson Condemns Sexual Harassment of U.S. Supreme Court Judge Thomas by Radical Feminist Movement," *Bottom Line* 9, no. 2, 1 Box F+, Folder D.3 Mildred Fay Jefferson Papers, Schlesinger Library, Radcliffe Institute, Harvard University.
27. Hevesi, "Mildred Jefferson," B19.
28. Anne Merrewood, "A New Iconoclast: You Might Not Like What She Says, but Mildred Jefferson Speaks Her Mind," *Chicago Tribune*, July 22, 1990, 3.
29. Edgar Williams, "Abortion Foe Turns to Politics: Boston Doctor Says It's Where You Get Things Done," *Philadelphia Inquirer*, March 1984, B3.
30. Dudden, "Women's Rights Advocates and Abortion Laws," 103.
31. Mildred Fay Jefferson, "Abortion: Self-Defeat Solution," March 8, 1972 Box 22, Folder 12, Mildred Fay Jefferson Papers, Radcliffe Institute, Harvard University.
32. Jefferson, "Abortion: Self-Defeat Solution."
33. Jefferson, "Abortion: Self-Defeat Solution."
34. Jefferson, "Abortion: Self-Defeat Solution."
35. Jefferson, "Abortion: Self-Defeat Solution."
36. Jefferson, "Abortion: Self-Defeat Solution."
37. Jefferson, "Abortion: Self-Defeat Solution."
38. Blackmun and the Supreme Court of the United States. *U.S. Reports: Roe v. Wade*, 116–66.
39. Blackmun and the Supreme Court of the United States. *U.S. Reports: Roe v. Wade*, 116–66.
40. Blackmun and the Supreme Court of the United States. *U.S. Reports: Roe v. Wade*, 116–66.

41. Blackmun and the Supreme Court of the United States. *U.S. Reports: Roe v. Wade*, 116–66.
42. Williams, "Abortion Foe Turns to Politics," B3.
43. Williams, "Abortion Foe Turns to Politics," B3.
44. Williams, "Abortion Foe Turns to Politics," B3.
45. Prisock, *African Americans in Conservative Movements*, 99.
46. Mildred Jefferson, "Where Did All the Money Go?" January 3, 1984 Box 22, Folder 12, Mildred Fay Jefferson Papers, Radcliffe Institute, Harvard University.
47. Jefferson, "Where Did All the Money Go?"
48. Prisock, *African Americans in Conservative Movements*, 98.
49. Edgar, "Abortion Foe Turns to Politics," B3.
50. Edgar, "Abortion Foe Turns to Politics," B3.
51. Mildred F. Jefferson, "Pro-Life Movement," in *All About Issues*, March 1989, Mildred Fay Jefferson Papers Box 22, Folder 12, Mildred Fay Jefferson Papers, Radcliffe Institute, Harvard University.
52. Mildred Fay Jefferson, "Faith on the Line in the New Civil War," *Lux in Tenebris*, Winter 1990, Box f+, Folder D.3, Mildred Fay Jefferson Papers, Radcliffe Institute, Harvard University.
53. Jefferson, "Faith on the Line in the New Civil War."
54. Jefferson, "Faith on the Line in the New Civil War."
55. Mildred Fay Jefferson, "Casualties of War," *Good News: The Bimonthly Magazine for United Methodists*, May/June 1991, Box 22, Folder 12, Mildred Fay Jefferson Papers, Radcliffe Institute, Harvard University.
56. Jefferson, "Casualties of War."
57. Mildred Fay Jefferson, "The Nature of the Race/Class Factor in Abortion," December 12, 1991 Box 22, Folder 12, Mildred Fay Jefferson Papers, Radcliffe Institute, Harvard University.
58. Jefferson, "The Nature of the Race/Class Factor in Abortion."

REFERENCES

Blackmun, Harry A., and the Supreme Court of the United States. *U.S. Reports: Roe v. Wade, 410, 113, 1973*. Washington, DC: Library of Congress, 1973, 116–66.

Bloomer, Fiona, Claire Pierson, and Sylvia Estrada. "The Biomedicine of Abortion." In *Reimagining Global Abortion Politics: A Social Justice Perspective*, edited by Fiona Bloomer and Claire Pierson, 31–50. Bristol, England: Policy Press, 2018.

Dudden, Faye E. "Women's Rights Advocates and Abortion Laws." *Journal of Women's History* 31, no. 3 (Fall 2019): 102–23.

Haugeberg, Karissa. *Women against Abortion: Inside the Largest Moral Reform Movement of the Twentieth Century*. Urbana: University of Illinois Press, 2017.

Holland, Jennifer L. "Abolishing Abortion: The History of the Pro-Life Movement in America." *American Historian*, November 2016, 1–5.

Karber, Robert N. "The National Right to Life Committee: Its Founding, Its History, and the Emergence of the Pro-Life Movement Prior to *Roe v. Wade*." *Catholic Historical Review* 97, no. 3 (July 2011): 527–57.

Manis, Andrew M. "Culture Wars." In *The New Encyclopedia of Southern Culture: Volume 10 Law and Politics*, edited by James W. Ely and Bradley G. Bond, 177–82. Chapel Hill: University of North Carolina Press, 2014.

National Right to Life Committee. "National Right to Life Remembers Dr. Mildred Jefferson." YouTube Video, 11:26, June 23, 2011, https://www.youtube.com/watch?v=UB30-QazcNg.

Orr, Judith. *Abortion Wars: The Fight for Reproductive Rights*. Bristol, England: Policy Press, 2017.

Pepe, Laura. "Abortion in Ancient Greece." In *Symposium 13*, edited by Michael Gargarin and Adriaan Lanni, 39–63. Vienna: Austrian Academy of Sciences Press, 2013.

Priscock, Louis G. *African Americans in Conservative Movements: The Inescapability of Race*. New York: Palgrave Macmillan, 2018.

Van de Walle, Etienne. "Toward a Demographic History of Abortion." *Population: An English Selection* 11 (1999): 115–31.

Vieweg, W. Victor R. "Review: *Against All Odds: The Legacy of Students of African Descent at Harvard Medical School before Affirmative Action, 1850–1968*." *Journal of the National Medical Association* 97, no. 9 (September 2005): 1307.

Williams, Daniel K. *Defenders of the Unborn: The Pro-Life Movement before "Roe v. Wade."* New York: Oxford University Press, 2016

Archives

Mildred Fay Jefferson Papers, Schlesinger Library, Radcliffe Institute, Harvard University, Cambridge, Massachusetts.

Mildred Fay Jefferson Files. The History Makers Digital Archive. Thehistorymakers.org.

NAKED TRUTHS

Dr. Joycelyn Elders, Public Health, and Sex Education in the 1990s

TEDI A. PASCARELLA

> But when it was over, I wasn't positive people knew who I was much better than they had when it started. After only fifteen months as surgeon general, I'm not sure they ever really did get to find out.
> —Dr. Joycelyn Elders, Joycelyn Elders, MD[1]

Dr. Joycelyn Elders, medical professional and public health advocate, rose against innumerable odds to the highest medical position in the United States of America under President Bill Clinton: surgeon general. Elders and her ideas regarding safe sex and birth control, for example, are central topics of the culture wars of the late twentieth century. Moreover, Elders and her outspoken truths, backed by experience and scientific evidence, came under fire by conservative critics and reveal the intersections of politics, religion, class, and race in American life. Elders resigned after fifteen months in Washington. She continued to navigate her role as a public intellectual outside of governmental administration after she left the Clinton administration by injecting meaningful ideas about universal health care and knowledge about human sexuality into public spaces. She inserted herself as an authority into the larger conversations that defined the culture wars of the Clinton era and beyond.

In the era of the AIDS epidemic, the youth of America came together to create an unbreakable chain across the nation. This was demonstrated with the 1986 national campaign called Hands Across America. From the visual of arms stretching across America, it was apparent that youths represented the future, but as explained in Ava DuVernay's documentary *13th*, the campaign's commercial (televised on Music Television, MTV) ignored some of the larger issues adolescents and young adults would have to face.[2] Moreover, according to 13th, which aims to explain and contend with some of the loopholes of criminalization used throughout the twentieth century, Nixon's "War on Drugs," Reagan's agenda to militarize that term, and Clinton's crackdown on crime created larger fissions in society regarding cultural practices that ultimately impacted Elders in her capacity as surgeon general under President Bill Clinton. Hands Across America, as a jumping-off point in telling the story of Dr. Elders, her humble beginnings, and her rise to "power," reveals some of the nuanced ways that the culture wars dealt with Elders's attempts to implement accessible, informative, effective health care and sex education in American schools and nonprofit organizations.[3]

The culture wars feature prominently in the historiography of the 1990s. Though polarities in value systems of different groups existed throughout the twentieth century, times of technological innovation aggravated cleavages in modes of thinking, especially societal issues steeped in religious connotations, including abortion, homosexuality, and gun laws.[4] Music and television made it easier than ever before for conflicts over language regarding sex, sexuality, and other sex-related topics, including sexually transmitted diseases, entered the public consciousness and on a global scale. Lisa Duggan, editor of *Sex Wars: Sexual Dissent and Political Culture*, argues that "sex wars" evolved during the mid-1980s—Elders, therefore, was caught in a crossfire of public discourse and change.[5] Eventually, Elders and her ideas were deemed controversial by conservative and even moderate congressional members: thus, Elders was dismissed as and even considered harmful to some in Washington.

What makes a public intellectual? How does one intervene to deal with the world of the late twentieth century, amid the culture wars of American identity? What is the role of the public intellectual in evaluating differing ideologies and coming to consensus to produce the best possible outcome for American citizens? These are some of the questions that Elders faced during her time as surgeon general. According to Dwain Hebda of *Arkansas Business*, Elders "left Washington unbowed" and encouraged dialogue on difficult, seemingly uncomfortable subjects.[6] Though Elders resigned from her position as surgeon general in 1994, her work has recently been recognized by many and has resurfaced as an overlooked historical narrative, and her medical and health-oriented practicality has been regarded by some as revolutionary.

Elders (formerly Minnie Joycelyn Lee) was born to poor farming parents in 1933. The eldest of eight children, she grew up in "rural, segregated, poverty-stricken" Arkansas.[7] Education was hard to come by, as the children were preoccupied with the cotton harvest seasons. When they did attend school, it was segregated, and a long journey of thirteen miles from home.[8] In her autobiography, *Joycelyn Elders, M.D.: From Sharecropper's Daughter to Surgeon General of the United States of America*, she expresses the influence of her formative childhood years, which in turn set the scene for her future career and decisions as a medical professional and public intellectual. For instance, Elders prefaces her autobiography with a dedication to her mother, Haller Jones, who instilled "four gifts of wisdom" in her children that assisted Elders in not only surviving but developing into the professional she would later become, as well as setting the scene for her "unconventional" medical approaches: "If you want to get out of the fields, get something in your head. Recognize the truth and speak out against wrong doing. Don't use up your future trying to recapture your past. Do your best; that's good enough."[9] Furthermore, in Elders's autobiography, she notes that her medical knowledge as a child in her home of Schaal, Arkansas, was extremely limited. She says, "In Schaal, if somebody got sick or hurt, people didn't necessarily associate that with going to doctors. Doctors cost money, and for the most part Schaal didn't run on a money economy . . . either you pulled through or you died. There wasn't much else."[10] Though Elders's childhood was characterized by a type of simplicity that shaped her worldview, the family life that surrounded her was positive and encouraging. Elders recalls that there was no lack of Christian morality in Schaal—there were several churches, including Sweet Home Baptist, Calvary Methodist, AME Zion, Church of Christ, Assembly of God, and Church of God in Christ, present in the community.[11] Ironically, conservative religious overtones would come into play during the latter years of Elders's career.

For Elders, there was a measure of hope once she "earned a scholarship to the all-black liberal arts institution of higher education at the Philander Smith College in Little Rock. While she scrubbed floors to pay for her tuition, her brothers and sisters picked extra cotton and did chores for neighbors to earn her $3.43 bus fare, most of that money going to classes on biology and chemistry."[12] The African American medical field in the late nineteenth and early twentieth centuries not only developed out of the need to deliver health care to both rural and urban areas, but also with advances in technology and the development of the medical profession, including staff like doctors and nurses. Elders had never imagined becoming a "professional" in her adolescent years—she imagined herself becoming a store clerk—but race and class impacted this severely. Elders recalls, "The only problem was that no store clerk I had ever seen was black. Around Schaal, indoor work was white. Except for maids. Maids worked inside, but maid work didn't exactly seem like 'being something.'"[13] Midwife practices and birth control availability were not easily accessible either. Sex education and contraception were often misunderstood and not readily obtainable. The economic, racial, political, and religious asymmetries constructed within the American system existed as vestiges of slavery and Jim Crow, and so it is not surprising that Elders did not meet a doctor until she was sixteen years old:

Her ambitions changed when she heard Edith Irby Jones, the first African American to attend the University of Arkansas Medical School, speak at the college sorority. . . . After college, Elders joined the Army and trained in physical therapy at the Brooke Army Medical Center at Fort Sam (Houston, Texas). After discharge in 1956, she enrolled at the University of Arkansas Medical School on the G.I. Bill. Although the Supreme Court had declared separate but equal education unconstitutional two years earlier, Elders was still required to use a separate dining room—where the cleaning staff ate.[14]

In addition to Texas, her time in the army took her to army hospitals in San Francisco, California, and Denver, which further influenced her as she witnessed the health and treatment of not only American citizens but veterans in particular.[15] Elders earned a master's degree in biochemistry, became assistant professor of pediatrics at the University of Arkansas in 1971, full professor in 1976, and "combined her clinical practice with research in pediatric endocrinology," publishing well over one hundred papers, most dealing with problems of growth and juvenile diabetes.[16]

Elders's experiences at school, in higher education, and in the military further colored her intellectual philosophies on health and the necessity of creating a universal health care system to combat ageism, classism, and racism. Not only did Elders interact with the "vestiges of institutional and societal discrimination" during her school years, she was determined to extinguish the root of poverty in Arkansas, that of "emotionally immature young adults becoming parents to unwanted children" due to the lack of health facilities and knowledge available.[17]

During the first wave of the feminist movement at the beginning of the twentieth century, women's organizations began to more publicly address women's issues as human rights issues for the first time in American history. More often than not, many of these issues occupied space within the parameters of Christian moralism. For instance, exploring the ways in which the Young Men's Christian Association (YMCA) and Young Women's Christian Association (YWCA) influenced the American value system at large is far-reaching and inclusionary but also complex, troublesome, and propagandistic. With the First World War on, the *War Work Bulletin* promoted women entering the workforce in droves. The bulletin informed women of their duties at home and on the home front by illustrating that for every male fighter in the war overseas, there was a woman worker in America, and the way to support her was through the YWCA.[18]

It is impossible to ignore the effect of eugenics on the early twentieth century. Eugenics as a popular but pseudoscientific belief system permeated not only intellectual circles but popular culture, down to local American newspapers. Racial hierarchical ideology created an even worse situation when it came to race relations in America. For African Americans, sterilization was one consequence of this system.

Adah Thoms, president of the National Medical Association (NMA) and activist in the YWCA, was quick to not only serve but also to engage in fiery commentary, expressing her views on Wilsonian diplomacy at home. Thoms proved to be a great mouthpiece for the medical community, but she also held tremendous significance as a female intellectual. Like Du Bois, Thoms felt the frustrations of the Great War as well as of the Paris 1919 peace conference. During the middle of the war, Thoms spoke to an audience, saying that "whether [President Wilson] meant to include us or not makes no difference. We are included, and there is no power outside ourselves that can keep us from sharing with the rest of mankind the liberty and freedom for which democracy stands."[19] By 1918, Thoms, not so subtly, alluded to her frustration and confusion. In writing to the chair of the Red Cross, Jane A. Delano, Thoms fought to challenge the United States Army Nurse Corps: "How an association as great as the Red Cross and with such noble ideals as it represents can take time to make a distinction in color, a thing over which we have no control, and for which we are not responsible, is beyond my comprehension."[20] Thoms's words are typical of the times in which she wrote. Despite the horrid environment of race relations and uncertainty in the future of American life and politics, a ray of sunshine peeking out from under that dreary cloud were the New York YWCAs.

Nannie Helen Burroughs, secretary to the Woman's Convention of the National Baptist Convention, approached Wilson's hypocrisy even more directly. Though the convention was divided on the war effort, Burroughs decried the policies that dictated the presence of the war rather than those supporting servicemen and nurses, Black or white. As a result of her criticisms and challenges to Wilson, the War Department decided Burroughs was a threat to national security. She was later placed on a list of harmful individuals, and her correspondence and personal contacts and affairs were monitored.[21]

Though some of the institutionalized ideologies of eugenics were disguised as Christian morality and uplift within the mantras of the Red Cross, Army Nurse Corps, and the YWCA, African American women creatively formed a sound foundation throughout the city, but especially sought refuge in the Harlem community. Thoms's organization, the National Nurses' Headquarters and Registry, was placed in Harlem's YWCA, and by 1918, 229 members (43 of whom were under the age of eighteen; by the end of the year, the membership total had reached 1,156, including 187 girls) had been able to participate in social clubs and public activities.[22] The leaders of the African American YWCA in Harlem also sought to reverse or at least lessen mainstream racial violence with education.

By 1937, this YWCA offered lessons on "Negro History," literature, music, science, drama, and athletics. There were also groups that focused on several other topics such as international politics, national politics, and careers issues.[23] The African American YWCA of Harlem was created out of resistance and necessity, but it also operated with some of the YWCA ideals still intact. More specifically, it operated on the grounds of Black Christian morals rather than the dominant culture of whiteness. In Schaal, Arkansas, Elders was not exposed to the ideas of Black intellectualism until her time at college. However, her earliest pushes for positivism in the direction of education came specifically from her mother.

Discrimination expressed similarly as in the anecdote above illustrates the ways in which America's racial hierarchy was cemented. In addition, inequality at the level of nursing staff also reflected limitations faced by the Black community. Though it is a disservice to overgeneralize, studies have been shown that African Americans suffered from higher rates of mortality than those of white Americans. Moreover, this speaks to the very long history, dating back to slavery, of the lack of equal opportunity and access to health care, careers, food, shelter, and education across the nation. Infant mortality rates among African Americans also speak to the limited access to proper health facilities that provide education and resources on reproduction, contraception, birth, and care for children. Midwives were commonly used for births in rural areas through the Second World War.

During the 1980s, Elders began to see larger general connections between sexual health and overall health. Specifically, "she saw that young women with diabetes face health risks if they become pregnant too young," with the potential consequences of spontaneous abortion and congenital abnormalities in the infant; Elders began helping patients control fertility and advising them on the safest times to start a family.[24] A CNN news article from 2005 describes Elders engaging with "politically sensitive subjects such as teen sexuality, abortion, and legalization of drugs."[25] The phrase "politically sensitive" reflects the context of Elders's resignation under the pressure of public outcry and opposition. Elders's views on legalization of marijuana for medical use and possession in small amounts came from crossroads of race criminalization and the lack of health resources among African Americans: "Black people are almost four times more likely to be arrested for cannabis possession than whites despite the fact that black people and white people use cannabis at roughly the same rate," Elders wrote as an honorary board member of Doctors for Cannabis Regulation.[26]

In 1987 she was appointed by Clinton as Arkansas director of public health. Elders was struck by the problems she faced in this position:

> She initiated a project to reduce the level of teen pregnancy through availability of birth control, counseling, and sex education at school-based

clinics; achieved a 10-fold increase in early childhood screenings from 1988 to 1992 and a 24 percent rise in the immunization rate for two-year-olds; and expanded the availability of HIV testing and counseling services, breast cancer screenings, and around-the-clock care for elderly and terminally ill patients.[27]

She hoped to "reduce teen pregnancy by making birth control and sex education more readily available to teenagers. She also widened the scope of HIV testing and counseling in the state."[28] Clinton recognized the successes that Elders produced for the state of Arkansas, and her ambitions to serve the United States and provide its citizens with improved health were subsequently elevated to the national stage.

In 1993, Elders was appointed surgeon general, the first African American to hold the position and the second woman to do so.[29] Janice M. Irvine, author of *Talk about Sex: The Battles over Sex Education in the United States* and associate professor of sociology at the University of Massachusetts Amherst, approaches the history of sex education from a cultural perspective. Irvine argues that public discussion about sex in American history, from nineteenth-century moral protector Anthony Comstock onward, has been petrified in a culture war because sex education debates involve children and their innocence.[30] Information that can and cannot be discussed and disseminated in a public fashion, particularly in the school setting, became the crux of the sex education debate.

Moreover, Irvine argues that words and language are the center of sex education "dilemmas," which most prominently began in the 1960s. Relics of the culture wars from the 1960s continued to surface in the late twentieth century, especially because popular culture was being instantaneously transmitted through media outlets such as MTV, but openly talking about sex in a realistic manner remained largely taboo, even when the speaker was the surgeon general: "Elders did not masturbate in public; she was fired for discussing how teachers might talk about masturbation. The fear that sexual language will trigger social chaos has historically fueled initiatives to regulate sexual speech. Sex education has been at the center of these conflicts."[31]

Though second-wave feminism and the sexual revolution of the 1960s furthered new conversations about sexuality, the educational aspect of sexual health was not consistently accessible or coherent. Hence, Elders aimed to standardize sex education and its approaches in a comprehensive way throughout the United States of America. The organized regulation of sex education in schools and nonprofit organizations was part and parcel of Elders's mission of tackling misconceptions about sex, health, and reproductive systems.

Moreover, Elders's end goals, and the reasons for appointing her in the first place, were to not foster ignorance, shame, and social problems because of silence on these topics, but to support positive communal understandings and to implement abstinence, contraception, pregnancy, abortion, sexual activity, disease, relationships, and diversity programs.[32] In 1993, Elders published a commentary on the "natural partnership" of schools and health. When the Lakeview School District applied a school-based clinic with Elders's guidance, the superintendent, Leon A. Phillips, shared that not only were there no pregnancies the next year, but "the reality is that children see sexual messages everywhere—even selling cars has sexual connotations these days."[33] Phillips agreed with Elders that the education of children was a moral issue in promoting wellness, in contrast to its framing by conservative groups.[34]

Elders's resignation in 1994 was a timely subject in media. A *New York Times* article refers to the White House as surrendering to "Republican pressure by forcing the resignation of Surgeon General Joycelyn Elders, whose outspoken views about drugs and sexuality had made her the target of a conservative campaign to oust her from office."[35] It is difficult to ignore the cultural context in which Elders was criticized—AIDS and awareness of AIDS was at its apex, affecting people of all sexual orientations, particularly those living in poverty. As a result of limited proper care facilities and economic disparity, African American communities endured institutional racism linked to drug use, higher mortality rates, and violence. Furthermore, "as teenage pregnancy and high infant mortality become national dilemmas," as reported in 1992, "reproductive health for all African American women assumes critical importance. For many women who are young, single, and poor, reproductive health must be defined within the context of basic survival and quality-of-life issues."[36]

Elders was both equipped and appointed to face and eradicate the problems plaguing public health at the turn of the 1990s, rather to throw them to the wayside with palliatives. She chose to face the issues head-on: "You wonder why we're poor [as a state (Arkansas)]," she said. "The most common cause of poverty is children becoming parents before they become adults. I thought, we've got to prevent our children from having children, whatever we need to do."[37]

The World Health Organization defines "sexual health" as:

> a state of physical, emotional, mental and social well-being in *relation* to sexuality; it is not merely the absence of disease, dysfunction or infirmity. Sexual health requires a positive and respectful approach to sexuality and sexual relationships, as well as the possibility of having pleasurable and safe sexual experiences, free of coercion, discrimination, and violence. For sexual health to be attained and maintained, the sexual rights of all persons must be respected, protected, and fulfilled.[38]

As a public intellectual, Elders's leadership was ahead of her time, but it also allowed her to act as a strategic mouthpiece for advocating sexual health as part and parcel of *overall* health. While schools and health-oriented facilities offered education-based programs, preparedness to deal with safe sex operated hand in hand with abstinence, according to Elders.

Elders's bottom-up approach of creating educational programs with other experts and representatives reflected her position that homes, communities, and churches were the first layer of change and interaction at which her politics were to be set in motion.[39] Elders stipulated that although the United States had one of the highest rates of adolescent births (four times that of Canadian adolescents), it had declined 40 percent since 1995.[40] Furthermore, her strategy as a public intellectual not only encompasses the reality that abstinence is not the only reality for young people, but also that condoms and other forms of birth control must be accessible within a healthy society and as part of overall health for young people.

Her resignation came as some news organizations were preparing to report that at a United Nations conference on AIDS, Elders "had condoned the idea of teaching school children to masturbate as a way of avoiding the spread of the AIDS virus." In fact, Elders "had intended to relate that masturbation is a natural part of human sexuality," not that schoolchildren should be taught how to masturbate.[41] The Elders resignation, as a result, was more than just a reaction to words and language but a political decision by the Clinton administration.

Though Clinton's long relationship with Elders had stemmed from her successes in his home state of Arkansas, the White House was pressured to dismiss her by many right-wing influences. A "Statement on the Resignation of Joycelyn Elders as Surgeon General" was published on December 9, 1994:

> Dr. Joycelyn Elders is a physician of outstanding ability, energy, and commitment. As a pediatrician, she dedicated her life to improving the health of children. As Surgeon General, she worked tirelessly to reduce teen pregnancy and AIDS and to improve the health of all Americans, especially our children. Dr. Elders' public statement reflecting differences with administration policy and my own convictions have made it necessary for her to tender her resignation.[42]

For the fifteen months Elders was surgeon general of the United States of America, she occupied the most powerful governmental medical office in the nation. However, for Clinton, Elders became "more of a political liability than an asset."[43] The culture wars over reproductive rights were closely guarded by conservatives and Christian fundamentalists.

Opinions about Elders within the historical record exist on both sides of the political spectrum, leaving Clinton and Elders in the middle. Some publications went as far as describing Elders as "too in the nation's face," as being "just too much," and as an omnipresent "noisy lady."[44] Nevertheless, despite the opinions of religious groups and the media at large, Elders pushed for readily available birth control. Elders believed that "[Black] ministers were up on the pulpit saying the birth control pills were black genocide," a theme that was prominently featured in the historiography of the Black church and an ideology of Marcus Garvey himself. Moreover, as a Black intellectual of the second half of the twentieth century, Elders criticized some of the ideas put forth earlier in the century.

Birth control is a substantial aspect of the nurses' job, the suffragettes' struggles, and the activists' mission. This centrality was shaped by not only feminism but also popular culture. While it may be surprising to see church organizations supporting birth control, many church leaders understood the implications of bringing another child into the world when the parents both have to earn livable wages in order to continue providing for their family. Elders understood this. Jessie Rodrique explains the significance of having church groups support the birth control movement in Harlem:

> The Grace Congregational Church of Harlem both supported the work of the Birth Control Clinical Research Bureau and urged churches to give more attention to the sex education of young people and supported the work of Harlem's Katy Ferguson Home for unwed mothers. George Schuyler, another popular advocate of birth control, wondered how to regard the growing frankness of youth in regards to questions of sex, companionate marriages and the growing practice of pre-nuptial sex experience.[45]

Black leadership worked with white suffragists and other trailblazers, like Margaret Sanger, but many African Americans were wary of giving too much of their power away:

> During the early twentieth century, African Americans of different socioeconomic classes embraced the possibilities of eugenics for racial improvement, and Thelma Berlack Boozer in a 1934 *New York Amsterdam News* piece, "argued that reproductive control could resolve many of the social problems facing the race and society at large: 'More well-born babies, fewer ill-born babies, and sterilization of those unfit to become parents will aid society in solving some of its major problems.'"[46]

Of a January 26, 1933, birth control lecture at Sanger's Harlem Branch Birth Control Clinic, Dr. Marie Levinson noted that the all-female audience on January 26, 1933, "showed considerable interest in contraception, and their questions reflected a range of fears and misunderstandings about reproduction."[47] Sanger's approach in Harlem was a localized one in which Black nurses could participate in educating patients about birth control. Many American-born and immigrant Blacks as well as a surprising number of white women visited the clinic, and most of the foreign-born women (most from the British West Indies) represented more than half of the cases from 1925 to 1929 (about 189 of the 321 Black women patients).[48] A National Public Radio (NPR) podcast episode titled "Was Margaret Sanger Out to Control the Black Population" brings to the surface many of the misconceptions about Sanger. Historian and founder of the Papers Project Esther Katz addresses some of the "misconceptions":

> Leaders of the Black community certainly admired Sanger and wanted her help. Everyone from W. E. B. Du Bois to Martin Luther King Jr. all asked for her help and she worked closely with leaders in the Black community to provide the resources that the Black community needed to allow women there to control the number of children that they had.[49]

Like many first-wave feminists, both Black and white, there were numerous points of contention and opposing opinions on health, motherhood, child-rearing, and family-raising. In 1903, a *Good Housekeeping* article titled "The White Woman and the Negro" addressed the racial differences highlighted by eugenicists. The author, Ellen Barret Ligon, attempted to justify different "types" of black bodies, including types such as the gentleman or the scrounger: "The southerner has no antipathy for the negro as a human being or an individual; he merely declines to take him as a social equal."[50] Supremacist ideas based on racial hierarchy would no doubt have influenced Sanger's choices in how she operated her newfound business. New inquiries and challenges continued to emerge as part of identity regarding the woman's duty within and without the sphere of domesticity, as an "American" as well as a New Woman living during and after the Great War.

Birth control was a contested areas of women's rights and human rights, not just in America but also in the West Indies, where many Black intellectuals, including Garvey, spent time further spreading and understanding the Pan-African movement. The Black Cross Nurses were part of Garvey's Universal Negro Improvement Association and African Communities League (UNIA) in 1914. As a humanitarian initiative coordinated by Henrietta Vinton Davis in Philadelphia by 1920, the nurses were on a mission to address the health care needs of the Black community. Their community-based aid also brought them to the Caribbean as part of Garvey's work. Nancy Lurkins, author of "'You Are the Race, You Are the Seeded Earth': Intellectual Rhetoric, American Fiction and Birth Control in the Black Community," writes that many Black women did not necessarily listen to or follow the intellectual rhetoric of Du Bois or Garvey.[51] Perhaps more important to everyday women were the notions of being the "ideal woman" in white-dominated space and society and what "Black woman" implied in terms of wifehood, motherhood, nationhood, sexuality, and sexual pleasure.[52] Lurkins further comments on the work of historian Jamie Hart, author of "Who Should Have the Children? Discussions of Birth Control among African-American Intellectuals, 1920–1939." While Hart contends that Garvey's religious views affected his anticontraceptive position, Lurkins adds that perhaps his views on contraception had more to do with racial purity in combating white control while developing the Black community as a separate entity.[53] With this, Garvey molded his stance with religiously inspired eloquence that developed from a Catholic upbringing but general spirituality as a pillar of the Black church.

African Americans flocked to the rhetoric crafted by intellectuals including Washington, Du Bois, and Garvey as well as prominent woman leadership like Terrell, Thoms, and Burroughs. The ideas of Pan-Africanism were applied in an American way to bring awareness to Black history, oppression, and injustice not only globally but in Wilson's America. Coupled with first-wave feminism, the New Negro movement, the New Woman movement, and humanitarian reforms leading up to the New Deal, the Black Hospital movement flourished during the 1910s and 1920s. Though there would be a whole host of problems to face, including institutionalized and widespread racism from across the US, the Black community and congregational organizations aided the fight for better health care and better education as well as opportunities for professionals in the medical field. Nurses and doctors working in all-Black hospitals were able to care for rural communities in a systematic way for perhaps the first time. However, from Elders's experiences from the 1950s onward, there was more to be concerned about regarding the state of health throughout the nation.

In an *Ethics and Behavior* article, Elders recalls the unfortunate and stained legacy of the US Public Health Service (USPHS) at Tuskegee University, started in the 1930s. President Bill Clinton offered an apology for the "staggering number of researchers, policymakers, administrators, and agencies committing grievous errors for decade after decade," regarding the syphilis study that involved years of untreated Black men, which lasted until 1972.[54] According to Elders, despite the USPHS not being recognized under the Nuremberg Code and its response to medical abuses after the Holocaust, "President Clinton's apology set a new culture moving through research structures," and "if medical care becomes a right, then people will not feel pushed to go to extremes to acquire it."[55] Similarly, though Clinton's apology came before those from the American Medical Association or the National Medical Association, it was a great move toward not only education for all children in the kindergarten through twelfth-grade system but desegregation of knowledge—"if patients do not understand what you are saying, they cannot do what you say."[56] According to Elders, this is also true of birth control, safe sex, and contraception, as well as healthy relationships and quality-of-life.

The institution of slavery vis-à-vis the Black body prompted many intellectuals, including Garvey, to consider what birth control meant for Black populations in terms of control and the move toward positivism, in which African Americans would be able to create their own futures through independence and the reclamation of past traumas in order to forge ahead. Sociologist Angelique Harris regards the Black church as the most important institution within the African American community at large. Elders understood this importance well due to her time as a child in Schaal, Arkansas. Furthermore, Harris explains that "blacks have the highest HIV/AIDS rates, accounting for over half of all HIV/AIDS diagnoses in the US," and "this statistic is disproportionately high concerning that blacks were 12.3% of the total US population in 2000."[57] Harris is also critical of the way religious communities dealt with the realities of HIV/AIDS. The illness was commonly misconceived as purely a "white" issue or a "homosexual" issue, but "Rev. Sarah Wesley, the Director of Church and Community Mobilization of The Balm in Gilead, contends that many black churches still, 'are not looking at HIV/AIDS because it has to do with sex, has to do with drugs, has to do with homosexuality.'"[58]

In a *New York Times Magazine* article published in 1989, Elders shares an anecdote that helped to strengthen her views on the importance of birth control availability for young people. During her time as a pediatric resident, Elders treated a young patient for a thyroid ailment. The patient was extremely hesitant to be released, and Elders was puzzled, but when she learned that the patient was being molested by family members, the matter became clear to Elders and also encouraged her to begin the intensive work of creating public health and sex education programs:

> Again, Elders pauses, to say that her patient was not black. In so doing, she asks one to imagine the threshold of fear and shame the young white teenager had had to vault, in the South of the early 1960's, to confide her agony to a black person, even if the person was a woman, and a doctor.[59]

These hurdles and debates further exemplify the complicated, fraught nature of the culture wars and the place of public intellectuals such as Elders. The position of Elders as public intellectual involved her constantly engaging in dialogues and working through the intersections of race, class, and gender. As a Black woman and a doctor, statistics such as 6,500 babies being born to teenage mothers in 1986 and amounting to almost 20 percent of Arkansas's total births spurred her involvement to decrease the pregnancy rates among teenagers, which were increasing faster among white females than Black.[60] Furthermore, as a public intellectual, Elders was prepared to meet resistance in Washington to what she had learned in Arkansas and elsewhere. She did so by engaging with the public, as well as experts within and outside her field.

A short article in *Christianity Today*, published in 1993, shows that the partisanship regarding Elders's appointment to surgeon general was not black and white. The article, titled "No Respect for Elders: Conservatives Irate over Clinton Nominee's Views," presents some of the ways in which religion and Elders's own presence in the church stirred support in her favor. For example, Ezra Earl Jones, general secretary of the United Methodist Church's General Board of Discipleship, wrote that Elders "exemplifies, through her words and actions, the church's dedication to healing ministries."[61] Since Elders's appointment, church leaders have initiated talks about sex as part of youth, relationship, and family-planning programs. Though Elders aimed to implement these types of programs in public schools around the country, church groups had begun to recognize the pragmatism of discussing sexuality, such as in the case of Reverend Roxan Craft:

> Craft points out an instance where she had placed condoms, along with other AIDS relevant information, in the church, and described a conversation she had with a deaconess at that church about the condoms: people just picked them up, looked at them, and quietly put them in their pocket or pocketbook and never said anything.[62]

Sex education courses did not do away with risky sexual activity, but in some conservative circles (and in many cases, the overwhelming general mainstream), anything related to sex was regarded as taboo and was to be left to the private confines of the locker room or the bedroom rather than the public square.

In the introduction to her autobiography, Elders recalls the congressional hearing that preceded her resignation. She describes the linkage of sex and silence in popular culture: "When I was growing up in Schaal, Arkansas, sex was so secret that no adult ever mentioned it, period."[63] Elders's pursuit of the medical profession exposed her to the commonalities in her state regarding lack of health knowledge. She says that her journey from being a naïve child to becoming a well-educated doctor allowed her to treat severe cases of misunderstanding regarding sexual development in her work; for example, "at one time I had more experience talking to parents and children about sex than any doctor in the state and probably as much as anyone in the country."[64] Elders notes that during her confirmation for the position of surgeon general, many people were fixated on the shock value of abortion and could not bear the discussion of sex education in the public square, further alluding to the morbid state of public health knowledge and the demands of the niceties of language.

In 2016, Joycelyn Elders was invited to the Olympia, Washington YWCA to deliver a celebratory keynote talk. A news article featured in the local newspaper, *The Olympian*, covered an interview with Elders and the "Women of Achievement" event she was there to speak at. She was asked how sex education and the decriminalization and legalization of marijuana have evolved in recent years. Elders replied with cautious optimism:

> People are more open to sex education today, because of the years of open discussion that we have had. I think Hillary Clinton understands that ignorance about sexuality is not bliss. She knows that we must educate our children for protection, so that they can not only survive, but also thrive, and so that they can grow up healthy, educated, and motivated and have hope. I support legalization of medical marijuana and decriminalization for small amounts of possession of marijuana.[65]

Elders's successes resurfaced again in presidential politics during the 2000s. In light of the 2016 presidential race, Elders believes that quality-of-life and positive public policies geared toward equality are the types of ideals medical practitioners should work for and that politicians should serve.[66] To Elders, not giving up is "fighting well" and "being willing to weather a short-term impact in pursuit of a long-term outcome."[67] Education, according to her expertise, will always come from the exchange of ideas, especially traditionally unconventional ones. In an article for *Contemporary Pediatrics*, Elders is introduced as a pediatric endocrinologist and emeritus professor at the University of Arkansas for Medical Sciences: "She keeps busy between advocacy meetings with former surgeons general and health care advocacy lectures around Little Rock." In the article, she urges whoever the next surgeon general is to use the spotlight of the bully pulpit, as is has great power to create plans, reports, and calls to action with experts in the field.[68] As a public intellectual, Elders recognized the significance of consistency and its importance in health education.

Elders continued to be widely recognized by her commitment to ending teenage pregnancy during the 1990s—"Her wish came true: teen pregnancy rates dropped."[69] Her dedication as a physician is a noteworthy part of her legacy, in regards to which she says that "the politicians have to be about what they have to be about. But physicians have a higher calling. 'I feel that the surgeon general's first responsibility is to the health of all the people in this country. You should always be true to that basic underlying fact.'"[70]

To Elders, and to many, education is the key to creating a healthy, productive society. "If I could make any changes at all to the current healthcare system, you know I would start with education, education, education. You can't educate people that are not healthy. But you certainly can't keep them healthy if they're not educated.'"[71] In the 2010s, Elders's ideas based on decades of research and patient consultation did not seem so delusional, outlandish, or provocative but were considered rather commonplace pillars of a healthy society. According to Elders, medical professionals should approach the "crisis of creativity" in order "to think out of the box and develop a health care system that is available, affordable, assessable, high quality, and culturally competent."[72] Throughout her career, Elders recognized her responsibility as a public intellectual in delivering not only competency but comprehensive, well-rounded, thoughtful agendas. In a letter to *Crisis* commemorating the legacy of Dr. Martin Luther King Jr., Elders acknowledged that "good health demands active involvement" and strategic nonviolence to accomplish change, especially in the "early, routine, and preventative health care" of Black Americans.[73] Her leadership as a public intellectual in looking back toward the history of Black intellectualism continues a tradition of breaking status quo for the greater good of all citizens. As a trailblazer, Elders's life reveals that fighting for a seat at the table is propelled through perseverance.

NOTES

1. Elders and Chanoff, *Joycelyn Elders, M.D.*, 8.
2. DuVernay, *13th*.
3. *A War for the Soul of America: A History of the Culture Wars*, written by Andrew Hartman, associate professor of history at Illinois State University, explores the culture wars from the 1960s onward. Hartman introduces words of Patrick Buchanan, in which his speech before the 1992 Republican National Convention used thematic rhetoric of the culture wars. Buchanan describes these cultural conflicts placed around different groups' belief systems as being struggles, "as critical to the kind of nation we will one day be as the Cold War Itself" and "war for the soul of America." Hartman, *A War for the Soul of America*, 1.
4. The fifth chapter of *A War on the Soul of America*, "The Trouble with Gender," mentions Elders as part of the political atmosphere of the 1990s, led by President Bill Clinton and Hillary Clinton: "Hillary, the personification of liberal feminism, was the prototypical successful career woman. When she led a task force on healthcare reform in her capacity as First Lady, conservatives responded with outrage, not only because they opposed a more socialized healthcare system but also because they hated it that Hillary did not assume the

matriarchal role expected of those in her position. Bill, for his part, cut his political teeth working on the 'acid, amnesty, and abortion' campaign of George McGovern. Although many political commentators correctly placed the Arkansas Democrat in the center of the political spectrum, particularly on crime and the economy, Clinton's feminist-infused cultural liberalism, including his support for legal abortion, was alien to a Christian Right in no mood to appease him. When the newly elected president's intentions to lift the ban on gays in the military were made public in 1993, conservative evangelicals swamped Congress with nearly half a million calls. When his surgeon general Joycelyn Elders provocatively stated that teaching masturbation in schools would be appropriate, conservatives riding high on their 1994 midterm successes compelled the president to fire her. And when news leaked that Bill had oral sex with a young White House intern by the name of Monica Lewinsky and then committed perjury by denying the affair during grand jury testimony, apoplectic conservatives in the House impeached him." Hartman, *A War for the Soul of America*, 169–70.

5. Duggan and Hunter, *Sex Wars*, 1.
6. Hebda, "Dr. M Joycelyn Elders."
7. US National Library of Medicine, "Dr. M. Joycelyn Elders."
8. US National Library of Medicine, "Dr. M. Joycelyn Elders."
9. Elders and Chanoff, *Joycelyn Elders, M.D.*, vi.
10. Elders and Chanoff, *Joycelyn Elders, M.D.*, 24.
11. Elders and Chanoff, *Joycelyn Elders, M.D.*, 9.
12. US National Library of Medicine, "Dr. M. Joycelyn Elders."
13. Elders and Chanoff, *Joycelyn Elders, M.D.*, 14.
14. US National Library of Medicine, "Dr. M. Joycelyn Elders."
15. Encyclopaedia Britannica, "Joycelyn Elders."
16. Encyclopaedia Britannica, "Joycelyn Elders."
17. Hebda, "Dr. M Joycelyn Elders."
18. Weisenfeld, *African American Women and Christian Activism*, 122.
19. Weisenfeld, *African American Women and Christian Activism*, 144.
20. Weisenfeld, *African American Women and Christian Activism*, 144.
21. Weisenfeld, *African American Women and Christian Activism*, 127.
22. Weisenfeld, *African American Women and Christian Activism*, 164.
23. Weisenfeld, *African American Women and Christian Activism*, 164.
24. US National Library of Medicine, "Dr. M. Joycelyn Elders."
25. CNN, "Then and Now: Joycelyn Elders."
26. Nathan, Elders, and Adinoff, "21st Century Reefer Madness."
27. Encyclopaedia Britannica, "Joycelyn Elders."
28. CNN, "Then and Now: Joycelyn Elders."
29. *American Sex*, "Dr. Joycelyn Elders."
30. Irvine, *Talk about Sex*, 6, 13.
31. Irvine, *Talk About Sex*, 7.
32. Irvine, *Talk About Sex*, 4.
33. Elders, "Schools and Health."
34. Elders, "Schools and Health."
35. Jehl, "Surgeon General Forced to Resign."

36. Weisenfeld, *African American Women and Christian Activism*, 123.
37. Hebda, "Dr. M Joycelyn Elders."
38. Ford et al., "The Need to Promote Sexual Health in America," 579.
39. Elders, "The Call to Action," 1004.
40. Elders, "Coming to Grips with the US Adolescent Birth Rate."
41. Jehl, "Surgeon General Forced to Resign by White House."
42. Weekly Compilation of Presidential Documents, Statement on the Resignation of Joycelyn Elders.
43. *People's World*, "This Week in History."
44. *National Review*, "Joycelyn Elders, R I P," 16.
45. Jessie M. Rodrique, "The Afro-American Community and the Birth control Movement, 1918-1942" (PhD diss., University of Massachusetts Amherst, 1991), 100, 105.
46. Ayah Nuriddin, "The Black Politics of Eugenics," *Nursing Clio* (blog), June 1, 2017.
47. New York University, "Looking Uptown: Margaret Sanger and the Harlem Branch Birth Control Clinic," The Margaret Sanger Papers Project.
48. New York University, "Looking Uptown."
49. NPR and WBUR Boston, "Was Margaret Sanger Out to 'Control' the Black Population?," *Here and Now*, podcast audio, August 17, 2015.
50. Ellen Barret Ligon, "The White Woman and the Negro," *Good Housekeeping*, November 1903.
51. Nancy Lurkins, "'You Are the Race, You Are the Seeded Earth': Intellectual Rhetoric, American Fiction, and Birth Control in the Black Community" (master's thesis, Eastern Illinois University, 2008), 48.
52. Lurkins, "'You Are the Race,'" 48.
53. Lurkins, "'You Are the Race,'" 49.
54. Elders, "The Legacy of the U.S. Public Health Service," 482, 483.
55. Elders, "The Legacy of the U.S. Public Health Service," 484.
56. Elders, "The Legacy of the U.S. Public Health Service," 484.
57. Harris, *AIDS, Sexuality and the Black Church*, 3.
58. Harris, *AIDS, Sexuality and the Black Church*, 58.
59. Barnes, "The Crusades of Dr. Elders," 2.
60. Barnes, "The Crusades of Dr. Elders," 2.
61. Lawton, "No Respect for Elders."
62. Harris, *AIDS, Sexuality and the Black Church*, 58.
63. Elders and Chanoff, *Joycelyn Elders*, 4.
64. Elders and Chanoff, *Joycelyn Elders*, 4.
65. *Olympian*, "Former Surgeon General Elders to Speak."
66. *Olympian*, "Former Surgeon General Elders to Speak."
67. Cope, "Joycelyn Elders on 'Fighting Well.'"
68. "An Elders Stateswoman," *Contemporary Pediatrics*.
69. "An Elders Stateswoman," *Contemporary Pediatrics*.
70. "An Elders Stateswoman," *Contemporary Pediatrics*.
71. CNN, "Then and Now: Joycelyn Elders."
72. Elders, "The Politics of Health Care."
73. Elders, "Dr. Elders' Rx for the Health of the Nation," 24.

REFERENCES

American Sex Podcast. "Dr. Joycelyn Elders: Former Surgeon General and Sexual Health Revolutionary." Episode 12. Americansexpodcast.com. First broadcast October 2017.

Barnes, Steve. "The Crusades of Dr. Elders." *New York Times Magazine*, October 15, 1989.

CNN. "Then and Now: Joycelyn Elders." July 18, 2005. http://www.cnn.com/2005/US/07/18/cnn25.tan.elders/index.html.

Cope, Mary Kincy. "Joycelyn Elders on 'Fighting Well.'" *Dell Medical School: Rethink/New Perspectives on Health*, May 2019.

Duggan, Lisa, and Nan D. Hunter. *Sex Wars: Sexual Dissent and Political Culture*. New York: Routledge, 1995.

DuVernay, Ava, dir. *13th*. Kandoo Films/Foward Movement, 2016.

Elders, Joycelyn. "The Call to Action." *Child Abuse and Neglect* 23, no. 10 (October 1999): 1003–9.

Elders, Joycelyn. "Coming to Grips with the US Adolescent Birth Rate." *American Journal of Public Health* 102, no. 12 (December 2012).

Elders, Joycelyn. "Dr. Elders' Rx for the Health of the Nation." *The Crisis*, 1995, 24.

Elders, Joycelyn. "The Legacy of the U.S. Public Health Service Syphilis Study at Tuskegee, a Presidential Apology, and the Patient Protection Affordable Care Act: Just a Beginning in Health Care Reform." *Ethics and Behavior* 22, no. 6 (November 2012): 482–85.

Elders, Joycelyn. "The Politics of Health Care." *Social Research* 73, no. 3 (Fall 2006): 805–18.

Elders, Joycelyn. "Schools and Health: A Natural Partnership." *Journal of School Health* 63, no. 7 (September 1993): 312–15.

Elders, Joycelyn, and David Chanoff. *Joycelyn Elders, M.D.: From Sharecropper's Daughter to Surgeon General of the United States of America*. New York: Morrow, 1996.

"An Elders Stateswoman." *Contemporary Pediatrics* 25, no. 9 (September 2009): 152.

Encyclopaedia Britannica. "Joycelyn Elders." Last modified 2020. https://www.britannica.com/biography/Joycelyn-Elders.

Ford, Jessie V., Megan B. Ivankovich, John M. Douglas Jr., Edward W. Hook III, Lynn Barclay, Joycelyn Elders, David Satcher, and Eli Coleman. "The Need to Promote Sexual Health in America: A New Vision for Public Health Action." *American Sexually Transmitted Diseases Association* 44, no. 10 (October 2017): 579–85.

Harris, Angelique. *AIDS, Sexuality and the Black Church: Making the Wounded Whole*. New York: Peter Lang, 2010.

Hartman, Andrew. *A War for the Soul of America: A History of the Culture Wars*. 2nd ed. Chicago: University of Chicago Press, 2019.

Hebda, Dwain. "Dr. M Joycelyn Elders." *Arkansas Business* 33, no. 33 (August 2016): A25-A27.

Irvine, Janice M. *Talk about Sex: The Battles over Sex Education in the United States*. Berkeley: University of California Press, 2002.

Jehl, Douglas. "Surgeon General Forced to Resign by White House." *New York Times*, December 10, 1994, 1–4.

Lawton, Kim. "No Respect for Elders: Conservatives Irate over Clinton Nominee's Views." *Christianity Today*, September 13, 1993.

Nathan, David L., Joycelyn Elders, and Bryon Adinoff. "21st Century Reefer Madness." *Psychiatric Times* 36, no. 4 (April 2019).

National Review (New York). "Joycelyn Elders, R I P." December 31, 1994, 46–25.

The Olympian (Olympia, WA). "Former Surgeon General Elders to Speak at YWCA Celebration." Interview by Jerre Redecker. October 25, 2016. http://www.theolympian.com/news/local/article110459687.html.

People's World (Long View Publishing). "This Week in History: Dr. Joycelyn Elders Testifies to Congress." July 23, 2018. https://www.peoplesworld.org/article/this-week-in-history-dr-joycelyn-elders-testifies-to-congress/.

US National Library of Medicine. "Dr. M. Joycelyn Elders." Changing the Face of Medicine. Last modified June 3, 2015. https://cfmedicine.nlm.nih.gov/physicians/biography_98.html.

Weekly Compilation of Presidential Documents, Statement on the Resignation of Joycelyn Elders as Surgeon G, S. Misc. Doc., at 2490 (December 19, 1994).

Weisenfeld, Judith. *African American Women and Christian Activism: New York's Black YWCA, 1905–1945*. Cambridge, MA: Harvard University Press, 1997.

WHAT SHE KNOWS FOR SURE

Oprah Winfrey and the Tradition of Black Spiritual but Not Religious Writing

TEJAI BEULAH

Oprah Winfrey is one of the most significant women in recent US history. She has influenced nearly every aspect of American society as a talk show host, producer, actress, magazine editor, philanthropist, educator, literary critic, owner of the cable television station OWN: The Oprah Winfrey Network, and as an author. Winfrey has done this mainly using personal narrative, a fundamental aspect of African American intellectual and cultural traditions. Winfrey is responsible for popularizing the personal narrative in American culture first through her role as host of *The Oprah Winfrey Show*, a position she occupied for twenty-five years from 1986 to 2011. More recently, Winfrey has enhanced her personal narrative approach in her spirituality-themed books. This chapter turns to Winfrey's monographs to analyze her preeminence in American society within the larger context of African American intellectual and cultural history.

There have been a select number of academic studies of Oprah Winfrey and her influence. Cecilia Konchar Farr wrote one of the first critical texts. Her 2004 *Reading Oprah: How Oprah's Book Club Changed the Way America Reads* celebrates the genius of the bottom-up teaching style used by Oprah in her book club, as a monumental cultural phenomenon, by emphasizing both the literary content of Oprah's choices and her ability to generate mass sales for the books she chose. Marcia Z. Nelson's 2005 *The Gospel According to Oprah* is a discussion of the pastoral effectiveness of Oprah as demonstrated in her ability to tell a story and do good deeds. Eva Illouz delivers a provocative critique of the Oprah brand with her 2003 book *Oprah Winfrey and the Glamour of Misery: An Essay on Popular Culture*.

One of the first important scholarly anthologies on Oprah, *The Oprah Phenomenon* (2007), edited by Jennifer Harris and Elwood Watson, includes essays concerning the Oprah phenomenon and race, gender, and class, along with various other topics. One essay from the volume worth highlighting is Denise Martin's "Oprah Winfrey and Spirituality." Martin's work is an important precursor to this chapter because she does an excellent job of naming "faith, African spirituality, African humanism, Eastern spirituality, and metaphysical studies" as the central components of Oprah's spirituality. This essay adds another important lens though which to view Oprah as a spiritual thinker, specifically within the tradition of "spiritual but not religious" or SBNR writing.[1]

Finally, Kathryn Lofton's 2011 *Oprah: The Gospel of an Icon* argues that Winfrey is a preacher who presents her audiences with the message that in order to live their best lives—spiritually, emotionally, physically, and financially—they should purchase the wide array of items that she endorses. Essentially, Lofton views Oprah as both a metaphor and as the physical embodiment of prosperity Gospel preaching. While Lofton, like each of the scholars above, offers unique and invaluable readings of Oprah Winfrey's influence on American culture and religion, these earlier scholars published their works before a significant shift in Winfrey's career and thinking, and before the rapid growth of scholarly studies on the belief system of SBNR.

Between 2014 and 2019, Oprah Winfrey published three books.[2] Much of the material included in these books is culled from Winfrey's monthly editorial, "What I Know for Sure," featured in *O: The Oprah Magazine*, as well as from her interviews with recording artists, actors, writers, spiritual leaders, and successful entrepreneurs who participated on her network shows, *Oprah's Master Class* and *Super Soul Sunday*. Therefore, except for Oprah's introductory commentaries, much of the content of these works is unoriginal. Rather than solely producing original essays and writings, as an author Oprah functions as a curator of spiritual insights and thoughts from the lives of her guests and from her own autobiography. Lofton points out that while Oprah still endorses products to help her audience "live their best lives," Oprah's spiritual writings have more substantive recommendations for living a whole, healthy life. Oprah's writings convey that she is more concerned that people are living lives with joy, wisdom, and intention. Oprah's books offer scholars of African American intellectual and cultural history an opportunity to expand the field to consider the unique contributions from Black women and men who fit the description of "spiritual but not religious" and who produce writings—personal narratives and meditations—that affirm that particular worldview. This chapter is one such contribution to this expansion.

The year 2014 proved to be a critical year for scholarship on SBNR. Historical theologian and SBNR expert Linda A. Mercadante's book *Belief without Borders: Inside the Minds of the Spiritual but Not Religious* stands out among those published. Mercadante defines SBNR as those individuals who are "looking to develop their own spirituality apart from traditional structures."[3] She further explains SBNR's function both within and outside of religious institutions. Mercadante studies the lives of over eighty SBNRs, and while her subjects vary across gender and generation, her book leaves the impression that SBNRs are mostly white people. Mercadante explains that she had difficulty recruiting Blacks and other people of color for her study; there is substantial evidence to suggest that the concept of SBNR has long resonated with African Americans.

Those familiar with the careers and writings of W. E. B. Du Bois (1868–1963), Zora Neale Hurston (1891–1960), Ella Jo Baker (1903–1986), and James Baldwin (1924–1987) would agree that these Black activists, artists, and thinkers maintained an SBNR perspective generations before Linda Mercadante and other scholars defined the belief system.[4] Another critical figure in early SBNR writing is Howard Thurman (1899–1981), singled out here because there is a distinct genealogy of thoughts and ideas that begins with him and ends with Oprah Winfrey. Howard Thurman, Maya Angelou, Alice Walker, and Susan L. Taylor are critical forebears to Oprah's emergence as a Black spiritual writer who is unattached to traditional American Christianity. Oprah's books bear a strong resemblance to the projects of Thurman, Angelou, Walker, and Taylor in the way that she uses the material of her distinctly African American life and teases out universal truths to offer lessons in spiritual living for her diverse audiences. This is, essentially, what defines the tradition of Black spiritual but not religious writings.

Oprah's writings demonstrate a strong intellectual kinship with Thurman and Walker, but the influence of Maya Angelou and Susan L. Taylor on her three published books runs deep. Winfrey appears to mimic Angelou's and Taylor's writing and publishing styles, and this imitation is another critical aspect of the Black intellectual and cultural tradition. Ralph Luker's study of Martin Luther King Jr. and Vernon Johns—a mentor and friend of the King family—explores how King "quoted," "merged," and "sampled" the ideas of Johns into his own speeches and writings.[5] There is evidence to suggest that Oprah "sampled" the styles of Angelou and Taylor. However, the content of Oprah's work along with the writings of Angelou, Taylor, and Walker all find their roots in the creative spiritual thought of Howard Thurman.

Before unpacking the highlights of Howard Thurman's spiritual projects, it is important, especially in a chapter on a Black woman intellectual, to provide some additional justification for the use of a Black male thinker here. The available scholarship on Thurman significantly downplays the influence of women on Thurman's thought and the extent to which Thurman shaped the thinking of women scholars. Thurman scholars, who are mostly Black men, rely too much on Nancy Ambrose, Thurman's formerly enslaved grandmother, as the woman who shaped his intellectual development the most. Ambrose did have a profound impact on Thurman's thinking about the Bible, the Negro spirituals, ecclesiology, and race in the United States. However, Olive Schreiner, a white South African writer, also deeply influenced Thurman's intellectual creativity and embrace of pacifism.[6] In addition to naming his first daughter Olive, in honor of Schreiner, Thurman edited and published the only surviving collection of Schreiner's papers.[7]

In his autobiography, Thurman wrote fondly of his engagement with students at Spelman College, the premier undergraduate intuition for Black women. Thurman often served as a chapel preacher and spiritual director at both Spelman and Morehouse, his alma mater. He also had a profound influence on pioneering woman religious scholars beyond the undergraduate level, such as Katie Geneva Cannon (1950–2018), a forerunner of womanist scholarship in the field of religious studies, who heavily relied on Thurman's writings in constructing her influential text, *Black Womanist Ethics* (1988). Finally, Howard Thurman's second wife, Sue Bailey Thurman, provided him great intellectual companionship, in addition to a wonderful family life. Sue Bailey Thurman was an accomplished educator and activist alongside her husband, and a deeper engagement of her life and work is needed and necessary.[8] Considering Howard Thurman's affinity for Olive Schreiner, his work with Spelman students, his choice of a wife, and even his collaboration with two daughters, Olive and Anne, in his publishing projects, his inclusion in this work opens the door for a more complete interpretation of his influence and relevance to Black women thinkers. Further, prior to the emergence of Martin Luther King Jr. (1929–1968), James Cone (1938–2018), and Delores Williams (b. 1937), Howard Thurman was the most influential Black theologian of the twentieth century.[9]

Thurman's career as a theologian is distinguished from those of King, Cone, and Williams in three ways. First, Thurman did not pursue a doctorate degree in theology, though he produced over twenty books on theology and spiritual life. His text *Jesus and the Disinherited* (1949) remains influential in the canon of Black theology. Second, though an ordained minister like King and Cone, Thurman developed a reputation as a spiritual mystic. Thurman wrote extensively about experiencing God in nature, in the kindness and warmth of other people, and in his own solitude.[10] Finally, the extent of Thurman's roles as a university chaplain at Howard University and Boston University, as an educator at Morehouse and Spelman Colleges, and as the pastor of the first interracial and interreligious church in the US allowed him to have an immeasurable influence on many well-known scholars and activists, including James Farmer Jr. (1920–1999), who founded the Congress of Racial Equality (CORE) at Thurman's urging.[11] A close study of many other civil rights organizations demonstrates that Thurman was essential to the spiritual formation of many of their leaders.

Thurman's autobiography, *With Head and Heart* (1981), examines his lifelong quest to face "the timeless issues of the human spirit" as a Black man living in a country that defined him as a second-class citizen.[12] Thurman's life story is also shaped by his attempt to work both within and beyond the borders of the Black churches and religious institutions that shaped him and employed him. In addition to his ordination in the Baptist faith, Thurman embraced elements of Quakerism, Eastern religions, and transcendental meditation to help him deal with the harsh realities of race in the US, the profound grief he experienced after losing both his father as a small boy and his first wife as a young adult, and a lifelong struggle with shyness and insecurity. Thurman's eclectic and experimental approach to both the Christian religion and universal spirituality made him the ideal leader of the Church for the Fellowship of All Peoples.

Thurman's church, founded in 1944 in San Francisco, gave him the space to develop as a spiritual practitioner of various religious and spiritual rituals. The Church for the Fellowship of All Peoples was intentionally an interracial and interfaith community. Thurman led the congregation in silence, fasting, meditation, and other practices that helped them to connect with God as individuals and as a community that was intentional about worshiping and working together at the height of the Jim Crow era.[13] Further, Thurman and his parishioners developed spiritual lives that were unbounded by traditional religious doctrines. The congregation believed that as "Children of God," they could use their spiritual formation toward social transformation.[14] Thurman's experience as a pastor shaped the tenor of his writing projects, which are mostly compilations of prayer-meditations, reflections on spiritual disciplines, and the role of music, particularly the famed Negro spirituals, in spiritual development.[15]

Thurman left San Francisco in 1953 to become dean of Marsh Chapel at Boston University. During his first year at Boston, he taught a course titled "Spiritual Disciplines and Resources." That experience prompted him to write the book *Disciplines of the Spirit* (1963). Thurman explains: "The purpose of this book is to examine certain specific aspects of human experience. These aspects are chosen because of their universality and because of their significance for tutoring the human spirit. There are five such areas in the discussion: commitment, growth, suffering, prayer, and reconciliation."[16]

Although Thurman emphasized "the human experience" and the "human spirit," he used a wide variety of thinkers and writers to help his students and broader audiences to understand his thinking on the disciplines that he singled out. For example, there are biblical references, passages from novels, and insights from both the philosopher John Dewey and from Olive Schreiner, Thurman's intellectual hero. Thurman employs personal narrative whenever he offers examples to prove his points. The chapters include stories from his childhood in the segregated community of Daytona Beach, Florida, his varied experiences as a lecturer and pastor in predominately white spaces, and his relationship with the family dog. While Thurman's writing style is much more scholarly than those of Oprah and the other writers examined below, his emphasis on cultivating deep spiritual living for all human lives is what establishes him as a critical forerunner in the tradition of Black SBNR thinkers and writings.

Maya Angelou (1928–2014), Oprah's "spiritual mother," fits within this tradition not only because of her relationship with Oprah but also because of the parallels between her life and Howard Thurman's. There is no evidence that she ever attended the church that Thurman led. However, Angelou became San Francisco's first Black woman streetcar conductor the same year that Thurman began pastoring in the city. Therefore, it is reasonable to assume that the precocious young Angelou—she was sixteen at the time—would have read about the pastor of a predominately white yet racially and culturally diverse congregation in the daily newspaper.

Their common residency in San Francisco is just one of the many connections that Angelou and Thurman shared. Angelou and Thurman were both raised in the South. Though born in Saint Louis, Maya Angelou spent the majority of her childhood in Stamps, Arkansas. Like Thurman, Angelou maintained a marked commitment to Christian traditions and institutions. She wrote extensively about her lifelong devotion to Christianity, and she was a longtime member of Mt. Zion Baptist in Winston-Salem, North Carolina.[17] However, where Thurman incorporated Eastern spirituality into his rituals and practices, Angelou was an adherent of the Unity Church.[18] Angelou also had long associations with college campuses. She frequently lectured at universities throughout the US and abroad, and her reputation as a teacher led to an appointment as the Reynolds Professor of American Studies at Wake Forest University in 1981. Again, it is unclear if any of these common links in the lives of Thurman and Angelou ever created a moment in which their paths crossed. It is clear, however, that she was an avid reader of Howard Thurman. In a review of Thurman's *Meditations of the Heart* (1953), Angelou proclaims, "I have read Howard Thurman and been informed, influenced, and girded by his courage, intelligence, and abiding love."[19] Thurman's thoughts and ideas on the spiritual life and social transformation permeate Angelou's writings.

Angelou mastered the art of the personal narrative. While she is mostly known for her multiple memoirs and poetry books, she wrote extensively on the spiritual life in *Wouldn't Take Nothing for My Journey Now* (1993), *Even the Stars Look Lonesome Tonight* (1997), and *Letter to My Daughter* (2008).[20] Angelou, like Thurman, maintained a universal approach to her audiences. For example, in the introduction to *Letter to My Daughter*, Angelou states, "I gave birth to one child, a son, but I have thousands of daughters. You are Black and White, Jewish and Muslim, Asian, Spanish-speaking, Native American and Aleut. You are fat and thin and pretty and plain, gay and straight, educated and unlettered, and I am speaking to you all."[21] While the latter book is gender specific, the lessons that she provides in each of her works are important for "sons" as well.

Because Angelou wrote for broad audiences, her reflections and meditations differ slightly from Thurman. Throughout each of the above works, Angelou emphasizes traditional spiritual disciplines like prayer and reconciliation. However, in *Wouldn't Take Nothing for My Journey Now*, she writes about the spiritual benefit of developing a personal style. Angelou writes: "Style is as unique and non-transferable and perfectly personal as a fingerprint. It is wise to take time to develop one's own way of being, increasing those things one does well and eliminating the elements in one's character which can hinder and diminish the good personality."[22] Angelou's ability to spiritualize everyday matters, like approaches to personal style and the cultivation of excellence, made her a popular public speaker and a frequent guest on Oprah's talk show and on her network's shows *Super Soul Sunday* and *Oprah's Master Class*. Angelou appeared on these shows as a venerated elder who used her life as a lesson book on overcoming, preserving, and loving. Like Thurman, Maya Angelou's influence was broad and expansive. And, though she clung to her Christian faith, Angelou's willingness to affirm the humanity and beliefs of all peoples makes her a vital voice in the Black SBNR tradition.

Other Black SBNR writers who share an intellectual and spiritual kinship with Howard Thurman and Maya Angelou include Alice Walker (b. 1944) and Susan L. Taylor (b. 1946), both of whom are friends, collaborators, and conversation partners with Oprah Winfrey. Each of these thinkers has quoted the words and ideas of Thurman and Angelou in their writings and public addresses. For example, Walker's Pulitzer Prize–winning novel *The Color Purple* is perhaps one of the clearest examples of Thurman's influence on her thought—Thurman shines through the character, Shug Avery, who experiences God through nature and through her own pleasures, particularly the color purple.[23]

In some cases, Walker, Taylor, and Winfrey have each endorsed or directly influenced the work of Thurman and Angelou. For example, on the cover of the 1981 reissue of Thurman's book *Meditations of the Heart*, a quote from Alice Walker reads, "In those midnight hours when morning seems weeks away, the words of Howard Thurman have kept watch with me."[24] Both Susan L. Taylor and Oprah Winfrey had a profound influence on Maya Angelou's first essay collection, *Wouldn't Take Nothing for My Journey Now*. In the acknowledgements, Angelou thanks Taylor for prompting her to write essays for *Essence*. Several of those pieces are included in the book. Further, the book is dedicated to Oprah Winfrey, "with immeasurable love," a testament to their well-publicized mother-daughter relationship.[25]

Walker, Taylor, and Winfrey, like Thurman and Angelou, have each adopted the practice of addressing how their spiritual beliefs and practices helped them to overcome suffering and live healthy, purpose-driven lives. Walker has frequently written about overcoming poverty, growing up in the segregated south, and suffering a childhood accident that left her eye disfigured. Taylor connected to her readers through stories of her experiences with single parenthood and depression. Oprah's weight-loss battle was often the topic of discussion on *The Oprah Winfrey Show*, and she includes lessons from that particular struggle in her writings.

Of this group, Walker has the most nontraditional approach to religion. She stopped practicing Christianity as a teenager, and she has spent the last several decades studying Eastern religions and practices.[26] Like Maya Angelou, Taylor has had a long affiliation with the Unity Church and New Thought organizations.[27] Winfrey is a self-described "nontraditionalist," who still maintains many of the rituals she learned in the southern, Black Baptist church in which she was raised. While Oprah no longer attends church regularly—her definition of a "nontraditionalist"—she maintains a daily prayer ritual, often includes her favorite biblical passages in her writings, and appreciates the preaching of Bishop T. D. Jakes and Joel Osteen.[28] Like Thurman's and Angelou's, Walker's writings offer creative insights and ideas for spiritual living to universal and broad audiences from her unique southern, African American perspective. Like Angelou, Walker has had a profound influence on Winfrey's life and career. Oprah's acting debut was in the film adaptation of *The Color Purple*.

While Walker is primarily known for *The Color Purple*, her essay collection *In Search of Our Mother's Garden: Womanist Prose* (1983) is important to consider here. In the opening pages of the book, Walker provides a four-part definition of the term "womanist," or a Black feminist. First, a womanist exhibits "womanish . . . outrageous, audacious, courageous or willful behavior."[29] Second, Walker explains that a womanist is:

> committed to survival and wholeness of entire people, male and female. Not a separatist, except periodically, for health. Traditionally universalist, as in: "Mama, why are we brown, pink and yellow, and our cousins are white, brown, and beige?" Ans.: "Well, you know the colored race is just like a flower garden, with her color flower represented."[30]

Third, a womanist "loves music. Loves dance. Loves the moon. Loves the Spirit. Loves love and food and roundness. Loves struggle. Loves the Folk. Loves herself. Regardless."[31] Finally, Walker concludes, "Womanist is to feminist as purple to lavender."[32]

Walker's definition of "womanist" is important because it emphasizes an earlier point about the definition of the Black SBNR writing tradition. Walker draws from her unique experience as a Black woman to make claims for the universal survival, wholeness, and wellness of all people while also offering insights into the sources and resources, or the spiritual disciplines, that sustain human life for Black women specifically. However, it is also clear in *In Search of Our Mother's Garden* that Walker believes that Black women's approach to living, learning, and learning offers liberation for them as a marginalized group, and for others who are oppressed.

The essays included in Walker's volume are quite different from the essays found in the works of Thurman and Angelou. Walker offers no prayers or reflections on personal style. Instead, she writes about the significance of Black women taking the time to develop as artists and writers, about her own work of recovering the work of Zora Neale Hurston, and on the significance of Black lesbians living into their fullness as visible, human beings. However, like Thurman and Angelou, Walker draws deeply on her own autobiography for stories of everyday encounters with the divine. Further, she details her career as a civil rights activist, as she also believed that spiritual transformation was key to social change.

Walker's term "womanist" is most closely associated with the work of Black women theologians, ethicists, and biblical scholars. These thinkers and writers have embraced womanism as a way to interpret Christianity from the perspectives of Black women.[33] On the one hand, Walker's rejection of Christianity makes it ironic that womanism has become so central to Christian thought.[34] On the other hand, womanism's emphasis on universalism made it likely that Black women of various traditions would embrace the term.[35] Whereas Walker's writings have offered Black Christian women an outlet within the field of theological education, Oprah has cited Walker's writings as influential to her development as a Black woman, and it is clear that the two writers share a spiritual affinity.[36]

Walker's writings have also had a significant impact on the thought of Susan L. Taylor. Taylor served as editor in chief of *Essence* magazine from 1981 to 2000. Her monthly column, "In the Spirit," addressed the subjects of faith, self-esteem, and health for Black women, the target audience of the magazine. Taylor's columns included references to the work of Walker, Angelou, and Thurman. During Taylor's tenure as editor in chief, "In the Spirit" became the hallmark column of the publication. Her essays are credited with expanding the readership of *Essence* to over five million readers, and for enabling Taylor's rise as a lecturer. Between 1993 and 2008, she published four books that set the stage for Oprah's style as an author. Taylor's first book, *In the Spirit: The Inspirational Writings of Susan L. Taylor*, is a collection of essays culled from her monthly columns in *Essence*. While Taylor explains that some of the pieces were written specifically for the book, the volume also contains "some previously published ones that have been expanded, and a few of my and our readers' favorites."[37] Taylor's intention for the volume is to express "the truth" that "by cultivating a deep inner awareness, we develop the wisdom and faith necessary to create happy and fulfilling lives."[38] This intention undergirds each of Taylor's published books.

Her second book, *Lessons in Living* (1995), is another essay collection of inspirational writings that explores the themes that shaped her monthly column in *Essence*. What distinguishes the book, however, is its emphasis on spiritual lessons to help readers learn to "love and honor themselves."[39] Taylor's third book is unique in that it is coauthored with her husband, Khephra Burns, another Black SBNR. Their 1997 volume, *Confirmation: The Spiritual Wisdom That Has Shaped Our Lives*, includes fourteen chapters on topics such as responding to God's call to grow spiritually, facing fear, love, forgiveness, and prayer. In each of these chapters, Taylor and Burns coauthor an introductory essay on the topic at hand, and then they provide quotes from twenty to thirty writers, poets, artists, philosophers, activists, and entrepreneurs who have offered words of wisdom on how to address the overarching theme of the chapter. The thinkers quoted in Taylor and Burns's book not only vary in terms of their career paths but also come from different faith traditions, different continents, and different times. Taylor's latest book, *All about Love: Favorite Selections from In the Spirit on Living Fearlessly*, follows the same premise of her first. It is another collection of her editorials from her extensive career at *Essence* magazine.

As of 2019, Oprah Winfrey has authored three books that developed out of her "What I Know for Sure" column and her network television shows, *Super Soul Sunday* and *Oprah's Master Class*. Oprah Winfrey's body of writings clearly demonstrates a "sampling" of Susan L. Taylor's approach to publishing and a continuation of a tradition of Black spiritual but not religious writing. Oprah's first book, *What I Know for Sure*, was published in 2014. That year also saw a spike in theological publications on SBNRs. The year also stands out because of Maya Angelou's death on May 28 at the age of eighty-six. In a tribute to Angelou quoted by ABC News, Oprah Winfrey honored her "mentor, mother/sister, and friend" by explaining:

> She was always there for me, guiding me through some of the most important years of my life. The world knows her as a poet but at the heart of her, she was a teacher. "When you learn, teach. When you get, give" is one of my best lessons from her. She walked through the world

with unshakeable calm, confidence and a fierce grace. I loved her and I know she loved me. I will profoundly miss her. She will always be the rainbow in my clouds.[40]

Oprah's emotional tribute to Maya Angelou becomes even more poignant when one considers that *What I Know for Sure* was published four months after Angelou's death. Oprah, who learned a lot from Maya Angelou, had compiled a book on lessons in living much like Angelou's *Wouldn't Take Nothing for My Journey Now*. Oprah had learned from Angelou, and her book allowed her another medium through which she could teach those lessons.

Oprah begins *What I Know for Sure* in the same manner that Taylor began *In the Spirit*, which begins with Taylor explaining how she gets her ideas for column. She explains, "I write about what I'm challenged by, what I might be struggling through and trying to awaken within myself. And because every day comes with a new trial, there is always something new to discover."[41] Oprah opens her collection of essays by explaining how the famed film critic Gene Siskel stumped her with a question during an interview. He asked simply, "What do you know for sure?" And while Oprah did not have an immediate answer, she explains how the question became the "central question of my life: At the end of the day, what exactly do I know for sure?"[42] Oprah offers various answers to that question and categorizes her responses under the following themes: joy, resilience, connection, gratitude, possibility, awe, clarity, and power. Each of the essays contains nuggets of wisdom filled with personal anecdotes, and they are written in the conversational yet instructional style that has defined Oprah's communications career.

Likewise, Oprah's second collection, *The Wisdom of Sundays: Life-Changing Insights from Super Soul Conversations* (2017) bears a striking resemblance to Taylor's second and third books, *Lessons in Living* and *Confirmation: The Spiritual Wisdom That Has Shaped Our Lives*. Like Oprah's former work, *The Wisdom of Sundays* offers another round of "lessons in living." However, like Taylor's *Confirmation*, the book includes selected quotes from a wide variety of influential thinkers who worked with Oprah on her show *Super Soul Sunday*. The show, and the book that originated from it, perfectly represent Oprah as an SBNR intellectual and cultural producer.

Super Soul Sunday first aired on October 16, 2011, on the Oprah Winfrey Network. According to Oprah's website, the show "delivers insight and inspiration from renowned thought leaders to awaken viewers to their best selves and discover a deeper connection to the world around them . . . each week, enjoy mind-nourishing conversations between Oprah and top thinkers, authors, and spiritual luminaries."[43]

Kathryn Lofton's *Oprah: The Gospel of an Icon*, mentioned earlier in the chapter, was published eight months before the launch of Oprah's show. While

Lofton's portrayal of Oprah's religious representation in the US—as a preacher of consumerism in the age of the prosperity gospel—is valid, Oprah's *Super Soul Sunday* shifted Lofton's reading of her religious influence by showing the depth of her thinking on spiritual matters. *The Wisdom of Sundays* is a helpful companion to the show because Oprah curates select episodes into a single volume.

Oprah begins *The Wisdom of Sundays* by explaining, "I believe part of my calling on Earth is to help people connect to ideas that expand their vision of who they really are and all they can be."[44] She goes on to explain that in fulfilling that calling, she "began to envision a truly transcendent book—with words you can hold in your hand, be inspired by, and carry with you forever."[45] In these brief opening lines, Oprah employs the language of religion—"calling"—and connects it to a universal sense that all people need to connect to certain "ideas" to help them live lives of self-awareness and purpose. Like Taylor's *Confirmation*, Oprah begins each of the ten sections of *The Wisdom of Sundays* with a personal essay on her experience with the idea or the theme of the chapter. Following her personal essay, Oprah then provides lengthy quotes from her interviews with well-known figures including Shonda Rhimes, Arianna Huffington, Iyanla Vanzant, Anne Lamott, and scores of others.

In addition to the interviews, Oprah's book includes numerous nature photos. Oprah provides a lengthy explanation for including them. She writes:

> Many of the images you'll see were taken at my home in Santa Barbara, where I feel the presence of God, and the connection to All that is greater than myself, mostly deeply. Morning walks with my dogs represent a form of prayer for me, taking time to delight in the glory of nature that surrounds me . . . these photos represent to me both the majestic abundance of our shared world and the unseen details we often miss in our lives. Like spirituality itself, the simplest things, when appreciated with reverence, take on an entirely new meaning.[46]

This quote, more than any other from Oprah's writings, connects Oprah to Howard Thurman and Alice Walker, both of whom wrote extensively about experiencing God in nature. Thurman was so connected to an oak tree in the woods behind his childhood home that he devoted several paragraphs to discussing the tree in his autobiography.[47] The protagonist of *The Color Purple*, Shug Avery, speaks at length about experiencing God in nature. After explaining to her female friend and lover, Celie, how she believes that she experiences God in trees and in sexual pleasure, she declares that "God love admiration." Shug explains to a questioning Celie that God is not vain for loving admiration, but she believes that God loves to share in the goodness of life. Shug then proclaims,

"I think it pisses God off if you walk by the color purple in a field somewhere and don't notice it."⁴⁸ While Oprah is not as sassy as Shug and she makes no real claim to a special relationship with a tree as Thurman did, it is clear from these passages that Winfrey, Thurman, and Walker connect their experiences of God to all of life, including nature and animals.

The inclusion of the pictures is the main difference between Oprah's *The Wisdom of Sundays* and Taylor's *Confirmation*. Oprah's book also stands out because, ever the entrepreneur, she created a podcast and a short film series to complement the book. Perhaps Oprah's constant creation of products for public consumption adds more validity to Kathryn Lofton's reading of Oprah as a religious figure? If Lofton wanted to update and expand her book on Oprah, she could certainly make that claim. However, the content of the personal essays included in Oprah's *What I Know for Sure* and *The Wisdom of Sundays*, show that Oprah is doing more than endorsing products; she is preaching universal spiritual ideas. She returns to many of those same ideas in her latest book, *The Path Made Clear: Discovering Your Life's Direction and Purpose* (2019).

In many respects, *The Path Made Clear* is the sequel to *The Wisdom of Sundays*. Oprah, seemingly following the publishing example of Susan L. Taylor, returns to her own autobiography and her interviews to teach her audiences how to understand and live out purpose in their lives. In each of the ten chapters, Oprah offers questions for her readers to consider in order to prove her point that a person must understand who they are (their "being") before they can understand their vocation (their "doing"). While Oprah includes several personal anecdotes containing life lessons she learned from Maya Angelou, echoes of Walker and Thurman are present in the text. Oprah includes photographs featuring scenes from nature in the book, another connection to Walker, while it is also clear that Oprah has read from Thurman's body of work as well.⁴⁹ In one section of the book, Oprah declares:

> I believe every one of us is born with a purpose. No matter who you are, what you do, or how far you think you have to go, you have been tapped by a force greater than yourself to step into your God-given calling. This goes far beyond what you do to earn your living. I'm talking about a supreme moment of destiny, the reason you are here on earth. Each one of us has an essential role in the whole of humanity. All you have to do is follow your path to answer the call.⁵⁰

Oprah does not directly quote Thurman here. However, Oprah linked the discovery of one's life purpose as essential for all of humanity. This is classic Thurman thinking. In a 1980 baccalaureate address at Spelman College, Thurman explained:

> There is in every person something that waits and listens for the sound of the genuine in herself. . . . There is something that waits and listens for the sound of the genuine in yourself. Nobody like you has ever been born and no one like you will ever be born again—you are the only one. And if you miss the sound of the genuine in you, you will be a cripple all the rest of your life. Because you will never be able to get a scent on who you are.[51]

Thurman then proceeds to offer the women of Spelman three lessons on how to discover "the sound of the genuine" within themselves. Thurman understood the significance of knowing one's purpose in life, and this is a lesson that he has bequeathed not only to his various audiences but also to the Black SBNR writing tradition, of which Oprah Winfrey is the current leading contributor.

This chapter has attempted to expand the field of African American intellectual and cultural history by considering the unique contributions of Oprah Winfrey, one of the most influential and significant women in the history of the US, by considering Oprah as a writer. It has teased out an intellectual genealogy that begins with Howard Thurman, Maya Angelou, Alice Walker, and Susan L. Taylor, spiritual writers who do not limit themselves to traditional and organized religion when addressing the matter of spiritual truth and spiritual wellness. It is hoped that this chapter will spark new ways of reading the works of each of the writers featured, particularly Oprah Winfrey. Her writings demonstrate that there is much more to learn from "what she knows for sure."

NOTES

1. For more information on the SBNR movement, see Linda A. Mercadante, *Belief without Borders: Inside the Minds of the Spiritual but Not Religious* (New York: Oxford University Press, 2014).

2. Oprah also authored a cookbook during this time. See *Food, Health, and Happiness: 115 On-Point Recipes for Great Meals and a Better Life* (New York: Flatiron Books, 2017).

3. Mercandate, *Belief without Borders*, 4.

4. Two important texts by scholars writing about the SBNR community include Robert Fuller, *Spiritual but Not Religious: Understanding Unchurched America* (New York: Oxford University Press, 2001), and James Emery White, *The Rise of the Nones: Understanding and Reaching the Religiously Unaffiliated* (Ada, MI: Baker Books, 2014).

5. See Luker, "Quoting, Merging, and Sampling the Dream."

6. See Thurman, *With Head and Heart*, 225–26.

7. Thurman's project on Schreiner is titled *A Track to Water's Edge: The Oliver Schreiner Reader* (New York: Harper and Row, 1973).

8. Sue Bailey Thurman was a scholar, a museum founder, and an author. As of 2019, she has not been the subject of a major study outside of works on her husband, Howard Thurman.

9. King is singled out here because of his overwhelming influence on the US and countries around the globe. Both James Cone and Delores Williams have had significant influence on theological education by founding the fields of Black theology and womanist theology, respectively.

10. For examples of Thurman's reflections, see *The Centering Moment* (New York: Harper and Row, 1969)

11. Thurman's influence on James Farmer is examined in Ben Voth, *James Farmer: The Great Debater* (Lanham, MD: Lexington Books, 2017).

12. Thurman, *With Head and Heart*.

13. For more information on Thurman's church, see Howard Thurman, *Footprints of a Dream: The Story of the Church for the Fellowships of All Peoples* (New York: Harper, 1959).

14. Thurman, *Footprints of a Dream*.

15. For example, see Thurman, *Deep River and the Negro Speaks of Life and Death*.

16. Thurman, *Disciplines of the Spirit*, 9.

17. Angelou's pastor spoke of her as a congregant at the time of her death in 2014. See Michael Hewlett, "Eulogy Showed 'Human Side of Angelou,' Her Pastor Says," *Winston-Salem Journal*, June 13, 2014, https://www.journalnow.com/news/local/eulogy-showed-human-side-of-angelou-her-pastor-says/article_e36a16a1-3d7c-5328-a9d6-119037bf290c.html.

18. Maya Angelou's relationship with the Unity Church is documented on the church's website. See "Maya Angelou and Unity," http://www.unity.org/archives/articles/maya-angelou-and-unity.

19. Maya Angelou's review of Thurman's book *Meditations of the Heart* is found on the Penguin Random House Publishing site. The publisher reissued the work in 1999. The review can be found at https://www.penguinrandomhouse.com/books/204158/meditations-of-the-heart-by-howard-thurman/9780807010235/.

20. Maya Angelou's spiritual writings, along with her poetry, are critical pieces in her literary canon and deserve more attention for future scholarly work.

21. Angelou, *Letter to My Daughter*, xii.

22. Angelou, *Wouldn't Take Nothing*, 28.

23. See Walker, *The Color Purple*, 197.

24. See Thurman, *Meditations of the Heart*.

25. Angelou, *Wouldn't Take Nothing*, ix.

26. For more information on Alice Walker's beliefs, see the 2007 article "Alice Walker Calls God 'Mama,'" https://www.beliefnet.com/wellness/2007/02/alice-walker-calls-god-mama.aspx.

27. Susan Taylor discusses her affiliation with the Unity Church throughout her book *In the Spirit*.

28. Oprah discusses her beliefs in Barbranda Lumpkins Walls, "Spirituality According to Oprah," *AARP Bulletin*, October/November 2015, https://www.aarp.org/entertainment/style-trends/info-2015/oprah-winfrey-belief-series.html.

29. Walker, *In Search of Our Mother's Gardens*, xi.

30. Walker, *In Search of Our Mother's Gardens*, xi.

31. Walker, *In Search of Our Mother's Gardens*, xii.

32. Walker, *In Search of Our Mother's Gardens*, xii.

33. For examples of womanist theology, see Delores Williams, *Sisters in the Wilderness: The Challenge of Womanist God-Talk* (Ossining, NY: Orbis, 1993), Katie G. Cannon, *Black*

Womanist Ethics (Eugene, OR: Wipf and Stock, 1988), and Wilda Gafney, *Womanist Midrash: A Reintroduction to the Women of the Torah and the Throne* (Louisville, KY: Westminster John Knox Press, 2017).

34. In addition to rejecting Christianity, Walker is also a bisexual woman, and some conservative Black women Christian scholars have rejected womanism because of the thought's association with Walker. For examples, see Monica Coleman, "Roundtable Discussion: Must I Be Womanist: With Response," *Journal of Feminist Studies in Religion* 22, no. 1 (Spring 2006): 86–134.

35. For example, the edited volume *Deeper Shades of Purple: Womanism in Religion and Society*, edited by Stacey M. Floyd-Thomas, shows that Black womanist thinkers come from varied faith traditions, and some identify as Latinx.

36. Oprah Winfrey discusses Alice Walker's influence on her life in an interview featured on makers.com: https://www.yahoo.com/lifestyle/oprah-winfrey-media-mogul-philanthropist-083416378.html.

37. Taylor, *In the Spirit*, xiii.

38. Taylor, *In the Spirit*, xiii.

39. Taylor, *Lessons in Living*, Nook book location 18/110.

40. Oprah Winfrey's tribute to Maya Angelou can be found here, https://abcnews.go.com/Entertainment/oprah-winfrey-remembers-mentor-maya-angelou/story?id=23901061. Accessed June 28, 2019.

41. Taylor, *In the Spirit*, xiii.

42. Winfrey, *What I Know for Sure*, Kindle location 18 of 1583.

43. See "About," Super Soul Sunday, accessed June 28, 2019, http://www.oprah.com/app/super-soul-sunday.html.

44. Winfrey, *The Wisdom of Sundays*, Kindle location 9 of 240.

45. Winfrey, *The Wisdom of Sundays*, Kindle location 9 of 240.

46. Winfrey, *The Wisdom of Sundays*, Kindle location 10 of 240.

47. Thurman, *With Head and Heart*, 7–8.

48. Walker, *The Color Purple*, 197.

49. One example of Winfrey's familiarity with Thurman is found in her baccalaureate address at Harvard University in 2013. Coverage of the address can be found at https://www.essence.com/news/oprah-gives-inspiring-commencement-speech-harvard/.

50. Oprah Winfrey, *The Path Made Clear: Discovering Your Life's Direction and Purpose* (New York: Flatiron, 2019), Kindle location 10 of 208.

51. Howard Thurman, "The Sound of the Genuine," Spelman College Baccalaureate Address, Spring 1980, The Crossings Project: Crossings Reflection #4 at the University of Indianapolis, http://uindy.edu/eip/files/reflection4.pdf.

REFERENCES

Angelou, Maya. *Letter to My Daughter*. New York: Random House. 2008.
Angelou, Maya. *Wouldn't Take Nothing for My Journey Now*. New York: Random House, 1993.
Floyd-Thomas, Stacey M., ed. *Deeper Shades of Purple: Womanism in Religion and Society*.
    New York: New York University Press, 2006.

Luker, Ralph. "Quoting, Merging, and Sampling the Dream: Martin Luther King and Vernon Johns." *Southern Culture* 9, no. 2 (Summer 2003).

Taylor, Susan. *In the Spirit: The Inspirational Writings of Susan L. Taylor*. New York: Amistad, 1993.

Taylor, Susan. *Lessons in Living*. New York: Anchor Books, 1995.

Thurman, Howard. *Deep River and the Negro Speaks of Life and Death*. Richmond: Indiana Friends United Press, 1975.

Thurman, Howard. *Disciplines of the Spirit*. Richmond: Indiana Friends United Press, 1963.

Thurman, Howard. *Meditations of the Heart*. Boston: Beacon Press, 1981.

Thurman, Howard. *With Head and Heart: The Autobiography of Howard Thurman*. New York: Harcourt Brace Jovanovich, 1979.

Walker, Alice. *The Color Purple*. New York: Harcourt Brace Jovanovich, 1982.

Walker, Alice. *In Search of Our Mother's Gardens: Womanist Prose*. New York: Harcourt Brace Jovanovich, 1983.

Winfrey, Oprah. *What I Know for Sure*. New York: Flatiron Books, 2014.

Winfrey, Oprah. *The Wisdom of Sundays: Life-Changing Insight from Super Soul Conversations*. New York: Flatiron Books, 2017.

Part IV

Black Women's Patriotism: The National Good, Military Service, and Everyday Intellectualism

SUMMARY

Part IV considers the role of Black women public intellectuals in what is often deemed an anti-intellectual arena, the US military. Much has been written about whether or not the modern US military is indeed "anti-intellectual," and there are indeed actors at all levels, in all of the services, who not only slip into but actively pride themselves on their anti-intellectualism. Retired general Alfred M. Gray Jr., one-time commandant of the United States Marine Corps, for example, famously complained in 1987 about "too many intellectuals" at the top of the armed services and said that what the military needed was not intellectuals but "old-fashioned gunslingers." Though some have argued these remarks were taken out of context, they are indicative of a perception held by many: that the military needs more brawn than brains. For some, the military is not a place for intellectuals. Authors in this section outline how, for generations, African American women intellectuals have fought for a place in the military, battling prejudice based on both gender and their race. They do this not to be the next big "gunslinger" or even necessarily to "serve their country," though no one can question their patriotism. Many Black women join the military as a sensible path to self-betterment and upward mobility in a society that often limits options for Black women.

In "'Know Where You Are Going and . . . Remember Where You Came From': Black Women in the Army during World War II," Sandra Bolzenius writes how, "desperate for additional military personnel during World War II, the War Department opened its ranks to women, including Black women, for the first time in its history." The creation of the Women's Army Corps (WAC) injected fresh context into the nation's traditional intellectual debates over the role of women in war; which women might qualify to serve; and how deep democracy must extend in society in order to be genuine. Black women understood how fundamental their presence as uniformed members of the military was to these discussions.

Activist Mary McCleod Bethune was perhaps the most prominent of these Black women. Her powerful voice and connections provided private and public forums to discuss the significance of Black WACs to the cause of all Black women. Black WACs, however, also had their say. From officers to privates, they regularly asserted their rights as African Americans, as women, and as soldiers. Personal letters, testimonies from disciplinary hearings, and recorded interviews in which they detail their arguments showcase the intellectual framework for their actions. Clearly, through their unique experiences, Black WACs understood what classically trained intellectuals typically did not: that policies that seemingly included African Americans and women individually often nevertheless excluded Black women. Bethune and other noted Black women activists knew this, and they used their national outreach efforts to promote Black WACs' importance to the war effort and the civil rights movement. Meanwhile, Black WACs' discussions of their marginalization in the military and strategies to resist it typically took place in the intimate spaces of their segregated barracks. By war's end, this combined intellectual discourse, grounded in the high status of members of the armed forces during wartime, produced remarkable consequences for Black women, the armed forces, the civil rights movement, and the nation. Bolzenius's chapter examines that discourse, arguing that its roots were firmly nurtured by both the intelligentsia of World War II and the ordinary Black women who served in the WAC.

In Tanya L. Roth's "Seizing Opportunity: African American Women in the Postwar Military," we shift from an exploration of women during the "good war," to women during the Korean War era, a conflict sometimes known as the "forgotten war." Roth writes, "During World War II, as the military branches began to experiment with utilizing womanpower, only the army permitted African American women into the ranks." Many of these women's time in the service embodies the long tradition of African Americans participating in national defense as a way to claim their citizenship rights. When the war ended, government leaders began to reimagine the military's role in the postwar world. While Congress authorized the permanent use of women beginning in 1948, just six weeks later President Harry S. Truman enacted Executive Order 9981 to desegregate the armed forces. While military leaders did not move quickly to integrate male troops, the women's services accomplished racial integration within two years, guaranteeing African American servicewomen full access to the same equal pay and benefits as white servicewomen. Roth's chapter examines how African American women of the post-WWII military conceptualized military service in terms of economic and equal opportunity, rather than in the longer tradition of patriotism and citizenship.

"'Regardless of What Life Presents You': Black Women Public Intellectuals in the Post-Vietnam US Military," by Carol Fowler and Melissa Ziobro, concludes this section of the volume. It is based on the authors' analysis of more than two hundred veterans' oral history interviews in addition to academic historiography. Fowler and Ziobro suggest the most often cited reasons for serving include patriotism and pride, yes, but also economic empowerment, college tuition, and travel. The chapter concludes with a powerful quote from Bettie Jean Vaughan of Texas, who served in the US Army from 1977 to 1980:

> My main interest is African-American History. I don't think enough is being taught. . . . The world needs to know about the contribution that women have made. I'm researching, even as far back as the Civil War—even before we were allowed to go to Iraq or Afghanistan—the contribution that women have made as far as the military, even as far back as Harriet Tubman.

This section surely contributes to this effort.

Chapter 13

"KNOW WHERE YOU ARE GOING AND ... REMEMBER WHERE YOU CAME FROM"

Black Women in the Army during World War II[1]

SANDRA BOLZENIUS

In the winter of 1942, Lieutenant Dovey Johnson embarked on an unprecedented assignment: to recruit Black women for the newly established Women's Army Auxiliary Corps. The United States' entry into World War II had compelled the War Department to, for the first time in its history, open its forces to women. The fact that it invited Black women, which was not altogether a given in the 1940s, gave force to Johnson's message to potential recruits of the significance of their new platform to advance democracy. "The way we think and work for the common good today," she reminded them, "reveals just how much we want a decent world in which to live after this conflict is ended."[2] Johnson's entreaties echoed those of club leaders half a century earlier, who had urged Black women to unite in common purpose "for the good of women and men, for the benefit to *all* humanity."[3] The intervening five decades had witnessed contentious debates among leaders as how to best advance their goals for themselves and ultimately the nation. As a means for advancing these goals, they could not have anticipated the Women's Army Corps (WAC).

This chapter situates the first years of the WAC, from 1942 to the end of World War II in 1945, in Black women's intellectual history through an analysis that foregrounds related discussions, strategies, and actions. Given that the new platform arrived with a suddenness that afforded few movement leaders lead time to evaluate its pros and cons, this chapter draws on the voices of a wide spectrum of Black women, from enlisted and commissioned WACs to citizens both prominent and ordinary. Accordingly, this analysis rejects notions that intellectual discourse is the sole preserve of academia, giving weight instead, as expressed in *Toward an Intellectual History of Black Women*, to "ideas necessarily produced in dialogue with lived experiences."[4] Subjugated by both their race and sex, Black women were well-positioned to recognize the contradictions between the War Department's stated mission to defend democracy and its directives that assured the subordinate status of its minority and female troops. Through their unique lens, described by Elizabeth Alexander as "an insider's knowledge but an outsiders' keen eye," African American women reflected on, questioned, and challenged the "patriarchal and racial norms" that governed Black WACs during the war.[5] Though largely excluded from the academy that conferred intellectual credibility, these women's efforts to carve out this new military path contributed to intellectual discourse.

To uncover Black women's perspectives and strategies, historian Martha Jones suggests investigating "not only what were women doing, but what were they thinking, what sort of ideas were they producing."[6] Drawing from arenas as diverse as leadership conferences and barracks banter to personnel correspondence and courts-martial testimonies, this chapter examines why African American women considered an institution that historically had been hostile to Black male soldiers as well as hesitant about its new female recruits to be a pathway to their goals of social and economic justice. Why did 6,500 Black women take their chances with the racially segregated and previously all-male United States Army? What strategies did they employ to counter military directives that subordinated them due to their sex, race, and rank? Why did their civilian sisters stand by them, and what actions did they take on their behalf? How did the intersectionality of identities give rise to a military derivation of Jim Crow, "G.I. Jane Crow"? How successful were they in gaining respect, asserting their rights, and breaking down barriers for themselves, the race, and the nation through service in the military, and what knowledge did they produce? The military personnel crisis of World War II opened a previously closed site to women. What Black women did with this opening during this pivotal transitional period marks the first years of the WAC as a critical space to examine the development of Black women's intellectual history.

What were Black women who enlisted thinking? According to Martha Putney, a pioneer scholar of Black WACs, "all had enrolled with the expectation of doing something to help the war effort."[7] An officer during the conflict, Putney may have overstated the totality of the commitment to this altruistic purpose, yet military records and postwar recollections lend credence to her contention. "I think the thing that really sustained and enabled all of us," offered veteran Violet Gordon many years later, "was that underneath the adventurous aspect of it was a sense of duty: it was our country, that we were at war and that there was a purpose to all of this."[8] For African Americans, this purpose extended from victory over fascism abroad to victory over discrimination at home, as symbolized in the war's popular Double V campaign.[9] "If ever there was a time our race should fight for our right[s]," exhorted Sergeant Thelma Robinson, "it's now." For Robinson and others Black WACs, the women's corps was the place to make a stand.[10] In addition to military service providing a direct route to assist the war for democracy and according personnel recognition as patriots, the new women's corps offered training in marketable skills. At a time when 70 percent of employed Black women were trapped in service jobs, with the majority serving as domestic servants, the skill training offered in the WAC was key to postwar employment options and thus their future economic security.[11] On the other hand, the War Department's segregation policies and deplorable treatment of Black male soldiers, whose history of service expanded over every American war, offered few reasons for such optimism. Nevertheless, nearly 6,500 Black women were among the 140,000 total women who enlisted in the WAC during World War II, while untold millions of Black female civilians supported them throughout the conflict.[12]

To be sure, the WAC presented unique and uncertain prospects for American women, regardless of race. The army had always used the services of women, primarily as nurses and support staff, yet by classifying women as employees rather than soldiers, it exempted them from the honored status of active duty support and the veteran benefits due male personnel.[13] Only perilously insufficient numbers of male soldiers compelled first the War Department to reconsider its rigid gendered classifications, and then Congress, to agree to a military corps of women, though they were wary of the threat that this corps posed to social conventions. On May 14, 1942, Congress passed a bill to establish the Women's Army Axillary Corps (WAAC), though within a year, they replaced the WAAC with a more functional version: the Women's Army Corps (WAC). The latter solidified female members' status as soldiers and their connection with (though not in) the main male forces, though their mission remained the same: to learn the skills required to free male soldiers for combatant duties.[14]

Consequently, the WAC presented particularly incredible prospects for African American women, beginning with their recognition as potential recruits. The Women Accepted for Voluntary Emergency Service (WAVES), Women's Reserve of the United States Coast Guard (SPARS), and marines also called on women to enlist, yet they categorically refused to accept Black women.[15] Only the WAC invited them to enlist, and therefore only the WAC offered them training in skills rarely available to them as civilians, even during the war's severe labor shortage.[16] Civilian employers desperate to hire female workers regularly rejected Black female applicants, leaving most to toil in fields or in other people's households for meager pay and stagnant career prospects.[17] That the WAC publicity featured training in over a hundred "important jobs" therefore proved an incentive to many. The purported uniformity of army pay, promotions, and policies likewise appealed to citizens hemmed in by a racist patriarchal hierarchy, the legacies of slavery, and the brutality of Jim Crow. Then there was the traditional honor, respect, and visibility of the military uniform. Black women were only too aware that such honor and respect did not necessarily transfer to Black servicemen, though the War Department's announcement two years before that it would employ African American troops "on a fair and equitable basis" helped assuage concerns.[18] Black women had long strategized for ways to gain job skills, fair pay, recognition as valued citizens, and opportunities to advance the ideals of democracy. The WAC seemed to incorporate all of these goals.

While the WAC platform was new, the battles Black women mounted from it during World War II were part of a long history of defending their character and asserting their rights as citizens. Enthusiastic participants of the women's club movement that swept the country during the nineteenth century, albeit in segregated fashion, during the war Black women organized community groups to discuss their circumstances, strategize on setting boundaries on unacceptable treatment (often by leveraging their labor), and collaborate on actions.[19] Recognizing their goals as beneficial to all, they increasingly considered the centrality of their role in achieving them. By the 1890s, educator Anna Julia Cooper articulated this vision through calls for, in historian Mia Bay's rendering, "an outspoken and gender-conscious antiracism."[20] An outgrowth of these sentiments and the club movement, the 1896 establishment of the National Association of Colored Women, later the National Association of Colored Women's Clubs (NACWC), marked the pinnacle of African Americans' united organizing initiatives.[21] The impetus to establish the NACWC was a well-publicized attack that maligned Black women as "having no sense of virtue and of being altogether without character."[22] Members responded by uniting under the NACWC umbrella and celebrating their role as the spiritual souls of their communities on whom the success of the race depended. Affirming their pivotal role in military terms, Josephine Ruffin, one of its founders, asserted that "the battle for womanhood is the battle for race."[23]

Led by women whose educational and economic privileges did not spare them from patriarchal and racial subjugation, the NACWC encouraged all Black women to recognize their role in "lifting as we climb." It was an audacious mission for persons bearing the burdens of multiple oppressions, yet one that epitomized their pride in their unique position at core crossroads of their communities, the nation, and the world.[24] "Black women may have been the only group in America," argued Paula Giddings, "able to see not only the degradation but the triumph of transcending what the system would make of them."[25] The NACWC offered much, and often exacting, guidance. It encouraged members to model respectable behavior, mobilize locally, and avoid divisive party politics that they believed had a corrupting influence on their men.²⁶ Heralding the role of African American women as pivotal to fundamental social change, the NACWC emerged as the largest civil rights organization in the United States.²⁷

By the 1920s, the rise of Jim Crow violence, northern migration, and the Black middle class took its toll on the NACWC, with its emphasis on respectability and uplift. Black women, including association leaders, considered additional, if not necessarily alternative, strategies suited for an era of increasing urbanization and militancy. For instance, the failure to gain southern Black women's enfranchisement through the Nineteenth Amendment substantiated distrust in partnerships with white women and encouraged the formation of ties to organizations focused on race rather than women. Many African American women joined the National Association for the Advancement of Colored People (NAACP) to fight segregation.²⁸ Others gravitated to groups with agendas ranging from racial separation to interracial labor organizing. Meanwhile, young Black women increasingly eschewed the strict morality standards of the NACWC in favor of personal and sexual liberation. While the NACWC was alarmed by provocative fashions and entrainment, these new options broadened these women's views of feminine respectability and emboldened strategies in keeping with a modern age that was impatient for real change. The 1930s Great Depression and the New Deal government programs that excluded most African American women encouraged tacking toward organizations that prioritized race, while in the North, the right to vote inspired interest in partisan politics and national campaigns.²⁹ Clearly, Black women were seeking more audacious agendas than the NACWC offered. In 1935, organizations that met this need included the National Council of Negro Women (NCNW), founded by the celebrated activist Mary McCleod Bethune.

Dedicated to ushering professional Black women into important decision-making positions, the NCNW's goals reflected lessons that Bethune had learned during her extraordinary rise from poverty to prominence. Bethune believed in the power of education (she founded the now named Bethune-Cookman University), network building (the means by which she met Franklin and Eleanor Roosevelt before their move to the White House), and accessing positions to influence policy. Her roles as president of the NACWC, director of negro affairs in the National Youth Administration, and a "Black Cabinet" advisor to President Roosevelt, among others, convinced Bethune of the strategic importance of accessing leadership positions for professional Black women.

Bethune had her detractors. Leaders of the NACWC and of the Ladies Auxiliary of the International Brotherhood of Sleeping Car Porters, another prominent organization in the 1930s, criticized the NCNW's emphasis on professionals when most Black women were economically struggling menial laborers.³⁰ The ever-practical Bethune maintained her membership in the NACWC, sought a coalition with the auxiliary, and poured her energies into the NCNW in the belief that women in positions in authority would bring attention to Black issues. Bethune considered the government to be the most effective conduit for this purpose. It had the financial and legislative power to set bold agendas and was reliant on public sensitivities, including those of recently enfranchised Black women in northern states.³¹

Bethune could not have predicted the establishment of the WAC, and yet the NCNW she founded eight years earlier was tailor-made for it. The WAC paralleled the NCNW's key strategy of advancing the role of educated Black women through government-backed positions. By offering training to recruits without marketable skills, the WAC extended to less-privileged women the same opportunities that the NCNW sought for professional ones. The WAC was still in its planning stages when Bethune stepped in as semi-official advisor to its future Black volunteers. No one was better prepared for the role.³²

The War Department's decision to racially segregate the corps was disappointing but not unexpected and therefore did not deter Bethune's commitment to the WAC. Instead, Bethune made clear both to its director, Oveta Culp Hobby, and to the public that she expected the inclusion of Black women to lead to the racial integration of the corps, a goal she designated "the other half of the battle."³³ Meanwhile, with her emphasis on leadership positions, Bethune targeted the officer program as pivotal to the success of her plan. Nearly single-handedly, she secured Black WACs' placement in the program, headed off a plan that would have limited their training, and handpicked the first forty Black candidates, including two of her protegees, Dovey Johnson and Harriet West.³⁴ Bethune was also a tireless advocate for enlisted members. Having urged them to volunteer, she felt a deep commitment to them—and they to her. According to Putney, Black WACs considered the septuagenarian their surrogate mother, knowing that, like so many other veterans of women's club movements, she was devoted to their struggle.³⁵

This powerful legacy of her forebearers, including her mentor Bethune, persuaded a reluctant Dovey Johnson to enlist in the WAC, though not without some prodding from another longtime clubwoman, her grandmother: "Grandma thought it was alright for me to go into the WAAC," Johnson later noted, "because Mrs. Bethune had something to do with it."³⁶ When she tried to submit her application to her local South Carolina recruiting office, however, the well-qualified Spelman College graduate encountered a soldier who refused to accept it, ordered her to leave, and threatened her with arrest if she did not immediately comply. Years later, Johnson recounted how the event transformed her commitment as a Black woman to serve in the WAC.

Up until that moment, Dr. Bethune's vision and my belief in her had spurred me on. Now I was angry—livid in fact—that the army for which she'd handpicked me had turned me away. How dare he tell me that I couldn't fight for America, I was an American, through and through, and I believed in the war effort. Whatever we women could do in the fight, I wanted to be a part of.[37]

Despite the significance of the unique platform and Bethune's entreaties to volunteer, enlistments of Black women remained low throughout the war. Many refused to consider the WAC because of the War Department's segregation policy. They knew of the army's mistreatment of its Black male personnel and could only guess that it would be the same for them. Rumors that the army was recruiting women to act as male soldiers' companions also discouraged enlistments, as did questions about what sort of women would volunteer for the ultra-masculine domain of the army.[38] In many Black communities, recalled Millie Veasey, joining the WAC "was just a taboo."[39] Meanwhile, the wartime labor shortage had improved Black women's civilian employment possibilities, including access to coveted factory jobs, though more typically they secured service work that paid better than it had in the past. Others did not feel that they could leave home due to family obligations, particularly those necessitated by poverty. Their earned wages, unpaid labor at home, and female caregiver responsibilities made them indispensable. As illustrated by Johnson's appalling reception at her recruiting office, the military did its part to stem the number of female Black recruits. During its first year, the corps rejected 40 percent of Black applicants on medical grounds, compared to 25 percent of white applicants.[40] For these reasons, Black WAC enlistments peaked at 4 percent during the war.[41] As Violet Gordon described the era, enlisting as a woman "was such a bold step."[42]

The boldness of the step swelled support for those who took the chance and enlisted from a wide spectrum of civilian Black women. The Delta Sigma Theta sorority and the Young Women's Christian Association were among the organizations that protested the appointment of Hobby as director of the corps because of concerns over how the wife of the former Texas governor, with her own deep southern roots, would treat her Black troops. Alpha Kappa Alpha, another sorority that opposed the appointment, invited the director to speak at Howard University. Each of these groups secured Hobby's guarantee that the WAC would follow the army's new policy directing fair treatment regardless of race.[43] Opera star Marian Anderson visited Black WACs. Journalists reported on them. Florence Murray, the author of the *Negro Handbook*, ensured their inclusion in her compendium of contemporary data and statistics.[44] Ordinary citizens also demonstrated their support for their military counterparts. A group of friends in Atlanta, Georgia, were "so proud to see a black woman in uniform," recalled Private Dorothy Miller, that they treated her and two other WACs to home-cooked meals and nights on the town.[45] Not all Black women could or would enlist, but many understood that those who did were there for them too.

Archival records suggest that Black WACs in uniform recognized an obligation to make their service count for themselves, other African Americans, and the nation. "I am deeply conscious of the war against fascism and have dedicated myself to do all possible to bring the day of victory closer," wrote one to the *Chicago Defender*.[46] Not all of them managed to do their part without an occasional nip of alcohol or slip of the tongue. At Fort Devens, Massachusetts, Private Johnnie Murphy faced disciplinary hearings for drinking, cursing, and tardiness, yet her bold protest against her detachment's relegation to menial labor reveals a similarly fierce dedication to the democratic ideals of the war. Knowing the risks, she told her officers, "I would take death before I would go back to work" and turned herself in for a court-martial.[47] The NACWC's "lifting as we climb" motto had lost much of its vitality since its inception fifty years earlier, yet the sentiment clearly left an indelible imprint on the struggle. Despite their history of subjugation (or perhaps because of it), Black WACs were fighting for themselves and for others. A 1943 article penned by commissioned officer Ina McFadden underscored this commitment as the mission of Black WACs: "Whatever the past has been, however dark the present, the future must be free for us and all of the people of the world."[48]

Black women also enlisted for personal reasons. Many saw the WAC as an escape from domestic service. Women such as Mary Daniels Williams, who realized that "I was going nowhere fast" in her cleaning job, enlisted, expecting army training to unlock postwar employment options.[49] Some already had careers. Vera Campbell was a New York City podiatrist who knew that the military could use her expertise.[50] Alice Young had a government office job with a good salary but hoped to study nursing. She volunteered to train as a medical technician. Women like Millie Veasey, who faced a community taboo against female soldiers, enlisted anyway. Feeling the pull of adventure that has long enticed men into soldiering, and the encouragement of her foremothers to claim her destiny, Veasey reasoned that "if there were black soldiers in the army, then why not black women in the army."[51] Though personal goals, such ambitions perfectly aligned with the overarching goals of Black women's movements. In fact, they held significance beyond any personal advantage they might afford. Opening doors of their choosing and walking through them evoked Anna Julia Cooper's celebrated vision, as expressed in 1892: "Only when the black woman can say 'when and where I enter, in the quiet, undisputed dignity of my womanhood ... then and there the whole Negro Race enters with me.'"[52]

Pioneers on an uncharted path, Black women recognized a responsibility to set the WAC on the right course. For most, this meant countering stereotypes. "We knew we had to do the best," maintained Elsie Woods, "to be the best we could be in order to prove ourselves."[53] Setting the right course also required setting limits on the treatment they would accept. Veteran Dorothy Miller recollected an incident at Camp Forrest, Tennessee, where white WACs appeared at her barracks looking to hire a laundress. Members of her unit replied that they did not know of anyone interested in the job but would appreciate hearing when they found one (presumably in their white unit), "because we need someone to do ours." Recounting the story with apparent bemusement many years later, Miller described a scene of startled white women who "hauled tail" after that.[54] At Fort Lewis, Washington, a Black WAC overheard a dispatcher on the radio order a snowplow to "clear the nigger WAC area." Her officer reported the offensive comment to her superiors, which prompted an immediate apology from the dispatcher.[55] Assigned by a white WAC captain to clean the nurses' quarters at Douglas Air Base in Arizona, Private Henrietta Stevenson inquired as to whether enlisted men had previously performed the task. Learning that none had, Stevenson reminded her officer of the WACs' mission to replace men in their military duties and declined the assignment.[56] In these instances and others, Black WACs successfully established boundaries by asserting their status as military personnel, a point that same grade pay economically bolstered.

The pervasiveness of discrimination meant that Black WACs had to carefully choose their battles. During a rare integrated WAC officer candidate program, a white southerner related to Martha Putney her mother's certain disapproval if she knew that her bunk was next to a "nigger's."[57] Putney held back, knowing that "if I opened my mouth, I knew I'd be the one who [would] be pushed out." Soon after, the southerner, seeking to make amends, began mopping her bunkmate's area. Catching her in the act, Putney remarked, "Your mother ought to see you now." That broke the ice, and for the remainder of the program, the two swapped stories of regional racial relations.[58] The WAC's adherence to racial segregation greatly impeded similar connections between its Black troops and others, thereby assuring that perverse portrayals of Black WACs would fester on military posts. At Camp Maxey in Texas, civilian office workers shunned Private Veasey when she arrived, letting her know that "they didn't want a Black person in there." Transferred to another office where the white personnel appreciated her clerical expertise, Veasey shined, so much so that her former officemates asked her to return. "You're a good worker," they told her. "We need you." Veasey stayed where she was.[59] More often than not, Black WACs had little recourse, yet they also attempted to set boundaries. Discriminatory treatment by white civilian clerks, for instance, inspired individual boycotts.[60] Some Black WACs showed distain for permanent menial duties by reporting late to work.

Though this cast them in a poor light, it gave them and their dissatisfaction more visibility than usually gained from by-the-book approaches that officers could easily ignore. Thus, tactics that did not necessarily meet even the looser respectability standards that emerged during the 1920s did, in their modified form for the military, prove useful. When a white enlisted man warned Private Lois Floyd, "Where I come from, they don't argue." Floyd shot back that if he tried anything, "You'll never live to tell about it."[61] Others risked dismissal from the service, and some protested by leaving the service. Publicly assailing the racism she encountered, Private Ana Aiken explained her resignation in an article published in the Black press: "The prejudice that exist tears down the assistance that we can offer toward the promotion of a better world to live in."[62] The WAC's uncharted path was daunting to most Black women, promising for others, and especially challenging for those in military uniform whose presence alone threatened established paradigms.

In her autobiography published in 1940, a founder of the NACWC and its first president, Mary Church Terrell, then approaching her eighties, lamented that while Black men and white women had "only one handicap to overcome," Black women had "two—both sex and race."[63] The experiences of Black WACs during World War II illustrate how this concept manifested itself in the military. In the early 1940s, the War Department prepared extensively for an increase in the number of African American troops and the introduction of female troops, but it did not prepare for troops who were both Black and female. Segregated by race and subordinated to the male forces by sex, Black WACs occupied the lower, marginalized rungs of both categories. Furthermore, their multitiered status required post commanders to locate separate living quarters, duty stations, training programs, and base facilities for them. Saddled with these logistical complexities, commanders, most of whom already had no interest in dealing with these unusual troops, tended to blame the women. Unable to find a post willing to accept three army-trained surgical technicians, one exasperated officer declared, "They're one of those things the poor—they are always with us."[64] Astoundingly, given the shortage of WACs throughout the war, the War Department prioritized segregating these troops over employing them where servicewomen were most needed. All the while, Black WACs attempted to contribute to the war effort as soldiers, even at the risk of disciplinary actions. In a letter to Eleanor Roosevelt, an unnamed enlisted WAC stationed at Fort Clark, Texas, cautiously said that though members of her unit were "all very willing though to offer our services for the causes," they were not given the opportunities to do so.[65]

Black WACs found little support among their all-female corps' leadership. Colonel Hobby's initial assurances of equal treatment quickly gave way to strict adherence to segregation and a ready acceptance of stereotypes that portrayed Black women as intellectually deficient and morally questionable. When barracks overflowed with untrained Black recruits, she and her staff attributed the overcrowding to Black women's reputed inferior abilities rather than the failure of Hobby and her staff to properly train and employ them. Though she sent white WACs abroad, Hobby blocked Black WACs from posting overseas where, she feared, encounters with Black male soldiers could not be properly monitored.[66] In the spring of 1943, WAC staff officers concluded that Black recruiters' public appearances in cities and towns were inhibiting white women from enlisting and recalled of Lieutenant Johnson and other Black WAC recruiters from the field.[67] Apparently, race alone indicated to the staff officers which women likely possessed the respectable feminine qualities that the officers desired. On rare occasions, interracial friendships pierced through policies, yet the absence of Black WACs' references to gender solidary with white WACs suggests the acknowledged futility of such an effort.

The majority of Black WACs' grievances pertained to assignments, in large part due to the imperative to gain skills in order to qualify for postwar jobs offering decent economic security. With so much on the line, many Black WACs who were relegated to menial labor made their desire for other assignments known. WAC staff officer Maddie Treadwell dismissed their protests by insisting that white WACs in these assignments expressed similar complaints.[68] Black WACs, however, were not protesting menial labor, which enlisted soldiers could expect to perform at some point in their service, but the wholesale assignments of their units to *permanent* menial labor. They deeply resented jobs they saw as "maid work" with links to slavery. The army denied charges of racial discrimination even as its dissemination of duties demonstrated racial and gender biases. During the war, 70 percent of WACs, mostly white, were assigned to office and communications jobs while two-thirds of Black WACs worked at some point during their service as hospital orderlies, mopping floors and waiting on patients and staff.[69] A requisition from Camp Murphy, Florida, is telling. It requested white WACs for its office and administrative positions and Black WACs for menial service jobs. If the latter request could not be filled, it instructed, "no colored WAACs are desired."[70]

If the War Department assumed that Black WACs would quietly accept this situation, it miscalculated. These women were not, as sociologist Brenda Moore attests, "mere passive objects in an institution that had only recently opened its doors to them."[71] In this respect, these women were better prepared for the army than the army was for them. African American women, after all, represented uncharted territory to the War Department, one that its officers knew little about and had virtually no idea how to navigate. In contrast, Black WACs arrived at military posts equipped with a sense of purpose, an armory of well-honed strategies, a rearguard of civilian Black women, and an inspiring legacy of activism. Also in their corner were Black men who rallied around the Double V campaign and had for decades participated in campaigns in shows of racial unity. During the war, the War Department learned that Black women were a force to reckon with, especially those with the status of soldiers.

Nevertheless, when questions emerged about their status as soldiers, Black WACs found that they were ultimately on their own, fighting against, as Terrell lamented, two handicaps, "both race and sex." While white Americans during World War II increasingly came to terms with Black men and white women serving in the military, many refused to consider Black WACs legitimate soldiers. "Those negroes joined the wacs because white women are in the wacs," charged a white Chicago man convinced that "whatever white people do they want to do. Monkey sees monkey does." So pernicious and immoral were Black women, he insisted that they would not be able to "stop this indecency if they want[ed] to."[72]

Black women were aware of the multiple sites of oppression—commonly referred to today as intersectionality—as a phenomenon that both plagued and inspired African American women. In the late nineteenth century, Anna Julia Cooper addressed its perplexities when challenging the then-popular ideal of "true womanhood," which espoused separate gendered spheres—men in the public arena and women at home. Cooper decried the emphasis on women's domesticity, which ignored the reality that most Black women had to leave their homes to find work. She found little support among her male counterparts. Often accepting patriarchal conventions, these men also critiqued women who ventured into the public "male" space, even to speak out against injustice.[73] Four decades later, during World War II, Pauli Murray provoked similar derision when pursuing a law degree at Howard University. Male professors and fellow students questioned her presence, as a woman, in the program. The experience sparked Murray's examination of the "disproportionate burdens" of women of color, which she called "Jane Crow." In 1963, she introduced this idea to the public in response to the male organizers of the March on Washington's refusal to allow female speakers on the public stage.[74] Situated within this sixty-five-year intellectual trajectory were the nation's first Black servicewomen. Like their contemporaries—Cooper, Terrel, Bethune, and Murray—they, too, grappled with the phenomenon, though within a military context and through a "GI Jane Crow" construct.

Shortly after the war, Dovey Johnson met Murray and shared the frustrations of her "outsider status as a black woman in a white man's army." Murray does not specify the military in her 1963 speech, yet her arguments relate to the loneliness of Black WACs' challenges to the military's gender and race policies even though these same policies also subordinated both white WACs and Black male personnel.[75] Murray noted that despite marginalized Americans' "common interest, . . . the dichotomy of the segregated society has prevented them from cementing a natural alliance."[76]

White WACs who were either unaware of their white privilege or accepted it as the natural order expressed bewilderment over Black WACs' complaints about menial duties that the white WACs were spared, occasionally due to the arrival of Black WACs who replaced them. Black men rallied behind the Black WACs' charges of racism, yet they did not always appreciate these women's unique circumstances, the extensiveness of their contributions, or even their role as soldiers. From their patriarchal perch, Black legionnaires in Boston urged leniency in the case of the Fort Devens WACs on the basis that women are "more frail, impulsive and sensitive than men."[77] Though more well meaning than the white male *Boston Herald* commentator who concluded that "Wacs really aren't soldiers," their sentiments mirrored his to a tee.[78]

Bethune was no stranger to demeaning images of Black women, yet having achieved success by working in the system, she advised others to do the same. Greeting the first graduating class of officers in 1942, she effused jubilant pride with a bit of caution. "We are seeking equal participation," she said, adding, "We are not going to be agitators."[79] For Black WACs, when simply serving in the military could provoke outrage among white Americans, the line between participation and resistance was not always clear.[80] "Just because you're in the uniform," an Alabama police officer warned two Black WACs whose refusal to vacate seats on a bus violated Jim Crow protocol, "you think you're smart. You're still a God-damn nigger down here in the South with us." He then proceeded to beat them. Their commanding officer at Camp Sibert expressed less outrage over their treatment than support for concessions to local mores.[81]

Where was the line between accommodation and resistance when military policies, rooted in oppressive civilian customs, subordinated Black women? Hailing from diverse regions and socioeconomic backgrounds, Black WACs held various views on where that line fell and how to best negotiate it as soldiers. They did not always agree. For instance, a plan to establish an all-Black WAC regiment at Fort Des Moines appealed to many of the officers, who assumed that a separate regiment without white WACs would increase their leadership and assignment opportunities. Others vehemently opposed the plan as yet another layer of segregation. Among them was Dovey Johnson, who in daring defiance, removed their insignia to declare that she would rather resign her commission than submit to further separation from the main forces. Several others felt the same and, with Bethune's backing, they prevailed.[82]

Another incident at Fort Des Moines illustrates the pressure on Black WACs to conform to the system and the risks involved when they instead stood up to it. In this case, a Black WAC officer reported three others for fraternizing with enlisted men in their quarters. The resulting charges led to the dismissal of Captain Francis Futrell. Seeking reinstatement through the NAACP, Futrell noted that the post's Black WAC officers did not have a club where they could socialize as did the other troops, and in any case, the army generally turned a blind eye to fraternization. She suspected therefore that her accuser reported her (and the army dismissed her) because of her outspoken advocacy of Black WACs. The motivations of the informant may only be guessed. Putney suggests that she was trying to avoid disciplinary charges for her own unbecoming conduct. According to Johnson, she was "a black stool pigeon who sold her soul for advancement in the white man's army."[83] More charitably, she may have believed that those who showed themselves to be compliant participants rather than agitators could boost the army's favorable impressions of Black women. Whatever the reasons, the informant remained in the WAC while the outspoken Futrell did not.

Differences in strategies according to rank were common among Black WACs, given the presence of a military hierarchy that paralleled civilian class distinctions. This came with important differences for African American women who generally recognized an intertwined solidarity and, among privileged women, an obligation to stand up for their less fortunate sisters.[84] Though often condescending, it tended to be genuine for women not long removed from an enslaved past. Aware of the social, psychological, and economic trap of subsistence menial labor and subject to much of the same malevolent treatment no matter how many degrees they earned or languages they spoke, privileged Black women recognized a connection and therefore a responsibly to others in service of the sisterhood. As officers, however, they also had a responsibility to assure their troops' compliance with directives that fundamentally were in service to a white male patriarchy. Lastly, they had a duty to their troops' advancement and morale, yet they did not have the authority to upgrade assignments or stem the racism they and their troops encountered.[85] Enlisted women typically understood this predicament and appreciated officers who looked out for them. Looking back, Veteran Essie Wood remembered that her officers "were never distant from you."[86] Those who proved distant earned the ire of their troops, not only as officers but as Black women who had betrayed them and their shared history of struggle. She "should be tarred and feathered," insisted one WAC about her officer in a letter to the NAACP, especially because the officer knew that "the Negro WAC has a hard way to go."[87]

The effects of officers' conflicting responsibilities were arguably born most by Harriet West, one of the two most highly ranked and profiled Black WAC officers of the war. A Bethune protegee, West briefly served as a WAC staff officer before transferring to the adjutant general's office, and she was routinely called on to investigate complaints by Black WACs before situations got out of hand. West managed to avert crises, but not resolve problems. As mentioned, Black officers, including West, had little authority to address the root causes of the complaints. That noted, West's reports gave short shrift to the enlisted women's grievances. Summarizing her observations, she wrote that the WACs "complained that they came in the Army to get away from the kitchen, but with their limited qualifications and capabilities, it has been impossible to use them in skilled occupations."[88] At one point, she tracked down the author of a letter alleging mistreatment of Black WACs at Fort Riley, Kansas, including mistreatment by one of the author's Black WAC commanders. Referencing Lieutenant Verneal Austin, Sergeant Thelma Robinson pointedly remarked, "And then your own selling you out." In a postscript to the letter, she added, "Someone must fight for our rights and I'm sure I'll win. If not me, then others will carry on and in the end our black WACs will come into their own."

Despite powerful statements connecting the role of Black WACs to the advancement of civil rights that Robinson interspersed throughout her letter and later during her conference with West and her immediate officers, West focused on the sergeant's "disturbing influence." Considering Robinson's extensive record of complaints as well as incidents of drinking and "jitterbugging out in the road," West recommended her removal from the company. In fact, there was little else to be done. Robinson's complaints were legitimate, while Lieutenant Austin, who others also bitterly complained about, had at least tried to be lenient with her. The problem was that neither she nor West had the authority to change the demoralizing dynamics. Robinson was a capable and hardworking leader who had enlisted "with the intention to get ahead," yet after an intense conference with her officers, she relented, "I just lose something—I just can't express how I feel."[89] Many Black WACs expressed the same.

In April 1943, West acknowledged on a radio broadcast that the segregated army "does not represent an ideal of democracy," though she believed that by enlisting, Black WACs were making a "contribution to its realization."[90] Part of this realization required that Black women succeeded in the WAC, an achievement the military measured by advancement in rank. The quandary for officers was what price were they willing to pay. Black WAC officers at Fort Clark, Texas risked their rank when protesting their new commander's segregation of the chapel. Much to their officers' dismay, the Black WACs organized a sit-in of Black personnel at a white service on Easter.[91] A lieutenant stationed at Camp Rucker, Alabama, attempted to improve her troop's assignments, only to have her commander, tired of her regular requests, suddenly disband her unit.[92]

Where then was the line between participating and agitating? When War Department investigators asked if discrimination existed at Fort Devens, a beleaguered Black WAC lieutenant played it safe. Though her troops had mutinied over their discriminatory orderly assignments, she replied, "Maybe I don't know what discrimination is," to which the investigator helpfully proffered, "Well, . . . it is not segregation."[93] When sent a list of complaints from Fort Des Moines WACs, Major Charity Adams, the highest-ranking Black WAC on the post, returned a review that concluded that racial discrimination did not exist there. "Fulfilling a role with which she did not necessarily identify," suggests Brenda Moore, "Major Adams was merely a black Wac carrying out orders."[94] In fact, both Adams and West also stood up for their troops. These were highly capable women who were dedicated to democracy. They also understood that to get ahead in the military—and to prove that Black WACs could rise in rank—they had to operate according to the dictates of a faulty system.[95] To much acclaim, both left the service as lieutenant colonels, the highest rank available to WACs, but at what costs?[96] West acknowledged, "My girls think I am giving them a bad deal because I have not, as they think, stood up for them in general." However, West did not believe that the army was the "place to fight race problems," a view that aligned with the War Department's 1940 insistence that it was not a "social laboratory" and could not therefore be expected to tackle issues of race.[97] In this, West could not have differed more from other Black WACs and the civilians who stood behind them.

Civilian Black women took little notice of rank, focusing instead on the gender and race issues that those in uniform faced. They wanted to know, for instance, why the WAC transferred white but not Black WACs overseas, failed to ensure safe accommodations for Black WACs traveling on military orders in the same way as they did white WACs, and deactivated the Black WAC band at Fort Des Moines. Furious over the policies that excluded these servicewomen, African American civilian women took action. One of the most successful of these actions was a national campaign to reactivate the Fort Des Moines Black band. Arguing that the War Department's limitation of one band per post did not take into account the segregation policy that banned Black musicians from the post's white WAC ensemble, they forced the intervention of the Secretary of War Henry Stimson. Subsequently, Stimson reversed the ban at Fort Des Moines. Throughout the war, civilian women coalesced with other civil rights organizations, galvanized letter-writing campaigns, and held fundraisers in support of Black WACs. Their efforts were essential to their sisters on the front lines of their struggle in the military.

The well-publicized 1945 Black WAC strike at Fort Devens, Massachusetts, provides an illustration of the collaboration between Black WACs and civilian women. Prior to the work stoppage, Private Harriet Warfield had written about the volatile situation to her aunt, who rushed the letter to her local Philadelphia NAACP office. Its executive secretary, Carolyn Moore, immediately alerted Thurgood Marshall, the organization's chief attorney. Back at Fort Devens, WACs were pressing for collective action, including Private Anna Morrison, who warned, "If we don't try to get something better now, we never will get it."[98] Nearly all of the orderlies joined the strike, and four took the court-martial that propelled it onto the national stage.

Reporters Constance Curtis of the *Amsterdam News* and Leotha Hacksaw of the *Pittsburgh Courier* covered the case.[99] Prominent female leaders from across the country declared their support of the four, among them Lucille Milner, the secretary of the American Civil Liberties Union; Jane Hunter, the president of the Ohio State Federation of Colored Women; and the entire leadership of the California State Association of Colored Women. Rebecca Stiles Taylor, the Georgia stalwart of the NACWC and later the NCNW, featured the defendants in her *Chicago Defender* column headlining the commentary, "Four Negro Wacs Call for Justice. Will They Be Heard?"[100] Locally, Jane Parker of the Red Cross and Boston's NAACP members Florence Luscomb and Ruby Hurley worked behind the scenes to aid the cause.[101] Closely monitoring developments, Bethune corresponded with the War Department and the NAACP to ensure a just outcome, financed the eminent civil rights lawyer Charles Houston to investigate the circumstances that led to the work stoppage, and regularly discussed the case in the press and with NCNW members. Florence Murray included a report of the incident in her 1945–46 edition of the *Negro Handbook*.[102] Ordinary Black women helped flood the War Department with letters demanding justice. One woman published "A Negro's Prayer" in dedication to the four WACs "for their stand against discrimination."[103] The defendants' relatives buoyed spirits with good wishes from home. Strangers donated money and spoke out about the case in public forums. Meanwhile, in their trial open to the public, the four at the center of the controversy detailed their treatment and defended their action in statements that went public. Both the Black and white press covered their officer's alleged comment that Black WACs were there to do the "dirty work."[104]

During her trial, Morrison explained that she had risked the court-martial to "help my people." This perplexed the prosecutor, who did not understand how "her people" had anything to do with her decision.[105] African Americans understood though, and African American women got it even more. "The cause of our four WACs belongs to the entire group," declared Stiles Taylor. And it did. It belonged to the WACs on trial who had risked prosecution to expose the army's treatment of their detachment and to the prominent female leaders and ordinary women who supported them, through actions or in spirit. As the facts unfolded, other Americans began to understand the reasons for the strike, yet the root factor was one that that did not—and perhaps could not—fully register with them: the conditions of GI Jane Crow.

Confronting discrimination was a risky venture, yet Black WACs took their chances—and usually lost. Officers found the Fort Devens WACs guilty, dismissed the women's complaints of racism at post-exchanges as unfortunate misunderstandings, refused to reinstate Captain Futrell, and labeled the organizers of the Fort Clark chapel sit-in "saboteurs." On the other hand, by initiating such challenges, these women ultimately won, courtesy of the US military protocols.

The bureaucratic nature of the War Department required the documentation of even minor incidents. This requirement provided Black WACs risking disciplinary action with, at minimum, an official platform to air their grievances and have them recorded. For many, the trade-off was worth it. "I feel that the investigation has not been in vain," Sergeant Robinson told West, "as it will bring to light a great many things." The outspoken Captain Futrell may have suspected that her prospects for reinstatement were dim, yet by pursuing her case, she guaranteed that her side would be on record. High-level inquiries about the Fort Devens strike, including from President Franklin Roosevelt, prompted an exhaustive investigation that produced a seven-hundred-page report containing dozens of transcribed interviews of Black WACs. Court-martial records of this case and others reveal insightful information by and about these women. Disciplinary protocols that permitted defendants to tell their side of the story, which required accurate transcriptions, in turn assured accounts of Black WACs' experiences, motivations, and strategies. A portion of these have survived to this day. Many are detailed, and most are in the women's own words.

The Black civilian women who supported their military counterparts during World War II likewise contributed to the intellectual history of the first WACs. Prominent leaders followed Black WACs' triumphs and challenges, as noted in conferences and meeting notes, newsletters, and press releases. Ordinary women demonstrated their solidarity with Black WACs by celebrating their achievements in the press, protesting their unjust treatment in letters to officials, coalescing with other groups to strengthen their efforts, and at times, putting themselves at risk. For example, the Red Cross worker at Fort Devens submitted her observations insisting on anonymity. Black female civilians' interest in the WAC attests to a recognition of the WAC's central, if largely unnoticed, role in many of the war years' most contentious debates, from the nation's commitment to democracy to the inclusion of African Americans and of women in the military. Black WACs lent clarity to that role.

Black women also made their mark on the military. First, by enlisting in the thousands, those in uniform overwhelmed the War Department's personnel classifications. Officers at the nation's most diversified post had to organize separate accommodations, duty stations, and timetables for Black and white men and for Black and white women. These subcategories required yet another division to suitably accommodate enlisted personnel and officers. Inefficiency turned to dysfunction after postwar troop reductions, which led to the racial integration of the WAC, as Bethune had predicted, in 1950, four years before the completed integration of male soldiers.

Second, by donning the uniform, Black WACs occasionally brought public attention to the discrimination that African Americans regularly faced, yet that non-Black civilians seemed unaware of. For instance, in 1945 Kentucky police officers brutally attacked three Black WACs for violating the state's segregation laws. A white Oregonian was so angry over the beatings and the army's subsequent court-martial of the victims for disrupting civil laws that he insisted that Jim Crow not apply to military personnel. Likewise, a white woman, appalled by the prosecution of Fort Devens Black WACs over their protest of menial labor, asked President Roosevelt, "Are we going to be as cold and inhuman in our practices as Hitler?"[106] The answer was decidedly no, at least when the Black women involved were soldiers whose situations attracted public attention. In both of these cases, officers dropped the charges. When asked about the reasons for dismissing the Fort Devens verdict, the women's commander explained that "a re-trial of those women would have been considered by a great many people in this county and would have placed the War Department in a still more difficult position."[107] The uniform gave visibility to Black WACs that their civilian counterparts in similar circumstances rarely had.

Third, by asserting the rights of those who had enlisted in the WAC, African American women gradually convinced officials that they could not simply ignore Black WACs' desire to help the war effort as soldiers. Hence, in early 1945, Hobby at last dispatched Black WACs overseas, and the War Department, apparently eager to avoid a repeat of the Fort Devens debacle, carefully planned the transfer of Black WACs to Gardiner General Military Hospital in Chicago. Over the vociferous objections of local residents—including the previously mentioned man who reduced Black WACs' motives to monkey-see-monkey-do aspirations—the War Department sent a unit of various skills and ranks and thereafter monitored the women's treatment.[108] With Martha Putney as their commander, the women successfully carried out their mission with morale high.

Two years after World War II ended, an NCNW spokesperson delivered a stirring message proclaiming that the "Women's Army Corps will be high up in the annals of history, and as part of that grand organization, the Negro woman cannot and will not be overlooked.[109] In fact, in the postwar backlash against changes to the status quo, white Americans did largely overlook Negro women, who historian Jacqueline Jones argues, lost most of their wartime gains.[110] The exceptions were those who served in the WAC.

Recognizing that "neither the concept nor the reality of fairness was operative in the corps, but neither was U.S. society's treatment of its blacks fair,"

Putney surmised that "many blacks got a better deal in the WAC than society offered them in the civilian sector."[111] Some gained skills, over eight hundred gained overseas experience as part of the 6888th Postal Battalion, and all who left the service in good standing gained benefits through the Servicemen's Readjustment Act of 1944. Known as the GI Bill, it entitled veterans to government-backed school tuitions, housing and business loans, and lifelong health care. Many used the GI Bill to pursue professional degrees. Dovey Johnson studied law. Anna Morrison, one of the Fort Devens defendants assigned to clean hospitals, became a licensed practical nurse. Martha Putney, who earned a doctorate in history through the GI Bill, credited veterans' health care and mortgage loan guarantees for propelling many into "a part of the nucleus of an expanding black middle class."[112] From this position, and in the spirit of their foremothers, these women helped their communities and, therefore, the nation. Morrison contributed to her church. Johnson, as a lawyer, took on cases of African Americans. Putney laid much of the scholarly groundwork for the study of World War II's Black WACs. If not all Black WAC veterans were as successful as those who responded to inquiries, all were part of the force that expanded the struggle into the military. Jacqueline Jones has further argued that "if black women did not achieve any long-lasting economic gains as a result of the war, they did begin to test the limits of their own collective strength in way that would reverberate into the future."[113] This is true, though in many ways military service gave Black WAC veterans a jump start.

By war's end, Black WACs and their sister champions had produced a remarkable array of knowledge that, though little noticed at the time, would have far-reaching consequences for Black women, the armed forces, the civil rights movement, and the nation. Together, they laid the GI Jane cornerstone of the civil rights movement on which Black women in all US services stand. By literally sitting down at Fort Devens, on an Alabama bus, in a Kentucky bus station, and during segregated services at Fort Clark's chapel, these women evoked the sit-in tactic used to great effect during civilian protests in the following decades. Furthermore, the War Department's marginalization of Black WACs during World War substantiates Pauli Murray's contention that state policies do not have to specifically exclude race or gender to fundamentally, in Jane Crow fashion, exclude women of color. Within the hierarchal constraints of the military, Black WACs also proved that such multi-segmentations based on race and gender simply did not work to anyone's advantage. The Department of Defense integrated women into the regular army in 1978.

Two decades after the integration, Violet Gordon attended a WAC reunion, where she marveled at changes that she "would never have envisioned in 1942." Impressed, Gordon expressed her respect to the younger generation of servicewomen.

It is mind-boggling to see a whole amphitheater of women representing all branches of the service (which was not true at the time that the WAC was formed) and to see the range both in age and rank . . . representing all colors, all races, and all ranks. . . . The final touch was the fly over of the Air Force with women pilots! It was a great moment, a great moment![114]

The young generation of servicewomen, however, were more intrigued by those who pioneered this path for them during World War II and asked if they had messages for Black women in the military. To this, Essie Woods replied that she did: "Know where you are going and . . . remember where you came from."[115]

NOTES

1. Interview, Essie Dell O'Bryant Woods, April 2, 2001, Essie Dell O'Bryant Woods Collection (AFC/2001/001/04741), Veterans History Project, American Folklife Center, Library of Congress, 13.

2. McCabe and Roundtree, *Justice Older Than the Law*, 71–72.

3. Josephine St. Pierre Ruffin, Address, First National Conference of Colored Women, July 29–31, 1895, in Lerner, *Black Women in White America*, 443.

4. Bay et al., *Toward an Intellectual History of Black Women*, 4; see also Cooper, *Beyond Respectability*, 12, 16.

5. Referencing Zora Neale Hurston, Alexander infers the insight of Black women. Alexander, "A Prehistory of African-American Studies."

6. Alexander, "A Prehistory of African-American Studies," time marker 55:00.

7. Putney, *When the Nation Was in Need*, 118.

8. Interview, Violet Hill Askins Gordon, March 25, 2002, Violet Hill Askins Gordon Collection (AFC/2001/001/00146), Veterans History Project, American Folklife Center, Library of Congress, 3–4.

9. Putney, *When the Nation Was in Need*, 118; Meyer, *Creating GI Jane*, 30.

10. Letter, "Baby Sis" (Thelma Robinson) to her sister, Fort Riley, Kansas, October 2, 1943, contained in the report of Harriet West, "Report on Field trip to Fort Riley, Kansas," October 27, 1943 in Harriet West Waddy, "Interim Report: Number 2," Army Women's Museum Archives, Ft. Lee, Virginia.

11. In 1940, 70 percent of employed female African Americans, compared to 22.4 percent of white women, worked in service jobs. The next largest proportion of Black workers engaged in agricultural, approximately half of them as "unpaid family workers." United States Department of Labor, "Negro Women War Workers," 16. Also see Jones, *Labor of Love*, 235–40, and Moore, *To Serve My Country*, 8–13.

12. Hartmann, *The Home Front and Beyond*, 31; Moore, "From Underrepresentation to Overrepresentation," 117.

13. Putney, *When the Nation Was in Need*, vii–viii.

14. Hartmann, *Home Front and Beyond*, 34–35; Morden, *Women's Army Corps*, 4–5; The WAC bill, passed on July 1, 1943, retained gender restrictions on women soldiers' command (limited to female troops), dependency benefits, assignments (gender appropriate), and rank (capped at lieutenant colonel for all but the corps director, a colonel. Morden, *Women's Army Corps*, 6, 12–15.

15. Moore, *To Serve My Country*, 2.

16. The US Navy and Coast Guard accepted their first Black recruits, all officers, in late 1944 and the US Marine Corps not until 1949. MacGregor, *Integration of the Armed Forces*, 86–88.

17. Jones, *Labor of Love*, 235–40.

18. Lee, *Employment of Negro Troops*, 75.

19. Jones, *Labor of Love*, 56–57, 215–16.

20. Mia Bay, "The Battle for Womanhood Is the Battle for Race: Black Women and Nineteenth-Century Racial Thought," in Bay et al., *Toward an Intellectual History of Black Women*, 89.

21. The NACW transitioned to the NACWC in 1904.

22. Giddings, *When and Where I Enter*, 93.

23. Bay, "The Battle for Womanhood Is the Battle for Race," 90. Ruffin founded the National Federation of Afro-American Women in 1895 and a year later joined with the Colored Women's League to form the NACWC.

24. Cooper, *Beyond Respectability*, 6.

25. Giddings, *When and Where I Enter*, 87.

26. White, *Too Heavy a Load*, 51, 54; Bay, "The Battle for Womanhood," 89. See also Cooper, *Beyond Respectability*, 22.

27. Stephanie Shaw, "The Creation of the National Association of Colored Women," in Hine, King, and Reed, *"We Specialize in the Wholly Impossible,"* 441.

28. White, *Too Heavy a Load*, 60, 145–46.

29. White, *Too Heavy a Load*, 124–30.

30. White, *Too Heavy a Load*, 148–57.

31. White, *Too Heavy a Load*, 244–46, 141, 152.

32. Moore, *To Serve My Country*, 52–53.

33. Moore, *To Serve My Country*, 61.

34. Putney, *When the Nation Was in Need*, 1–2; Moore, *To Serve My Country*, 52–59.

35. Putney, *When the Nation Was in Need*, 51; Moore, *To Serve My Country*, 16–17.

36. Sims-Wood, *We Served America, Too!*, 55.

37. McCabe, *Justice Older Than the Law*, 57.

38. Putney, *When the Nation Was in Need*, 30, 38; Meyer, *Creating GI Jane*, 6, 36.

39. Interview, Millie L. D. Veasey, Veterans Historical Project, Oral History Collection, June 25, 2000, 6; Putney, *When the Nation Was in Need*, 33.

40. Putney, *When the Nation Was in Need*, 40.

41. Treadwell, *Women's Army Corps*, 596.

42. Gordon, Veterans History Project, 2.

43. Putney, *When the Nation Was in Need*, 29; Address, Director Oveta Culp Hobby to the Alpha Kappa Alpha Sorority, Howard University, "The Role of Our Federal Government,"

July 6, 1942, Historical Background, War Department, Bureau of Public Relations, Records of the War Department General and Special Staffs 165, box 21, NARA.

44. Murray, *The Negro Handbook*, 325. Two others under the same title, one published in 1942 and the other in 1944, complete the series.

45. Interview, Dorothy Miller, Veterans Historical Project, February 8, 2001, 2.

46. Letter from a WAC stationed at Fort Des Moines ["name withheld"] to John H. Sengstacke, Editor of the *Defender*, January 8, 1944, as quoted in Litoff and Smith, *We're in This War, Too*, 76; also see Putney, *When the Nation Was In Need*, 13–14.

47. Testimony, Anna Morrison, in the General Court-Martial, United States v. Young, et al., (CM 278502), March 19–20, 1945, Ft. Devens, Massachusetts [hereafter, "*US v. Young*"], United States Army Judiciary, Department of the Army, Arlington, VA, 241.

48. Ina M. McFadden, "Women on Their Own," *Pulse*, February 1943.

49. Moore, *To Serve My Country*, 12.

50. Putney, *When the Nation Was in Need*, 13.

51. Veasey, Veterans Historical Project, 7.

52. Giddings, *When and Where I Enter*, 13, 82.

53. Woods, Veterans History Project, 13.

54. Miller, Veterans Historical Project, 12.

55. Interview, Judy McKinnon, Women's Veterans Historical Project, February 9, 2001, 5.

56. Interviews, Henrietta Stevenson Ingram, February 3, 1999, Women Veterans Historical Project (Greensboro: University of North Carolina), 7.

57. In Putney's rendition to Sims-Wood, she writes that the recruit said, "Negro," followed by "she didn't say Negro" in parentheses. Putney, *When the Nation Was in Need*, 54–55; Sims-Wood, "*We Served America Too!*," 155–56.

58. Before departing the program, the white WAC left Putney a wrapped gift with a note signed, "A reconstructed southerner." Sims-Wood, "*We Served America Too!*," 157.

59. Veasey, Veterans Historical Project, 8–9.

60. Interview, Juanita Porter, March 14, 1945, "Investigation of WAC Detachment, Lovell General and Convalescent Hospital, Fort Devens, Massachusetts," May 4, 1945 [hereafter War Department Investigation], File 333.9 (2) Lovell General Hospital, General Correspondence, 1939–1947, Record Office of the Inspector General, Group 159, National Archives, College Park, MD, 21.12.

61. Interview, Lois Floyd, War Department Investigation, 7.

62. "Disillusioned by Jim Crow Washington Girl Quits WAC," *Afro-American* (Washington, DC), March 10, 1945.

63. Rosalyn Terborg-Penn, "Discontented Black Feminists," in Hine, King, and Reed, "*We Specialize in the Wholly Impossible*," 500.

64. Lt. Colonel Edward R. Whitehurst, Chief, Enlmt Br SGO to Chief of Pers SGO, Surgeon General—and Cpt. Sisson, March 7, 1945; War Department Investigation.

65. Putney, *When the Nation Was in Need*, 75–96.

66. Treadwell, *Women's Army Corps*, 599.

67. Treadwell, *Women's Army Corps*, 594.

68. Treadwell, *Women's Army Corps*, 598; "WAC Group Confined in Discipline Action," *Atlanta Constitution*, March 1945.

69. Meyer, *Creating GI Jane*, 72; As early as August 1943, the Medical Department had deemed hospital orderly duties unsuitable for women due to the long hours and heavy

lifting it required. Treadwell agreed. Calling it a job for the "lowest aptitude," she concluded that it was "the only hospital job on which women were admittedly unsuccessful." Treadwell, *Women's Army Corps*, 345–46.

70. Meyer, *Creating GI Jane*, 80.

71. Moore, *To Serve My County*, 19.

72. Letter, "A White American" to Mr. Chas E. Gilkey and Dr. Homer A. Jack, Chicago, Illinois, July 30, 1945, National Archives for Black Women's History, RG 38, Series 3, Box 2, File 7.

73. Bay, "The Battle for Womanhood," 89.

74. Pauli Murray, "Jim Crow and Jane Crow," in Lerner, *Black Women in White America*, 593–99; Cooper, *Beyond Respectability*, 88.

75. McCabe, *Justice Older Than the Law*, 84.

76. Murray, "Jim Crow and Jane Crow," 593, 595.

77. Letter, American Legion Post #16 to the Judge Advocate, Boston, March 23, 1945.

78. Bill Cunningham, "WAC Decision Unity Threat," *Boston Herald*, April 5, 1945.

79. Putney, *When the Nation Was in Need*, 51.

80. Meyer, *Creating GI Jane*, 93.

81. Testimony of Pvt. Roberta McKenzie, December 23, 1944, "Discrimination in the U.S. Armed Forces, 1918–1955," NAACP Papers, Reel 25, Part 9, Series B, 1940–1955, microfilm; Meyer, *Creating GI Jane*, 93–94.

82. Putney, *When the Nation Was in Need*, 14–16.

83. Putney, *When the Nation Was in Need*, 22–23; McCabe, *Justice Older Than the Law*, 86.

84. White, *Too Heavy a Load*, 69–72.

85. Putney, *When the Nation Was in Need*, 13.

86. Woods, Veterans History Project, 8.

87. Letter, signed "a disgusted Service Woman," to the NAACP, April 10, 1945. (Note on letter reads "Wac at Devens," "Discrimination in the U.S. Armed Forces, 1918–1955," NAACP Papers, Reel 19, Part 9, Series B, 1940–1955.

88. Report, Harriet West Waddy, (ud) FIC.2012.107 Album 709–11. US Army Women's Museum, Fort Lee, VA.

89. West, "Report on Field Trip to Fort Riley."

90. Meyer, *Creating GI Jane*, 75.

91. Putney, *When the Nation Was in Need*, 75–96; Ft. Clark, TX servicewoman to Mrs. Roosevelt, who forwarded the letter to Colonel Hobby on May 2, 1943, RG 165, Stack 390, Row 31, Comp 4, Shelf 03–4, Entry 54, Box 49, folder 291.2, NA.

92. Putney, *When the Nation Was in Need*, 96.

93. Interview, Stoney, 55, April 6, 1945.

94. Moore, *To Serve My Country*, 75.

95. Meyer, *Creating GI Jane*, 92.

96. Yet she was also the one with rank, the first to make major in 1944 and the highest-ranking Black WAC when she left service as lieutenant colonel in 1959.

97. Meyer, *Creating GI Jane*, 93; Lee, *Employment of Negro Troops*, 142.

98. Interview, Anna Morrison, War Department Investigation, 573.

99. Constance Curtis, "6 WACs Face Possible Death Penalty," *Amsterdam News*, March 17, 1945; Leotha Hacksaw, "New Evidence in WAC case," *Pittsburgh Courier*, March 31, 1945.

100. Letter, Lucille B. Milner to Thurgood Marshall, March 23, 1945, "Discrimination in the U.S. Armed Forces, 1918–1955," NAACP Papers, Reel 19, Part 9, Series B, 1940–1955; "Devens WAC Strike Ends; Six Fac Court-Marital," *Afro American, Baltimore, MD*, March 24, 1945; Harry McAlpin, "Fate of 'WAC four' Riles Country's Leaders to Action," *Cleveland Call and Post*, March 31, 1945; letter, California State Association of Colored Women Inc. to Henry L. Stimson, April 9, 1945, RG 407, Stack 270, Row 41, Comp 35/2–3, Box 1063, Entry 363, File: 291.2, NARA; Rebecca Stiles Taylor, "Four Negro WACs Call for Justice. Will They Be Heard?," *Chicago Defender*, March 31, 1945.

101. Strom, *Political Woman*, 181; Memorandum, Robert L. Carter to Mr. Wilkins, "WAC Strike in Massachusetts," March 15, 1945. "Discrimination in the U.S. Armed Forces," NAACP Papers.

102. Murray, *The Negro Handbook*, 351, 356.

103. Poem, Ruth M. Apilado, "A Negro's Prayer," Negro Journal of Letters, ud, from the scrapbook of Alice Young Porter, courtesy of Stacie Porter.

104. "Colonel Voiced Bias, Colored WAC Testifies," *Washington Star*, March 20, 1945.

105. *US v. Young*, 120, 126.

106. Crookham, City Editor of the *Journal* to Secretary of War Stimson, Portland, Oregon, March 21, 1945; Weymer to Roosevelt, March 21, 1945; Emily Weymer, San Jose, California, to Roosevelt, March 21, 1945.

107. Another was the Kentucky Fort Knox bus station in the fall of 1945.

108. Letter, "A White American" to Mr. Chas E. Gilkey and Dr. Homer A. Jack, Chicago, Illinois, July 30, 1945, National Archives for Black Women's History, RG 38, Series 3, Box 2, File 7.

109. "Talk to Be Made at the New York Public Library Commemorating National Negro History Week on 13 February 1947," in the "Brief History of Negro Women the Army," Mary McLeod Bethune Council House, NABWH_001_S05_B38_F54, p. 4.

110. Jones, *Labor of Love*, 257.

111. Putney, *When the Nation Was in Need*, 135.

112. Putney, *When the Nation Was in Need*, 138.

113. Jones, *Labor of Love*, 235.

114. Gordon, Veterans History Project, 10.

115. Woods, Veterans History Project, 13.

REFERENCES

Alexander, Elizabeth. "A Prehistory of African-American Studies." Keynote speech, Toward an Intellectual History of Black Women: An International Conference, April 29, 2011, Columbia University, New York. https://www.socialdifference.columbia.edu/events-1/toward-an-intellectual-history-of-black-women-an-international-conference.

Bay, Mia, Farah J. Griffin, Martha S. Jones, and Barbara D. Savage, eds. *Toward an Intellectual History of Black Women*. Chapel Hill: University of North Carolina Press, 2015.

Cooper, Brittney. *Beyond Respectability: The Intellectual Thought of Race Women*. Champaign: University of Illinois, 2017.

Giddings, Paula. *When and Where I Enter: The Impact of Black Women on Race and Sex in America*. Toronto: Bantam Books, 1985.

Hartmann, Susan M. *The Home Front and Beyond: American Women in the 1940s.* Boston: Twayne Publisher, 1982.
Hine, Darlene Clark, Wilma King, and Linda Reed, eds. *"We Specialize in the Wholly Impossible": A Reader in Black Women's History.* Brooklyn: Carlson Publishing, 1995.
Jones, Jacqueline. *Labor of Love, Labor of Sorrow: Black Women, Work, and the Family from Slavery to the Present.* New York: Vintage Books, 1986.
Lee, Ulysses. *The United States Army in World War II, Special Studies: The Employment of Negro Troops.* Washington, DC: Office of the Chief of Military History, 1966.
Lerner, Gerda, ed. *Black Women in White America: A Documentary History.* New York: Vintage Books, 1973.
Litoff, Judy Barrett, and Davis S. Smith, *We're in this War, Too: World War II Letters from American Women in Uniform.* New York: Oxford University Press, 1994.
MacGregor, Morris J., Jr. *Integration of the Armed Forces, 1940–1965.* Washington DC: Center of Military History, 1981.
McCabe, Katie, and Dovey Johnson Roundtree. *Justice Older Than the Law: The Life of Dovey Johnson Roundtree.* Jackson: University Press of Mississippi, 2009.
Meyer, Leisa D. *Creating GI Jane: Sexuality and Power in the Women's Army Corps during World War II.* New York: Columbia University Press, 1996.
Moore, Brenda L. "From Underrepresentation to Overrepresentation: African American Women." In *It's Our Military, Too! Women and the U.S. Military,* edited by Judith Hicks Steihm. Philadelphia: Temple University Press, 1996.
Moore, Brenda L. *To Serve My Country, to Serve My Race: The Story of the Only African American WACs Stationed Overseas during World War II.* New York: New York University Press, 1996.
Morden, Bettie, E. *Army Historical Series: The Women's Army Corps, 1945–1978.* Washington, DC: Center of Military History, United States Army, 1992.
Murray, Florence. *The Negro Handbook, 1946–1947.* New York: Current Books, 1947.
Putney, Martha S. *When the Nation Was in Need: Blacks in the Women's Army Corps during World War II.* Lanham, MD: Scarecrow Press, 1992.
Sims-Wood, Janet. "*We Served America Too!* Personal Recollections of African American Women in the Women's Army Corps during World War II." Ph.D. diss., the Union Institute, 1994.
Strom, Sharon. *Political Woman: Florence Luscomb and the Legacy of Radical Reform.* Philadelphia: Temple University Press, 2001.
Treadwell, Mattie E. *The United States Army in World War II, Special Studies: The Women's Army Corps.* Washington, DC: Office of Chief of Military History, 1954.
United States Department of Labor. "Negro Women War Workers." Percent of Negro Women among Total Employed Workers in Specified Occupational Groups, April 1940 and April 1944.
White, Deborah Gray. *Too Heavy a Load: Black Women in Defense of Themselves, 1894–1994.* New York: W. W. Norton, 1999.

Archives

General Court-Martial, United States v. Young, et al., (CM 278502), March 19–20, 1945, Ft. Devens, MA, United States Army Judiciary, Department of the Army, Arlington, VA.

Harriet West Waddy Collection, US Army Women's Museum, Fort Lee, VA.
Lt. Col. Milton S. Musser to the Inspector General, "Investigation of WAC Detachment, Lovell General and Convalescent Hospital, Fort Devens, Massachusetts," May 4, 1945, File 333.9, Lovell General Hospital, General Correspondence, 1939–1947, Record Office of the Inspector General, Group 159, National Archives, College Park, MD.
Mary McLeod Bethune Council House, Washington, DC.
National Association of Colored People Papers, Part 9. "Discrimination in the U.S. Armed Forces, 1918–1955." (microfilm)
Record Group 165: Records of the War Department General and Special Staffs, National Archives, College Park, MD.
Record Group 407: Records of the Adjutant General's Office, National Archives, College Park, MD.
Veterans History Project, American Folklife Center, Library of Congress, Washington, DC (digital collection).
Women Veterans Historical Project, Greensboro, NC: University of North Carolina (digital collection).

Chapter 14

SEIZING OPPORTUNITY

African American Women in the Postwar Military

TANYA L. ROTH

In the spring of 1943, the year-old Women's Army Auxiliary Corps (WAAC) needed more women. Three months before the WAAC lost its auxiliary status to become more fully integrated into the United States military, Major Harriet West went on the radio to advertise WAAC service as a patriotic wartime job. In particular, West hoped to recruit more African American women like herself to the WAAC, aiming to convince them that the opportunities in service outweighed the challenges that came with joining a segregated institution. West addressed the problem of segregation head-on, arguing that choosing to participate in the segregated WAAC should not be considered "a retreat" from the larger effort to gain equal rights as American citizens. Instead, she suggested to her audience that by enlisting in the women's services, African American women would make "our contribution to its realization."[1] West argued that by engaging in wartime public service, Black women would redefine Americans' conceptions of Black women's citizenship, a major intellectual shift with important implications for equal rights.

While it is not common to think of military service as a form of public intellectual discourse, it is a crucial way to understand the significance of Black women's military service. For men, military service has been both obligation and opportunity. The use of the draft in the twentieth century meant that many men experienced military service that was foisted on them. Black men had this same experience, but for them, military service offered an opportunity as well: a way to prove that they, too, were citizens deserving of the same rights and benefits as white servicemen. Yet because women have never been drafted, women's military service has always been a choice. Women who made that choice became part of the process of reimagining Black women's citizenship. During World War II and the Cold War, military service became a significant avenue through which Black women could engage in the intellectual discourse shaping what it meant to be a citizen with equal rights.

World War II saw the use of womanpower on an unprecedented scale, but this reliance did not alter military leaders' insistence on racially segregating all personnel. Additionally, Black women, like African American men, were admitted on a 10 percent quota. Beginning in 1942, as the WAAC developed and transitioned into a fully military unit known as the Women's Army Corps (WAC) in 1943, journalists in many African American newspapers also embraced African American women's service. The WAC offered Black women the same claims on citizenship rights that Black male veterans had long sought. Some criticism centered on the fact that the WAAC/WAC embraced military segregation and racial quota policies and that a southern woman (Colonel Oveta Culp Hobby of Texas) was chosen to lead the WAAC. Ultimately, however, the military opportunities for African American women emerged as more significant to these journalists. The first group of WAAC recruits included forty African American women, as compared to four hundred white women, all selected out of thirty thousand total applicants of both races.[2] With the 10 percent quota and segregation policies firmly in place throughout the war, approximately four thousand African American women served in the military by war's end—4 percent of the permitted total.[3]

By entering the armed forces during World War II, African American women gained economic opportunities often unavailable in the civilian world. They participated in the tradition of military service as a means to secure citizenship rights. After the Civil War, supporters of the Fifteenth Amendment cited African American soldiers' service as a reason why Black men deserved the right to vote. That connection persisted in World War II, historian Douglas Bristol Jr. writes: "African Americans sought to fight in combat during World War II in order to link their military service to their claims for equal citizenship."[4] World War II was an important turning point in claiming that equality, following a half century in which the military had shrunk in size, reduced peacetime service opportunities, and used new tools such as standardized tests to shape the recruit pool more formally. According to historians Sherie Mershon and Steven Schlossman, these changes heightened racial discrimination, reducing the numbers of African Americans in the ranks prior to World War II and further underscoring segregation. By the 1940s, "Such formal, institutionalized practices as racial segregation, limitations on the careers of black officers, and the exclusion of blacks from specialized technical occupations had become firmly entrenched."[5] Despite such limitations, when war came, military and government leaders tended to call on African Americans to do their patriotic duty, just as West did in 1943.[6]

The connection between military service and claims of equal citizenship is most evident during wartime because of the intense need for Americans in defense work. World War II demonstrates this connection particularly well, since more than 11.5 million men—more than 60 percent of the active military force—were drafted during the conflict.[7] On the other hand, all World War II servicewomen were among the 40 percent of servicemembers who volunteered. While not all women joined the military in World War II for purely patriotic reasons, love of country was a strong pull, in addition to the benefits of a steady job, living quarters, and training opportunities. For African American servicemen and women, patriotism took on double meaning; they joined that fight not just to win the war, but to fight against discrimination and segregation as per West's suggestion.

Women's service remained patriotic after the war, but a new focus emerged as government and military leaders made the military's use of womanpower permanent and eliminated racial quotas and segregation. Military service became a source of economic opportunity for American women, always as volunteers who were never compelled to serve as an obligation of citizenship. Servicewomen continued to support the nation as they had in wartime, but often did so specifically because the Cold War offered them a career path unlike any in the civilian world, one that had equal pay to and offered the same benefits as their male counterparts. If a woman could get into the services, military service offered better opportunities than many other career paths in the Cold War United States. As military leaders imagined how women could support the country in service, they simultaneously created an institution in which women's sex mattered more than their race, at least on paper. Accordingly, for African American women, military service created an anomalous opportunity.

Immediately after World War II, military leaders, members of Congress, and the president all engaged in efforts to reimagine national defense. Even as servicemen and women began returning home in late 1945, these leaders recognized a need to be prepared for future emergencies. Two world wars within a generation signaled a need for prudence. Additionally, with American troops scheduled to engage in postwar occupations in Europe and Asia, it would not be possible to restore the military to what its prewar state. The goal for many military leaders was to build on wartime successes to create an institution that would be more efficient moving forward. The 1947 National Security Act eliminated the War Department and created the Department of Defense as an umbrella framework for the army, marine corps, navy, and the newly created air force.[8] With this newly centralized approach to national defense, military planners could begin reimagining national defense in the postwar nuclear world they had helped create.

Even before the National Security Act passed, military leaders reexamined their segregation policies, which had been challenged consistently during the war. The US Navy's Granger Inquiry, begun before the war ended in 1945, came to many of the same conclusions as the navy's concurrently running Committee on Negro Personnel: it was time to allow African Americans to serve in "all general-service positions on all ships and at all shore stations." Further recommendations asserted the need for continued desegregation and officer education throughout the navy.[9] While the changes had mixed results, African American women experienced immediate benefits: beginning in 1946, they could join the navy for the first time. Previously, because of the navy's segregation policies, Black women had not been allowed to join the wartime navy women's reserve, Women Accepted for Volunteer Emergency Services (WAVES). Very few Black women—about seventy—joined in 1946, because of both high enlistment standards and decreasing personnel demands at war's end. However, the presence of so few African American women meant that the new Black WAVES lived in a racially integrated environment and participated in job assignments on an integrated basis, unlike Black servicemen, or Black women who had served in the wartime WAC.[10]

However, army leadership firmly believed that racial integration would hurt efficiency. In addition to interviewing white officers and noncommissioned officers who had spent some of the war working with a few European-based "experimental racially mixed infantry companies," the leadership also surveyed another 1,700 enlisted white men who were unrelated to the experimental project. Soldiers who had not worked with Black platoons thought desegregation undesirable; those who had worked with Black platoons saw desegregation as a possible good. Amid split opinions over the research results, some worried what members of Congress might think of the possibility of racial integration.[11] In early 1946, the Gillem Board recommended that the army recruit African Americans more heavily and more fully employ them throughout the army. The board did not recommend full desegregation, but it had in mind an arrangement more like that of the experimental integrated infantry, grouping some Black units along with white ones. Ultimately, however, the board recommendations mostly focused on keeping segregation in place, with African Americans and whites grouped in different units and living in separate facilities. Although the Gillem Board's results became policy, many officers did not respond well and failed to institute the changes. Two years later, few Gillem Board recommendations had been implemented.[12]

In addition to re-evaluating racial segregation, military leaders debated allowing women to continue their service. The legislation authorizing the Women's Army Corps in 1943 specified that the organization would disband within six months of the war's end. The debates about changing that rule began almost immediately in 1945, although early legislation drafts did not go far. Even though military leaders were clearly evaluating segregation policies at the same time as the legislation went through Congress, the Women's Armed Services Integration Act said nothing about race, and members of Congress did not discuss race as they considered the proposed law. The focus remained solely on women and whether the nation needed their service in peacetime. This meant questioning whether women should be included only in the reserves, worrying over the problem of motherhood and marriage, and addressing fears about women commanding men. No one asked about classifying women's roles by their race, perhaps assuming that existing racial policies would remain in effect.

When the Women's Armed Services Integration Act became law in June 1948, allowing women to serve in all military branches, military leaders created a new type of segregation based on sex. The Women's Army Corps remained a separate organization within the military. The marine corps and navy continued to apply World War II–era titles like the Women Marines and WAVES but neither they nor the air force—which termed its new organization Women in the Air Force (WAF)—created fully separate organizations. All branches appointed a director to manage women's service, including the WAC director, Women Marines director, WAF director, and WAVES director. Only 2 percent of the total armed forces could be female, and women could advance no higher than colonel (army, air force) or captain (navy, marines), ranks that would be held only temporarily by the women serving as directors; when a woman left her role as director, she dropped back a rank for the remainder of her career and retirement. Pay would be rank based: a woman at any given rank would make the same as a man in that rank. In short, women would make equal pay, which was unheard of in the private sector.

A number of restrictions limited what looked like fantastic, forward-thinking career opportunities. In addition to the rank limitations, other provisions were built on assumptions that women should aspire to be wives and mothers one day. Servicewomen could get married and remain in service, but in the first five years of women's postwar service, it was so common for women to take a "marriage discharge" that many veterans recall that leaving was *mandatory* upon marriage, even though it was not.[13] Within a few years, this policy disappeared, mostly because too many women tried to leave before completing their enlistment term. However, any woman who got pregnant or became a mother through adoption or marriage was required to leave the services.[14] The belief was that military service should not interfere with such a higher calling for women's lives in any way. Combat and combat support roles remained off-limits, as they were deemed unfeminine roles that were unsuitable for Uncle Sam's nieces, and were reserved only for men.

Although the law imagined the uses of womanpower in limited ways, the Women's Armed Services Integration Act, signed by President Harry Truman, was forward-thinking because it recognized that women could be vital to the nation's defense. By creating a system that based pay on rank, the new law created a space where women could find some measure of equity and economic equality with their male counterparts. The benefits came at some cost, because pregnant women and mothers would lose their jobs. Rank limitations also had long-term implications on women's career potential, eventually creating scenarios in which women had to leave the military because they could no longer advance to the next level. And the question remained as to what women's service would look like: it was clear that women would not serve in or anywhere close to combat, but would perform work that they seemed well-suited for, roles that would be appropriate in the civilian world. Beyond that, the goal would be to find the best places to use women based on their unique skills.[15] But at the end of the day, women were there to stay.

The women's service components had barely begun recruitment planning efforts when President Truman ordered the desegregation of the US military on July 26, 1948. Executive Order 9981 specified that "there shall be equality of treatment and opportunity for all persons in the armed services without regard to race, color, religion or national origin."[16] This policy change came directly from the results of his 1946 President's Committee on Civil Rights, a yearlong project in which committee members researched not just military segregation but the status of civil rights in the United States. In their final report, "To Secure These Rights," published in the fall of 1947, committee members noted that "the armed forces have recently adopted policies which set as explicit objectives the achievement of equality of opportunity," providing evidence from the services to this effect. The authors continued, noting, "However, despite the lessons of the war and the recent announcement of these policies, the records of the military forces disclose many areas in which there is a great need for further remedial action."[17]

Further, the authors explained that "studies made within the last year disclose that the actual experience has been out of keeping with the declarations of policy on discrimination. In the Army, less than one Negro in 70 is commissioned, while there is one white officer for approximately every seven white enlisted men."[18] The navy, meanwhile, had the same ratio for white officers, but "less than one [Black officer] to 10,000 Negro enlisted men," while the marine corps had no Black officers and the coast guard had only one.[19] For enlisted personnel, most African Americans could be found in the lowest ranks and duties. Beyond numbers, discrimination remained a big problem in the military. "The armed forces, in actual practice, still maintain many barriers to equal treatment for all their members. . . . There is much that remains to be done, much that can be done at once."[20] This situation resulted in a moral and practical issue: "Morally, the failure to act is indefensible. Practically, it costs lives and money in the inefficient use of human resources."[21]

The commission's far-ranging recommendations began with the premise that the government had a responsibility to take the lead in civil rights matters. The belief that the government should "safeguard the civil rights of all Americans" undergirds all their recommendations.[22] In terms of the military, commission members argued that it was imperative for the federal government to take the lead to not only tackle segregation but also "to see that discrimination and prejudice are completely eliminated from the armed services."[23] Commission members called on Congress and the administration "to end immediately all discrimination and segregation based on race, color, creed, or national origin, in the organization and activities of all branches of the Armed Services."[24] Not only did the authors believe it was morally wrong to continue segregation and allow discrimination in the military, these problems would inhibit military success. Going further, the commission members called for legislation to ensure that any member of the armed forces would be protected from discrimination "by any public authority or place of public accommodation, recreation, transport, or other service or business."[25]

President Truman did not immediately act on the commission's recommendations. Although he used the information in the report as background for a message to Congress about civil rights in February 1948, he did not yet request legislation to end military segregation and discrimination. In his message, President Truman explained that he was tasking the Department of Defense to think about how they might end "discriminatory practices within its jurisdiction."[26] Then he did nothing until the summer. Meanwhile, members of Congress continued to consider the Women's Armed Services Integration Act, the major political parties were in the thick of a presidential election year, and the Democratic National Convention began in early July.

Truman acted just six weeks after the Women's Armed Services Integration Act became law, bypassing Congress to eliminate segregation in the military. Executive Order 9981 capitalized on the newly restructured armed forces, the decision in late June to reinstate the draft, and the permanent integration of womanpower.[27] While he did not offer a specific plan to accomplish this goal, his order created a President's Committee on Equality of Treatment and Opportunity in the Armed Services to provide follow-up research and support and specified that "this policy shall be put into effect as rapidly as possible, having due regard to the time required to effectuate any necessary changes without impairing efficiency or morale."[28] A few days later, Truman confirmed that the intention of the executive order's call for "equality of treatment and opportunity for all persons" was to desegregate the military; moreover, the vagueness of the executive order was intentional, giving latitude, rather than guidance, to the armed forces.²⁹ Given the vagueness of the executive order, most members of the Republican-controlled Congress ignored the executive order. In the service branches, without real guidance or instructions, it remained to be seen how seriously this new directive would be taken.

Although Executive Order 9981 represented a major policy shift, it created immediate change not primarily for servicemen, but for servicewomen. For Black servicemen, segregation remained a reality through the Korean War and beyond. However, coming as it did just as the women's services began to create their postwar accession plans, Executive Order 9981 played an important role in women's postwar military integration.

Initially, the women's components followed the policy set by their individual branches because they lacked other specific directives to help implement Executive Order 9981. Even so, the women's services desegregated much more efficiently and earlier than the rest of the armed forces, even though the Fahy Committee, the group authorized to help carry out Executive Order 9981, largely ignored the women's services. This oversight likely had two root causes: on the one hand was the myth that since women were now fully integrated into the military, there was no need to consider them separately. Although theoretically true, this was not actually the case. While women worked in the predominantly male institution, often working alongside men, they lived with other women and tended to have some degree of leadership from women officers—depending on which service branch they joined—from initial training through the duration of their careers. While limited in their power, the directors of the women's components had the responsibility of administering womanpower themselves. In the years following the Women's Armed Services Integration Act, women in the armed forces served alongside men in many ways but were also uniquely segregated on the basis of sex.

The reality was that very few women served in the military in 1949 and 1950 as the Fahy Committee pushed the services to desegregate, and even fewer African American women. By 1950 and the start of the Korean War, only 15,000 women served across all branches.³⁰ In 1949 the navy's WAVES had one Black woman officer and six Black enlisted women out of 1,700 women total; by 1950, that number had risen to twenty-five enlisted women, but no Black women officers served outside of the Navy Nurse Corps.³¹ In 1949, the WAC—the largest of the services—had only six Black women officers and 208 Black enlisted women. Thus, not only were the numbers of women small overall, but the numbers of Black women were miniscule in relation to women's service and to the military as a whole. They were of small consequence to an organization most concerned about how desegregation might affect combat and unit cohesion—factors that might have appeared irrelevant when it came to women, who were all classified as noncombatants.

Even though the Women's Armed Services Integration Act became law in mid-1948, most of the women's services would not begin heavy recruiting efforts until 1949 or 1950, and when they did so, they struggled to recruit women in the numbers they desired. In addition to cultural messages about the desirability of marriage and motherhood, recruitment standards posed some barriers to potential servicewomen. In 1950, a woman at the minimum age of eighteen would have been born in 1932, right in the middle of the Depression. As retired air force general Jeanne Holm points out, the Depression lowered birth rates, which lessened the pool of possible applicants. By the early 1950s, there were about five hundred thousand "unmarried women ages eighteen to twenty-four who were not at school or working" in the United States.[32] Additionally, the intellectual, moral, and physical enlistment requirements limited who could be accepted. All the women's services required high school diplomas, and some (like the WAVES) required a college degree in order to be commissioned as an officer upon entering (it was also possible to attend Officer Candidate School after enlisting in some cases).[33]

During World War II, enlistment standards had already been a concern when it came to recruiting Black women. At that time, segregation and discrimination were also paramount concerns, but when African Americans still learned in segregated schools and "separate but equal" reigned, military leaders faced challenges recruiting their quota of Black women. For example, by 1950, only 9.2 percent of African American women attended four years of high school, with only 3.2 percent attending up to three years of college and a scant 2.4 percent finishing four or more years of college.[34] This dramatically limited the pool of African American women eligible to enlist or be commissioned. Holm notes that because Black men were drafted, there was no problem recruiting Black men, but the WAC had never hit its 10 percent quota for African American women even during the war.

If these numbers were small, they nonetheless mattered. From a practical perspective, segregation became harder to justify with so few Black women in service. When Truman established Executive Order 9981, the newest of the military branches—the air force—decided to act right away. By late 1949, the WAF had made plans to eliminate all-Black training units, instead incorporating African American women directly into training "flights" alongside white women. That same year, the marine corps enlisted its first Black women, simultaneously creating its first racially integrated unit (men remained segregated). In the Women Marines, leaders planned to maintain a small, elite corps of women and believed segregation would be impossible given that reality—but they also worried that since the marines trained in the South, local recruits would be unaccustomed to integrated facilities. "No one was quite certain how white women, unaccustomed to mixing with blacks, would react to an integrated barracks situation."[35] The Women Marines leaders arranged the first integrated platoon's barracks by recruits' geographic point of origin, although no details exist as to how women responded. Black and white women from the North bunked with one another, while southern white and Black women—both used to a society in which Black women were relegated to invisibility—would also live side by side. The intention behind this arrangement was to lessen the possibility of problems that might arise should northern Black women, unaccustomed to the Jim Crow South, push back against southern resistance to integration.

While air force, marine corps, and navy leaders began integrating Black women in 1948 and 1949, army officials fought integration as an institution well past 1950, although the WAC became racially integrated by late 1950.[36] Until that year, enlisted African American women joined a segregated battalion that was led by African American women. Outside of this assignment, they experienced some integrated opportunities, including Officer Candidate School and specialist training. Yet segregation persisted into early 1950 in "work assignments, housing, eating arrangements, and social gatherings."[37] Even with this remaining segregation, the WAC sometimes remained the best opportunity for African American women who wanted to serve, in part because they admitted more women. Mary Teague tried to join the WAVES first but was told they were not taking Black women, and the WAF had "filled their quota. So I ended up in the first black (WAC) basic training company for women after World War II."[38] Eventually, Teague witnessed the desegregation of Fort Lee, but when she received a new assignment on the West Coast, she entered a base where segregation persisted and where commanders would not put her in charge of white women. "Then I noticed that the white women were getting promoted faster than the women in my unit." While she complained, and an investigation occurred, nothing changed—except that she received a new assignment to Japan, which Teague believed was a result of her whistleblowing efforts—a way to remove someone that her leadership perceived as a problem.[39] Desegregation of the women's services thus happened unevenly and with mixed results.

Teague's experience highlights the conflict between ideals and reality when it came to both women's service and Black women's service. Officially, sex was a larger consideration than race for all servicewomen, but when women recount their experiences, it becomes clear that for many, race and gender both shaped their military service. Military leaders frequently hoped to achieve certain ideals, which were often expressed most clearly in recruiting materials and publicity efforts meant to highlight military service as a beneficial career for women. For example, during the congressional debates over the Women's Armed Services Integration Act, many military leaders discussed the possibility of moving women into a number of new roles, which would be determined based on women's potential. While this did happen, many servicewomen worked in traditionally feminine jobs; these jobs were differentiated from similar jobs in the civilian world primarily by location, such as Europe or Asia, along with the guarantee of pay equality based on rank. Similarly, even after desegregating the women's services, local commanders could find ways to circumvent policies or make excuses as to why a woman could or could not have a specific job or receive a promotion. Officially, race-based discrimination did not exist, but policing discriminatory behaviors—and reporting problems without recrimination—remained problematic, as Teague experienced.

By the early 1950s, although sex theoretically mattered more than race for women who joined the armed forces, many women's experiences demonstrate that in the military, a global organization with a diverse range of personnel, racial discrimination and prejudice often remained salient features of their experiences. For example, in 1952 a white WAF observed that although her basic training flight included four African American women, the women's race was always noted on official paperwork, and the four women always seemed to be kept together.[40] Similarly, on overseas assignments in Germany—a place that was theoretically integrated—Black servicewomen encountered "unfair treatment, menial assignments, segregated living quarters, and failure to receive promotion."[41] Holm, writing three decades later in the early 1990s, points out that just because the armed forces integrated officially, that "did not solve the problems of discrimination against blacks nor end institutional racism any more than integration would solve the problem of discrimination against women or end sexism in the armed forces."[42]

By eliminating racial segregation, the US government placed the armed forces at the forefront of social change in America. It was change that would continue to take years to accomplish. Prior to *Brown v. Board of Education* in 1955, and even during the civil rights movement that followed, military service, even though imperfect, nevertheless offered Black women opportunities and advantages that they could not always find in the civilian world. Although numbers of Black servicewomen remained small during the Cold War, African American women consistently took advantage of military service as a career opportunity—if they could get in. From 1950 to 1960, when statistics are available, the number of African American WACs rose from 648 to 1,183. No statistics were kept during the 1960s, but by 1972, only 2,453 Black women served as WACs. By 1974, more African American women served in the WAC than had served in World War II, and within four years that number had risen to more than 14,000, largely as a result of wider social changes, some of which emerged from the civil rights movement and Vietnam War.[43]

In the women's services, military leaders shaped utilization policies around white, middle-class gender ideals, all while claiming that a woman's race played no part in determining what job she would hold. In some cases, this was true. African American WAC Susie McArthur's aptitude test results matched up with the career she anticipated, based on her past training. "Since I had gone to school for stenographer-secretary, I knew that's what I wanted to do, so the test just proved that I would be suited for that field."[44] While McArthur reflected that racism and racial discrimination did exist in the armed forces, she did not seem to feel that such attitudes shaped her access to military opportunities during her twenty-six-year career with the army. When she entered the WAC in the mid-1960s in the midst of the civil rights movement, she anticipated, "I'm going to get in here, and I'm going to have to really fight, but . . . it was entirely different." Ernestine Johnson also believed her identity as a woman, not just as an African American, affected many of her experiences in the WAF, as she encountered male supervisors who "thought I had too much authority."[45] Doris "Lucki" Allen, whose WAC career encompassed both the Korean and Vietnam Wars, noted that she lost out on a promotion because "I would not go out with my boss . . . it had nothing to do with my race or color—it had to do that I wouldn't go out with him."[46] The reality was that women's integration created many new scenarios in the armed forces, including ones that gave male commanders the opportunity to manipulate their female personnel and affect their careers. At times, it could be hard to distinguish whether discrimination happened primarily because of sex or skin color, but African American servicewomen pointed to both as causes during their time in service.

While encouraging women's military service as a patriotic activity worked during World War II, many women pursued military careers during the Cold War because they saw benefits for themselves. While Holm suggests that military service was not actually a good career opportunity because the pay was low and the jobs tended to be feminine, for many women the military offered economic security, the possibility of education, a way out of their communities, and even adventure.[47] Dorothy Spencer joined the WAC in 1962 because military service was an economic opportunity. Many were drawn to the military because of—or in rare occasions, despite—family and friends' military connections, in addition to a desire for other benefits. Doris Allen, for example, joined the services with a sense of wanting to get back at the military for what service had done to her brother; however, she also spent some time under her sister's command, noting that her sister was the best commander she ever had.[48] Joycestane Malcolm's cousin was an officer, but a high school boyfriend bet her she couldn't get into the military. Once she enlisted, it was the ideals that stayed with her. "The doors that I walked in when we got there: 'Through these portals pass the most important women on Earth.' That I'll always remember."[49] In an age when few women, and even fewer African American women, served in the military, word of mouth was a powerful means by which African American women identified military service as a job option, with family and friends playing a significant role in the process. In some cases, a father, uncle, or sibling had served; in others, a friend wanted to enlist and talked someone else into joining them. Ozell Barksdale entered because her high school friend Eloise Siewert wanted to join the navy but didn't want to do so alone. Ozell and Eloise wound up speaking with a marine corps recruiter and were so impressed with her that they chose that branch instead.[50]

Many African American women joined the military for economic reasons. Some women needed a job, and the military offered just that. Juanita Johnson and Luevenia Mitchell both joined for financial reasons, although Mitchell wanted the money to go to school eventually.[51] Future WAF major Clara Johnson, who had completed some college, struggled to find work in the private sector "because there was just nothing available for a young black female."[52] Several Black women veterans explain that they chose military service because it was hard to find jobs in the 1950s and 1960s. Eighteen-year-old Brenda Johnson couldn't find a job and, having been told to get a job or move out, she joined the air force.[53] Mary Dooley, the oldest of eleven children, knew college was not an option for her because of the cost, making the military an attractive alternative. Norma Busby spent a year at university before realizing that her parents, with six other children, could not afford to send her; instead of starting her sophomore year of college, she enlisted in the air force that fall.[54]

Even more than just a steady income, the educational opportunities that Black women could pursue during and after military service offered major incentives for entering the armed forces. The possibility of both a job *and* future education made military service doubly enticing. Gertrude Edwards planned to attend nursing school and took the entrance exam for a school in Virginia, earning the highest score ever recorded. When she needed emergency surgery on her appendix, she lost her nest egg paying for the operation. "My brother-in-law told me about going to the military." The nursing school promised they would hold her spot no matter how long it took, and she felt she would have better opportunities in the services.[55] Although initially assigned to the motor pool—a job she hated—Edwards managed to transfer to the hospital and gained valuable experience that helped her when she left the service. In 1968, at the age of eighteen, Linda Hicks was having a hard time finding a job and "decided that joining the military would be a good choice . . . and then I could also go to college."[56] Although Barbara Seldon really wanted to go to college in the early 1960s, her parents did not have the money. She notes that "it was hard for women to find a job," and she had no skills that would help her find a good job. Barbara and her friend Penny "were exploring what we could really do, and one day we saw a sign that said, 'See the world and get an education: Join the Army.'"[57]

Once in the military, African American women's experiences of discrimination varied widely depending on when and where they entered and served, their engagement with the civilian world during training, and even their own prior experience with segregation in civilian life. Because basic training became racially integrated by 1950, many women developed friendships with white women, something that was new to some of them. Clara Johnson noted that "I was always impressed with my female colleagues in that I was the only person of color and they were readily accepting. And this was something that you find very odd, strange, particularly in the early 50s."[58] That Johnson saw the relationship as "strange" reflects the broader experience Black servicewomen had of the Jim Crow South or experiencing a still-segregated nation outside of military bases. For some women, this was the world they knew. Virginia Bailey, born and raised in Louisiana, noted that "the military had to be equal and fair at that time. They treated us equal. I was treated okay in the military as a black female." Military leaders could not police racist thoughts that white personnel might have, but they could reinforce desired behaviors through integration policies. Still, that did not mean that Bailey and other servicewomen never experienced discrimination.: "I had racism from my coworkers, but it didn't bother me because I grew up in the '60s, so it didn't really bother me."[59] Bailey did not elaborate further, but other servicewomen also note discriminatory experiences. Early in her thirty-year career, Doris Allen and three other Black women secured an audition for the military band. At the end of the audition, however, they were told "Sorry, we don't have any negroes in the band." Because Allen joined in 1950, it's possible she witnessed one of the last gasps of the army's resistance to racial integration, but the timing is unclear.[60] Allen explained that she saw a lot of prejudice during her military career, "against me as a woman, me as a WAC, me as a soldier with the rank of specialist, me as an intelligence technician, and me as a Black woman, but all of the prejudices were overshadowed by a wonderful camaraderie and lots of love and lasting friendships. I wouldn't trade it for a million."[61]

Travel and movement into quarters with a diverse range of women opened some recruits' eyes to a world they had never known. Norma Busby, born and raised in Ohio, never saw separate Black and white restrooms until a plane layover in North Carolina on her way to basic training. "But I was defiant and I refused to go into the black restroom and so I went into the white restroom. They looked at me, the people in the restroom, but they didn't say anything." Coming into the military, she had not experienced prejudice firsthand, although she was aware that it was present in Cincinnati growing up. Over the course of her military career, she would travel the world, but she noted "having traveled as much as I did, I can't say that I was very aware of a black and white situation. It was really a very pleasant situation."[62]

Mary Dooley, on the other hand, grew up in the South in Louisiana, and basic training was her first experience being around white people. "I wasn't familiar with white people. The schools that I went to were completely segregated, small schools. Ride a bus to go to school, pass the white schools, look at the kids, and wonder if they knew that they had to be smarter than we were." During training, her policy was to keep quiet. "I didn't say anything unless I had to," as she lived in an integrated barracks, where she was the only Black recruit. At her basic training in the mid-1950s, "everything was white. When we went to the cafeteria, there were some black cooks," but she was the only African American woman in her unit.[63] Gertrude Edwards grew up in Virginia and "never knew very much about segregation, because we lived in a [rural] community and black and white farmers worked together . . . it was not until I went away to the military that I really faced segregation." On the way to training in Texas, other white recruits began teasing her on the train, and she couldn't disembark to eat because of segregated restaurants across the South.[64] Yet some showed kindness to Edwards, the only Black woman in the group of recruits, and brought food back to her.

Edwards's experience speaks to the challenges military leaders faced in reconciling their racial integration efforts in a Jim Crow nation. While military policy could, to some degree, control how servicemen, and women, behaved with one another on a racially integrated base, when servicewomen stepped off based, they were once again subject to civilian rules about where Black bodies could be. Loretta Johnson was warned not to go off base with her three white friends, but they went anyway. Restaurants refused to serve the four women because of Loretta's presence, until they found a Mexican restaurant where the proprietor "said he would serve us, but we had to eat in the park." Later, when she went to West Palm Beach, Florida, for flight attendant training, her first attempt to call a cab ended with a white cab driver instructing her to call the Black cab company. Recounting these experiences, Johnson reflected, "I'm so glad I wasn't stationed in the south."[65]

Southern training locations posed a problem, and West Palm Beach figured into Mary Dooley's negative experiences as well. She and four white friends tried to go downtown and could not get a white or Black cab driver to take their group, ultimately relying on the base's free ride stand. While downtown, the white girls decided to try drinking from both the white and Black drinking fountains, and Dooley did the same. By the time they returned to base, the base commander had been notified and called an assembly, telling the recruits, "When you go downtown, you do as they do in Rome . . . we couldn't do anything that was going to create a problem for him . . . that was the end of that." Dooley did not venture into town again during her training, opting to use her time studying. It was in those moments that Dooley discovered she had been wrong in assuming that white people were smarter than her. "I began to realize they're no smarter than I am—they can't do no more than I can do because my grades were high.... And that helped me deeply. It helped my soul. It brought me a long-ways."[66]

While most African American servicewomen experienced discrimination in their off-base interactions with the civilian world, some found that even a racially integrated military might lead to tensions. WAF Sergeant Ernestine Johnson was assigned to Tokyo in the early 1950s when the WAF—but not the WAC—had fully racially integrated. "According to Thomas, [General Douglas] MacArthur, the Supreme Allied Commander, 'sent MPs up to Tokyo to investigate what the black WAFs stationed there were doing.' MPs also harassed her male African-American friends."[67] In her career as an air force flight attendant, Mary Dooley enjoyed traveling across Europe regularly, but a 1955 incident in Iceland stands out. On a layover at Keflavík, Iceland, she noticed that an airman followed her everywhere. When asked, he replied that he had been assigned to do so. Neither the airplane captain nor any of the plane's other personnel had anyone following them, and the reasons for her shadow remained unclear until she returned stateside. "The reason is the US had a contract . . . with Iceland that they would not station any Negroes in Iceland because they didn't want to mix the people."[68]

Even considering such experiences, many African American women veterans viewed their military careers as a positive time in their lives. For Juanita Johnson, military service was "the first opportunity I had to actually live with and work with Caucasians, and so I really had an opportunity to get to know people other than the people of my race. So that was a plus."[69] Many of the women who entered the services to pursue their education did so with the GI Bill and went on to diverse careers. In short, while military service may not have been a panacea for completely ridding the nation of racism and segregation, African American women nonetheless found many ways in which military service propelled them to what they wanted to achieve. In Dorothy Spencer's estimation, "There's no greater—in my opinion—no greater opportunity to serve your country than in the military."[70]

Ruth Lucas's career exemplifies the possibilities of military service. She joined the military in 1942, one of the first African American women to arrive and one of the first to attend the Joint Forces Staff College during the war. Although few women remained in service after World War II, Lucas continued her military career, switching to the air force after the Women's Armed Services Integration Act passed. In 1962, as she celebrated twenty years of military service—a rare feat—*Ebony* magazine profiled her as part of an article commemorating twenty years of women's military service. This article praised military service as an opportunity that Black women should consider, citing Lucas as a prime example of the possibilities women could find. "Negro women have been in the forefront of the women's services and have welcomed the opportunities for travel, education and exciting service for their country." As a lieutenant colonel in 1962, Lucas was not only the highest-ranking Black woman in the nation, but the only rank higher than hers in the women's services was colonel, which could only be held by one woman at that time. As the article's authors noted, Lucas's rank was just below that of the "head of the entire 10,000 member Women's Army Corps."[71]

Seven years later, *Ebony* writers returned to celebrate Ruth Lucas, now the first African American woman colonel. In 1967, new legislation finally removed rank limitations on all servicewomen, which meant that career servicewomen like Lucas could hope to extend their careers further. With her promotion to colonel in 1968, Lucas became the highest-ranking African American woman in the US military, a status that she kept until 1991.[72] Stationed at the Pentagon in 1969, Lucas's career centered on helping servicemen with their education. "Most people don't realize that among all the servicemen who enter the military annually, about 45,000 of them read below the fifth-grade level, and more than 30 percent of these men are black," she said. "Right now if I have any aim, it's just to reach these men, to interest them in education, and to motivate them to continue on."[73]

Colonel Lucas's long military career put her in a unique class of servicewomen. Most servicewomen, regardless of skin color, only remained in the armed forces for a few years, taking advantage of a military career as a springboard to other opportunities. Although Lucas considered other career options at various points in her time with the military, "I decided that I could best utilize my training right here in the service. One year slipped into another, and, well, when my promotion came . . . it just seemed to cap off all my previous experiences." In the military, Lucas had found not just a career but a calling as an educator. Having entered the military with an education degree from Tuskegee Institute, the air force helped her complete her master's degree at Columbia University. Reflecting on her experiences, Lucas concluded, "The important thing is that the Air Force offered me an opportunity to learn and develop, and I believe I've taken advantage of the opportunity."[74]

In the first two decades of the Cold War, the number of African American servicewomen certainly remained small, and discriminatory behavior persisted, despite efforts to eliminate it. But Black servicewomen continued to find their way to military service, feeling the benefits outweighed problems they might face and taking full advantage of the opportunities available. In or out of the military, discrimination and prejudice remained a part of daily life for African Americans, but military service offered Black women a new opportunity, grounded in ideals of racial—and sexual—integration. For most servicewomen, the realities of military service did not match those ideals, but military careers, whether brief or long, brought Black women into contact with whites on a more equal basis than had been previously possible. Black servicewomen never expected that military service would offer them an idealized version of American life, but they did expect that their time in the military would give them some measure of financial independence, a job, and the ability to imagine and build new futures for themselves.

NOTES

1. Quoted in Meyer, *Creating GI Jane*, 75.
2. Holm, *Women in the Military*, 28.
3. Holm, *Women in the Military*, 78.
4. Douglas Walter Bristol Jr., "Terror, Anger, and Patriotism: Understanding the Resistance of Black Soldiers During World War II," in Bristol and Stur, *Integrating the US Military*, 13.
5. Mershon and Schlossman, *Foxholes and Color Lines*, 24.
6. Mershon and Schlossman, *Foxholes and Color Lines*, 25.
7. "Research Starters: U.S. Military by the Numbers," National World War II Museum, accessed July 15, 2019, https://www.nationalww2museum.org/students-teachers/student-resources/research-starters/research-starters-us-military-numbers.
8. "Declaration of Policy, Section 2," *The National Security Act of 1947*, Public Law 253, *US Statutes at Large* 61 (1947), https://research.archives.gov/id/299856.
9. Mershon and Schlossman, 138.
10. Holm, *Women in the Military*, 78.
11. Mershon and Schlossman, *Foxholes and Color Lines*, 142, 143.
12. Mershon and Schlossman, *Foxholes and Color Lines*, 146–48, 149, 151.
13. Veterans Joan (Eastwood) Neuswanger and Polly Hazelwood both recalled that women could not be married, for example. Joan (Eastwood) Neuswanger interview with Mary Jo Binker, 13 (File 331365); Women's Memorial Foundation Collection, Alexandria, VA. Polly Hazelwood interview with Tanya L. Roth, October 26, 2009. For history on the marriage discharge policy, see Witt et al., "A Defense Weapon Known to be of Value," 2–3.
14. Public Law 625 in *United States Statutes*, 361, article (b) of Section 107. Repeated in each title of the law to apply to all service branches.
15. For a list of specific provisions in the Women's Armed Services Integration Act—Public Law 80-625—see Holm, *Women in the Military*, 119–20.
16. Executive Order 9981, "Establishing the President's Committee on Equality of Treatment and Opportunity in the Armed Services," July 26, 1948, Truman Library, https://www.trumanlibrary.gov/library/executive-orders/9981/executive-order-9981.
17. The Report of the President's Committee on Civil Rights, "To Secure These Rights," 1947, 41; Harry S. Truman Presidential Library, http://www.trumanlibrary.org/civilrights/srights1.htm.
18. "To Secure These Rights," 42.
19. "To Secure These Rights," 42.
20. "To Secure These Rights," 46.

21. "To Secure These Rights," 46.
22. "To Secure These Rights," 99.
23. "To Secure These Rights," 102.
24. "To Secure These Rights," 162.
25. "To Secure These Rights," 163.
26. Mershon and Schlossman, *Foxholes and Color Lines*, 167.
27. Holm, *Women in the Military*, 119.
28. Executive Order 9981, "Establishing the President's Committee on Equality of Treatment and Opportunity in the Armed Services," July 26, 1948, Truman Library, https://www.trumanlibrary.gov/library/executive-orders/9981/executive-order-9981.
29. Mershon and Schlossman, *Foxholes and Color Lines*, 184.
30. Holm, *Women in the Military*, 149.
31. Witt et al., "A Defense Weapon Known to be of Value," 240.
32. Holm, *Women in the Military*, 154.
33. Holm, *Women in the Military*, 134.
34. Center for Education Statistics, Thomas D. Snyder, ed., "Table 4: Years of School Completed by Persons 25 Years Old and Over, by Race and Sex: April 1940 to March 1991," *120 Years of American Education: A Statistical Portrait* (US Department of Education, Office of Educational Research and Improvement. National Center for Education Statistics), https://nces.ed.gov/pubs93/93442.pdf.
35. Stremlow, *A History of the Women Marines*, 31.
36. Witt et al., "A Defense Weapon Known to be of Value," 49.
37. Witt et al., "A Defense Weapon Known to be of Value," 240.
38. Quoted in Witt et al., "A Defense Weapon Known to be of Value," 49.
39. Witt et al., "A Defense Weapon Known to be of Value," 50–51.
40. Witt et al., "A Defense Weapon Known to be of Value," 241.
41. Witt et al., "A Defense Weapon Known to be of Value," 240.
42. Holm, *Women in the Military*, 79.
43. "Table 5: Strength of Black Members of the Women's Army Corps, 1945–1978," in Morden, *The Women's Army Corps*, 415.
44. Susie McArthur Papers, Susie (Stephens) McArthur interview with Hermann Trojanowski, 2001, WV0199.5.001; Betty H. Carter Women Veterans Historical Project, Jackson Library, University of North Carolina at Greensboro, July 31, 2019, http://library.uncg.edu/dp/wv/results5.aspx?i=2690&s=5.
45. Witt et al., "A Defense Weapon Known to be of Value," 150.
46. Dr. Doris "Lucki" Allen interview with Debora Cox, Doris I. Allen Collection (AFC/2001/001/109035), Veterans History Project, American Folklife Center, Library of Congress, https://memory.loc.gov/diglib/vhp/bib/loc.natlib.afc2001001.109035.
47. Holm, *Women in the Military*, 154.
48. Dr. Doris "Lucki" Allen interview with Debora Cox, Doris I. Allen Collection (AFC/2001/001/109035), Veterans History Project, American Folklife Center, Library of Congress, https://memory.loc.gov/diglib/vhp/bib/loc.natlib.afc2001001.109035.
49. Joycestane Brant Malcolm Papers, Joycestane Malcolm interview with Eric Elliott, 1999, WV0126; Betty H. Carter Women Veterans Historical Project, Jackson Library,

University of North Carolina at Greensboro, http://libcdm1.uncg.edu/cdm/singleitem/collection/WVHP/id/4283/rec/1.

50. Ozell Barksdale interview with Colonel Eleanor Wilson, 2004, p. 1. Ozell Barksdale Collection, Women in Military Service for America Foundation, Arlington, VA.

51. Juanita Johnson Papers, Juanita Johnson interview with Eric Elliott, 2002, WV0239; Betty H. Carter Women Veterans Historical Project, Jackson Library, University of North Carolina at Greensboro, http://libcdm1.uncg.edu/cdm/singleitem/collection/WVHP/id/4453/rec/1; Luevenia Mitchell Papers, Luevenia G. Mitchell interview with Hermann J. Trojanowski, 2001, WV0200; Betty H. Carter Women Veterans Historical Project, Jackson Library, University of North Carolina at Greensboro, http://libcdm1.uncg.edu/cdm/singleitem/collection/WVHP/id/4434/rec/1.

52. Clara Johnson interview with Ruth Stewart, Clara C. Johnson Collection (AFC/2001/001/42843), Veterans History Project, American Folklife Center, Library of Congress, https://memory.loc.gov/diglib/vhp/bib/loc.natlib.afc2001001.42843.

53. Brenda Johnson interview with Carlton Cartwright, Brenda Cornette Johnson Collection (AFC/2001/001/89411), Veterans History Project, American Folklife Center, Library of Congress, https://memory.loc.gov/diglib/vhp/bib/loc.natlib.afc2001001.89411.

54. Norma Busby interview with Viennease Dennis, Norma Wilma Dean Busby Collection (AFC/2001/001/48743), Veterans History Project, American Folklife Center, Library of Congress, https://memory.loc.gov/diglib/vhp/bib/loc.natlib.afc2001001.48743.

55. Gertrude Edwards interview with James Scollen, Gertrude Johnson Edwards Collection (AFC/2001/001/87242), Veterans History Project, American Folklife Center, Library of Congress, https://memory.loc.gov/diglib/vhp/bib/loc.natlib.afc2001001.87242.

56. Linda Hicks interview with William Alexander, Linda Diane Laudermilk Hicks Collection (AFC/2001/001/54719), Veterans History Project, American Folklife Center, Library of Congress, https://memory.loc.gov/diglib/vhp/bib/loc.natlib.afc2001001.54719.

57. Barbara Seldon interview with Daniel Brightwell, Barbara Ann Purifoy Seldon Collection (AFC/2001/001/58370), Veterans History Project, American Folklife Center, Library of Congress, https://memory.loc.gov/diglib/vhp/bib/loc.natlib.afc2001001.58370.

58. Clara Johnson interview with Ruth Stewart, Clara C. Johnson Collection (AFC/2001/001/42843), Veterans History Project, American Folklife Center, Library of Congress, https://memory.loc.gov/diglib/vhp/bib/loc.natlib.afc2001001.42843.

59. Virginia Bailey interview with Winter Bailey, Virginia Faye Bailey Collection (AFC/2001/001/03456), Veterans History Project, American Folklife Center, Library of Congress, http://memory.loc.gov/diglib/vhp/bib/loc.natlib.afc2001001.03456.

60. Dr. Doris "Lucki" Allen interview with Debora Cox, Doris I. Allen Collection (AFC/2001/001/109035), Veterans History Project, American Folklife Center, Library of Congress, https://memory.loc.gov/diglib/vhp/bib/loc.natlib.afc2001001.109035.

61. Dr. Doris "Lucki" Allen interview with Kate Scott, 2004, "Information for Computer Registration," Doris "Lucki" Allen Collection, Women in Military Service for America Foundation, Arlington, VA.

62. Norma Busby interview with Viennease Dennis, Norma Wilma Dean Busby Collection (AFC/2001/001/48743), Veterans History Project, American Folklife Center, Library of Congress, https://memory.loc.gov/diglib/vhp/bib/loc.natlib.afc2001001.48743.

63. Mary Dooley interview with Bernard Watson, Mary L. Ballard Dooley Collection (AFC/2001/001/72536), Veterans History Project, American Folklife Center, Library of Congress, https://memory.loc.gov/diglib/vhp/bib/loc.natlib.afc2001001.72536.

64. Gertrude Edwards interview with James Scollen, Gertrude Johnson Edwards Collection (AFC/2001/001/87242), Veterans History Project, American Folklife Center, Library of Congress, https://memory.loc.gov/diglib/vhp/bib/loc.natlib.afc2001001.87242.

65. Loretta Johnson interview with Gwendolyn Coley, Loretta Cecilia Johnson Collection (AFC/2001/001/74506), Veterans History Project, American Folklife Center, Library of Congress, https://memory.loc.gov/diglib/vhp/bib/loc.natlib.afc2001001.74506.

66. Mary Dooley interview with Bernard Watson, Mary L. Ballard Dooley Collection (AFC/2001/001/72536), Veterans History Project, American Folklife Center, Library of Congress, https://memory.loc.gov/diglib/vhp/bib/loc.natlib.afc2001001.72536.

67. Witt et al., "A Defense Weapon Known to be of Value," 50.

68. Mary Dooley interview with Bernard Watson, Mary L. Ballard Dooley Collection (AFC/2001/001/72536), Veterans History Project, American Folklife Center, Library of Congress, https://memory.loc.gov/diglib/vhp/bib/loc.natlib.afc2001001.72536.

69. Juanita Johnson Papers, Juanita Johnson interview with Eric Elliott, 2002, WV0239; Betty H. Carter Women Veterans Historical Project, Jackson Library, University of North Carolina at Greensboro, http://libcdm1.uncg.edu/cdm/singleitem/collection/WVHP/id/4453/rec/1.

70. Dorothy Spencer interview with Sacorya Kay, Dorothy E. Spencer Collection (AFC/2001/001/84469), Veterans History Project, American Folklife Center, Library of Congress, https://memory.loc.gov/diglib/vhp/bib/loc.natlib.afc2001001.84469.

71. "Women in Uniform," *Ebony* magazine, December 1962, 63.

72. "Ruth A. Lucas," Connecticut Women's Hall of Fame, https://www.cwhf.org/inductees/politics-government-law/ruth-a-lucas#.XUHXKehKhPY.

73. "Air Force's Education Expert," *Ebony*, November 1969, 88–89.

74. "Air Force's Education Expert," 90.

REFERENCES

Bristol, Douglas Walter, Jr., and Heather Marie Stur, eds. *Integrating the US Military: Race, Gender, and Sexual Orientation Since World War II*. Baltimore: Johns Hopkins University Press, 2017.

Holm, Jeanne. *Women in the Military, Revised Edition: An Unfinished Revolution*. Novato, CA: Presidio Press, 1993.

Mershon, Sherie, and Steven L. Schlossman. *Foxholes and Color Lines: Desegregating the U.S. Armed Forces*. Baltimore: Johns Hopkins University Press, 1998.

Meyer, Leisa D. *Creating GI Jane: Sexuality and Power in the Women's Army Corps during World War II*. New York: Columbia University Press, 1996.

Morden, Bettie J., and Center of Military History. *The Women's Army Corps, 1945–1978*. CMH pub 30-14. Washington, DC: Center of Military History, US Army, 1990.

Stremlow, Colonel Mary V. *A History of the Women Marines 1946–1977*. Washington DC: History and Museums Division, Headquarters, US Marine Corps, 1986.

Treadwell, Mattie E. *The United States Army in World War II: The Women's Army Corps.* Washington, DC: Office of the Chief of Military History, Department of the Army, 1954.

Witt, Linda, Judith Bellafaire, Britta Granrud, and Mary Jo Binker. *"A Defense Weapon Known to Be of Value": Servicewomen of the Korean War Era.* Hanover, NH: University Press of New England, 2005.

Archives

Veterans History Project, American Folklife Center, Library of Congress, Washington, DC.

Chapter 15

"REGARDLESS OF WHAT LIFE PRESENTS YOU"

Black Women Public Intellectuals in the Post-Vietnam US Military

CAROL FOWLER AND MELISSA ZIOBRO

When one hears the term "intellectual" used to describe a person, what image comes to mind? Perhaps that of an academic or perhaps an elder statesperson. Perhaps someone with spectacles, or suede elbow patches, and a lot of time to pontificate. An intellectual is defined as "a person of superior intellect" or one "who places a high value on or pursues things of interest to the intellect or the more complex forms and fields of knowledge, as aesthetic or philosophical matters, especially on an abstract and general level."[1] But another definition of the word "intellectual" is simply "an extremely rational person; a person who relies on intellect rather than on emotions or feelings."

Anti-intellectuals, on the other hand, are "opposed to or hostile toward intellectuals and the modern academic, artistic, social, religious, and other theories associated with them" or believe "that intellect and reason are less important than actions and emotions in solving practical problems and understanding reality."[2] Much has been written about whether or not the modern US military is "anti-intellectual," and there may indeed be individuals at all levels, in all of the services, who not only slip into but actively pride themselves in their anti-intellectualism. Retired general Alfred M. Gray, one-time commandant of the US Marine Corps, for example, famously complained in 1987 about "too many intellectuals" among the leadership of the armed services and said that what the military needed was not intellectuals but "old-fashioned gunslingers."[3] Though some have argued that these remarks were taken out of context, they are indicative of a perception held by many: that our nation's warfighters are more brawn than brains, that they actively prioritize physical over mental strength and agility.

We posit that many African American women in the modern military, however, do not want to be "gunslingers." They almost always see their military service not as an adventure but as a sensible path to self-betterment and upward mobility in a society that often limits their options. They enlist seeking personal advancement, economic empowerment, college tuition, and travel. They enlist because they want to expand their horizons and become more informed global citizens. They often rise through the ranks and become leaders and mentors, in the military and when they return to civilian life. They are Black women public intellectuals. This chapter, which is not limited to but focuses on the post-Vietnam era to address a dearth of existing sources, is based on the authors' analysis of more than two hundred veterans' oral history interviews, in addition to the academic historiography.

There is a body of literature related to both anti-intellectualism in America generally and in the military specifically. Richard Hofstadter's 1963 *Anti-Intellectualism in American Life*, though decades old, is probably still the standard of general works, though there are many more recent books that contemplate the impacts of the internet age. Consider, for example, Charles Pierce's *Idiot America: How Stupidity Became a Virtue in the Land of the Free*, A. J. Angulo's *Miseducation: A History of Ignorance-Making in America and Abroad*, Mark Bauerlein and Adam Bellow's edited volume *The State of the American Mind: 16 Leading Critics on the New Anti-Intellectualism*, and Susan Jacoby's *The Age of American Unreason in a Culture of Lies*.

Retired US Army colonel Lloyd J. Matthews has written what is perhaps the most succinct yet thorough analysis of the US military's relationship with intellectualism. Matthews graduated from the US Military Academy, earned an MA from Harvard University and a PhD from the University of Virginia, and graduated from both the Armed Forces Staff College and the US Army War College. He served overseas in places including Germany and Vietnam. He was a battalion commander; editor of *Parameters*, the US Army War College quarterly; and associate dean of the US Military Academy. He is the editor or coeditor of seven books: *Assessing the Vietnam War*, *The Parameters of War*, *The Challenge of Military Leadership*, *The Parameters of Military Ethics*, *Newsmen and National Defense*, *Challenging the United States Symmetrically and Asymmetrically*, and *Population Diversity and the U.S. Army*. Additionally, he is the author of some one hundred articles, features, reviews, and monographs on military topics in such journals as *Parameters*, *Army Magazine*, *Military Review*, and *Airpower Journal*.[4]

In other words, he is himself a true soldier and scholar. In his 2002 two-part series, "The Uniformed Intellectual and His Place in American Arms," he acknowledges that there is a "current of anti-intellectualism that has coursed through American arms from its earliest beginnings." This military anti-intellectualism is not a new phenomenon, nor is it a uniquely American one. As Matthews notes,

> Going back to medieval and even to classical times, a sharp distinction emerged between the so-called Active Man and Contemplative Man.... The division has remained a prominent feature of the British, French and American military traditions, with the Contemplative Man often the victim of condescension if not outright scorn by powerful men of deeds who molded the early value system of the profession of arms during a time when the only cerebral quality found useful was likely to be guile.[5]

While military anti-intellectualism is not exclusively American, Matthews points out that "the contemplative officer in this country receives a double whammy. Not only is she or he a citizen of a country itself notorious for its anti-intellectual tendencies, but he has come into a military establishment that in many respects has been more retrograde in its receptivity to ideas than the European militaries."[6] He continues,

> There are reasons for our anti-intellectual heritage, of course, revolving mainly around the rough-hewn and homespun life incident to establishing ourselves as pioneers on the shores of a savage continent and then advancing the frontier across a dangerous wilderness extending some 3,000 miles.... Such hardy folk are apt to be a bit earthy, more like John Wayne than Alec Guinness. But our pioneer days are long past, and though we as a people have excelled in the scientific and engineering aspects of cognitive endeavor, we still can't quite let go of the notion that thinking for thinking's sake is just not macho.[7]

African American women have a long history in the US military. For most of the eighteenth and nineteenth centuries, the United States military employed women only occasionally, in what it considered gender-appropriate roles.[8] African American women, battling biases against both their gender and their race, still found ways to support the military causes they championed. Most commonly, civilian women, white and Black, often known as "camp followers," cooked, cleaned, and mended for military men during the Revolutionary and Civil Wars, much as they had done for civilian men in times of peace.[9] These women could be found in both the British and Continental Armies during the War for Independence. The role of "camp followers" has been discussed at length in Michael Lee Lanning's *African Americans in the Revolutionary War*, Carol Berkin's *Revolutionary Mothers: Women in the Struggle for America's Independence*, and Alan Gilbert's *Black Patriots and Loyalists: Fighting for Emancipation in the War for Independence*. The best account of Black women's service in the Civil War may well be the memoir of Susie King Taylor. Born a slave in Georgia, she recorded her experiences traveling with her husband's Union Army encampment in her 1902 memoir, *Reminiscences of My Life in Camp with the 33rd U.S. Colored Troops*. She contributed to the war effort by serving as a laundress, teacher, clerk, and more.[10] Most women were never compensated for these types of services. Taylor, wrote:

> I was very happy to know my efforts were successful in camp, and also felt grateful for the appreciation of my service. I gave my services willingly for four years and three months without receiving a dollar. I was glad, however, to be allowed to go with the regiment, to care for the sick and afflicted comrades.[11]

During the Revolutionary and Civil Wars, some women, both white and Black, also acted as nurses, despite popular concerns about the close contact with males this work required. The US Army Medical Department reports,

> During the Civil War, black nurses such as Sojourner Truth, an emancipated slave, worked in Union hospitals caring for the sick and wounded. Similarly, Harriet Tubman, when she was not serving as a laundress, cook, scout, spy or guide for the Union Army, also nursed soldiers. Like all Civil War nurses, Tubman did not receive a pension until 30 years after the end of the war. As many as 181 black nurses, both female and male, served in convalescent and U.S. government hospitals in Maryland, Virginia, and North Carolina during the Civil War.[12]

An official Army Nurse Corps did not become a part of the Medical Department until 1901. The Navy Nurse Corps followed in 1908. It would be many years before these military nurses received rank, pay, or benefits equal to those offered to male soldiers and sailors,[13] and it would be many more years before African American women could enlist as military nurses. Though a few Black women served in the military as nurses during World War I after the 1918 influenza pandemic ravaged the ranks of white nurses and swelled the number of men in hospitals, the Army Nurse Corps remained formally closed to Black women until 1941.[14]

Even then, the army had a strict quota for African American nurses. Only three hundred African American women could serve in the Army Nurse Corps at a time (of forty thousand total nurses). Many of the Black nurses were assigned to care for German prisoners of war, which the nurses found incredibly insulting, as they had not volunteered to care for the enemy. By the end of World War II, only some five hundred African American nurses had served in the army, though thousands had applied.[15]

On the other hand, women, both Black and white, served as spies from the nation's inception. Mary Elizabeth Bowser (also known as Mary Jane Richards Denman), for example, was born into slavery on the Richmond plantation of John Van Lew. Though freed by Van Lew's family after his death, she and some other members of her family stayed in their service. John Van Lew's daughter, Elizabeth (a Quaker and an abolitionist), sent Bowser to school in Philadelphia sometime in the 1850s. Bowser returned to Richmond, married Wilson Bowser days before the Civil War broke out, and settled just outside the city. When Elizabeth Van Lew began a spy ring in the city, she enlisted Mary's help. This freed slave, who had once lived in the North, willingly entered servitude in the home of Confederate president Jefferson Davis himself. Quietly, and at great risk to herself, she gathered intelligence that she passed back to Van Lew, who in turn passed it along to her contacts in the North. Much of what we know about Bowser's daring wartime service comes from Elizabeth Van Lew's records.[16] As Lois Leveen writes in her popular dramatized account of Bowser's life,

> Few details about Mary Bowser are known today. In the 19th century, little effort was made to record the daily lives of most slaves, free blacks, or women of any race. The scant facts about Mary Bowser (Richards) that survive cannot tell us what we most want to know: What experiences in freedom would make her risk her life in a war she couldn't be sure would bring emancipation?[17]

Whatever her motivations, in 1995 the US government inducted Bowser (Richards) into the Military Intelligence Corps Hall of Fame at Fort Huachuca, Arizona.[18]

In addition to serving as cooks and laundresses, nurses and spies, white and Black women during the Revolutionary and Civil War eras also disguised themselves as men and took up arms. While details are scant, the Women in Military Service for America Memorial Foundation provides the example of one "William Cathey," who enlisted in the army in Saint Louis, Missouri, in 1866. "William" was described by the recruiting officer "as 5'9" with black eyes, black hair, and a black complexion." According to the memorial foundation,

> the cursory examination by an Army physician missed the fact that William was actually Cathay Williams, a woman. . . . "William Cathey"

served from November 15, 1866, until her discharge with a surgeon's certificate of disability on October 14, 1868. Despite numerous and often lengthy hospital stays during her service, her sex was not revealed until June 1891, when Cathay Williams applied for an invalid pension and disclosed her true identity. She did not receive the pension, not because she was a woman, but because her disabilities were not service related. Cathay was probably the first black woman to serve in the U.S. Regular Army.[19]

More would follow, but not quickly. The exigencies of twentieth-century warfare certainly propelled the military, like the private sector, to find additional formal opportunities to employ women—they were just rarely Black women. During the First World War, women served in their traditional roles as nurses but also assumed more nontraditional jobs in the face of personnel shortages. The Army Signal Corps, for example, employed a few hundred women as switchboard operators, with some, called "Hello Girls," deploying overseas and serving just behind the battle lines.

Some three hundred women served as contracted administrative clerks with the marines, and the navy had enlisted an astounding eleven thousand "Yeomannettes" by December 1918. These women mostly served in secretarial and clerical roles, many in Washington, DC, but some occasionally became translators, drafters, fingerprint experts, ship camouflage designers, or recruiting agents.[20] Placing women in these noncombatant roles freed more men to fight.

The military allowed few African American women into these new jobs, however. There were no Black "Hello Girls," for example, and Blacks made up only fourteen of the aforementioned eleven thousand "Yeomannettes."[21] Undeterred, Black women, according to Dr. Chad Williams of Brandeis University,

> contributed to the war effort in significant ways and formed the backbone of African-American patriotic activities. Clubwomen, many under the auspices of the National Association of Colored Women (NACW), led "liberty loan" campaigns, held rallies, and provided crucial material and emotional support for black troops. Women joined war service organizations such as the YWCA and the Red Cross as well as establishing their own groups, like the Women's Auxiliary of the New York 15th National Guard, to meet the specific needs of black soldiers.[22]

Except for the nurses, most of the military women mustered out soon after the Armistice of 1918. While battle-hardened career officers like World War I chief signal officer Major General George Owen Squier cited women's value in freeing up men for the fighting front, they usually couched their praise of women in terms of their suitability as replacements for men in noncombatant roles. They did not suggest that women would be a valuable part of the military under other circumstances.[23] This concept of women as mere replacements for men in noncombatant roles exemplifies the historic chauvinism of the military. Why was the military historically gender restricted?[24]

Americans, men and women both, had long idealized a woman's place in the home (though race and socioeconomic status nonetheless often forced women to labor outside of it). In the late nineteenth and early twentieth centuries, the women's rights movement helped to challenge traditional gender roles and restrictions on women in the workforce and otherwise, but competition for jobs during the Great Depression had more or less ended society's relative tolerance of the feminist activities of the Progressive Era.[25] For example, a poll conducted in the 1930s showed that 82 percent of both men and women surveyed disapproved of a married woman working outside the home if she had a husband capable of supporting her. Not surprisingly, the poll also showed that the women who sought employment most frequently were married women whose husbands' salaries alone could not support the family. Twenty-six states went so far as to enact laws against employing married women.[26] Women were to work only if they absolutely had to. The idea of women working outside the home if it wasn't absolutely necessary, especially in the traditionally masculine military, seemed "unfathomable" to many in interwar America.[27]

During the Second World War, however, the "unfathomable" became a reality as the military once again struggled to fulfill wartime quotas. According to historian Russell Weigley, after entering World War II, the military quickly approached "the limit of the numbers it could remove from the economy without endangering a basic conception of the Allied war effort, that America was to be the industrial arsenal for all the Allied powers."[28] The military was simply removing too many men from critically important industrial jobs, even with women flooding into the civilian workforce. It became clear to many in the military that meeting manpower goals without endangering the industrial sector could be accomplished by enlisting women. In the modern military, there were many noncombatant roles that they could fulfill. As Dwight Eisenhower explained, "The simple headquarters of a Grant or Lee were gone forever. An Army of filing clerks, stenographers, office managers, telephone operators, and chauffeurs had become essential, and it was scarcely less than criminal to recruit these from needed manpower when great numbers of highly qualified women were available."[29]

Thus the military again welcomed women into its ranks during World War II. The army became the first of the services to enlist women in May 1942, with the navy, coast guard, and marines following the army's lead in July 1942, November 1942, and February 1943, respectively.[30] This decision to permit women to enlist in the military was preceded by much heated debate over whether or not "women generals would rush about the country dictating orders to male personnel and telling the commanding officers of posts how to run their business,"[31] and "who then will do the cooking, the washing, the mending—the humble home tasks to which every woman has devoted herself?"[32]

Bipartisan objections to women's military service abounded, with Republicans and Democrats alike denigrating the idea.[33] Senators Francis T. Maloney (D-CT) and John A. Danaher (R-CT) led the dissenters, suggesting women did not want to serve. Maloney protested that "there has been no strong clamor for the plan from women's groups."[34] Another opposing senator went so far as to claim that the bill "cast a shadow on the sanctity of the home."[35] Despite the emotional turmoil the idea obviously caused for some, the practical need for women in the military could not be denied.

Still, despite the military's need for women's service, World War II veteran Violet Caudle shared that, for many women, "It was a disgrace to join the military. If you were a woman, it wasn't the thing that was done. He (her father) was afraid of what the neighbors would say."[36] The military engaged in a public relations campaign to convince nervous Americans that allowing women into the military would not tear apart the fabric of society. The 1943 book *What You Should Know about the Navy*, for example, heartily endorsed WAVES (Women Accepted for Volunteer Emergency Services), stating, "Today, the WAVES are as much a part of the Navy ashore as the ocean's billows, from which they got their name, are a part of the scenery afloat."[37]

Removing legal barriers to women's military service and convincing the populace that it was socially acceptable did not ensure "smooth sailing" for women in the military during World War II (or in the decades that followed, for that matter). Winifred Quick Collins, one of the first female officers in the navy, confirms that both women in the navy and their counterparts in the other services had limited upward mobility and experienced sexism and sexual harassment.[38]

Rumors about the promiscuity of women in the military abounded. For example, sailors often joked about joining the navy to "ride the WAVES."[39] This "slander campaign" gained such notoriety during World War II that both First Lady Eleanor Roosevelt and Representative Edith Nourse Rogers publicly denounced the rumors as a "Nazi-inspired" attempt to undermine the American war effort.[40] One military woman, Dorothy Austell, recalled her understanding that Hitler was "putting propaganda out saying that all the women are getting pregnant, discouraging women to go into the military, and they're making the people believe that that's really happening."[41] Secretary of War Henry L. Stimson also addressed the issue, saying

My attention has been attracted to sinister rumors aimed at destroying the reputation of [women in uniform]. I refer to charges of immorality.... I wish to state that these rumors are absolutely and completely false.... I emphasize that I have made a thorough investigation of these rumors. They are completely false.[42]

Even General George Marshall entered the fray, publicly denouncing the unfounded rumors that could prove detrimental to the war effort if they discouraged enough women from serving.

Whether "Nazi inspired" or domestic in origin, the cloud of moral suspicion lingered even as former military women reentered civilian life in the postwar era. History shows women removing their military service from their civilian resumes lest their character be questioned. Despite these hardships, women served quite successfully during World War II and would not be turned out of the services again as they had after World War I. The Women's Armed Forces Integration Act of July 30, 1948, made women permanent participants in the military, at peace and at war (albeit with many restrictions, slowly lifted over time).[43]

African American women who answered Uncle Sam's call during World War II faced resistance based on their gender, but they also entered (like their male counterparts) a frustratingly racially segregated military world that seemed antithetical to the war's purported goal of freeing the world from Nazism and fascism. For example, while the Women's Army Auxiliary Corps (WAAC) accepted Black women right from its start in 1942, "recruitment of black women was limited to ten percent of the WAAC population—matching the black proportion of the national population." Enlisted women were almost always segregated by race, and while officers generally trained in integrated units, they, like the enlisted women, almost always lived under segregated conditions. During the war, some 6,520 Black women served in the WAAC/WAC.[44]

It was no better in the other services. Black women could not join the WAVES until October 19, 1944. While the first two Black WAVES officers, Harriet Ida Pickens and Frances Wills Thorpe, were sworn in December 22, 1944, of the 80,000 WAVES in the war, a mere 72 Black women served, generally under integrated conditions.[45] And while the coast guard technically opened the SPARS (from the coast guard motto *Semper Paratus*, "Always Ready") to Black members on October 20, 1944, only a few actually enlisted.[46]

Charity Adams Earley, the first Black woman commissioned as an army officer and the commander of the only all-Black Women's Army Corps (WAC) unit to serve overseas during World War II, recalled her devotion to fighting this hypocrisy in her memoir, *One Woman's Army: A Black Officer Remembers* the WAC. From her enlistment in 1942 and throughout her storied career, she waged her campaign with optimism, writing in her memoir, "Don't advertise when you are down. When people believe that you are down, they press down; when they think you are up, they push up." Adams Earley retired in 1946 with the rank of lieutenant colonel, second only in rank to the WAC director.[47]

Adams Earley's 6888th Central Postal Directory Battalion was active from 1945 to 1946 and employed 855 women. The battalion's nickname was "Six-Triple Eight," and its motto was "No Mail, Low Morale" (sometimes given as "no mail, no morale").[48] They were tasked with sorting and clearing a two-year backlog of mail in England and France. Veteran of the 6888th Lena King recalled, "The mail was stacked almost to the top of the hangar."[49] Working conditions were suboptimal, carried out in cold, dirty, dark, and rat-infested aircraft hangars with broken windows. The work could also be frustrating. For example, there were some 7,500 pieces of mail addressed to Robert Smith, due to how common that name was.[50]

The battalion worked three shifts a day, seven days a week, while bombs dropped all around them. King recalled, "They had asked if we could get it done in about six months. We were able to get it done in three months." Ultimately, they processed 65,000 pieces of mail per shift. One might expect these efforts to be met with gratitude by other soldiers, but that was not always the case. Lena recalled "I met one white American soldier. The first thing that came out of his mouth, he said, 'What are you doing here, n----r?' All we were doing . . . we're trying to get letters to people like him." Another 6888th veteran, Essie Dell O'Bryant Woods concluded, "We came from an era that the young people today would not understand. We expected it, it wasn't—we knew, but we knew we had to do the best, be the best we could be in order to prove ourselves." Colonel Edna Cummings of the US Army advocated for the 6888th to receive a Congressional Gold Medal, which they did in 2021. As she told CBS News, "During a time where they were denied basic liberties as Americans, they still wanted to serve the United States."[51]

Not until after World War II was won by a racially segregated military would President Harry S. Truman sign Executive Order 9981 and end racial segregation in the United States armed forces.[52] However, military women would continue, for decades, to serve under various gendered restrictions. Those interested in doing further research into or reading on the history of women in the United States military will find the collections of the National Archives, Library of Congress, Smithsonian Institution, the Women in Military Service for America Memorial, United States Army Women's Museum, Texas Woman's University Library, and Naval History and Heritage Command to be useful starting points.

There are many published memoirs available as well, covering over 150 years of women's service. See for example Sara Ann Allen, ed., *Daughters of Pallas*

Athene: Cameo Recollections of the Women's Army Corps; Bernadine Bailey, *The Youngest WAC Overseas*; Jane Blair, *Hesitation Kills: A Female Marine Officer's Combat Experience in Iraq*; Sylvia Bugbee, *An Officer and a Lady: The World War II Letters of Lt. Col. Betty Bandel*; Ann Carl, *A WASP among Eagles: A Woman Military Test Pilot in World War II*; Tracy Crow, *Eyes Right: Confessions from a Woman Marine*; Cheryl Dietrich, *In Formation: One Woman's Rise through the Ranks of the U.S. Air Force*; Dottie Gill, *A Secret Place in My Heart: A Diary of a World War II WAC*; Sarah Edmonds, *Memoirs of a Soldier, Nurse and Spy in the Union Army: A Woman's Adventures in the Union Army*; Anne Bosanko Green, *One Woman's War: Letters Home from the WAC, 1944–1946*; Blanche Green, *Growing Up in the WAC: Letters to My Sister*; Joann Puffer Kotcher, *Donut Dolly: An American Red Cross Girl's War in Vietnam*; Judy Barrett Litoff, *We're in This War, Too: World War II Letters from American Women in Uniform*; Florence Nightingale, *Notes on Nursing: What It Is, and What It Is Not*; Elizabeth Pollock, *Yes Ma'am! The Personal Papers of a WAAC Private*; Janeta Velazquez, *The Woman in Battle: A Narrative of the Exploits, Adventures, and Travels of Madame Loreta Janeta Velazquez, Otherwise Known as Lieutenant Harry T. Buford, Confederate States Army*; and Selene H. C. Weise, *The Good Soldier: A Story of a Southwest Pacific Signal Corps WAC*.

For secondary sources, see the reference list that accompanies this chapter. Much of the literature focuses on the WWII period, but scholarship covering women's service both before and after are certainly available. Note that many of these texts discuss African American women's service. For works more specifically/singularly on the history of Black women in the US military, see Gerald Astor, *The Right to Fight: A History of African Americans in the Military*; Gail Buckley, *American Patriots: The Story of Blacks in the Military from the Revolution to Desert Storm*; Catherine Clinton, *The Black Soldier: 1492 to the Present*; James Controvich, *African-Americans in Defense of the Nation: A Bibliography*; Elizabeth F. Desnoyers-Colas, *Marching as to War: Personal Narratives of African American Women's Experiences in the Gulf Wars*; Charity Adams Earley, *One Woman's Army: A Black Officer Remembers the WAC*; Maureen Honey, *Bitter Fruit: African American Women in World War II*; Addie Hunton, *Two Colored Women, with the American Expeditionary Forces*; Martha Putney, *When the Nation Was in Need: Blacks in the Women's Army Corps During World War II*; Martha Putney, ed., *Blacks in the United States Army: Portraits through History*; and Phillip Thomas Tucker, *Cathy Williams: From Slave to Female Buffalo Soldier*.[53]

Much history remains to be written, though. Each and every day, Black women in the military continue to break down barriers placed before them. Their achievements, most of which have yet to make it into the academic historiography, are being covered in real time in newspapers, magazines, journals, and on the internet. For example, Dr. Irene Trowell-Harris became the first nurse to command an Air National Guard medical clinic in 1986, and in 1987 she became the first African American woman to serve as a general officer in the National Guard. Army sergeant Danyell Wilson became the first Black woman to earn the prestigious job of guarding the Tomb of the Unknowns at Arlington National Cemetery in 1997. Lillian Elaine Fishburne became the first African American female to hold the rank of rear admiral in the United States Navy in 1998. Michelle Janine Howard was the first African American woman to command a US Navy ship and the first to achieve two- and three-star rank. In 2014, Howard became the first woman—of any race, color, or creed—to become a four-star admiral in the US Navy.

Black women again made history in 2019 when on Saturday, May 25, a record thirty-four African American women cadets graduated from West Point Military Academy. All received a bachelor of science degree and commissions as second lieutenants in the US Army. A viral photo depicted these women in uniform. "My hope when young black girls see these photos is that they understand that regardless of what life presents you, you have the ability and fortitude to be a force to be reckoned with," said cadet Tiffany Welch-Baker.

Oral history interviews archived with the Library of Congress Veterans History Project allow rare insight into the motivations of Black women veterans. These veterans rarely say that they sought to be the next big "gunslinger" or to perform some physical feats. They frequently report that they saw their military service not as an adventure but as a sensible path to self-betterment and upward mobility in a society that limited their options. They enlisted seeking personal advancement, economic empowerment, college tuition, opportunities to travel, chances to expand their horizons, and to become more informed global citizens. They often rose through the ranks to become leaders and mentors, both during their time in the military and when they returned to civilian life. They are Black women public intellectuals.

Several of the Black women veterans interviewed said that they joined because they saw it as a patriotic duty, a way to give back to the country, or way to feel good about themselves. Native Missourian Gloria Jean Barnes, who in the 1970s joined the Air National Guard, enlisted after telling a friend of her husband's, "I wish I had something meaningful to do." He encouraged her to join the military, and she did. She reached the rank of technical sergeant and concluded that her time in the service "was good . . . I had a wonderful experience."

Illinois native Jacqueline Dancer Blount, who served in the coast guard from 1973 to 2002 (both in the reserves and on active duty) and ultimately attained the rank of yeoman first class, recalled finding a similar sense of purpose in the military. When asked what message about her service she might deliver to future generations, Blount replied,

> I would say that, one, I think as a true American, you as a future generation should always put your country first, put your fellow man first. The generation to follow will have to follow a pattern unlike what I followed. And I'm not talking about the fact that I am a black American, but the fact that just being an American is all important. I never put down on my list of when I'm applying for something, I never include the phraseology of African American. I know nothing about Africa. I've never been to Africa. I am a black American and I'm very proud.

Like Barnes and Blount, North Carolina native Nicole Douglas saw the military as a chance to do something meaningful with her life. She recalled that she entered the military in 1990 as an eighteen-year-old "who didn't have any direction, really," and noted, "The Army seemed like it was a great choice to go, it was actually the only available way out of the situation or the circumstances that I was in." She served in Operation Iraqi Freedom and rose to the rank of major.

Kemya Rence Willis of Indiana joined the army in 1987 and ended up serving in Operation Desert Shield/Desert Storm. She was discharged from the army in 1994 and recalled, "It was one of the most refreshing things that I had ever accomplished in my life. I felt so fulfilled . . . being able to bring that joy to my grandmother in accomplishing whatever. Now, I have served my country proudly. . . . I felt complete with myself."

Operation Enduring Freedom veteran Renita Weaver of Michigan enlisted in the army in 2003. She was twenty-nine and, since her family had preferred she wait until she earned her degree, she had waited to enlist. Weaver served a one-year deployment in Afghanistan and recalled, "It gave me the opportunity to work on improving myself as a person, as a soldier, as a mom, and being able to think, if I can make it through this, I can make it through anything." She also confessed, "I won't say it was easy; being a female soldier in combat is difficult. Your body goes through changes. I lost quite a bit of my hair. Your female clock even was off." Looking back, she shared that she is incredibly proud of the woman she became and felt she had come a long way from who she was before the military.

Many Black women veterans note that they joined the military specifically because good paying jobs were hard to come by for them in civilian life. Ohioan Norma Wilma Dean Busby, who served in the air force from 1952 to 1955, joined and served three years because, as the second of seven children, she knew her parents could not afford college. Busby attained the rank of airman second class and saved enough money to move her mother and younger siblings out of public housing. She recalled opening her first charge card, "which I thought was the greatest thing." Of her service overall, she noted, "I just loved every minute of it."

In the 1970s, Missouri-born Myrtis Smith Fields, a single mother raising three children after her husband died in a car crash, turned to the army. She felt it would provide her with a stable career, and she was willing to make the necessary sacrifices for her children, because "I wanted more for them. I wanted as much as possible for them." She served from 1974 to 2007 and earned the rank of sergeant first class.

Linda Warren, born in South Carolina, was a US Army medical corpsman during the Vietnam War era. As she recalled, "The army was an opportunity for me. Growing up, the eldest of nine children . . . the army was a means to escape, and to build a foundation, so I just had to leave. . . . I just wanted a different role for my life." She joined

> to escape poverty. I didn't want to end up like my mother. She always used to say to me, "I don't want you at 29 with nine kids. I want something better for you. I want you to have an education." She didn't have the means to send me to college. Back then they didn't have those special grants, or opportunities for people of color, especially a black woman. The army was my only way out at that time.

She wound up earning a degree as a sociologist. When she returned home from service, some of her former girlfriends from her hometown were dead. This reinforced, for her, that she had made the right decision. She noted, "It helped me to shift from one environment to a more prospering, more positive environment. It showed me that you don't have to live in poverty. You can reach for the stars. You can be whoever you want to be. And that's who I am now." In response to what advice she has for others, she shared,

> If anybody is lost, doesn't know which way to go, confused about their life or the choices of life and trying to build a relationship and a foundation, trying to establish a positive atmosphere for themselves, the military is the way to go. So, if you're not sure of your college, or what you want to do in terms of education, or skill building, I'm telling you the military is the choice. It will help you. Being in the military, I didn't have to worry about colleges' tuitions. I got paid while I was going to school. Even though I got pregnant . . . I went to school, and I was able to earn an income. It matured it, it placed me on a pedestal . . . I had control of my life. I wanted to make a difference in my children's lives.

Her three daughters went on to have careers as a nurse, a prosecuting attorney, and an investigator.

Rhonda Nunnally Watson of Virginia served in the US Army and the National Guard from 1977 to 2005. She is both an Operation Desert Storm and an Operation Iraqi Freedom veteran. She recalled, "I had two small children, and no good way to earn a living, so I joined the Army." She felt that "the service made me a much better person. It made me stronger, smarter, more independent, more aggressive, more assertive." She attained the rank of E-5 (sergeant).

Nicole Earley Watson of Ohio, a Cold War veteran, served in the US Navy Reserve from 1990 to 1994. She was assigned to a submarine division that was based in Groton, Connecticut. She was the only woman in the unit. She said she joined because she "wanted to do something positive, and I didn't want to go straight to college." She spoke candidly about the obstacles she encountered, though, confessing that her time in boot camp in Orlando, Florida, was filled with so much pressure and stress that her menstruation stopped. She ultimately used her education benefits to attend Sinclair Community College. Despite the stressors, overall, she concluded that the military was a worthwhile experience for her, saying,

> I learned how to be more of an independent person, instead ... of a dependent person. I was able to think on my own; and, no matter what's going on around me I can, I was able to stay focused on what I had to do and make sure the job was done ... to depend on solely myself, I mean even though we're together as a group as a team, but it made me, it motivated me to do better every day.

Veteran interviews from the early Cold War era through the present show that women consistently declare not just that they joined the military to find a sense of purpose, or to fulfill a patriotic duty, or for economic gain generally, but specifically to earn college tuition benefits, which had been available to veterans since the end of WWII.[54] Rosa B. H. Williams of Georgia, for example, served as a Cold War–era army nurse overseas in Germany and France, attaining the rank of major. She was, in fact, the first Black major to serve at Fort Gordon in Georgia. She declared that her reason for wanting to join the army was to have her college tuition financed. Wisconsin-born Effie Bell Baldwin, who served in the Army Signal Corps from 1986 to 1991 and was at one point stationed overseas in Germany, also said that she saw her service "as an opportunity to obtain money for college."

New Jersey–born Serrenia Odella White joined the New Jersey Air National Guard in 1972 and then the US Air Force and served until 1983. She is a veteran of both the Cold War and Operation Desert Shield/Desert Storm. A recruiter came to her high school and talked about tuition benefits. This was appealing since, as she recalled, "I didn't come from a very rich family . . . most of the time, no money at all." In the military, "I was all over the world; I stayed in the Air Force for ten years." She felt that "everything I wanted to do for my country, I did. And everything my country could do for me, they did." In response to a question about being a female in the service in the 1970s, she had this to say: "I had problems. Being a black woman, being recognized and being awarded . . . given top priority, in certain areas, I had problems with that. But being smart, and doing a job that has to be done . . . I felt pressure; I heard things." She credits the air force for her two years of college education as well as for finding her "inner self-esteem." After leaving the air force in 1989, she joined the army.

Indiana native Jeanne Williams was a Cold War–era soldier who enlisted in 1976 even though, as she recalled, "At the time there was a stigma about women joining the military." She achieved the rank of sergeant first class, and she used her tuition benefits to earn her bachelor's in business administration. At the time of her interview, she was interning for a licensure in mental health counseling. She also planned to attend a program in adaptive gerontology.

Sophia Webb was born in Trinidad and Tobago. She came to the United States and served in the US Marine Corps from 1982 to 2002, participating in Operation Desert Shield/Desert Storm and achieving the rank of sergeant. She used her GI Bill to pursue her master of science in business full-time for two years. She credits the military with having built her character and given her mental strength and endurance, in addition to financial benefits.

Dellia Rose Williams of Ohio enlisted with her sister in the air force in 1983. Dellia would serve in Operation Desert Shield/Desert Storm. She joined the Ohio National Guard, too, which paid for 90 percent of her education. While working with a security police unit in South Korea, she got entered in a contest "with all these tough security guys, and I won the medal. I got a pay raise; I got to move off base." She also earned the Expert Marksman medal with the M-16. As she remembered, "We kind of had to push ourselves. Physically we had to show that we could do the same kind of things that (men) could do. Mentally we had to show that we were smart enough to do the same things. Everywhere you went you were proving yourself." She said that she is afraid to think of where she would have ended up if she had not joined the military.

Floridian Casandra Williams, whose father served in the Vietnam War, enlisted in the army in 1988 and is an Operation Desert Shield/Desert Storm veteran. As she recalled, "I wanted to go attend college, and I got accepted into Savannah State. I was going on my Dad's GI Bill." Due to a change in the rules that would no longer allow her to go to school under her father's benefits, she "had to change my career direction, and I decided to go into the military." She did this because "I just wanted to go and do my time for the education, to get my GI Bill." She achieved the rank of specialist.

Georgia-born Michele Bowers Eason, who was in the army reserves from 1988 to 1996, achieved the rank of specialist, or E-4. When asked, "What made you enlist in the first place?" she proffered, "I enlisted to get money for school." Interviewer Stephanie McKinnell clarifies, "For the GI Bill. . . . Did you use it?" To which Michele replies, "Yes, I did. I used it well."

North Carolinian Lacia Alderman Flakes served in the army during Operation Iraqi Freedom, reaching the rank of staff sergeant. She entered the service straight out of high school, telling her interviewer, "I knew that I wanted to travel the world, and that was a good way to do it. And my intention was to join the Army, to get some college money." She intended to stay in only a few years, and then go to school, but instead served for fifteen years.

Flakes noted a desire to travel, along with college financing. This is another oft-cited motivation across generations of Black female veterans. What better way to broaden one's horizons then to get out and see the rest of the country, to get out and see the world? Kentucky-born Marethia Ann Williams, for example, enlisted in the Army Nurse Corps in 1989. She noted, "I wanted to travel . . . even though I joined at an old age: 36. They were taking nurses up to 52 when I joined." She enthused, "People in the community respect you. My kids respect the fact that I'm in the military . . . it's been a positive experience." Marethia achieved the rank of colonel.

Wallyne Volcy of Florida was born in Haiti and enlisted in the US Army in 1997. She served until 2006. Her first deployment was to Bosnia; she later served two tours in Iraq. She was attracted to the army because she wanted to travel. She also noted that she dealt with "sexual harassment . . . racism . . . sexism . . . People don't talk about it because a lot of times it's just brushed under the carpet." She recalled that most people in her unit were white males. Volcy described the difference between the sexism from the white males versus from the Black males. The Black males felt that "they should be able to see you on the side. Most of them were married, but they're still trying to pursue something, just because they have the rank." She concluded that, "The Army for me was not a walk in the park; it was fighting every day. It was a different fight every day. If I wasn't fighting racism, then I was fighting harassment." After Volcy became a noncommissioned officer, she found herself fighting for African Americans who, unlike her, were too afraid to speak up for themselves.

> If you start speaking up, they know you're going to get stopped in your tracks; you're not going to get promoted. You're not going to get any rank. The people in charge of you had to open that door for you. And

nobody wanted to say anything because of that. But to do that, you have to be able to live through that and let it happen.

Linda Taylor of Maryland served in the army, where she was commissioned in 1981. She came out of the service as a captain in 1993, after participating in Operations Desert Shield/Desert Storm. She initially joined the Army ROTC because of the potential for travel, the camaraderie, and the opportunity to give back something to the country. Overall, she felt her service a worthwhile experience. She recalled,

> I would have to say that I owe who I am and what I'm doing to the military. I learned to be a leader. It wasn't something that I was born with. The military provided so many challenges for me to overcome. I have excellent interpersonal skills, and I owe that all to the military. I attribute the military to the success that I now have as a civilian. I really do. It's a place that provides so much to a human being in terms of service, duty, honor; I'm grateful.

Jacqueline Blount, who as noted earlier served in the coast guard from 1973, recalled,

> At the time I was going to actually be separated from my husband. And a neighbor friend of mine came down in a hurry to say, "Jackie, I have an idea of how you can have a vacation every year for two weeks." And I said, "What?" And she said, "And get paid." I said, "Sounds good to me." And she said, "Okay, it's called the United States Coast Guard." I said, "Okay."

As she was still legally married to her husband at the time, she was required to get his permission for her to join.

Charonda Taylor of Delaware, an Operation Iraqi Freedom veteran, enlisted in the air force in 1999. She worked as an intelligence analyst, in Combat Mission Intelligence Support. She recalled, "I joined because I wanted to serve my country. I wanted to travel; I wanted an adventure. I felt like I'd been given a lot of opportunities from this nation, and I really just wanted to give back and serve." She deployed twice in support of Operation Iraqi Freedom, and her unit "actually dropped the first bombs in Iraq." They came home to a parade and were treated like war heroes, even asked to kiss babies, but she says she didn't feel like a war hero. Additional deployments followed. She felt the pressure of having to live up to the expectation of those who went before her and had it harder, such as her air force colonel grandmother, a Vietnam War veteran. "I not only have to do that best job that I can do. Not only did they fight for the right to fight for their country; they fought a war on two fronts, basically. Here I am, just fighting war, so you better do it well!"

Even when women perceived military service as personally advantageous in some ways, they took great personal risks when they donned their uniforms. Retired first sergeant Priscilla Harris Swan of Michigan served in the US Army Reserves and Michigan Army National Guard from 1985 to 2009. She is an Operation Iraqi Freedom veteran. Of her desire to enlist, she recalled, "I had wanted to get away and see a little bit of the world." In October 2004, her unit was activated for Operation Iraqi Freedom. When she got back, she had to deal with injuries, plus the problems from having to leave her school-age son home with family members.

These oral history excerpts allow only the briefest glimpse into the lives of these brave Black women veterans. They combine with the existing historiography to provide a fuller picture of the experiences and motivations of the average Black female veteran.

No woman has ever been drafted into the United States military. From the colonial era to the present, each and every one who has served, in any capacity, has volunteered. Though many express satisfaction in their service overall, they also face varying degrees of sexism, harassment, and sometimes violence while serving our nation. Black women bear a double burden and face obstacles and threats based on both their gender and their race. Still, they persist, and their stories deserve to be told, their sacrifices—and triumphs—understood. They worked for the military, but they made the military work for them too: expanding their horizons and seeking advancement, economic empowerment, college tuition, and travel.

Bettie Jean Vaughan of Texas, who served in the US Army from 1977 to 1980, notes,

> My main interest is African-American History. I don't think enough is being taught.... The world needs to know about the contribution that women have made. I'm researching, even as far back as the Civil War—even before we were allowed to go to Iraq or Afghanistan—the contribution that women have made as far as the military, even as far back as Harriet Tubman.

We hope that this chapter has contributed to this effort. The world might not think of Black female veterans when they think of Black women public intellectuals, but it should.

NOTES

1. "Intellectual," Dictionary.com, https://www.dictionary.com/browse/intellectual/.
2. "Anti-intellectual," Dictionary.com, https://www.dictionary.com/browse/anti-intellectual.
3. Reed, *Tarnished*, 55.
4. "Colonel Lloyd J. Matthews, USA Ret.," *The U.S. Army War College*, https://ssi.armywarcollege.edu/pubs/people.cfm?authorID=82.
5. Matthews, "The Uniformed Intellectual and His Place in American Arms Part I."
6. Matthews, "The Uniformed Intellectual and His Place in American Arms Part I."
7. Matthews, "The Uniformed Intellectual and His Place in American Arms Part I."
8. Hanson W. Baldwin, *What You Should Know about the Navy* (New York: W. W. Norton, 1943), 64; Rudi Williams, "Wartime Posters Drew Men, Women to Patriotic Duty," *Monmouth Message*, April 16, 1999, 6; Naval Historical Center, "WWI Era Yeomen (F)," May 6, 2000, http://www.history.navy.mil/photos/prs-tpic/females/yeoman-f.htm; Gruhzit-Hoyt, *They Also Served*, 125; Treadwell, *Women's Army Corps*, 10.
9. See Debra L. Newman, "Black Women in the Era of the American Revolution in Pennsylvania," *Journal of Negro History* 61, no. 3 (July 1976): 276–89; Berkin, *Revolutionary Mothers*.
10. Susie King Taylor, *Reminiscences of My Life in Camp: An African American Woman's Civil War Memoir* (Athens: University of Georgia Press, 2006). See more at Allison Espiritu, "Susan Taylor (Susie) Baker King (1848–1912)," Black Past, February 26, 2007, http://www.blackpast.org/aah/taylor-susan-susie-baker-king-1848-1912#sthash.g76MRvKY.pdf. See also Berkin, *Revolutionary Mothers*.
11. Kathryn Sheldon, "Brief History of Black Women in the Military," Women in Military Service for America Memorial Foundation, http://civilwarrx.blogspot.com/2017/01/brief-history-of-black-women-in.html.
12. US Army Medical Department, "Proud to Serve: African American Army Nurse Corps Officers," https://achh.army.mil/history/articles-blackhistory.
13. "Nurse Corps Role Vital," *Monmouth Message*, March 3, 1976, 12; Gruhzit-Hoyt, *They Also Served*, 1; Mike Wright, *What They Didn't Teach You about World War II* (Novato, CA: Presidio, 1998), 40; Treadwell, *Women's Army Corps*, 6; "Nurses and the U.S. Navy," Naval History and Heritage Command, accessed 20 December 2014, http://www.history.navy.mil/photos/prs-tpic/nurses/nurses.htm; Bellafaire, *The Women's Army Corps*, 27.
14. Eighteen African American nurses served for nine months at the end of World War I, according to Barbara Brooks Tomblin, author of *G.I. Nightingales: The Army Nurse Corps in World War II*, and Mary Sarnecky, author of *A History of the U.S. Army Nurse Corps*. Ted Gregory, "Forgotten War Nurses Keep Their Story Alive as the Surviving Black Army Nurses from World War II Dwindle, Their Contributions Remain Virtually Unknown," *Chicago Tribune*, May 28, 2001, http://articles.chicagotribune.com/2001-05-28/news/0105280153_1_black-nurses-ww-ii-phd; US Army Medical Department, "Proud to Serve."
15. Alexis Clark, "The Army's First Black Nurses Were Relegated to Caring for Nazi Prisoners of War," *Smithsonian*, May 15, 2018, https://www.smithsonianmag.com/history/armys-first-black-nurses-had-tend-to-german-prisoners-war-180969069/#pVyYvlkoY2l19pro.99.
16. Henry Louis Gates Jr. and Evelyn Brooks Higginbotham, eds, *African American Lives* (New York: Oxford University Press, 2004), 94; Karen Abbot, *Liar, Temptress, Soldier, Spy: Four Women Undercover in the Civil War* (New York: Harper Perennial, 2015).

17. Lois Leveen, *The Secrets of Mary Bowser: A Novel* (New York: William Morrow, 2012), i; see also Elizabeth Van Lew and David Ryan, *A Yankee Spy in Richmond: The Civil War Diary of "Crazy Bet" Van Lew* (Mechanicsburg, PA: Stackpole Books, 2001). It is heartening to note that despite the paucity of archival records about Mary Bowser's life, her story is making its way into children's and young adult literature. See, for example, Mary E. Lyons and Muriel Branch, *Dear Ellen Bee: A Civil War Scrapbook of Two Union Spies* (New York: Atheneum Books, 2000), Walter Hazen, *Hidden History: Profiles of Black Americans* (Dayton, OH: Milliken Publishing, 2004), and Lucia Raatma, *We the People: Great Women of the Civil War* (Minneapolis, MN: Compass Point Books, 2005).

18. Gates and Higginbotham, *African American Lives*, 94; Abbot, *Liar, Temptress, Soldier, Spy*.

19. Sheldon, "Brief History of Black Women in the Military."

20. Baldwin, *What You Should Know about the Navy*, 64; Williams, "Wartime Posters Drew Men, Women to Patriotic Duty," 6; Naval Historical Center, "WWI Era Yeomen (F)"; Gruhzit-Hoyt, *They Also Served*, 125; Treadwell, *Women's Army*, 10.

21. Navy History and Heritage Command, "The African American Experience in the U.S. Navy," accessed February 10, 2017, https://www.history.navy.mil/browse-by-topic/diversity/african-americans.html.

22. Chad Williams, "African Americans and WWI," New York Public Library, accessed February 10, 2017, http://exhibitions.nypl.org/africanaage/essay-world-war-i.html.

23. "Signal Museum Acquires 'Hello Girls' Uniform," *Monmouth Message*, March 23, 1972, 14; Morden, *The Women's Army Corps*, 4; Raines, *Getting the Message Through*, 170, 184–85, 302; Oveta Culp Hobby, "The Signal Corps WAC," *Radio News* 31 (February 1944): 246–47, 406. US Army Communications-Electronics Life Cycle Management Command Archives, Fort Monmouth, NJ.

24. Segal, "Women's Military Roles Cross-Nationally," 757; Miller "Not Just Weapons of the Weak"; *Kathryn Abrams*, "Gender in the Military."

25. Douglas, "WASPs of War"; Ryan, *Womanhood in America*, 315, 329; Bellafaire, *The Women's Army Corps*, 27.

26. Ryan, *Womanhood in America*, 315, 329.

27. Mary Trocchia, "The Introduction of the Skirt and Stocking Clad Soldier at Fort Hancock" (Sandy Hook, NJ: Gateway National Recreation Area, n.d.), 1.

28. Russell F. Weigley, *Eisenhower's Lieutenants: The Campaigns of France and Germany, 1944–45* (Bloomington: Indiana University Press, 1981), 13; see also Campbell, "Women in Combat," 313.

29. Weatherford, *American Women and World War II*, 98; Dwight D. Eisenhower, *Crusade in Europe* (New York: Doubleday, 1948), 132–33; Elizabeth R. Snoke, *Dwight D. Eisenhower: A Centennial Bibliography* (Fort Leavenworth, KS: US Army Command and General Staff College, 1990), http://www-cgsc.army.mil/carl/resources/csi/Snoke/SNOKE.asp; Treadwell, *Women's Army Corps*, 393. While evaluating Eisenhower's positive response toward women, one must note that Kay Summersby Morgan, a British woman commissioned to the WAC over WAC Director Hobby's protest, recounts her romantic relationship with Eisenhower during the war in *Past Forgetting: My Love Affair with Dwight D. Eisenhower* (New York: Simon and Schuster, 1976). Summersby served under Eisenhower for three and a half years, first as his driver and later as his secretary and military aide.

30. Collins, *More Than a Uniform*; Carol Stokes, "Women in Yesterday's Signal Corps," Gordon.army.mil, August 22, 2005, http://www.gordon.army.mil/AC/WWII/WOMEN.HTM; Nona Baldwin, "Bill to Put Women in the Army Is Passed," *New York Times*, May 13, 1942, 21; Treadwell, *Women's Army Corps*, 123.

31. US Congress. House of Representatives, *Sixteenth Anniversary of the Women's Army Corps: Extension of Remarks of Hon. Edith Nourse Rogers*. 85th Cong., 2nd sess., May 14, 1958; Morden, *The Women's Army Corps*, 5; Treadwell, *Women's Army Corps*, 45; *Army Almanac*, 167.

32. Stokes, "Women in Yesterday's Signal Corps"; Christopher J. Anderson, "Editorial," *World War II* (May 2006): 2; Douglas, "WASPs of War."

33. "Senate Sends Back New Bill for WAAC," *New York Times*, April 28, 1942, 18.

34. Baldwin, "Bill to Put Women in the Army Is Passed," 21.

35. Baldwin, "Bill to Put Women in the Army Is Passed," 21.

36. Violet K. Caudle, interview by Eric Elliot, Statesville, North Carolina, April 20, 1999. Jackson Library, University of North Carolina at Greensboro.

37. Baldwin, *What You Should Know about the Navy*, 64.

38. Collins, *More Than a Uniform*.

39. Gruhzit-Hoyt, *They Also Served*, xvi.

40. "Stimson Condemns Gossip about WAAC," *New York Times*, June 11, 1943, 6; Sherman, "'They Either Need These Women or They Do Not,'" 61; Weatherford, *American Women and World War II*, 91; Yellin, *Our Mothers' War*, 130; Violet K. Caudle, interview by Eric Elliot, Statesville, North Carolina, April 20, 1999. Jackson Library, University of North Carolina at Greensboro.

41. Dorothy B. Austell, interview by Hermann Trojanowski, Raleigh, North Carolina, September 18, 2000. Jackson Library, University of North Carolina at Greensboro.

42. "Stimson Condemns Gossip About WAAC," *New York Times*, June 11, 1943, 6.

43. For a timeline of "Women's Milestones in Naval History," see http://www.history.navy.mil/special%20highlights/women/timeline1.htm.

44. Sheldon, "Brief History of Black Women in the Military."

45. Sheldon, "Brief History of Black Women in the Military."

46. Sheldon, "Brief History of Black Women in the Military."

47. LTC Adams's papers are held at the Library of Congress, and a finding aid can be found at http://rs5.loc.gov/service/mss/eadxmlmss/eadpdfmss/2009/ms009089.pdf. Charity Adams Earley, *One Woman's Army: A Black Officer Remembers the WAC* (College Station: Texas A&M University Press, 1989).

48. Alexis Clark, "These Black Female Heroes Made Sure U.S. WWII Forces Got Their Mail," History, February 1, 2019, https://www.history.com/news/black-woman-army-unit-mail-world-war-ii.

49. Jim Axelrod, "An All-Black Women's Army Corps Unit from WWII Is Still Fighting for Recognition," CBS News, November 14, 2019, https://www.cbsnews.com/news/how-an-all-black-womens-army-corps-unit-still-fighting-for-recognition/.

50. "Women of the 6888th Central Postal Directory Battalion," Buffalo Soldier Educational and Historical Committee, accessed November 3, 2019, https://www.womenofthe6888th.org/.

51. Clark, "These Black Female Heroes"; Jim Axelrod, "An All-Black Women's Army Corps Unit from WWII Is Still Fighting for Recognition."

52. "Executive Order 9981," Harry S. Truman Library and Museum, accessed December 15, 2014, http://www.trumanlibrary.org/9981.htm.

53. The above section is in part adapted from Melissa Ziobro's chapter, "African American Women in the Public Square: Admiral Michelle Howard," in Hettie Williams's *Bury My Heart in a Free Land: Black Women Intellectuals in Modern U.S. History* (Santa Barbara, CA: ABC-CLIO, 2017).

54. For more, see "Education and Benefits History and Timeline," Veterans Benefits Administration, accessed October 28, 2019, https://benefits.va.gov/gibill/history.asp.

REFERENCES

Abrams, Kathryn. "Gender in the Military: Androcentrism and Institutional Reform." *Law and Contemporary Problems* 56 (Autumn 1993): 217–41.

Anderson, Karen. *Wartime Women: Sex Roles, Family Relations and the Status of Women during World War II.* Westport, CT: Praeger: 1981.

The Army Almanac. Washington, DC: Government Printing Office, 1950.

Bellafaire, Judith A. *Women in the United States Military: An Annotated Bibliography.* London: Routledge, 2010.

Bellafaire, Judith A. *The Women's Army Corps: A Commemoration of World War II Service.* Washington, DC: US Army Center of Military History, 1993.

Berkin, Carol. *Revolutionary Mothers: Women in the Struggle for America's Independence.* New York: Vintage Books, 2005.

Boot, Max. "A Necessary Man: Petraeus' Intellectualism Was Crucial to the U.S. Military. Now the Nation Loses His Skills." *Los Angeles Times*, November 13, 2012.

Breuer, William. *War and American Women: Heroism, Deeds, and Controversy.* Westport, CT: Praeger, 1997.

Campbell, D'Ann. *Women at War with America: Private Lives in a Patriotic Era.* Cambridge, MA: Harvard University Press, 1984.

Campbell, D'Ann. "Women in Combat: The World War II Experience in the United States, Great Britain, Germany, and the Soviet Union." *Journal of Military History* 57 (April 1993): 302–23.

Campbell, D'Ann. "Women in Uniform: The World War II Experiment." *Military Affairs* 51 (July 1987): 137–39.

Clark, Alexis. "These Black Female Heroes Made Sure U.S. WWII Forces Got Their Mail." History, February 1, 2019, https://www.history.com/news/black-woman-army-unit-mail-world-war-ii.

Cohen, Lizabeth. *A Consumers' Republic: The Politics of Mass Consumption in Postwar America.* New York: Vintage Books, 2003.

Collins, Winifred Quick. *More Than a Uniform: A Navy Woman in a Navy Man's World.* Denton: University of North Texas Press, 1997.

D'Amico, Francine J., and Laurie L. Weinstein, eds. *Gender Camouflage: Women and the U.S. Military.* New York: New York University Press, 1999.

Douglas, Deborah G. "WASPs of War." *Aviation History*, January 1999.

Farquhar, John T. "Building Air Force Intellectual Capacity: An Innovative Look at Creating Air University and the Air Force Academy, 1918–1955." *Air Power History*, Winter 2017, 29–36.

Feller, Carolyn M., and Debora R. Cox, eds. *Highlights in the History of the Army Nurse Corps.* Washington, DC: US Army Center of Military History, 2001.

Frank, Lisa Tendrich. *An Encyclopedia of American Women at War: From the Home Front to the Battlefields.* Santa Barbara, CA: ABC-CLIO, 2013.

Gilbert, Alan. *Black Patriots and Loyalists: Fighting for Emancipation in the War for Independence.* Chicago: University of Chicago Press, 2012.

Gruhzit-Hoyt, Olga. *They Also Served: American Women in World War II.* New York: Birch Lane Press, 1995.

Hofstadter, Richard. *Anti-Intellectualism in American Life.* New York: Knopf, 1963.

Kerber, Linda K. *No Constitutional Right to Be Ladies.* New York: Hill and Wang, 1998.

Kohn, Richard H. "Tarnished Brass: Is the U.S. Military Profession in Decline?" *World Affairs* 171, no. 4 (Spring 2009): 73–83.

Kovach, Karen. *Breaking Codes, Breaking Barriers: The WACs of the Signal Security Agency, WWII.* Fort Belvoir, VA: US Army Intelligence and Security Command, 2001.

Lanning, Michael Lee. *African Americans in the Revolutionary War.* New York: Citadel Press, 2000.

Marshall, Max L., ed. *The Story of the U.S. Army Signal Corps.* New York: Franklin Watts, 1965.

Matthews, Lloyd J. "The Uniformed Intellectual and His Place in American Arms Part I." Association of the United States Army, July 24, 2002. https://www.ausa.org/articles/uniformed-intellectual-and-his-place-american-arms-part-i.

Matthews, Lloyd J. "The Uniformed Intellectual and His Place in American Arms Part II." Association of the United States Army, August 14, 2002. https://www.ausa.org/articles/uniformed-intellectual-and-his-place-american-arms-part-ii.

McEuen, Melissa. *Making War, Making Women: Femininity and Duty on the American Home Front, 1941–1945.* Athens: University of Georgia Press, 2011.

Milkman, Ruth. *Gender at Work: The Dynamics of Job Segregation by Sex during World War II* Champaign: University of Illinois Press, 1987.

Miller, Laura L. "Not Just Weapons of the Weak: Gender Harassment as a Form of Protest for Army Men." *Social Psychology Quarterly* 60 (March 1997): 32–51.

Mitchell, Brian. *Women in the Military: Flirting with Disaster.* Washington, DC: Regnery Publishing, 1998.

Monahan Evelyn, and Rosemary Neidel-Greenlee. *A Few Good Women: America's Military Women from World War I to the Wars in Iraq and Afghanistan.* New York: Alfred Knopf, 2010.

Morden, Bettie J. *The Women's Army Corps, 1945–1978.* Washington, DC: Center of Military History, United States Army, 1990.

Percheski, Christine. "Opting Out? Cohort Differences in Professional Women's Employment Rates from 1960 to 2005." *American Sociological Review* 73, no. 3 (2008): 497–517.

Quester, George H. "Women in Combat." *International Security* 4 (Spring 1977): 80–91.

Raines, Rebecca Robbins. *Getting the Message Through: A Branch History of the U.S. Army Signal Corps.* Washington, DC: Center of Military History, United States Army, 1996.

Rao, Aruna, David Kelleher, and Rieky Stuart. *Gender at Work: Organizational Change for Equality.* Bloomfield, CT: Kumarian Press, 1999.

Reed, George E. *Tarnished: Toxic Leadership in the U.S. Military.* Lincoln: University of Nebraska Press, 2015.

Reskin, Barbara. "Bringing the Men Back In: Sex Differentiation and the Devaluation of Women's Work." *Gender and Society* 2 (March 1988): 58–81.

Ryan, Mary P. *Womanhood in America*. New York: New Viewpoints, 1975.

Segal, Mady Wechsler. "Women's Military Roles Cross-Nationally: Past, Present, and Future." *Gender and Society* 9 (December 1995): 757–75.

Serbu, G. G. "The Dangers of Anti-Intellectualism in Contemporary Western Armies." *Infantry* 99, no. 4 (November 2010): 44–47.

Sherman, Janann. "'They Either Need These Women or They Do Not': Margaret Chase Smith and the Fight for Regular Status for Women in the Military." *Journal of Military History* 54 (January 1990): 47–78.

Simon, Rita James, ed. *Women in the Military*. New Brunswick, NJ: Transaction Publishers, 2001.

Stiehm, Judith, ed. *It's Our Military, Too! Women and the U.S. Military*. Philadelphia: Temple University Press, 1996.

Thompson, George Raynor, and Dixie R. Harris. *United States Army in World War II: The Technical Services: The Signal Corps: The Outcome*. Washington, DC: Office of the Chief of Military History, Department of the Army, 1966.

Thompson, George Raynor, Dixie R. Harris, Pauline M. Oakes, and Dulany Terrett. *United States Army in World War II: The Technical Services: The Signal Corps: The Test*. Washington, DC: Office of the Chief of Military History, Department of the Army, 1957.

Tomes, Robert R. *Apocalypse Then: American Intellectuals and the Vietnam War, 1954–1975*. New York: New York University Press, 1998.

Treadwell, Mattie B. *United States Army in World War II: Special Studies: The Women's Army Corps*. Washington, DC: Office of the Chief of Military History, Department of the Army, 1954.

Viuc, Kara Dixon. *Officer, Nurse, Woman: The Army Nurse Corps in the Vietnam War*. Baltimore: Johns Hopkins University Press, 2010.

Weatherford, Doris. *American Women and World War II*. New York: Facts on File, 1990.

Williams, Vera S. *WACs: Women's Army Corps*. Osceola, WI: Motorbooks, 1997.

Wood, Donald N. *Post-Intellectualism and the Decline of Democracy: The Failure of Reason and Responsibility in the Twentieth Century*. Westport, CT: Praeger, 1996.

Yellin, Emily. *Our Mothers' War*. New York: Free Press, 2004.

Zeigler, Sara, and Gregory G. Gunderson. *Moving beyond G.I. Jane: Women and the U.S. Military*. New York: University Press of America, 2005.

Archives

Veterans History Project, American Folklife Center, Library of Congress, Washington, DC.

ABOUT THE EDITORS AND CONTRIBUTORS

EDITORS

Hettie V. Williams, PhD, has taught survey courses in US history, Western civilization, and upper division courses on the history of African Americans at the university level for more than fifteen years. Her teaching and research interests include African American intellectual history, gender in US history, and race/ethnicity studies. She is also the president of the African American Intellectual History Society (AAIHS). Currently, she is an associate professor of African American history in the Department of History and Anthropology at Monmouth University, where she teaches courses in African American history and US history. She has published book chapters, essays, and encyclopedia entries and edited/authored five books. Her latest publications include *Bury My Heart in a Free Land: Black Women Intellectuals in Modern U.S. History* (Praeger, 2017) and, with Dr. G. Reginald Daniel, professor of historical sociology at the University of California, Santa Barbara, *Race and the Obama Phenomenon: The Vision of a More Perfect Multiracial Union* (University Press of Mississippi, 2014). Williams has contributed opinion pieces, book reviews, and essays to media outlets such as *HuffPost*, *Daring Woman Magazine*, the *Asbury Park Press*, the *Star Ledger*, and the award-winning peer-reviewed blog *Black Perspectives*. She is a host on the New Books Network intellectual history channel and a research historian on "My Buddy: The WWII 369th Documentary Project." She also hosts a weekly podcast show with Monmouth University faculty called *This Week in Black History, Society, and Culture*.

Melissa Ziobro is a specialist professor of public history and the primary point of contact for the public history minor at Monmouth University. Her service to the university includes administration of the Monmouth Memories Oral History Program and the department's social media and newsletter. She serves as the campus coordinator for the National History Day program and the faculty advisor for the History and Anthropology Club. Ziobro currently serves as the president of Oral History in the Mid-Atlantic Region and as the editor for *New Jersey Studies: An Interdisciplinary Journal*, a joint venture of the NJ Historical Commission, Rutgers University Libraries, and Monmouth University. She works regularly with public history organizations such as the Monmouth County Park System, InfoAge Science History Learning Center and Museum, Monmouth County Park System, Monmouth County Historical Association, Monmouth County Historical Commission, Middlesex County Office of Culture and Heritage, and National Guard Militia Museum of NJ. She worked as a command historian at the US Army Communications-Electronics Command, Fort Monmouth, New Jersey, from 2004 to 2011.

CONTRIBUTORS

Omar H. Ali, PhD, is dean of Lloyd International Honors College and professor of comparative African diaspora history at the University of North Carolina at Greensboro. He is the author of *In the Balance of Power: Independent Black Politics and Third-Party Movements in the United States* (Ohio University Press, 2020) and *Malik Ambar: Power and Slavery across the Indian Ocean* (Oxford University Press, 2016). A graduate of the London School of Economics and Political Science, he received his PhD in history from Columbia University. Ali was selected as the Carnegie Foundation North Carolina Professor of the Year.

Simone R. Barrett, PhD, is research associate for the Robert M. Bell Center for Civil Rights in Education at Morgan State University in Baltimore, Maryland, a native of Baltimore, and a three-time graduate of Morgan State University. Her research on student-led civil rights protest and Baltimore politics has appeared in both academic and popular publications, including *Black Perspectives*, *USA Today*, and the *Baltimore Afro-American*. She is the author of the forthcoming book *Before Greensboro: The Unknown History of Student-Led Protests in Baltimore, Maryland*.

Tejai Beulah, PhD, is currently an assistant professor of history, ethics, and Black church and African diaspora studies at Methodist Theological School in Ohio, where she teaches courses in church history and African American religious and ethical studies. Her teaching and research interests include African American religious intellectuals, gender in US history, African American music and social movements, and race/ethnicity studies. She is currently at work on a monograph titled *Soul Salvation, Social Liberation: Race and Evangelical Christianity in the Black Power Era, 1968–1979*.

About the Editors and Contributors

Sandra Bolzenius, PhD, lived abroad for nearly twenty years, first as a soldier in the United States Army stationed in Germany and then as a teacher in international schools located in Africa, Europe, the Middle East, and Asia. Resuming her studies at Ohio State University, she received a PhD in history in 2013. Reflecting her interest in the dynamics of gender, race, and class, particularly as manifested in public policies, Bolzenius is the author of *Glory in Their Spirit: How Four Black Women Took on the Army during World War II* (University of Illinois Press, 2018). Her recent article "Asserting Citizenship: Black Women in the Women's Army Corps (WAC)" appears in the *International Journal of Military History and Historiography* (Special Issue: Women and the Second World War, 2019).

Carol Fowler, BS, is the National Guard Militia Museum of New Jersey's assistant curator and director of its Center for US War Veterans Oral Histories. Fowler is a graduate of the College of Saint Elizabeth. Prior to joining the museum staff to establish the oral history program in 2001, she was an associate producer of the Brookdale Community College television production *Triumphant Spirit Series: America's WWII Generation Speaks*. She then conducted veteran interviews for history professor Paul Zigo's project, the Center for WWII Studies and Conflict Resolution. Fowler, who mentors Monmouth University interns in oral history, has conducted over six hundred interviews with veterans from World War II to the present and has been commended by the Library of Congress Veterans History Project, which named her among the top fourteen oral history interviewers in the country. She also works with local community leaders and programs, including veterans' organizations and the Quilts of Valor award program for combat veterans.

Lacey P. Hunter, PhD, is currently a professor at Rutgers University–Newark in the Department of African American and African Studies. She teaches courses in African American history and life, hip hop culture, and interdisciplinary research and methods seminars. Her research focuses on the intersections of race, gender, politics, and spirituality for African American women during the Early National and antebellum periods. She is currently working on a manuscript that comes out of her dissertation, "Made in His Image: The Origins of African American Women's Jeremiad."

Tiera C. Moore is a spoken word artist, writer, military veteran, and community organizer with interdisciplinary interests in the histories, cultures, literatures, and philosophies of African peoples. A Phi Beta Kappa graduate of the University of North Carolina at Greensboro, where she received her undergraduate degree in African American and African diaspora studies and a master's degree with a focus on global studies, she has been coordinator of programing in Lloyd International Honors College at UNC Greensboro and has served as a director of Community Play!/All Stars Alliance in the Warnersville neighborhood of Greensboro.

Tedi A. Pascarella is an advanced graduate student at Monmouth University interested in the early modern Mediterranean, gender and empire, as well as environmental history. Her thesis work focuses on how the exploitation and trade of alum affected Mediterranean empires as well as the rise of England and the relationships of religion, race, ecology, and power. Pascarella is currently working on a biographical essay, "Laskarina 'Bouboulina' Pinotsis, Greek Heroine and Ship Captain," for an ABC-CLIO online reference work *Women Who Changed the World: Their Lives, Challenges, and Accomplishments through History*. Pascarella is also researching and writing toward a publication on women and leadership in Kenya for an upcoming book edited by Dr. Julius Adekunle.

John Portlock, PhD, instructs in American history at Maine College of Art in Portland, Maine. Interested in both twentieth-century African American history as well as American military history, he recently completed a dissertation on the antiwar strain inside the modern civil rights movement entitled "Before Riverside: Black Antiwar Activism, 1917–1967." He has taught classes ranging from the history of lynching in America to the political upheavals of the 1960s.

Lauren T. Rorie is an advanced graduate student in the Department of History and Anthropology at Monmouth University. She is focusing her studies on the Black Atlantic in the nineteenth and early twentieth centuries within the larger context of the global African diaspora.

Tanya L. Roth, PhD, teaches 9th–12th-grade history at Mary Institute and Saint Louis Country Day School (MICDS), an independent JK–12 school in Saint Louis, Missouri. She received her PhD in history from Washington University in St. Louis (2011). Her chapter "'An Attractive Career for Women': Opportunities, Limitations, and Women's Integration in the Cold War Military" appears in Douglas W. Bristol and Heather Marie Stur's *Integrating the US Military* (Johns Hopkins University Press, 2017). In 2019, she won the Edward M. Coffman First Manuscript Prize for *Her Cold War: Women in the U.S. Military*, published in 2021 by the University of North Carolina Press.

Marissa Jackson Sow, JD, is currently assistant professor of law at the University of Richmond and the director of the Ronald H. Brown Center for Civil

Rights in Virginia. She earned her BA from Northwestern University and a master of laws, with merit, from the London School of Economics. Sow also holds a JD degree from Columbia University. She has clerked for judges in the Eastern District of New York and the Sixth Circuit and has also taught at NYU Law. Sow has served as general counsel in the office of the mayor of New York.

Virginia L. Summey, PhD, is a historian and faculty fellow in the Lloyd International Honors College at the University of North Carolina at Greensboro, where she also received her PhD in United States history. She has written several articles on Judge Elreta Alexander and is the author of her biography, published by the University of Georgia Press in 2021.

INDEX

References to figures are in **bold**.

Abbott, Robert, 176
abolitionist movement: countering stereotypes of Black women, 30; divine retribution and, 30; empowerment of Black women, 45; intellectualism promoting, 9
abortion: as Black genocide, 230; criminalization of, 218; ethical and legal aspects pre-nineteenth century, 216, 217; historical practices, 216–17; liberalization of practices, 218; personhood of fetus and, 217–18; right to privacy, 227
abortion, scholarly studies: historical, 219, 232n11; religion and politics, 220, 232n13; social analyses discussing race, 219–20, 232n12
Abortion and Women's Choice (Petchesky), 219
Acheson, Dean, 188
ACLU (American Civil Liberties Union), 294
activist intellectual, 8, 11n10
Adams, Betty Livingston, 8, 47
Adams, Charity, 292
Afric-American Female Intelligence Society of America, 30, 56
African American education: bolstering love of liberty and knowledge, 36; denial as means for continuing enslavement, 34–35; importance for women, 33–34; pooling of resources for children's education, 35

African American Episcopal Church (AME), 52
African American Religion (Johnson), 207
African Americans: in American Revolution and War of 1812, 33; attitude toward birth control, 245–46; Black virtue discourse, 37; mortality rates of, 241; nationalist political beliefs, 158; overidentification with race, 158; performance and acceptance by white establishment, 114; potential demonstrated by accomplishments of women, 27; schools for in the nineteenth century, 34; sexual stereotypes, 117–18; Stewart on treatment of, 21–22
African Americans in Conservative Movements (Prisock), 228
African Americans in the Revolutionary War (Lanning), 330
African Baptist Church, 51
Age of American Unreason in a Culture of Lie, The (Jacoby), 328
AIDS epidemic, youth demonstrations during, 236
Aiken, Ana, 287
Alexander, Elreta Melton, 107–22; as activist, intellectual, and producer of knowledge, 119; advocating rehabilitative justice, 111; attacking jury selection process as racially biased, 117; background of, 66, 107, 109; Black Marxist critique of, 114, 115;

Alexander, Elreta Melton (*cont.*)
    challenging status quo of segregationist South, 108; civil rights activism, 108; contributions of, 119; as defense attorney for Charles Yoes, 117; embracing Black identity, 113–14; as first Black woman graduate from Columbia Law School, 107, 109, 113; on importance of education in childhood home, 66, 109; intellectualism of, 109; on interracial harmony, 118; Judgement Day deferred sentencing program for juveniles, 111; knowledge of history and religion, 110–11; as lawyer and judge in North Carolina, 107, 109–10; light skin as advantage for, 113; marriage, 109; as member of Black middle class, 112, 119; performance highlighting contradictions of segregated society, 115; race for North Carolina Supreme Court chief justice, 118; theoretical frameworks of activism, 108; wardrobe as performance, 115–16
Alexander, Elreta Melton, writings of: poetry embodying Christian ideology and racial injustice, 108; "A Student's Plan for Peace," 110; *When Is a Man Free?*, 110
Alexander, Sadie Tanner Mossell, 107, 108
All about Love (Taylor), 265
Allen, Doris "Lucki," 316, 318
Allen, Richard, 54
All Stars Project Inc., 160
All Stars Talent Show Network, 154, 156, 159–60
Alpha Kappa Alpha sorority, 284
Ambrose, Nancy, 258–59
American Anti-Slavery Society, 57
American Civil Liberties Union (ACLU), 294
American Girls' Art Club, 208
American intellectual history: activism of Black preaching women and, 46; African American women in context of, 3, 5, 6; dominant themes from 1865 to the present, 5
American Missionary Association (AMA), 76
America's First Black Woman Political Writer (Richardson), 5
Anderson, Gladys, 91
Anderson, Marian, 284

Andrews, William L., 53
Angelou, Maya: on art of personal narrative, 261–62; Black SBNR tradition and, 262; commitment to Christian traditions and institutions, 261; death of, 265; emphasizing traditional spiritual disciplines in works, 262; as first Black woman streetcar conductor in San Francisco, 261; influence on Oprah as SBNR, 258; as member of Mt. Zion Baptist Church, 261, 270n17; as Oprah's "spiritual mother," 261; parallels with Thurman, 261; review of *Meditations of the Heart*, 261; Reynolds Professor of American Studies, Wake Forest University, 261
Angulo, A. J., 328
Ansell, Dorothy, 334
antiabortion movement: African American women in, 216; Christian ethics and sin-shaping, 217; as defense of human rights, 220; neglected in studies of twentieth-century women's movement, 218–19; participants in, 215; seeking human life amendments to Constitution, 227
anti-intellectualism: defined, 327; literature on, 328; in US military, 329
Anti-Intellectualism in American Life (Hofstadter), 328
Anti-Slavery Society (England), 50
Anti-Slavery Society of New England, 23
Appiah, Kwame Anthony, 159
Araya, Peggy (neé Wilson), 94, 95
Army Nurse Corps (1901), 330, 346n14
Army Signal Corps (WWI), 332
Ar'n't I a Woman? (White), 7–8
Articulating Life's Memory (Stormer), 219
Artis, William, 204
assemblage, theory of, 116–17, 119
Austin, Verneal, 292

Back to Africa movement, 158
Baer, Hans A., 52
Bailey, Virginia, 318
Baker, Ella: on barriers to leadership roles for women in SCLC, 99; civil rights movement and, 66, 79, 89, 223; creating

SNCC as bridge from SCLC, 101; as public intellectual, 178; as SBNR writer, 258
Baldwin, Effie Bell, 341
Baldwin, James, 138, 258
Baldwin, Lewis, 72
Baltimore Afro-American (newspaper), 91, 93
Baltimore City NAACP, civil rights protests, 90
Baltimore Colored High and Training School, 95
Bando, Thelma: as Black woman intellectual, 66; as model for contemporaries, 96; support for civil rights protestors, 90, 95–96
Barksdale, Ozell, 317
Barnett, Bernice McNair, 101–2
Barstow, Anne Llewellyn, 52
Bascom, Marion, 99–100
Bass, Charlotta (Spears), 3, 176–91; articulating Black life in America, 191; as autodidact, 179; campaign for Congress, 190; conflict with *LA Sentinal* on Black employment at Kress store, 183–84; criticized as too moderate by *The Eagle* readership, 183; as editor of the *California Eagle*, 173, 184; faith and worldview of, 186–87; fighting segregation, 177; *Forty Years*, 180; ideational odyssey of, 179; influence and impact of, 177; interest in Soviet Union, 187; investigative journalism of, 184; joining Progressive Party, 185, 188; "On the Sidewalk," 184–85, 187, 188; Progressive Party vice-presidential nominee, 190–91; as public intellectual, 173, 177–78, 179; purchase of *The Eagle*, 176; on racial uplift, 178; as regional campaign director for Wendell Wilke, 185; revering institutions of higher learning, 177; selling *The Eagle*, 184; speaking uncomfortable truths to Blacks, 179; travel to Soviet Union, 189–90
Bass, Joseph: death of, 184; as editor of the *California Eagle*, 180–82; as owner/editor of the *Montana Plaindealer*, 180
Bates, Daisy Lee, 66, 89, 92–93
Bay, Mia, 7, 8, 46

behaving Black, 158
Belief without Borders (Mercadante), 257–58
Bell, Derrick, 160
Berea College (Berea, KY), 83–84
Berkin, Carol, 330
Bethune, Mary McLeod: accomplishments of, 72; as "Black Cabinet" advisor to Roosevelt, 78, 282; on Black soldiers, 80–81; "Certain Unalienable Rights," 80–82; challenging segregated seating at public events, 75; connection to Brown and Burroughs, 73–74; Daytona Literary and Industrial Training School for Negro Girls, 75; detractors of, 282–83; including liberal arts in curriculum, 72; influence on Howard Thurman, 75; Methodist Church and, 87n57; modeling Christian values, 72; National Council of Negro Women and, 282–83; neglect as Christian intellectual, 70; on "our group of women," 65, 73–74; personal sacrifices for career, 77–78; as public intellectual, 178; racial integration of WAC and, 283; as school builder and educator, 71; support for Black WAC during WWII, 275–76, 283–84
Bethune-Cookman University, 72, 282
Bevel, Diane Nash, 100
birth control: Black community interest in, 245–46; as contested area of women's rights, 246–47; criminalization of, 218; necessity for, 245
"Black Art and the Racial Mountain" (Hughes), 197–98
Black Atlantic, The (Gilroy), 47, 59n12
Black Atlantic discourse, 47–48
Black Christ, The (Douglas), 58
Black church (American): Moravians and, 49; public activism of women, 51–52, 57; women barred from leadership roles, 98; women's reformation of, 57
Black communities: barriers to economic mobility, 29–30; marginalization and subjugation of women, 25, 26, 39n26; racially restrictive legislation, 35; writing, oratory,

362   INDEX

Black communities (*cont.*)
 and activism of (1830s), 10. *See also* free Black communities
Black Cross Nurses, 246
Black female attorneys, 66
Black Feminist Thought (Collins), 6
Black Hospital movement, 247
Black intellectualism, 45, 178. *See also* Black preaching women as public intellectuals; public intellectualism of Black women
Black Manhattan (Johnson), 207
Black Marxism (Robinson), 112
Black middle class (bourgeoisie), 112
Blackmon, Traci, 71, 84, 85n16
Blackmun, Harry A., 226–27
Black Natural Law (Lloyd), 69
Blackness, stereotypical narrative of, 178
Black Patriots and Loyalists (Gilbert), 330
Black performance: acceptance into American mainstream and, 114–15; contradictions in segregated society, 115
Black Power movement, 150
Black preaching women as public intellectuals, 45–58; activism of, 45, 47; African diaspora and, 45; American intellectual tradition and, 46; autobiographies of, 17; Early Republic and, 46; feminist theology of, 47; ideas shaped by lived experience, 46; intersectional approach to empowerment, 47; as itinerant ministers, 17–18, 45; in National era, 45; as prophets, 47, 58
Black Religious Intellectuals (Thomas), 79
Black Skin, White Masks (Fanon), 151
Black virtue, discourse of, 37
Blackwell, Elaine, 91
Black/white alliances, 28–29
Black Womanist Ethics (Cannon), 259
Black women: beauty as form of empowerment, 116; civil rights movement and discrimination against, 98–99, 293; economic influence of, 32–33; education and teaching as cornerstone of racial virtue, 36; employment status (1940), 280, 298n11; historical scholarship on, 89; importance of education, 33–34, 36; interconnection of race and gender, 116; and internationalism, 200–201; intersectional approach to empowerment, 47; "Jane Crow" racial barrier, 94, 289; lack of defense against stereotypes, 30; leadership as feminist movement, 102; multiple consciousness of, 116; poetry of, 111; political respectability of, 96; Stewart on moral leniency of, 27–28; struggle as writers against racism and sexism, 7; syncretized spiritual belief of, 26; teaching as spiritual calling, 37; as unprotected population, 27
Black women, as visual artists: advancing New Negro agenda, 196; awakening race consciousness during Harlem Renaissance, 194; expatriate status in success of, 199–200; historical neglect as intellectuals, 195; paintings and sculptures exposing truths about Blackness, 200
Black Women in the Ivory Tower, 1850–1954 (Evans), 108
Black Women's Christian Activism (Adams), 8, 47
Black Women's Intellectual Traditions (Waters and Conaway), 195
Black Women Writing Autobiography (Braxton), 56
Blain, Keisha N., 194, 200–201
Bloomberg, Michael, 165
Blount, Jacqueline Dancer, 338–39, 344
Bolding, Phyllis, 149
Bond, Julian, 100
Book of American Negro Poetry, The (Johnson), 207
Boozer, Thelma Berlack, 245
Bowser, Mary Elizabeth (Mary Jane Richards Denham), 331, 347n17
Brand Plucked from the Fire, A (Foote), 53, 55
Braxton, Joanne M., 56
bridge leadership, in civil rights movement, 101
Bristol, Douglas, Jr., 306
Brown, Charlotte Hawkins: challenging social climate of the South, 76–77; inclusion of liberal arts in curriculum, 71;

modeling Christian values, 72; neglect as Christian intellectual, 70; "our group of women," 65; and Palmer Memorial Institute, 76; personal sacrifices for career, 77–78; relationship with Berea College, 83–84; as school builder and educator, 71; as teacher at Bethany Institute, 76; "What to Teach to Negro Americans," 83–84

Brown v. Board of Education (1955), 149, 315

Burns, Kephra, 263

Burroughs, Nannie Helen: chairing Committee on Negro Housing under Hoover administration, 76; as cofounder of Northeast Self-Help Cooperative, 76; as founder of Women's Convention of the National Baptist Convention, 75; inclusion of liberal arts in curriculum, 72; lack of education after high school, 74; "Making Your Community Christian," 82; modeling Christian values, 72; National Training School for Women and Girls, 75–76; neglect as Christian intellectual, 70; "our group of women," 65; personal sacrifices for career, 77–78; as political and economic theorist, 72–73, 85n23; as school builder and educator, 71; as threat to national security during Wilson administration, 240; using her faith to bring about social and political change, 81; "What Must the Negro Do to Be Saved," 82–83; on Wilson's hypocrisy, 240

Burrow, Rufus, 72

Bury My Heart in a Free Land (H. Williams), 3–4, 9

Busby, Norma, 317, 318; oral history, 339–40

Bush, George H. W., 165

"Buy Where You Can Work" campaign (Baltimore), 90

California Eagle (newspaper): on Black support of WWI war effort, 181–82; Charlotte Bass as publisher, 173; on integration of education, 180–81; Joe Bass's editorial control of, 180; Progressive Party support, 188; pushing Republicanism, 180; on race riots and lynchings of Black Americans, 182; "red" agenda of, 188

California State Association of Colored Women, 294

Cambridge Movement (civil rights protest), 97

Campbell, Vera, 285

camp followers, 329–30

Cannon, Katie Geneva, 259

Carby, Hazel, 7, 8

Carter, J. Kameron, 69

Casper, Monica J., 219

Caudle, Violet, 334

"Certain Unalienable Rights" (Bethune), 80–82

Chapman, Mark, 71, 79

Chicago Defender (newspaper), 176

Chisholm, Shirley: alignment with mainstream feminist movements, 132; as American hero, 123; anger toward anti-Black racism, 138–39; autobiographies, 124; Black feminism of, 133–35, 143n34; Black liberation theory, 137; body of work, 126–27; as catalyst for change, 129; catchphrases associated with, 126; congressional recognition of accomplishments, 143nn29–32; distorted narrative and branding by civil rights crusaders, 124; embracing personal rage, 137; on failures and racism of white liberals and progressives, 126; feminism and critical race theory, 132; as founder of National Congress of Black Women, 133; *The Good Fight*, 124; as hero of white liberal movements, 126; on liberal white resistance to Black education and power, 127; on militant rejection of oppression, 139–40, 145n100; misappropriation of likeness, words, and legacy, 124, 127; as nursery school teacher, 138; parks and monuments honoring her, 123, 142n5; on personal as political, 137, 145n48; posthumous iconic status, 126; as public intellectual, 3, 128, 130–31; on sexism as pernicious form of oppression, 131–32; stereotypes of, 137–38; sympathetic approach to aggressive

Chisholm, Shirley (*cont.*)
   sexism, 135; transcendence over labels and categories, 141; vision for racial and gender justice, 125, 126, 139; visual depictions of, 123–24; on women's liberation, 142n22; writings of, 120. See also *Unbought and Unbossed* (Chisholm)
Chisholm, Shirley, political activities: elections shattering race and gender barriers, 125; feminist politics and advocacy, 127; as first Black woman elected to House of Representatives, 128; as first woman to run for US president, 67; "folding chair" decolonizing table, 140; misogynistic campaign tactics used against, 134–35; as political moderate, 132, 144n56; refusing to play by Democratic Party rules, 144n73
Christianity: Black women preachers and, 46; Holiness tradition in, 45; reimagining Christ, 58; rejection by Alice Walker, 264
Christianity on Trial (Chapman), 79
Christian moralism: historical attitudes about abortion, 217; race and, 230; women's issues as human rights, 239
Church for the Fellowship of All Peoples, 260
City-Wide Young People's Forum (Baltimore NAACP), 92
Civic Interest Group (CIG), 93, 100, 101
civic righteousness, 8, 47
Civil Rights Act of 1964, 117
civil rights movement: assumptions of male superiority in, 89; bridge leadership by women mobilizing, 101; as church-based affair, 98; and Democrats, 220; gender exclusion in, 89, 101; liberal Democrat participants as pro-life supporters, 220; male discrimination against Black women, 98–99; similarities between paternalism and racial arrogance, 94; uplift and equality of Black women, 26; women oppressed by race, class, and gender, 89, 98; Woolworths sit-in, 117
civil rights movement, Morgan State College: Black female student involvement, 89, 90; Cambridge Movement, 97; integration of Northwood Movie Theater, 90–91, 95, 96, 98; parental respectability of protesters, 96; support from white students from nearby colleges, 96
Clark, Septima, 10
Clarke, Yvette, 128
Clinton, Bill, 247–48, 251n4
Clinton, Hillary, 251n4
Coates, Ta-Nehisi, 9
Cold War, military career paths for women, 307
Cole, Michael, 152
Collier-Thomas, Bettye, 7, 8, 47
Collini, Stefan, 9
Collins, Norma, 93–94
Collins, Patricia Hill: on multiple consciousness of Black women, 116; on public intellectual, 9; themes in Black women's feminist consciousness, 6–7; "What's in a Name? Womanism, Black Feminism, and Beyond," 195
Collins, Winifred Quick, 334
Colored Women's League, 299n23
Color Purple, The (Walker), 262, 267–68
Come Shouting to Zion (Frey and Wood), 49
Coming of Age in Mississippi (Moody), 56
Committee for a Unified Independent Party, 163
community investment by Black women, 32
Comstock Act (1873), 218
Conaway, Carol B., 195
Cone, James, 259
Confirmation (Taylor and Burns), 265, 267
Congress of Industrial Organizations (CIO), 184
Congress of Racial Equality (CORE), 91, 259
contraception. *See* birth control
Cooper, Anna Julia: as Black Christian public intellectual, 69, 70; call for gender-conscious antiracism, 281; on choice for Black women, 285; earning doctoral degree, 85n10; on intersectionality of gendered spheres, 289; as "womanist foremother," 70, 85n11
Cornish, Howard L., 97

Council on African Affairs, 183, 188
Craft, Roxan, 249
"Creation" (Johnson), 207
Crenshaw, Kimberlé, 116, 132
Crichlow, Ernest, 204
Crisis, The (magazine), 176, 198
Critchlow, Donald T., 220
Cugoano, Ottobah, 48
cultural postures and attitudes, Black-identified, 159
Culture Wars (Hunter), 223
culture wars: Black women in, 4; Elders as authority figure, 236, 237; historiography of 1990s and, 237, 251n3; traditionalist/modernist conflicts over morality, 222–23
Cummings, Edna, 336
Curtis, Constance, 294

Danaher, John A., 334
Daring to Be Bad (Echols), 219
Daughters of Conference (AME), 52
Davis, Angela, 178
Davis, Elva, 91
Davis, Henrietta Vinton, 246
Davis, Jefferson, 331
Daytona Literary and Industrial Training School for Negro Girls, 76
Defenders of the Unborn (D. K. Williams), 220–21
Delano, Jane A., 240
Delany, Martin, 178
Delta Sigma Theta sorority, 133, 134, 284
Dennison, Joyce, 94, 96
Department of Defense, US, 297, 307
Derby, Doris, 100
desegregation of armed forces: enlistment standards and, 313; Executive Order 9981 requiring, 276, 310, 311–12, 336; leadership of women officers, 312; social change and, 315; women's services and, 312, 336
Development School for Youth, 154, 157, 160
Diagne, Blaise, 198
diasporada, 210–11, 213n56
Disciplines of the Spirit (Thurman), 260–61

Dodson, Jualynne E., 47, 52
Dooley, Mary, 317, 319–20
Double V campaign (WWII), 279
Douglas, Aaron, 196
Douglas, Kelly Brown, 58
Douglas, Nicole, 339
Douglass, Frederick: American Anti-Slavery Society and, 57; jeremiadic discourse, 20; lack of higher education, 179; orations against slavery, 10; public intellectual tradition and, 69, 178
Du Bois, W. E. B.: on art as propaganda, 196–97; as Black intellectual, 10, 20, 69; "Criteria for Negro Art," 196; as editor of *The Crisis*, 176; on elevation of Blacks through Black art, 198; as internationalist, 199; launching first Pan-African Congress, 198; objecting to Savage's rejection by Fontainebleau School, 201–2; painting of, **199**, 207; on racial policies of Woodrow Wilson, 198; on "race women," 195; as SBNR writer, 258; on "talented tenth," 178, 198; visual arts advancing New Negro agenda, 196
Duggan, Lisa, 237
Duncan, Sara, 57
DuVernay, Ava, 236

Earley, Charity Adams, 335–36
Eason, Michele Bowers, 343
Echols, Alice, 219
ecological validity, 152
economic mobility barriers, Black vs. white population, 29–30
Edlin, Kenneth, 228
Edwards, Gertrude, 317, 319
Eisenhower, Dwight D., 333, 347n29
Elaw, Zilpha: as Black women preacher, 45, 52–53; conversion at camp meeting, 55; spiritual autobiography, 46, 53, 55
Elders, Joycelyn, 236–51; as Arkansas director of public health, 241–42; attending University of Arkansas Medical School on GI Bill, 239; autobiography of, 237–38; changing attitudes toward, 250; childhood of, 237; connections between sexual

Elders, Joycelyn (*cont.*)
  health and overall health, 241; on consistency in health education, 250; cultural context in criticism of, 243; discourses on sex education, 4, 237, 242–43; on importance of birth control, 245, 248; on masturbation, 244; military service of, 239; omission from consideration as public intellectual, 222; as public intellectual outside of government, 236, 248–49, 251; scholarship to Philander Smith College, 238; as University of Arkansas faculty member, 239
Elders, Joycelyn, as surgeon general in Clinton administration: congressional hearing preceding resignation, 249–50; as first African American woman surgeon general, 174; focus on sex education, 242–43; partisanship in appointment as surgeon general, 249; on Public Health Service abuses at Tuskegee University, 247; resignation as surgeon general, 236, 237, 243, 244; White House statement on resignation, 244
Elshtain, Jean Bethke, 6
Engendering Church (Dodson), 47
enslavement, self-writing as liberation from, 56
Equiano, Olaudah, 48, 50
Essence (magazine), 264
Ethiopia Awakening (Fuller exposition), 208–9
eugenics: African American support for racial improvement, 245; disguised as Christian morality and uplift, 240; as pseudoscientific belief system, 239–40; white vs. Black racial differences, 246
Evans, Sara, 219
Evans, Stephanie Y., 108
Even the Stars Look Lonesome Tonight (Angelou), 261

"Faith on the Line in the New Civil War" (Jefferson), 230, 234n52
Fanon, Frantz, 150, 152–53
Farmer, James, 134–35

Farmer, James, Jr., 259
Farr, Cecilia Konchar, 256
Fauset, Jessie Redmon, 206
Female Anti-Slavery Society, 57
Female Literary Society of Philadelphia, 56
feminism: of Chisholm, 132; intersectional, 133; women's issues as human rights, 239
feminist consciousness, Black: gender-specific sexualized violence in, 55; origin of, 7; spiritual autobiographies and, 54–55; Stewart and, 51
fetus. *See* personhood of fetus
Fields, Myrtis Smith, 340
Finney, Charles Grandison, 5
Fishburne, Lillian Elaine, 338
Fisk University (Nashville, TN), 93
Flakes, Lacia Alderman, 343
Flamming, Douglas, 177
Floyd, Lois, 287
Flunder, Yvette, 71, 84, 85n16
Foote, Julia: AME Zion Church and, 53; as Black woman preacher, 52, 53; on mother's enslavement, 55; spiritual autobiography of, 53, 55
Ford's Theatre (Baltimore, MD), student protests against segregated seating, 91
Forgotten Sisterhood, A (McCluskey and Laney), 73
Fort Devens, Black strike against, 293–95
Forten, James, 57
Forten, Margaretta, 57
Forty Years (Bass), 180
Foster, Ezola, 229
Franklin, Benjamin, 5
Frazier, E. Franklin, 78
free Black communities: complacency among well-to-do, 24; educational barriers of early nineteenth century, 34; high moral standard requirements, 24; importance of education for women, 33–34; private ownership of businesses and residences, 32; teaching as spiritual calling for women, 37
Free Speech and Headlight (newspaper), 177
Frey, Sylvia R., 49
Fried, Marlene Gerber, 219
Friedan, Betty, 132

Frund, Arlette, 5
fugitive slave laws, 35
Fulani, Lenora B., 148–66; Black and independent alliances for political reform, 16, 165; Black Power movement and, 150; Black vs. white feminism, 150; building network of independent political activists, 162–63; campaigns promoting structural political reforms, 163; as developmental psychologist, 148, 149, 166; development of postmodern independent Black leadership in US, 162; graduate degrees, 151; postmodernization of Black politics, 164; as postmodern revolutionary, 148–49, 167n3; programs created by, 157–58, 165; questioning efforts to reform traditional psychology, 151; racism and political power, 159; support for Ross Perot, 162; urging African Americans to diversify political options, 160; on Vygotsky, 153
Fulani, Lenora B., presidential election of 1988: challenging bipartisan control of electoral process, 160; challenging Democratic party claim to Black and Latino communities, 161; exclusion from presidential debates, 161; as first woman on presidential ballot in all fifty states, 67, 148, 161, 162, 167n2; as milestone in terms of gender and race, 161; New Alliance Party ticket, 160–61; six different running mates representing different constituencies, 160
Fulani, Lenora B., publications: *The Making of a Fringe Candidate*, 149, 165; "Poor Women of Color Do Great Therapy," 154
Fuller, Meta Warrick: birth and art education, 208; as Black visual artist during Harlem Renaissance, 195; *Ethiopia Awakening*, 208–9; ideas of New Negro era in works, 174; *Mary Turner: A Silent Protest against Mob Violence*, 209–10; as "race artist" and public sculptor, 210; racial uplift as recurring theme in works, 210. *See also* Black women, as visual artists

Futrell, Francis, dismissal from WAC, 291, 294

Gaines, Kevin K., 70
Gamin (sculpture), 202, **203**
Gardiner General Military Hospital (Chicago, IL), 296
Garrison, William Lloyd, 56, 57
Garvey, Marcus: anticontraception rhetoric of, 247; "Back to Africa" movement, 158, 198; on birth control for Black populations, 245, 248; counseling return to Africa, 178; Pan-African movement and, 246; Universal Negro Improvement Association, 182
Gates, Henry Louis, Jr., 160
Gergen, Kenneth, 159
GI Bill (Servicemen's Readjustment Act of 1944), 297, 320
Giddings, Paula, 7, 281
GI Jane Crow, 279, 289, 297
Gilbert, Alan, 330
Gilbert, Anne Hart, 48, 49
Gill, Tiffany, 308
Gillem Board, 308
Gilroy, Paul, 47, 59n12
Glaude, Eddie, 69
God's Trombones (Johnson), 207
Good Fight, The (Chisholm), 124
Goodman, Philip, 90, 95
Gordon, Linda, 218
Gordon, Violet, 279, 284, 297–98
Gospel According to Oprah, The (Nelson), 256
Graham, Shirley, 189
Gramsci, Antonio, 179
Grant, Jacquelyn, 98
Gray, Alfred M., Jr., 275, 327
Griffin, Farah J., 6, 46
Grimké, Sarah Moore, 5
Gronniosaw, James, 48
Gwynn Oak Amusement Park (Gwynn Oak, MD), 90, 97–98

Hagelin, John, 162
Hallinan, Vincent, 191

Hamer, Fannie Lou, 65, 89, 229
Hancock, Gordon, 73
Hands Across America campaign (1986), 236–37
Hansberry, Lorraine, 189
Hansen, Juanita M., 100
Harlem Institute for Social Therapy and Research, 154
Harlem Renaissance: art as messages of Black freedom, 196; Black women visual artists and race reform, 194, 195; as cultural movement, 196; purpose of visual art during, 195
Harmon Foundation, 206, 208
Harris, Angelique, 248
Harris, Irene Trowell-Harris, 338
Harris, Jennifer, 256–57
Harrison, Bonnie Claudia, 210
Harris-Perry, Melissa, 69
Hartman, Andrew, 251nn3–4
Hartmann, Betsy, 219
Hart sisters (Anne and Elizabeth), 48, 49
Haugeberg, Karissa, 215, 220, 221
Haywood, Chanta M., 46, 47
Heba, Dwain, 237
Height, Dorothy, 100
"Hello Girls" (switchboard operators), 332
H. G. Hill Supermarket (Nashville, TN), 93–94
Hicks, Helena (neé Sorrell), 92, 100
Hicks, Linda, 317
Higginbotham, Evelyn Brooks, 7, 8, 46–47, 83
high fashion, as power statement, 116
Hine, Darlene Clark, 7, 8
History of Mary Prince, a West Indian Slave, The (Prince), 50
Hobby, Oveta Culp: dispatching Black WACs overseas, 296; providing little support for Black WACs, 287–88; as WAC director, 283, 284, 306
Hofstader, Richard, 328
Holm, Jeanne, 313, 315, 316
Holmes, Eugene, 80
Holzman, Lois, 152, 153, 155
hooks, bell, 132

Hooper's Restaurant protest (Baltimore, MD), 93
Hoover administration, failing to implement *Negro Housing Report*, 76
Hope, John, 198
House Un-American Activities Committee, 188
Houston, Charles, 294
Howard, Michelle Janine, 338
Hughes, Langston, 197–98
human development, theories of, 152
Hunter, James Davison, 223
Hunter, Jane, 294
Hunter, Nan D., 237
Hunter-Gault, Charlayne, 137–38
Hunton, Addie W., 198
Hurley, Ruby, 294
Hurston, Zora Neale, 4, 258
Hutchinson, Anne, 5

identity politics, destructive effects of, 159
Idiot America (Pierce), 328
Illouz, Eva, 256
Incidents in the Life of a Slave Girl (Jacobs), 54
Independence Party of New York, 163
Independent Daughters of Hope, 52
independent voters, 163
In Search of Our Mother's Garden (Walker), 263–64
Institute for Urban and Minority Education, Columbia University, 160
intellectual tradition, 4–5, 194
Interesting Narrative of the Life of Olaudah Equiano, The (Equiano), 48
intersectionality: Black WACs and, 289; theory of, 116–17, 119, 132
In the Spirit (Taylor), 265
"Invisible Southern African American Women Leaders in the Civil Rights Movement" (Barnett), 101–2
Ipothia (Brooklyn College student group), 134
Irvine, Janice M., 242

Jackson, Ada, 189, 207
Jackson, Jesse, 69, 161

Jackson, Lillie Carroll: civil rights movement and, 66, 90, 91, 97; as Maryland SCLC chapter leader, 99; as president of the Baltimore City NAACP, 90
Jackson, Willie, 69
Jacobs, Alan, 68
Jacobs, Harriet, 9, 54
Jacoby, Susan, 328
"Jane Crow" (racial barrier), 94, 289. *See also* GI Jane Crow
Jefferson, Mildred Fay, 215–31; antiabortion activism, 228, 231; birth and pregraduate education, 221; changing Reagan's views on abortion, 224; conservatism conflicting with Black protest ideologies, 222; extreme right-wing worldview of, 229; as far-right conservative Republican opposing abortion, 223–24; as far-right culture warrior, 222; holistic arguments about abortion, 224–25; ideas shaping conservative politics, 231; intellectual contributions to antiabortion cause, 222; intersectional approach to abortion, 229–31; as Massachusetts Citizens for Life cofounder, 224; medical degrees, internships, and residencies, 221–22; as NRLC cofounder and president, 174, 222, 227; on personhood of fetus, 215, 216; positioning NRLC as major force in American politics, 228; pro-life movement and, 3, 4, 174, 216, 228; as public intellectual shaping antiabortion argument, 215, 220–21, 222, 223, 231; rightist ideologies and, 231; on secular humanism, 230
Jefferson, Mildred Fay, publications of: "Abortion: Self-Defeat Solution," 224–26; "The Casualties of War," 230, 234n55; "Faith on the Line in the New Civil War," 230, 234n52; "The Nature of the Race/Class Factor in Abortion," 230–31, 234n57; "Where Did All the Money Go?," 229, 234n46
Jefferson, Thomas, 5
Jenkins, Adah, 91–92
jeremiad, American: market revolution and, 20–21; political discourse in eighteenth and nineteenth centuries and, 19–20

jeremiadic tradition of Black women: American revolutionary ideals and experiences of free and enslaved Black women, 20; Black women's intellectual communities and, 20; core themes of, 26; rejecting African American stereotypes, 20; Stewart and foundations of, 19–38; valorizing Black womanhood in public forums, 20
Jesus, Jobs, and Justice (Collier-Thomas), 8, 47
Jesus and the Disinherited (Thurman), 259
"Jim Crow" laws, 94
Johnson, Amelia E., 108
Johnson, Brenda, 317
Johnson, Carole, 93–94
Johnson, Charles S., 196
Johnson, Clara, 317, 318
Johnson, Dovey: enlistment in WAC, 283–84; GI Bill and law degree, 297; on outsider status in white man's army, 289; recruiting Black women for WAAC, 278
Johnson, E. Patrick, 114
Johnson, Ernestine, 316, 319
Johnson, James Weldon: advocating peaceful protests, 210; attending Pan-African Congress, 198; *The Harp*, 205; publications of, 207; Weldon's portrait of, 207
Johnson, Juanita, 317, 320
Johnson, Loretta, 319
Johnson, Lyndon B., 117
Johnson, Mordecai, 69–70, 71–72
Johnson, Violet, 47
Jones, Edith Irby, 238
Jones, Ezra Earl, 249
Jones, Haller, 238
Jones, Jacqueline, 296, 297
Jones, Martha S., 6, 7, 46, 279
Joycelyn Elders, M.D. (Elders and Chanoff), 237–38
Judgement Day program, 111

Kennedy, Florynce, 107, 108
Killing the Black Body (Roberts), 219
King, Alveda, 222
King, Lena, 336

King, Martin Luther, Jr.: ethical and intellectual beliefs of, 72; misappropriation of words and legacy, 124; as public intellectual, 10, 69, 178; on role of Southern Negro women, 99; as theologian, 259; urging America to recapture revolutionary spirit, 187
Kinloch, John, 185
Knight, Gwendolyn, 204

Lane, William Preston, Jr., 91
Laney, Lucy, 73
Lang, Roslyn Garfield, 96–97
Lanning, Michael Lee, 330
Laughing Boy, The (Savage), 202–3
Lazard, Joshua L.: "Christian intellectual" definition, 70; omission of Black women as public intellectuals, 69–70; rebuttal of Lloyd's essay, 68, 69–70
Lee, Jarena: as Black woman preacher, 17, 52–53; on call to preach, 54–55; challenging male autonomy in Black church, 54; founding school for Black women in Burlington, NJ, 53; intersectional approach to Black empowerment, 9; joining American Anti-Slavery Society, 57; public intellectualism of, 5; spiritual autobiography of, 45, 46
legislation, racially restrictive (early nineteenth century), 35
Lessons in Living (Taylor), 265
Letter to My Daughter (Angelou), 261–62
Leveen, Lois, 331
Levinson, Marie, 246
Lewie, Reva, 97
Lewis, David Levering, 200
Liberator, The (journal), 56, 57
Library of Congress, Veterans History Project, 338–45
Life and Religious Experience of Jerena Lee, The (Lee), 45, 53, 54–55
"Lift Every Voice and Sing" (Johnson), 205
Lightfoot, Natasha, 49
Ligon, Ellen Barret, 246
Lloyd, Vincent, 68–69, 84n4
Locke, Alain, 200

Lofton, Kathryn, 257, 266–67, 268
Logan, Rayford, 80
Lorde, Andre, 149, 167n9
Los Angeles Sentinal (newspaper), 183–84
Lucas, Ruth, 320–21
Luker, Ralph, 258
Lurkins, Nancy, 246
Luscomb, Florence, 294
Lynch, Shola, 125, 142n18, 143n34
lynchings and race riots (1917–1919), 182

Making of a Fringe Candidate, The (Fulani), 149, 165
Making of Pro-Life Activists, The (Munson), 219
Making of the Unborn Patient, The (Casper), 219
"Making Your Community Christian" (Burroughs), 82
Malcolm, Joycestane, 316
Malcolm X, 179
Maloney, Francis T., 334
Mandela, Nelson, 124, 142n12
Marable, Manning, 178
March on Washington for Jobs and Freedom (1963), 100–101
market economy (new market), American jeremiad and, 20–21
Marrow, Gloria, 96
Marshall, George (General), 335
Marshall, Thurgood, 72, 293
Marx, Karl, 153
Maryland, women as civil rights leaders, 99
Mary Turner (Fuller), 209–10
Massachusetts Female Anti-Slavery Society, 57
Matthews, Lloyd J., 328–29
Mays, Benjamin Elijah, 69, 79
McArthur, Suzie, 316
McCluskey, Audrey Thomas, 73, 82
McDuffie, Erik, 190
McFadden, Ina M., 285
McKinnell, Stephanie, 343
Meditations of the Heart (Thurman), 261, 262
Meier, August, 95

Melton, Alain Reynolds, 108
Melton, J. C.: as Baptist minister, 66, 108; importance of education in home, 107, 109, 112
Memoirs of the Life, Religious Experience, Ministerial Travels and Labours of Mrs. Zilpha Elaw, an American Female of Colour (Elaw), 53, 55
Mercadante, Linda A., 257–58
Meredith, James, 98
Mershon, Sherie, 306
Methodist Church, segregation in, 81, 87n57
Military Intelligence Corps Hall of Fame (Fort Huachuca, AZ), 331
military service: African American women in gender-appropriate roles during the eighteenth and nineteenth centuries, 329–30; anti-intellectualism of, 327, 328–29; Black women in postwar military, 276, 305–22; burdens and obstacles for Black women, 345; economic and educational opportunities, 307, 317; equal citizenship claims in recruitment, 307; friendships with white women, 318; moral suspicion of former military women, 335; opportunities for Black men, 305; oral history interviews (Black women veterans), 338–45; as positive experience for African Americans, 320; public intellectualism and, 275, 305, 328; quotas for African American nurses, 330–31; racial discrimination experiences, 318–20; reimagining Black women's citizenship, 305–6; secondary sources on, 337; white vs. Black male sexism, 343–44; women as spies, 331; women replacing men in noncombatant roles, 332–34; women's reasons for joining, 275; women's service memoirs, 336–37. *See also* desegregation of armed forces; Women's Army Corps (WAC); *specific branches*
Miller, Dorothy, 285, 286
Milne, Seumas, 142n12
Milner, Lucille, 294
Mind and Society (Vygotsky), 153

Miseducation (Angulo), 328
Mis-Education of the Negro, The (Woodson), 112
Mitchell, Juanita Jackson: civil rights movement and, 90; as leader in Maryland SCLC chapter, 99; as legal council for Baltimore City NAACP, 90, 97
Mitchell, Luevenia, 317
Montana Plaindealer (newspaper), 180
Moody, Anne, 56
Moore, Brenda, 293
Moore, Carolyn, 293
moralism. *See* Christian moralism
Morgan, Kay Summersby, 347n29
Morgan State College (Baltimore, MD): Black women and civil rights movement at, 89–102; civil rights activities during WWII, 91; getting arrested as protest goal, 94–95; high school students joining protests, 93; mass arrest of civil rights protestors (1963), 90–91; shortage of women student leaders as role models, 100; student demands for improved facilities (1947), 91
Morrison, Anna, 293, 294, 297
Morrison, Toni, 4
Motley, Constance Baker, 107
Muhammad, Elijah, 79
Munson, Ziad W., 219
Murphy, Carl, 100
Murray, Florence, 284, 294
Murray, Pauli: Black freedom movement and, 79; as Black woman preacher, 46; on "Jane Crow" racial barrier, 94, 289–90; as public intellectual, 4
mutual aid societies, 52
mysticism, as feminist weapon, 52

NAACP. *See* National Association for the Advancement of Colored People (NAACP)
NACWC. *See* National Association of Colored Women's Clubs (NACWC)
Nader, Ralph (Green Party), 162
Nash, Diane, 94

National Association for the Advancement of Colored People (NAACP): Black women joining, 282; *The Crisis*, 176, 198; founders of, 10

National Association of College Women, 95

National Association of Colored Women (NACW, 1896–1904), 37, 281, 299n21, 332

National Association of Colored Women's Clubs (NACWC): declining membership of young women, 282; impetus for establishment, 281, 299n23; as largest civil rights organization in early twentieth century, 282

National Association of Women's Deans and Advisors of Colored Schools, 95

National Baptist Convention, Women's Convention, 75

National Congress of Black Women, 133, 134

National Council of Negro Women (NCNW): Bethune and founding of, 282–83; goals, 282; Height as president, 100; Thurman support for, 75

National Federation of Afro-American Women, 299n23

nationalist political beliefs, 158

National Medical Association (NMA), 240

National Nurses' Headquarters and Registry, 240

National Right to Life Committee (NRLC): Jefferson as cofounder and president, 174; as major force in American politics, 228; membership in late 1970s, 215

National Security Act (1947), 307

National Training School for Women and Girls (Washington, DC), 75–76

National Women's Political Caucus, 144n52

NATO (North Atlantic Treaty Organization), 188

Navy Nurse Corps (1908), 330

Negro Handbook, The (Murray), 284, 294, 300n44

Negro History Bulletin, 73

Negro Housing (Committee on Negro Housing), 76

Neimore, John, 176

Nelson, Jennifer, 219

Nelson, Marcia Z., 256

Nembhard, Jessica Gordon, 72–73

New Alliance Party, 160–61

Newcomb, James, 118

New England Anti-Slavery Society, 29, 56, 57

New Jersey Federation of Colored Women's Clubs, 57

Newman, Fred, 152, 153, 155, 156

New Negro, The (Locke), 200

New Negro movement, 174, 247

New Right: antiabortion activism, 220; conservative women's views on abortion, 220–21; minimizing Jefferson's contribution to antiabortion movement, 222

New Woman movement, 247

New York World's Fair (1939), 205

Niebuhr, Reinhold, 68

Nixon, Richard, "Southern Strategy" of, 118

North Atlantic Treaty Organization (NATO), 188

North Carolina Agricultural and Technical State University, 107

Northeast Self-Help Cooperative, 76

Northwood Movie Theater, integration of, 90–91, 95, 96, 98

Northwood Shopping Center (Baltimore, MD), protests and sit-ins, 92–93

NRLC. *See* National Right to Life Committee (NRLC)

Obama, Barack H.: presidential election of 2008, 162, 163; Winfrey's endorsement of, 4

October Revolution, ideals of, 187

Ohio State Federation of Colored Women, 294

One Woman's Army (Earley), 335–36

"On the Death of General Wooster" (Wheatley), 50

Operation Conversation: Cops and Kids, 157; police shooting of Sean Bell, 157

Oprah Phenomenon, The (Harris and Watson), 256–57

Oprah: The Gospel of an Icon (Lofton), 257, 266–67

"Oprah Winfrey and Spirituality" (Martin), 257
Oprah Winfrey and the Glamour of Misery (Illouz), 256
Oprah Winfrey Show, The, 256
organic intellectuals, 8, 11n10, 179
Orr, Judith, on abortion in ancient Egypt, 216
OWN: The Oprah Winfrey Network, 256, 266

Paine, Thomas, 5
Painter, Nell I., 7, 8
Palmer, Alice Freeman, 76
Palmer Memorial Institute (Sedalia, NC), 76
Pan-Africanism movement, 182, 247
parental respectability of protesters, 96
Parker, Jane, 294
Parks, Rosa, 10, 65, 89
participant-observer, Black intellectual as, 178
passing as white, 113
Pataki, George, 165
Path Made Clear, The (Winfrey), 268
patriarchal system, European origin of, 101
Patriot Party, 163
Patterson, Betty, 91
Patterson, Louise Thompson, 178, 189, 190
Paul, Sarah, 57
Paul, Thomas, 51
Pentecostalism, 54
performative leadership, 108
Perot, Ross, 162
Personal Power (Evans), 219
personhood of fetus: abortion as mortal sin, 215; existence of soul required for, 217–18; Jefferson and antiabortion movement, 216, 225
Petchesky, Rosalind, 219
Philadelphia Anti-Slavery Society, 57
Phillipps, Leon A., 237
Phyllis Schlafly and Grassroots Conservatism (Critchlow), 220
Piaget, Jean, 152
Pickens, Harriet Ida, 335
Pierce, Charles, 328

Planned Parenthood v. Casey (1992), 227
Player, Willa, 96
political respectability of Black women, 96
"Poor Women of Color Do Great Therapy" (Fulani), 154
Posner, Richard, 9
Preen, Mildred, 113–14
Pregnancy and Power (Solinger), 219–20
President's Committee on Civil Rights (1946), 310–11, 322n17
Pressley, Ayanna, 128
Prince, Mary: activist tradition and, 45; Black Atlantic discourses, 48; dictating narrative of her life to Susanna Strickland, 50; enslavement of, 50
Pringle, Thomas, 50
Prisock, Louis G., 228, 229
Progressive Era, feminist activities of, 333
Progressive Party: Bass as vice-presidential nominee, 190–91; Communist endorsement of, 188; as far-left intellectual redoubt of American politics, 188; founding convention at Independence Hall, 189
pro-life movement: defense of Christian moral values, 230; history before *Roe v. Wade*, 220
prophesying, gaining authority over male-dominated church via, 47
Prophesying Daughters (Haywood), 46
Protten, Rebecca: biography and accomplishments of, 48–49; Black Atlantic discourses, 48; marriage to Moravian missionary, 48, 49; occupying middle ground between slavery and freedom, 49
"Prove It on Me" (song), 56
Puar, Jasbir K., 116
public intellectualism, Christian: declining influence on popular culture, 68; Lazard's exclusion of Black women, 70–71; Lloyd on appropriate spokesmen for, 69; neglecting Black women intellectuals of early twentieth century, 65, 71; women's rights movement and decline of, 68, 84n2
public intellectualism and intellectuals: defined, 9, 11n10, 327; military as sensible path to self-betterment, 328; military

public intellectualism and intellectuals (*cont.*) relationship with, 328–29; military service as form of discourse, 305; in post-Vietnam military, 276–77, 327–45; role of, 237

public intellectualism of Black women: conservative Black women intellectuals omitted from studies, 222; distinctive tradition of, 6, 55; in eighteenth century, 5; feminist and racial justice work of Shirley Chisholm, 129, 130–31; foundation of, 9; Lloyd's recognition of, 69; moral and religious concerns, 6; neglect of Christian intellectuals, 65, 71; overview, 17–18; public address and self-writing in, 55; transformation of racial state as goal, 9; in US history, 3

Putney, Martha: on expectations of Black WACs, 279; on military benefits propelling Black veterans into middle class, 297; on treatment of Black WACs, 286, 297; on WAC attitudes toward Bethune, 283

race: American racial and gender inequalities, 22; consciousness and Black women visual artists, 194; intellectuals offering practical steps to racial uplift, 178; lack of biological evidence for racial differences, 159; "race women," 195, 200; riots and economic disparities (1830s), 21; Stewart on racial progress, 35

racial hierarchy (American): discrimination under, 241; ideology of, 240; power of privilege, 113

racism and racial prejudice, 29, 158

Rainey, Gertrude "Ma," 56

Randolph, A. Philip, 101

Randolph, Florence Spearing, 46, 47, 57

Rangel, Charles, 165

Reading Oprah (Farr), 256

Read's Drug Stores (Baltimore, MD), integration of, 92

Reagan, Ronald, 174, 224

Reconstructing Womanhood (Carby), 8

Reform Party, 163

rehabilitative justice, 111

Religion and the Pure Principles of Morality (Stewart), 21–23, 51

Religion Dispatches, 68, 84n3

religious moralism, 49. *See also* Christian moralism

Reminiscences of My Life in Camp with the 33rd U.S. Colored Troops (Taylor), 330

Remond, Sarah, 57

Reproductive Rights and Wrongs (Hartmann), 219

Republican Women (Rymph), 220

Reserve of the United States Coast Guard (SPARS), 280, 335

Revolutionary Mothers (Berkin), 330

Richardson, Beah, 190

Richardson, Gloria, 66, 90, 97

Richardson, Marilyn, 5

Righteous Discontent (Higginbotham), 8, 46–47

Right to Life Crusade (1980), 228

Roberts, Blain, 116

Roberts, Dorothy, 219

Robeson, Eslanda, 189

Robin, Corey, 9

Robinson, Cedrick, 112

Robinson, Jo Ann, 10

Robinson, Thelma, 279, 292, 295

Robnett, Belinda, 101

Rodrique, Jesse, 245

Roe v. Wade (1973): galvanizing antiabortion activists, 227–28; as nuanced decision on abortion issue, 226–27; pro-life movement before, 220

Rogers, Edith Nurse, 334

Roosevelt, Eleanor, 78, 334

Roosevelt, Franklin D., 78, 295

Ross, Loretta, 219

Ruffin, Josephine, 281, 299n23

Rymph, Catherine, 220

Salem Female Anti-Slavery Society, 57

Sanger, Margaret, 218, 245, 246

Savage, Augusta, 173, 201–5; aspirations of, 205; birth and early experiments with sculpture, 201; as Black visual artist during Harlem Renaissance, 194, 195; *The Harp*, **204**; Julius Rosenwald Fellowship for *Gamin*, 202, **203**; *The Laughing Boy*, 202–3; rejected by Fontainebleau School of Fine Arts because of race, 201. *See also* Black women, as visual artists

Savage, Barbara Dianne: on Bethune, Burroughs, and Brown as "Southern Black religious intellectuals," 71, 79; on Bethune and Burroughs as Christian public intellectuals, 73; on Burroughs as political and economic theorist, 72–73; on Frazier's criticism of Bethune, 78; on tradition of Black women's intellectualism, 6, 46; *Your Spirits Walk Beside Us*, 73, 79

Savage Studio of Arts and Crafts (Harlem, NY), 203–4

SBNR. *See* spiritual but not religious (SBNR) writing

Schlossman, Steven, 306

Schreiner, Olive, influence on Thurman, 259, 260

SCLC. *See* Southern Christian Leadership Conference (SCLC)

Scott, Coretta, 189

Seacole, Mary, 48

Second Baptist Church (Los Angeles, CA), 186

Second Great Awakening, 54

Second Pan-African Congress (London, 1921), 183

secular humanists, 230

Segregated Scholars, The (Wilson), 108

segregation, Black performance and contradictions in, 115

Seldon, Barbara, 317

self-life writing, 55, 56

Sesay, Chernoh, Jr., on Black intellectuals, 195

Sesquicentennial International Exposition (Philadelphia, 1926), 206

sex education: changing attitudes toward, 250; Elders discourses during Clinton administration, 4, 242–43; Irvine on, 242; as taboo in conservative circles, 249

sexual health (WHO definition), 243

sexualized violence, 55

Sex Wars (Duggan and Hunter), 237

Sharp, Susie, 118

Sharpton, Al, 69, 163

Shug Avery (character), 262, 267

Siewert, Eloise, 317

Silent Covenant (Bell), 160

Silliman, Jael, 219

Siskel, Gene, 266

Sisters of the Good Shepherd, 52

slave labor, 21

slave narratives, 53

Slowe, Lucy Diggs: as Bando's mentor, 95; civil rights movement and, 66, 90

Smith, Ruby Doris, 100

SNCC (Student Nonviolent Coordinating Committee), 93, 100

social change and armed forces, 315

social therapeutics, 160

social therapy, 153, 156–57

Sojourners for Truth and Justice (STJ), 190

Sojourner Truth (Painter), 8

Solinger, Rickie, 219–20

Souls of Black Folk (Du Bois), 10

Southern Christian Leadership Conference (SCLC): Baker creating bridge to SNCC, 101; women's leadership roles (Maryland chapter), 99

"Southern Strategy" of Richard Nixon, 118

SPARS (Reserve of the United States Coast Guard), 280, 335

Spears, Charlotta A. *See* Bass, Charlotta (Spears)

Spelman College, Thurman and, 259

Spence, Rosalie Cornish, 97

Spencer, Dorothy, 316, 320

spies, women as, 331

spiritual autobiographies, 53–54

spiritual belief, syncretized, 26

spiritual but not religious (SBNR) writing: Angelou and, 262; definition, 257–58; scholarship on, 257–58

spiritualism, 52

Squier, Owen, 332
State of the American Mind, The (Bauerlein and Bellow), 328
Steinem, Gloria, 132
Stevenson, Henrietta, 286
Stewart, James, 51
Stewart, Maria W., 19–38; adapting American jeremiad for Black women, 19–20; on African American improvement without nation's support, 36; on American racial and gender inequalities, 22, 25; on Anti-Slavery societies, 28; awareness of sexual politics, 51; birth, marriage, and career of, 18, 50–51; Black feminist thought and, 51; on Black women's education as cornerstone of racial virtue, 36–37; claims of divine authority for public speaking, 37–38; comparison of opportunities and resources for Black and white women, 29; criticism of Black male leadership, 24, 25; on elevating power of faith, 36; on elimination of racial prejudice in white communities, 29; as first Black woman political writer, 5; Hunter on significance of, 18; on hypocrisy of northern religious factions on slave labor, 36; informal education of, 34; on interlocking nature of race, gender, and class oppression, 51; intersectional approach to Black empowerment, 9; on moral leniency of Black women, 27–28; on motherhood, 31; on obligation of Black people to live up to high moral ideals, 23–24; positioning herself as living prophet, 23; as public intellectual and activist, 19; rejection of gender prejudice, 28; *Religion and the Pure Principles of Morality*, 21–23, 51; speaking to interracial crowd of men and women, 17; treatment of Black Americans contrary to US founding principles and Christian ethics, 21–22; on virtue and piety of Black women, 30; writing for *The Liberator*, 57
Stimson, Henry L., 334–35
St. Martin, Darla, 223
Stormer, Brian, 219
Student Nonviolent Coordinating Committee (SNCC), 93, 100
Super Soul Sunday (OWN show), 266–67
Swan, Priscilla Harris, 345

"Talented Tenth, The" (Du Bois), 72, 200
Talk about Sex (Irvine), 242
Taylor, Charonda, 344–45
Taylor, Clarence, 71
Taylor, George Edwin, 161
Taylor, Herman, 113
Taylor, Linda, 344
Taylor, Rebecca Stiles, 294
Taylor, Susan L.: affiliations with Unity Church and New Thought organizations, 263; *Confirmation*, 263; as editor in chief of *Essence*, 264; influence on Oprah, 258, 266; "In the Spirit" column, 264; as SBNR writer, 262; Walker's influence on, 264
Taylor, Susie King, 330
Teague, Mary, 314–15
Terrell, Mary Church, 287, 289
13th (DuVernay documentary), 236–37
Thomas, Clarence, 79, 230
Thompson, Hazel, 91
Thoms, Adah, 240
Thorpe, Frances Wills, 335
Thurman, Howard: Bethune's influence on, 75; as Black theologian, 259; as dean of Marsh Chapel, Boston University, 260; engagement with students at Spelman College, 258–59; on genuine self, 269; influence on Oprah, 267; influences on writings of, 258–59; parallels with Angelou's life, 261; as pastor of Church for the Fellowship of All Peoples, 260; as SBNR writer, 258–59; as spiritual mystic, 259
Thurman, Sue Bailey, 75, 259, 269n3
Thwaites, Elizabeth Hart, 48, 49
Time (magazine), 186
To Tell the Truth Freely (Bay), 8
To Turn the Whole World Over (Blain and Gill), 200–201
Toward an Intellectual History of Black Women (Bay, Griffin, Jones, and Savage): activism of Black preaching women, 46;

Black women as producers of knowledge, 119, 194; Black women's intellectual tradition, 6, 8–9, 89; on centrality of Black women to construction of freedom, 137; on devaluation of Black women, 130; on intellectual discourse, 278–79; lacking sustained discussion of Black women conservatives, 222; on plurality of Black women's roles, 195; reproductive rights battle, 108
transatlantic slave trade, 158
Treadwell, Maddie, 288, 300n69
Truman, Harry S.: Executive Order 9981 desegregating armed forces, 276, 310, 311–12, 336; President's Committee on Civil Rights (1946), 310–11, 322n17; signing Women's Armed Services Integration Act, 310
Truth, Sojourner, 57, 330
Tubman, Harriet, 57, 330
Turner, Mary, murder of, 209–10
Tuskegee University, USPHS syphilis study at, 247–48

Unbought and Unbossed (Chisholm): on ambivalence about election to Congress, 128; on complacency and resignation toward oppression, 139–40; harsh critique of, 131, 137–38; having nothing to lose as liberation, 136; on liberal white resistance to Black education and power, 127; as part memoir and part manifesto, 143n37; on policymaking without input from Black and Brown people, 126; on racism of civil rights crusaders, 131; on sexism as more pernicious form of oppression than racism, 131–32; vision for racial justice, 139; women's liberation and antiracist liberation, 133
Undivided Rights (Silliman, Fried, Ross, and Gutiérrez), 219
"Uniformed Intellectual and His Place in American Arms, The" (Matthews), 328–29
Universal Negro Improvement Association and African Communities League (UNIA), 182, 246

US Army, Black women in post-WWII, 276, 308. *See also* Women's Army Corps (WAC)
US Coast Guard, SPARS as reserve of, 280, 335
US Department of Defense: as successor to War Department, 307; women integrated into regular army, 297
US Marines, rejecting Black women recruits during WWII, 280. *See also* Women Marines
US Navy: Committee on Negro Personnel, 308; Granger inquiry, 308. *See also* WAVES (Women Accepted for Voluntary Emergency Service)
US Supreme Court. See *Roe v. Wade*

Van Lew, Elizabeth, 331
Van Lew, John, 331
Vaughan, Bettie Jean, 277; oral history, 345
Veasey, Millie, 284, 285, 286
Veterans History Project, Library of Congress, oral history interviews with Black women veterans, 338–45
Vieweg, W. Victor R., 221
Volcy, Wallyne, 343–44
Voting Rights Act of 1965, 167n1
Vygotsky, Lev, 151, 152–53

WAF. *See* Women in the Air Force (WAF)
Walker, Alice: as bisexual woman, 271n34; influence on Oprah, 258; nontraditional approach to religion, 263; rejection of Christianity, 264; SBNR writings, 263; Thurman's influence on SBNR writings of, 262; on womanist (womanism), 85n11, 263–64
Walker, David, 51
Wallace, Henry, 188
Warfield, Harriet, 293
War for the Soul of America, A (Hartman), 251nn3–4
Waring, Laura Wheeler, 174; birth and education of, 205; Black internationalist movement and, 206; as Black visual artist

Waring, Laura Wheeler (*cont.*)
during Harlem Renaissance, 195; collaboration with Fauset on articles about Africans in Algiers, 206; honors and awards, 206; institutions displaying works of, 207–8; study at Académie de la Grande Chaumière, 206; as teacher at Cheyney Training School for Teachers, 205–6. *See also* Black women, as visual artists
Waring, Laura Wheeler, works of: *Anna Washington Derry*, **197**, 206–7; capturing variations of Blackness in paintings, 207; *James Weldon Johnson*, 207; "Portraits of Outstanding American Citizens of Negro Origin," 208; *W. E. B. Du Bois*, **199**, 207
Warren, Linda, 340–41
War Work Bulletin (YWCA), 239
Washington, Booker T.: accommodationist educational philosophy, 72, 74; "Atlanta Compromise Speech," 74; industrial education for Blacks and, 178
Washington, Leon, 183–84
"Watchmen, The" (Jacobs), 68
Waters, Kristin, 195
Watson, Elwood, 256–57
Watson, Nicole Earley, 341
Watson, Rhonda Nunnally, 341
WAVES (Women Accepted for Voluntary Emergency Service): Black officers and enlisted personnel, 312, 335; endorsement of, 334; enlistment standards, 313; refusing Black women recruits in WWII, 280
Weaver, Renita, 339
Webb, Sophia, 342
Weigley, Russell, 333
Welch-Baker, Tiffany, 338
Welcome, Henry C., 93
Welcome, Mary Sue, 93
Welcome, Verda, 93, 97
Wells, Ida B.: as antilynching crusader, 71, 177; challenging stereotypical narrative of Blackness, 178; as public intellectual, 10
We Specialize in the Wholly Impossible (Hine), 8
West, Cornel, 69, 178
West, Harriet: as candidate for WAC officer program, 283; denying army as place to fight race problems, 293, 301n96; investigating complaints of Black WACs, 291–92; recruiting Black women into WAAC, 305
West Point Military Academy, Black female graduates (2019), 338
What I Know for Sure (Winfrey), 265–66
"What Must the Negro Do to Be Saved" (Burroughs), 82–83
What the Negro Wants (Logan), 80
"What the Negro Youth Expects of the White Youth in Their Tomorrow" (Brown), 77
"What to Teach to Negro Americans" (Brown), 83–84
Wheatley, Phillis: as Black Atlantic writer, 48; childhood and education of, 50; development of modernity and, 48; as eighteenth-century Black intellectual, 5, 178; lack of higher education, 179; poetry of, 50
When and Where I Enter (Giddings), 7
"Where Did All the Money Go?" (Jefferson), 229, 234n46
White, Deborah Gray, 7
White, Odella, 341–42
white privilege, Brown speech addressing, 77
Wilke, Wendell, 185
Williams, Annette, 229
Williams, Armstrong, 174, 222
Williams, Casandra, 342–43
Williams, Cathay ("William Cathey"), 331–32
Williams, Chad, 332
Williams, Daniel K., 220–21, 223
Williams, Dellia Rose, 342
Williams, Delores, 79, 259
Williams, Hettie V., 3–4, 9
Williams, Jeanne, 342
Williams, Marethia Ann, 343
Williams, Mary Daniels, 285
Williams, Roger, 5
Williams, Rosa B. H., 341
Williams, Smallwood (Bishop), 79
Willis, Kemya Rence, 339

Wilson, Danyell, 338
Wilson, Francille Rusan, 108
Wilson, Woodrow: Jim Crow ideologies, 198, 209–10; Thoms on, 240
Winfrey, Oprah: acting debut in *The Color Purple*, 263; book club teaching style, 256; endorsement of Obama, 4; influence on American culture, 4, 174–75, 256; Maya Angelou as "spiritual mother," 261, 262–63, 265–66; as nontraditionalist, 263; not viewed as public intellectual, 222; on purpose in life, 268; spiritual writings, 257; Taylor influencing, 266; Walker influencing, 264; weight-loss battle, 263
Winthrop, John, 5
Wisdom of Sundays, The (Winfrey), 266, 267; nature photos in, 267, 268
With Head and Heart (Thurman), 75, 260
Wittgenstein, Ludwig, 153
womanist (definition), 263–64
Woman's Body, Woman's Right (Gordon), 218
Women against Abortion (Haugeberg), 215, 221
Women in Military Service for America Memorial Foundation, 331–32
Women in the Air Force (WAF): eliminating all-Black training units, 313; establishment of, 309; racial discrimination, 315
Women Marines: leadership of, 309; racially integrated units, 313–14
Women of Color and the Reproductive Rights Movement (Nelson), 219
Women's Armed Services Integration Act (1948): creating sexual segregation within military, 309; enlistment standards, 313; military branch directors of women's service, 309; recruitment efforts following passage, 313; restrictions on rank, marriage, and roles of women, 309, 322n13, 355
Women's Army Auxiliary Corps (WAAC): establishment of, 280; recruitment of Black women, 278, 305; segregation of, 305, 336
Women's Army Corps (WAC): accommodation vs. resistance to military policies, 290; Black strike at Fort Devens as collaboration between WACs and civilian women, 293–95; civilian protests against Black discrimination, 293; deactivation of Black band at Fort Des Moines, 293; debate over women in war, 275–76; discriminatory gender restrictions, 299n14; integration into regular army, 297; patriarchal and racial norms of, 279; personnel classifications and Black enlistments, 295–96; racial integration of, 283, 296; racial segregation until the late 1950s, 286–88, 306, 314. *See also* military service
Women's Army Corps, Black WACs: Black women serving in (1950–1972), 315; bringing attention to racial discrimination, 296; countering stereotypes of Black women, 286; low enlistment by Black women during WWII, 284; marginalization in WWII, 297; not regarded as legitimate soldiers, 289; as pathway to social and economic justice, 279; rank and strategies of, 291–92; reasons for enlisting, 279–80, 285, 306; recognizing obligations of service, 285; setting boundaries, 286–87; sit-in protesting segregation of chapel at Fort Clark, 292; 6888th Central Postal Directory Battalion, 336; status as soldiers, 280, 299n14; training in marketable skills for postwar employment, 280–81; white belittlement of concerns, 290
women's club movement, Black, 54, 281
Women's Convention, National Baptist Convention, 75
Women's Home and Foreign Missionary Society, 57
women's rights movement: abortion rights as women's rights, 68; antiabortion movement neglected in histories of, 218–19; challenging traditional gender roles, 333; decline of public intellectuals and, 68, 84n2
Women's Study Club of America, 183
Wood, Betty, 49
Wood, Essie, 291
Woodhull, Victoria, 161

Woods, Elsie, 286, 298
Woods, Essie Dell O'Bryant, 336
Woodson, Carter G., 112
World Committee of the Defenders of Peace, 189
World Health Organization (WHO), on sexual health, 243
World War I: Army Nurse Corps, 330, 346n14; Black women's patriotic activities, 332; Navy Nurse Corps, 330; women encouraged to join work force, 239; women replacing men in noncombatant roles, 332–33
World War II: bipartisan objections to women's service, 334; Black WACs in 6888th Central Postal Directory Battalion, 336; Black women in US Army during, 275; Black women recruits rejected by navy, marines, and coast guard, 280; Double V campaign, 279; marginalization of Black WACs, 297; propaganda discouraging enlistment of women, 334–35; race riots during, 186; racial quotas and segregation, 306; women replacing men in noncombatant roles, 333–34
Wouldn't Take Nothing for My Journey Now (Angelou), 261, 262
Wretched of the Earth, The (Fanon), 151

Yoes, Charles, 117
"You Are the Race, You Are the Seeded Earth" (Lurkins), 247
Young, Alice, 285
Young Men's Christian Association (YMCA), 239
Young Women's Christian Association (YWCA), 239, 240–41, 284
Your Spirits Walk Beside Us (Savage), 73, 79

Zibro, Melissa, 276–77
zone of proximal development, 152

www.ingramcontent.com/pod-product-compliance
Lightning Source LLC
Chambersburg PA
CBHW030602230426
43661CB00053B/1812